PENGUIN BOOKS

THE KAISER'S BATTLE

On a visit to France and Belgium in 1967 Martin Middlebrook was so impressed by the military cemeteries on the 1914–18 battlefields that he decided to write a book describing just one day in that war through the eyes of the ordinary men who took part. The book, *The First Day on the Somme*, was published by Allen Lane in 1971 and received international acclaim. Martin Middlebrook has since written other books that deal with important turning-points in the two world wars; these are *The Kaiser's Battle, Convoy, The Peenemünde Raid, The Battle of Hamburg, Battleship* (with Patrick Mahoney), *The Schweinfurt-Regensburg Mission, The Nuremberg Raid, The Bomber Command Diaries* (with Chris Everitt), *The Berlin Raids, The Somme Battlefields* (with Mary Middlebrook), *Arnhem 1944* and *Your Country Needs You*. He has also written two books about the 1982 Falklands War, *Task Force: The Falklands War, 1982* and *The Fight for the 'Malvinas'*. Many of his books have been published in the United States and Germany, and three of them in Japan, the former Yugoslavia and Poland.

Martin Middlebrook is a Fellow of the Royal Historical Society. Each summer he takes parties of visitors on conducted tours of the First World War battlefields and to Normandy and Arnhem.

Martin Middlebrook

The Kaiser's Battle

PENGUIN BOOKS

PENGUIN BOOKS

Published by the Penguin Group
Penguin Books Ltd, 80 Strand, London WC2R ORL, England
Penguin Putnam Inc., 375 Hudson Street, New York, New York 10014, USA
Penguin Books Australia Ltd, Ringwood, Victoria, Australia
Penguin Books Canada Ltd, 10 Alcorn Avenue, Toronto, Ontario, Canada M4V 3B2
Penguin Books India (P) Ltd, 11 Community Centre, Panchsheel Park, New Delhi – 110 017, India
Penguin Books (NZ) Ltd, Cnr Rosedale and Airborne Roads, Albany, Auckland, New Zealand
Penguin Books (South Africa) (Pty) Ltd, 24 Sturdee Avenue, Rosebank 2196, South Africa

Penguin Books Ltd, Registered Offices: 80 Strand, London WC2R ORL, England

www.penguin.com

First published by Allen Lane 1978
Published in Penguin Books 1983
Reprinted as a Penguin Classic 2000

3

Copyright © Martin Middlebrook, 1978
All rights reserved

Printed in Great Britain by CPI UK

Contents

Plates

1. Field Marshal Sir Douglas Haig (Imperial War Museum)
2. General Sir Hubert Gough (Imperial War Museum)
3. Hindenburg, the Kaiser and Ludendorff (Imperial War Museum)
4. St Quentin from the air (W.N.C. van Grutten)
5. German ammunition dumps (W.N.C. van Grutten)
6. St Quentin (Bavarian State Archives)
7. Captured British tank (J. Schulte)
8. German storm troops (Imperial War Museum)
9. Gas casualties (Bavarian State Archives)
10. Captured British guns (N. Schubert)
11. British dead (Bavarian State Archives)
12 & 13. British prisoners (Bavarian State Archives)
14. British prisoners (Imperial War Museum)
15. German prisoners (Imperial War Museum)
16, 17 & 18. British wounded (Imperial War Museum)
19. King George V and Sherwood Foresters (Imperial War Museum)
20. Albert Basilica (Bavarian State Archives)
21. Albert Basilica (Imperial War Museum)
22. Prisoner document (W. H. Crowder)
23. Vadencourt British Cemetery (Commonwealth War Graves Commission)
24. Arras Memorial to the Missing (Commonwealth War Graves Commission)

Maps

Diagrams

Maps and diagrams by Illustra Design Ltd from preliminary drawings by Edward Sylvester.

Introduction

Several years ago I wrote a book describing in detail the opening day of the Battle of the Somme on 1 July 1916. On this day, divisions of the British and French armies made a carefully prepared attack on the German positions astride the River Somme. This book will describe in similar manner another one-day set-piece attack, but this time by the Germans against the British positions. The day was 21 March 1918 and the field of battle was also 'on the Somme', as the soldier put it, but farther east than the area of the 1916 fighting. Like the first day of the Battle of the Somme, 21 March 1918 was one of the great turning points of the First World War and, in the number of men involved, was probably the greatest battle of that war.

Every German soldier of 1914–18 had a Military Service Book in which were recorded details of the battles in which he had fought and of the quieter periods of trench warfare in which he had served. Those who survived the battle of 21 March 1918 had this simple title stamped in their books: '*Grosse Schlacht in Frankreich*' – 'The Great Battle in France'.

*

Many sound books have described what British historians later called 'The March Offensive' or 'The March Retreat'. All of these earlier works treat the first and subsequent days as one battle, and there is no reason why they should not, although it was the nature and the results of the first day's fighting which set the seal on what was to follow. Most of these books deal with events in a conventional military-history manner by describing them from the top of the military hierarchy downwards and, although they usually pay tribute to the front-line soldiers *en masse*, they never really tell the reader what Private Brown or Musketier Schmidt experienced or thought while in the battle. Other books which do give personal accounts of the battle provide understandably narrow views of it or, if intended to be comprehensive, fall into the trap of taking too much note of British regimental histories published after the war. As will be shown later, these often presented a distorted and over-heroic version of events.

I make no apology for devoting a complete book to just the first day of this battle, and I will be concentrating on the experiences of the individuals involved and on the nature of the fighting at small-unit level, although as much of what the senior commanders and the politicians were doing as will enable the reader to set the battlefield scenes in context will also be included.

I must add a few words on sources. Before any use can be made of personal contributions, it is always essential to establish a reliable framework of the orders of battle of units, of the plans and orders of leaders, and of the main events in the battle itself. In preparing this framework I have relied heavily upon the following sources: *Military Operations France and Belgium 1918, The German March Offensive and its Preliminaries*, compiled by Brigadier-General J. E. Edmonds and published in 1935 (this is referred to henceforth as 'the British Official History');* *Der Weltkrieg 1914–18*, Volume 14, published by the Oberkommando der Wehrmacht in 1944 (to be referred to as 'the German Official History'); and the War Diaries of the British Army units involved which became available at the Public Record Office in 1965. Unfortunately there are drawbacks to the use of all these sources. Because of the results of the fighting on the first day, the War Diaries of the front-line British battalions are in parlous state, as the British Official Historian acknowledges, and this work suffers accordingly, there being huge gaps in the descriptions of events at battalion level although it is perfectly sound when describing the plans and preparations of both sides. The German Official History turned out

---

* Most of the work on this particular volume of the Official History was carried out by Major-General H. R. Davies, who was commanding the 11th Division on the River Lys sector in March 1918, and Lieutenant-Colonel R. G. B. Maxwell-Hyslop, an officer in the Dorsetshire Regiment who was badly wounded and taken prisoner near Mons in August 1914, exchanged back to England in a paralysed state in 1916, but, following medical treatment, was able to perform a useful duty at G.H.Q. in France in 1918.

to be only a very general work and contains little detail below corps level. I have studied only the most original and reliable of the non–official published works; 'new' books based purely on library research do not appeal to me. *The Fifth Army* by General Gough, Godspeed's *Ludendorff* and *The Private Papers of Douglas Haig* are all useful, as is the more recently published biography, *Goughie*, by Anthony Farrar-Hockley; and my thoughts have been stimulated by some of the essays in John Terraine's *The Western Front 1914–18* and his book *Impacts of War 1914 and 1918*.

One unusual prime source of material has been the registers of the Commonwealth War Graves Commission cemeteries and Memorials to the Missing in France. These list all fatal casualties, and a study and analysis of those registers covering the area of this battlefield provided an unexpected research bonus.

My appeals, in 1975, for men involved in the battle brought an almost overwhelming response, and I now have the results of interviews or correspondence with 518 Britons and 129 Germans who were involved in the battle on 21 March 1918, the highest positions held being battalion commanders on the British side and company commanders on the German side. The sceptical reader will, with some justification, query the value of old men's memories. But it was a day that most of the survivors would never forget and the material available from them has been dealt with in a very careful manner. All offerings were judged against the background of the known activities of the man's unit, and the general rule was that if any one part of an individual account was found seriously incorrect no other part of it was used. Another sieve was the sixth sense that one develops on reading so many accounts or after many hours' interviewing; this soon tells when a man is going astray. A serious drawback in these personal accounts is the forgivable tendency for a man to present his own actions in the best possible light, while the man who has every reason to conceal his actions, such as the soldier who threw away his rifle and hid in a shell hole until the fighting was over or the one who may have been involved in a battlefield atrocity, rarely volunteers to help at all. I have tried to make allowances for such distortions.

Despite these limitations, sufficient remains to present a worthwhile account of the fighting on the first day of the German offensive. No one will ever be able to present a completely comprehensive view which is accurate to the last detail and, even if one could do so, the result would probably be so tedious as to be unreadable. What I am attempting to do is to dip into a variety of sources, select material that is considered to be reliable, and then give the reader a series of impressions of the experiences and emotions of the men who were involved and the nature of the fighting on what was one of the more important days of the First World War.

Winter Quarters

Soldiers who had first come to the trenches of the Western Front in the summer or autumn of 1917 say that the winter that followed was the coldest of the war. But such expressions as 'the coldest winter' or 'the wettest summer' are often used by men who for the first time in their lives have to campaign and exist entirely in the open. These recent arrivals on the Western Front never had to spend a second winter in the trenches and so they had nothing with which to compare the winter of 1917–18. Men who had seen earlier winters on the Western Front say that this one was not too bad at all; it is true that there were some cold spells, but it was a very dry winter and, because of that, there were snug trenches, dry feet and much gratitude.

War was no new event in Europe. For centuries the traditional time for campaigning had been confined to the summer months and armies usually retired to spend the winter in as comfortable quarters as they could find. Winter was a time for rest and recuperation, the gathering-together of fresh supplies, weapons and men, and the making of plans for the next campaigning season. The First World War armies could not go entirely into winter quarters and a certain strength had always to be left posted in the trenches. But the old tradition of using winter as a time for renewal and for planning the next round of operations was still valid, and even before the last struggles of the 1917 battles had petered out the leaders of both sides were hard at it, trying to decide what they could do in 1918 to secure success and, if possible, complete victory for their armies.

The situation and hopes of most of these leaders were more confused in the winter of 1917–18 than at any of their previous times of reassessment. 1917 had seen great changes in strengths and alliances and there were unprecedented pressures on some of the leaders; there was particular dissension in the British camp. The way ahead was clear to no one. Many thousands of words have since been written concerning the ideas that were under consideration at that time and the plans eventually made out of them. Although there will always be differences in opinion over the merits of the arguments deployed and the decisions ultimately taken, there are few gaps remaining in the factual elements of the story. Because the decisions taken lead directly to the battle fought on 21 March 1918, it is necessary in this first chapter to go over this ground again, but, because there is little difference between historians on this subject, a brief and simple résumé will suffice. It must be stressed that what follows is no more than a 'plain man's guide' to the plans being made in the New Year of 1918 and those readers who wish to study the finer points should refer to the recognised works on this subject.

*

By the New Year of 1918, the nations of Europe had been attempting to achieve their national ambitions and settle their political differences by sending their young men to fight each other to the death for a few days short of three years and five months. It was now becoming a true world war because most of the world's great nations had become involved. Germany was in partnership with the Austro-Hungarian and the Ottoman Empires. The 'Allies' consisted of Britain and France with their respective empires, Belgium, Italy, Russia (dropping out now) and the United States (just coming in), with minor support from several smaller countries. No one believed in an easy or a swift victory any more; such hopes had died progressively for both sides in Flanders and Champagne, at Loos and Verdun, and on the Somme and the Chemin des Dames. The process of learning had been an erratic one. The Germans had come to it first at Verdun in the spring of 1916, the British after the bitter disappointment of the opening of the Battle of the Somme that summer. The French had kept faith with the old idea that dash and skill could break through barbed wire and entrenched machine-guns until the Nivelle Offensive of April 1917 had broken the heart of the French Army.

The Allies had long-term hopes for another means of

waging war in their use of the old weapon of blockade which had been applied steadily against Germany and Austria since the beginning. Starvation was fast becoming a reality in the enemy homeland, but short rations can be made to go a long way and there was no victory in sight yet for the blockade. The Germans had tried their version of blockade in the form of unrestricted submarine warfare against Allied shipping but, although achieving much success in 1917, the German submarines were now in the process of being defeated. The new element – the air – was also being tried by both sides, not just over the traditional battlefield but by the long-range strategic bomber or airships against the enemy homeland in the hope of destroying industries and demoralising populations. But this new weapon would take years to develop in quantity, and this revolutionary idea of achieving victory would have to wait for another war before being put to a full test. Back on the battlefield, another new weapon had been tried, but only by the Allies. The tank had been in use since 1916 and had had its moment of glory in the first mass tank attack, by the British, at Cambrai in November 1917. But this triumph had turned to ashes with the successful counter-attack mounted by the Germans after the tank advance had run its course, and some of the British had temporarily lost faith in the tank's full potential.

The positions in which the two sides found themselves in that New Year of 1918 were as follows. For the Allies, the best that could be hoped for now was victory by attrition – to gather together a greater strength of forces than that of the enemy and then, by determined use of this force, to grind down the enemy until he collapsed. This deadly process had begun in the later stages of the Somme battle in 1916 and had continued throughout 1917. The Allied military leaders, particularly the British, believed that they had travelled far along this road and that the German Army on the Western Front was always on the verge of breaking.

In the game of numbers that was the basis of attrition, there had recently been two great changes for the Allies. Russia, weakened by huge war casualties and a revolution, was dropping out of the Alliance but this loss would eventually be more than made up by the joining of the United

States. The Americans had 'been in' since April 1917, although the first contingents of their troops were only now starting to arrive on the Western Front. But there was the glorious prospect for the old Allies that this would one day become a rejuvenating flood of fresh men backed up by the great industrial resources of the United States.

The Germans could look for no such reinforcements. True, the recent Russian collapse had enabled the Germans to bring back many of their divisions from the Eastern Front, but this was a once and for all bonus. Beyond this, they could look forward only to the annual classes of youths reaching military age but this was no more benefit than their enemies were also receiving each year. Man for man, the German army was the most skilful in the world, but it would cease to be a 'man for man' situation.

Until recently there had been six main areas of active land fighting. The Western Front in Belgium and France was by far the most important of these; the remainder can loosely be called 'the East' and can be quickly disposed of here.

The campaign against the Turks in Mesopotamia had almost fizzled out, while that in Palestine was going well for the British following their success at the Third Battle of Gaza at the end of October 1917 and the subsequent advance. Jerusalem had been captured on 9 December.

Two fronts on which the Austrians were the main enemy of the Allies were Salonika, in northern Greece, and in the barren plateaux and mountains of north-eastern Italy. Neither side was putting much effort into the Salonika campaign and a minor stalemate had existed there for many months. Italy was different. The Italian troops had been dealt a crushing surprise blow at Caporetto when the small German force sent to support the Austrians had put the Italian troops into a minor rout from which a new front had only just been stabilised. Italy had looked like dropping out of the war, and France and Britain were forced to send troops from the Western Front to keep their ally in.

Russia was as good as finished as a partner for the Allies. Her peasant army had suffered heavy losses over the years, the fighting of 1917 had definitely gone against her, and the long-festering grievances of her mass population against their Tsarist rulers had finally erupted. World war and revolution were too much for Russia to bear at one time, and the new Bolshevik leaders decided that their country had suffered enough. At the end of the year an armistice with the Germans was in force and peace talks were taking place. These would culminate in the Treaty of Brest Litovsk in March 1918, but Germany was already anticipating this and the railways of Eastern Europe were bringing back a steady flow of German troops to the West.

It had always been the hope of certain Allied leaders – the so-called 'Easterners' – that a properly planned and fully supported blow somewhere in the East might bring a major success and avert the necessity of fighting it out to the end on the Western Front. But the overall effect of these recent 'Eastern' operations gave little comfort. It is true that Turkey was not doing well, but the loss of Russia was a disaster and the weakness of the Italians had caused a reduction in the Allied forces on the Western Front.

The 'Westerners' were those Allied leaders who had said all along that the only way to victory was to defeat the German Army on the Western Front. To them, any troops sent to other theatres represented a diversion from the main effort and a delay in reaching victory. But 1917 had been a poor year on the Western Front. The Belgians had only a tiny army and could do little more than defend one corner of their own country; the French and British manned the remainder of that terrible battle line from the Belgian coast to Switzerland. The year had started with a voluntary German withdrawal from the 1916 Somme battlefield to a strong new position, the Hindenburg Line, eleven miles farther east. The French and the British had both mounted major attacks in April. The French, under a new commander, Nivelle, had been cut to pieces on the Chemin des Dames between Rheims and Soissons and their front-line troops had mutinied; they would defend their trenches but they were not prepared to take part in any further attacks. The French Army had then gone on to the defensive for the remainder of the year.

The British, under the dogged and determined command of Field-Marshal Sir Douglas Haig, had borne the main strain for the remainder of 1917. Their spring attacks at Arras had at last gained the prominent feature of Vimy Ridge and had improved the position in front of Arras, but at heavy cost. Then had come the series of battles around Ypres, sometimes called the Third Battle of Ypres but popularly known as the Battle of Passchendaele. The early, limited attacks in the summer had been successful, but the subsequent efforts over the sodden ground beneath the Passchendaele Ridge in the worst fighting conditions of the war brought heavy casualties and a great loss of spirit among the British troops taking part. It was said that it was necessary to keep attacking until the French recovered from their mutinies and Haig and his intelligence staff insisted that the German Army was at last reaching breaking point. But, when the Germans counter-attacked so successfully after the British tank attack farther south at Cambrai at the end of November, they recaptured most of the ground won by the British tanks and even some of the old British front line. As the British Official History says, 'this brought home to many soldiers that the German army was by no means "dead" as some people fondly imagined.'*

Britain had suffered approximately 860,000 casualties on the Western Front in 1917, and the French 590,000.† Despite these appalling losses, the line of the Western Front remained unchanged from the one that had existed after the Germans withdrew to the Hindenburg Line early in the year, except on large-scale maps which showed small gains in front of Arras and Ypres – five miles at Arras, about the same at Ypres.

The Germans on the Western Front had stood on the defensive for the whole year, had done so, in fact, ever since breaking off their attacks on Verdun in July 1916. Their casualties on the Western Front in 1917 had been 850,000 men. Besides holding their lines in the West, the Germans had knocked Russia out completely, had pushed back the

* Page 34.

† 'Casualties' include dead, wounded, sick and prisoners. A rough calculation is that between one quarter and one third of all casualties were fatal but that many of the lightly wounded and sick would recover to fight again. Possibly half of all 'casualties' were thus men who were put out of action for good, but these are rough and ready proportions.

Italians, had caused the French to mutiny and had been responsible for much bloodletting in the British Army. But they were tired after more than three years of war, as indeed were all who had been involved since the beginning.

*

We come now to the subject of numbers, for it was on the strengths of armies that the plans for the coming year would

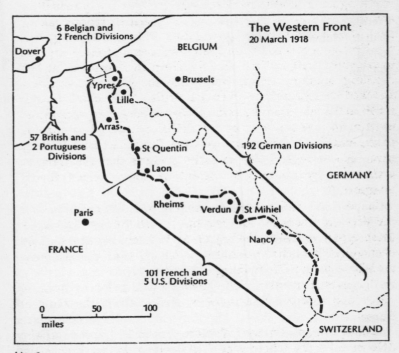

Map 1

be based. The largest military unit that remained permanently together was the division, consisting of from nine to twelve battalions of fighting infantry and the immediate supporting arms, and with a total strength of around 15,000 men. The infantry division was the currency in which the value of armies was reckoned. The situation on the Western Front is set out in the following table, which shows the numbers of infantry divisions available to the various armies at three separate times – the end of October 1917 when the Battle of Passchendaele was coming to an end, the end of the year, and the day before the Germans mounted the first offensive of 1918.

Infantry Divisions on the Western Front

	31 October 1917	31 December 1917	20 March 1918
French	104	98	98
British (Home)	52	47	47
British (Empire)	10	10	10
Belgian	6	6	6
United States	2	5	6
Portuguese	2	2	2
Total Allied	176	168	169
German	150	171	192

Even the above figures do not represent the true position of superiority that the Germans could expect to enjoy. The French had few reinforcements available for their divisions; five had already been broken up for lack of men, and General Pétain, the French Commander-in-Chief, was forecasting that as many as twenty-five more of his divisions might have to go in 1918 if the French became involved in heavy fighting. The Belgian divisions were very weak with negligible reinforcements behind them. The Americans were arriving at a much slower pace than had been promised, the delay being due in part to a shortage of shipping but also to the decision by the American Army to equip with French field guns, which were in short supply, rather than with the British types of gun which were actually being manufactured in quantity in American factories. When they did arrive, the American divisions were very keen but completely inexperienced and it would be some months before they could take a fully effective role.*

* The six United States divisions in France on 20 March 1918 would be the 1st (Regular), 2nd (Regular and Marine), 26th, 41st, 42nd and 93rd Divisions.

On the British front, the poor Portuguese were an unhappy contingent with little enthusiasm for fighting conditions so far north. Their original strength in men had fallen almost by half and they broke at once when they were attacked by the Germans later in the year. Probably the best Allied divisions on the Western Front were the ten British Empire divisions – five Australian, four Canadian and one from New Zealand. All but the New Zealanders were still completely volunteer units and their fighting ability was of a high order. There was also a South African Brigade which formed part of the 9th (Scottish) Division. These South Africans will be met again later in the book.

The ordinary British divisions were in a depressed state as regards manpower. It is recorded that they were more than 70,000 men below establishment by the end of the Battle of Passchendaele with the casualties of Cambrai still to come. It is probable that the average division was short of 2,000 men, mostly infantry, by the end of the year, with some divisions being in a far worse state than the average. Haig was telling his government that if he did not receive substantial reinforcements at once he might have to disband as many as half of his divisions if the British Expeditionary Force had to fight hard in the coming year. Such a position would have been a catastrophe for the Allies, and, while it is possible that Haig was overstating his case to achieve a purpose, the question of British reinforcements was of vital importance to the campaigns of the coming spring and summer. This will be dealt with in more detail shortly.

For once it was the Germans who were in a strong position. For years, they had held off all Allied attacks on the Western Front with an inferior number of divisions. Now there was the great reinforcement of troops arriving from the Eastern Front and a smaller one from Italy, from where the Germans brought back four divisions after their victory at Caporetto while the French and British had sent eleven divisions from

The 26th was made up of National Guard (similar to British or French Territorials) units from New England. The 41st never fought as a division but was split up to provide depots. The 42nd was the famous Rainbow Division of National Guardsmen from every state in the union. The 93rd was a wartime-raised division of coloured soldiers; it too never fought as a complete unit.

the Western Front to Italy. Moreover, all the German divisions were battle-hardened and most were in the process of being brought up to full strength. On New Year's Day 1918, the German military commanders could look forward to a period of several months when their side would have a clear superiority over the Allies and the opportunity to take the initiative on the Western Front. But that favourable position would last for only a limited time; when the Americans really arrived in force, the last German chance for victory would be gone.

*

It is necessary to look more closely at the strength of the British Expeditionary Force and at the two men who controlled its destiny but who were in grave conflict at that time over the future role of the British soldiers.

Field-Marshal Sir Douglas Haig, the Commander-in-Chief, was a confirmed 'Westerner'. He also strongly believed that not only would the final decision be reached in the West but that the decision would come only through constant offensive action against the Germans. There had been plenty of such action. The British offensives had started in 1915 and, at first, had usually been made in conjunction with a French attack, but the efforts of that year, at Neuve Chapelle, Aubers Ridge, Festubert and Loos, had made little impact on the Germans.

British Casualties*

Neuve Chapelle, March 1915	–	12,892 men
Aubers Ridge and Festubert, May 1915	–	28,267 men
Loos, September and October 1915	–	61,713 men

Since Haig had become Commander-in-Chief at the end of 1915, he had mounted four more offensive battles – the Somme, Arras, Passchendaele and Cambrai. Two of these,

---

* It is probable that the British Army system of reporting casualties may have resulted in these figures being too high, in that many men who became detached from their units and were reported as 'missing' turned up safely later but after the casualty return had been submitted. For this reason, these casualty figures may be too high but probably by no more than 5 per cent.

the Somme and Passchendaele, had been nothing less than all-out attempts, pushed with the utmost vigour and determination, to break the German Army. The British casualties had been enormous.

The Somme, July to November 1916	–	415,000 men
Arras, April and May 1917	–	139,867 men
Third Ypres (Passchendaele), June to November 1917	–	250,000 men
Cambrai (including the German counter-attack), November and December 1917	–	70,264 men

The Germans had lost heavily too, but their casualties were not recorded as diligently as were those of the British. There arose a controversy after the war, a controversy which has never been resolved, based on the belief that more casualties were suffered by the defending side in these battles than by the attackers, and every scrap of statement or casualty return that would support this view was brought into the argument. The supporters of Haig were naturally the same people who supported this view. What was important was whether these offensive battles had brought the Germans near to breaking point at a cost to the British that could be borne. It is true that part of the reason for the constant British attacks had been the need to help the French in order to relieve them from the German pressure at Verdun in 1916 and because of the French mutinies in 1917, but there is plenty of evidence that Haig was a strong believer in the doctrine of the offensive and was quite happy to keep using his army in this way. He was always an optimist, and his papers contain many references in 1916 and 1917 to the near breakdown of the Germans as a result of his attacks and the need for just one more effort to finish off the enemy. As has been stated already, however, the German counter-attack at Cambrai had shown that there was little evidence yet of the Germans breaking, and coming events in 1918 would dramatically reinforce this.

Haig, the 'Westerner', the optimist, the believer in the offensive, could take little comfort from the situation in which he found himself at the end of 1917. Five of his divisions had recently been sent to Italy, the remainder of his exhausted army were well under strength, and the reinforcement camps in France were empty. But Haig had not lost faith in his old policy of attack. At a meeting of the British War Cabinet on 7 January 1918, at which the possibility of the Germans attacking the French was being discussed, Haig stated, 'In my opinion, the best defence would be to continue our offensive in Flanders, because we would then retain the initiative and attract the German Reserves against us. It is doubtful whether the French Army can now withstand for long a resolute and continued offensive on the part of the enemy.'* In other words, Haig was actively seeking to mount yet another offensive on the grounds that the French Army, which had been virtually resting for most of the past year, was not yet fit to defend itself. It was a bleak prospect for the British soldiers who had only just finished fighting in the mud of Passchendaele that their leader was proposing to start all over again on the same sector of the front.

One man was taking steps to see that Haig did not find such an excuse to mount yet another offensive. David Lloyd George had been Prime Minister of a Coalition Government since late 1916. He was no pacifist and wanted as much as anyone to lead Britain to victory, but not at the cost of unlimited casualties. He sought constantly to control the freedom of action of the military and to see that offensive actions were limited to a specific purpose. In this, he had not been very successful in 1917. But, if he could not always be looking over Haig's shoulder at G.H.Q. in France, Lloyd George had at least one weapon. Through the War Cabinet and the Army Council, he could control the flow of troops to France, whether as complete new units or as reinforcements, and in the closing months of 1917 Lloyd George had reduced that flow to a minimum. This is why Haig's divisions were under strength and his reinforcement camps empty.

The reader might well ask why did not Lloyd George simply replace Haig, as he was quite entitled to do, for Britain was certainly not a military state. The thought must have crossed Lloyd George's mind on many occasions, but there were difficulties. Haig was well supported by Field-

* *The Private Papers of Douglas Haig 1914–1919*, page 278.

Marshal Sir William Robertson, Chief of the Imperial General Staff and hence chief military adviser to the Government, and Haig also had his supporters among the politicians. The morale of the civilian population and of the front-line soldiers would also have been badly shaken if Haig had been dismissed, because wartime propaganda had brazenly given the impression that the British offensives had resulted in clear-cut victories.

There were more than enough troops in England to make Haig's divisions up to strength. War Office returns for 1 January 1918 show that no fewer than 38,225 officers and 607,403 men were in England, fit, fully trained and immediately available for service in France. Just 150,000 of these men would have brought Haig's divisions up to full strength and provided a pool of reinforcements. It was these men that Haig was asking for when he told the War Cabinet of his future plans, but Lloyd George had had enough of offensives and, to stop Haig, he simply kept the reinforcements back at home.

For Haig, even worse was to come. Robertson was manoeuvred out of the post of Chief of the Imperial General Staff and replaced by General Sir Henry Wilson, an officer far more compliant to Lloyd George's will and no strong supporter of Haig. Then, when the French asked the British to take over a further section of the French-held front – the British had been steadily taking over such stretches since 1915 – Lloyd George agreed to do so, and Haig was accordingly instructed to extend his line to the south by twenty-five miles during January 1918. These measures, taken so soon after Haig had been forced to send five divisions to Italy, left the British Expeditionary Force in no fit state to mount a new offensive in 1918. Whether it could even defend itself against a German offensive was soon to be put to the test.

There is no doubt that this dissension between Commander-in-Chief in France and Prime Minister in London was one of the most critical phases of the war. There were many unpleasant side aspects to the affair which will not be followed up here, but it should be stated that, while one can sympathise with Lloyd George's undoubted humanitarian motives, the manner in which he achieved his ends is not

much to be admired. There was a particularly unsavoury
episode when Lloyd George allowed deliberately erroneous
figures about the strength of the British Expeditionary Force
to be given to Parliament. There was a good deal more
dignity in the way in which Haig conducted himself during
this period.

*

It was against this unhappy background of British dissension
that the Allied leaders consulted with each other in an attempt
to produce a common and successful policy for the coming
year. Their initial deliberations were made only in the
knowledge that the next few months would be a time of
relative Allied weakness. They would not know for several
weeks whether the Germans would attack at all, let alone
where such an attack would fall.

There was no truly centralised Allied military command
for the Western Front but there had recently been appointed
a 'Supreme War Council', which sat at Versailles. (The
French had wanted the Council to sit in Paris while the
British preferred a 'neutral' site and had suggested Boulogne;
Versailles, only just outside Paris, was supposed to be a
compromise.) The Council was to have permanent military
representatives from Britain, France, Italy and the United
States but the officers chosen were to be independent of
those countries' armies in the field. The first British military
representative was General Sir Henry Wilson, until he
became Chief of the Imperial General Staff in mid-February
1918; his place was then taken by General Sir Henry Rawlinson, who had, until then, been serving as an army commander
in France. These officers and their assistants were to prepare
plans and policies for periodic meetings of the political
leaders and military leaders, who would make decisions, in
harmony it was hoped, for the future.

The first full meeting of the War Council took place on
1 December 1917. The leaders did little more than survey
the position on the various fronts and the respective strengths
of the Allied and German armies. The permanent military
representatives were left then with the task of undertaking
further studies and of recommending policies for considera-

tion at the next full meeting. During the following weeks, no fewer than fourteen policy 'Notes' were produced and circulated, some being on such obscure subjects as the employment of Chinese labour companies and the reorganisation of Belgian infantry divisions. But the important Note Number 12 caused horror among the 'Westerners' when it urged that a major effort should be made to knock Turkey out of the war. Then came Note Number 14, recommending that a central reserve of French and British divisions be formed to counter any major attack by the Germans on the Western Front. On 24 January 1918, the principal British, French and American commanders on the Western Front met to consider their attitude to these proposals, which would all be coming up for consideration at the next full sitting of the Supreme War Council. During this preliminary discussion by the generals, there was some talk of Allied counter-offensives should the Germans attack. Haig made a very revealing remark when he said, 'Give us back the troops from Salonika [where there were 300,000 British troops] and we will commence offensives.' General Foch, Chief of the French General Staff, sharply retorted that they had been talking of 'counter-offensives' not new 'offensives'. The British Official History says that this preliminary conference 'resulted only in a somewhat acrid interchange of views without any definite understanding as to real unity of action.'*

The full Council met a week later. Foch accused Lloyd George of failing to see that Britain made a full effort – a clear reference to the reinforcements held back in England. Lloyd George retorted that since the opening of the Battle of the Somme in 1916 the British had done most of the fighting and had certainly suffered most of the casualties. Lloyd George fought hard for the proposed new effort in the East against Turkey; it had long been his favourite idea – anything rather than more offensives in France. The Western Front, however, was always first in the minds of the French; it was here, in their homeland, that the enemy had been sitting for over three years and they would not give support to the Turkish venture. The meeting concluded by deciding

* Page 70.

to attack Turkey, but only as long as the Western Front was not left short of troops and that no action at all against Turkey commenced for at least two months. The 'Westerners' had won this round in the long East-versus-West policy argument.

The French then asked the British to take over yet another stretch of the French line on the Western Front; this was in addition to the twenty-five miles that the British had only just taken over. This proposal was made by Clemenceau, the French Prime Minister, who was trying to use the authority of the War Council to force Lloyd George to get more troops out to France, and the Council did pass a suitably worded resolution to this effect. But Haig was not worried over this; Pétain, the French Commander-in-Chief, had already told his British colleague that he realised that this was a political move and the French Army would not insist that the British move even farther south.

Throughout all these debates there had been references to the forming of a 'General Reserve' behind the Western Front, with the British and French each contributing several divisions. This General Reserve was to be used to the best advantage of both armies in the event of a German attack on either. There was plenty of talk but little action. Everyone agreed that it was a fine idea but no one produced the necessary divisions. Haig, with his extended line and under-strength army, would have had grounds for much disquiet over this failure to find a General Reserve but he was assured by General Pétain that, in the event of the British front being attacked by the Germans, especially on Haig's right which was particularly weak, a French reserve would definitely move in behind the British and give support. Haig was satisfied with this arrangement; in fact Pétain's promise had been a condition of the recent British takeover of French line. When the Germans did attack this matter was to become one of vital importance.

That concluded the making of plans as far as the Allies were concerned. A fresh attempt to force Turkey out of the war was to be made but only in half-hearted fashion. Lloyd George had managed to keep the British reinforcements in England and Haig had not managed to obtain the new men with which to mount a fresh offensive. If the Germans attacked, they would be held and then counter-attacked by a General Reserve which was yet to be formed. The Americans were still coming.

Pity the poor British Expeditionary Force – worn out by three major battles in the last year, five of its divisions sent to Italy, dissension between its commander and those at home and kept short of men thereby, having just taken over twenty-five more miles of new front line and forced for its safety to depend on the charity of the French and a Central Allied reserve that did not exist.

*

When the German leaders came to consider their plans for 1918, they had the interesting and challenging problem of how best to use their new-found but temporary superiority in the West. The Germans certainly knew that the balance would turn against them later in 1918 and it was a clear case of where and how to strike before the Americans arrived in strength, if indeed it was decided to strike at all. There were four possible solutions open to the Germans:

1. They could recognise that they were unable to break the Western Front stalemate and that they would eventually be overwhelmed, and could accordingly ask the Allies for a compromise peace, what was sometimes called 'a peace of understanding'. The Germans had already done this, appropriately enough on Christmas Day 1917, but they had tried this approach several times before and had always been rebuffed. This recent approach had been no more than a mere formality insisted on by the Russians in the peace negotiations at Brest Litovsk and not expected to receive any more favourable answer than earlier attempts. The proud Allies had invested so much blood in this war that they were not going to settle now for much less than complete victory – the term 'unconditional surrender' was reserved for the Second World War but it was the mood of the Allies throughout the First. And why, said the Allies, should they settle for less now, with the Americans coming?

2. The Germans could recognise this reality and decide now

to stop the bloodshed by offering the unconditional surrender. But their pride, too, would not allow such a move, at least while their troops from the Eastern Front remained unused in the West.

3. The Germans could use their new strength to try once more for that elusive battlefield success and attempt to obtain a decisive victory before the Americans arrived in strength.

4. The long-shot hope for the Germans was that they might be able to exploit the advantage that every centralised force enjoys over an alliance – the advantage of unified command over possible dissension among allies. There was certainly plenty of scope for the latter.

The Germans had already made their decisions. They intended to fight on in the West. They intended to mount a massive offensive against the Allied positions on the Western Front, an offensive designed to knock out completely one of the Allied armies and at the same time place the maximum strain on inter-Allied loyalty.

The German with the most influence at this time was the formidable General Erich Ludendorff, who had, under Field-Marshal von Hindenburg, commanded the German forces at their great victory of Tannenberg and in the 1915 successes against Russia. When General von Falkenhayn had been removed from command in the West during the Battle of the Somme in 1916, the successful partnership of Hindenburg and Ludendorff had been brought back from Russia. Hindenburg became Chief of the General Staff and Ludendorff 'First Quartermaster-General', which was another title for Chief of Staff. In theory Hindenburg was the senior, but it was Ludendorff who took most of the important decisions.

Ludendorff's attitude at the end of 1917 was typical of that of the German military hierarchy. In his heart he knew that Germany could not win outright but he was one of the principal obstacles to the German Government's desire for peace. The civilians had long been ready to settle for the Allied terms. Ludendorff was not. The German Army was not yet ready to give up all its gains while Ludendorff had any say in affairs. It is known that in that New Year of 1918 Ludendorff was a little doubtful whether the Americans really would turn up in strength and be the deciding factor as so many said, but he was certainly not going to wait and see. He was preparing to attack on the Western Front. In all this – the rejection of peace on unfavourable terms and the intention to attack – Ludendorff had one, all-important supporter. Kaiser Wilhelm – grandson of Britain's Queen Victoria – was no mere figurehead and he was not yet prepared to give up his attempt to gain world glory for Germany through war.

The decision to attack had been taken at a conference on 11 November 1917 at Mons in Belgium. It is ironical that the location was the scene of the British Expeditionary Force's first clash with the Germans in 1914 and that the date was exactly one year before the end of the war. The initial decision was taken not by Hindenburg and the field army commanders but by Ludendorff with the chiefs of staff of the commanders. Such was the way of the German Army at that time – decisions by the staff, action by the field commanders. The British Official History comments:

> It is not without interest to note that neither the Kaiser nor the Crown Prince, nor even Hindenburg, was present at this moment-ous conference . . . The decision was taken by the General Staff, under the final covering authority of the Kaiser, without the slight-est reference to or interference from the Government in Berlin.*

Lloyd George would never have stood for that!

The vital questions following the main decision – the 'when' and the 'where' of the attack – were settled during subsequent weeks. The 'when' was an easy one: as soon as possible after the worst of the winter weather was over, in order to forestall any attack the Allies might be planning to make. Ludendorff wanted to start at the end of February or early in March at the latest. Where to attack was a more difficult problem. The German General Staff had plenty of plans, drawn up over the war years, for offensives in the West. A strong group within the staff wanted to attack the French on either side of Verdun – these attack plans were

* Page 138 footnote.

code-named *Castor* and *Pollux* – but this was decided against on the grounds that the British, a hundred miles away, would ignore this and be left intact. Three plans for attack on the British were looked at – one in the north on the Ypres sector and code-named *George*, another code-named *Mars* against Arras, and *Michael* against the British front at its junction with the French near the German-held town of St Quentin. The various arguments put forward in the German deliberations need not be recounted here. Ludendorff decided upon the old *Operation Michael* – the attack near St Quentin but extended in the north almost to Arras.

The main reasons for the choice of this sector were that the ground was likely to dry out more quickly here after the winter than in the British north and that the British and French defences and forces here were believed to be weak. There were thus the conditions for a tactical success, but the strategic aim was undoubtedly the destruction of the British Expeditionary Force. The German plan for the second stage after the front line had been broken through was to turn north-west and 'roll up' the British front from the south. Many British and German soldiers who took part in the fighting believed that the German plan was for a thrust westwards through Amiens and on to the coast but this was never the *original* German intention. The German plan was to break through, turn right, and then destroy the British piecemeal from the south or push them back against the Channel ports if the British chose to retire rather than stand and fight.

It was a truly ambitious plan but it contained great risks. Would the British break under such an attack? Would the French stand by and watch their ally defeated, or would they not come up from the south in strength and catch the Germans in rear? Ironically, *Operation Michael* was almost identical to Haig's original plan for the opening of the Somme attack in July 1916. If the map depicting the German plan is reversed it can easily be compared to Haig's plan to break through the German front on the Somme, take Bapaume and roll up the German front from the south. Haig's bold plan had ended in bloody disaster on the first day and been replaced by the slogging match of attrition in the subsequent stages of the battle. The comparison between Haig's plan for the Somme

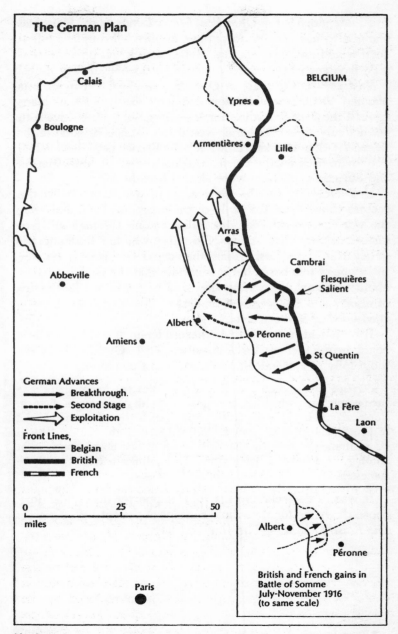

The German Plan

BELGIUM

Calais

Boulogne

Ypres

Armentières

Lille

Arras

Cambrai

Flesquières Salient

Abbeville

Albert

Péronne

Amiens

St Quentin

German Advances
Breakthrough
Second Stage
Exploitation

Front Lines,
Belgian
British
French

La Fère

Laon

0   25   50
miles

Albert

Péronne

British and French gains in
Battle of Somme
July–November 1916
(to same scale)

Paris

Map 2

and Ludendorff's for *Operation Michael* ends here. Haig had planned to use cavalry to exploit his breakthrough; Ludendorff would use only infantry. Haig's attack was on a sixteen-mile frontage; Ludendorff's would be on one of fifty miles!

Vast as was the scale of *Operation Michael*, yet more was planned. Various combinations of the old German attack plans against the British farther north – *George* and *Mars* – were to be actively prepared and would be launched soon after *Michael*; other attacks would keep the French occupied. When one looks back on the German plans, the scope, imagination and objectives of them were almost breathtaking.

Not everyone on the German side was happy with the sectors chosen and the scale of these grand plans, and after the war there was much discussion among German military historians over their merits. To judge whether Ludendorff's policy was the wisest choice that could be made is outside the scope of this book, but it is certain that the Germans were about to throw everything they had into this one last series of efforts and that a great amount of blood was about to be shed on the Western Front.

It remained to be seen whether Ludendorff and his soldiers could bring victory for Germany. D. J. Godspeed, in his biography of Ludendorff, makes this apt comment:

Perhaps in the mud and filth of the Western Front there was bred some virus which infected generals with delusions of victory. For nearly four years the British and French High Commands had had such delusions, and now Ludendorff assured the Kaiser: 'It will be an immense struggle that will begin at one point, continue at another, and take a long time. It is difficult but it will be successful.'*

It was in deference to his royal supporter that Ludendorff chose the name for the whole concept of the spring offensive: *Die Kaiserschlacht* – 'The Imperial Battle'.

* From *Ludendorff*, page 194.

The Attackers

It was in a very ordinary part of France that this first great battle of 1918 was to be fought. It did not even have a distinctive name, as had battlefields like Ypres, the Somme or Verdun. The southern part was in what may loosely be called the Somme region, because the river, mostly in canalised form, flows to the west through it, but this area is well to the east of the fighting on the Somme in 1916. The area of the coming battle was bounded on the south by the wide and marshy River Oise. In the centre there was a low but extensive ridge, almost a plateau, again running from east to west, but this high ground is not distinguished by a name. Then the ground falls away again in the north into Artois and the valley of the River Scarpe near Arras, though that well-known city was to be just beyond the northern limits of the battle. Probably the best description of the area would be to call it the Cambrai–St Quentin Front, but even that would not be completely satisfactory.

The main feature of the landscape was its wide but rolling nature, especially on the uplands away from the rivers. The rich topsoil was naturally well drained by the chalk beneath and there was no need for ditches or hedgerows. It was fine agricultural land which had grown wheat and sugar beet before the war. There were a few dense woods, but not enough to be major factors in the coming fighting as they had so often been on the Somme farther west in 1916. It was easy country for digging trenches and for excavating deep dug-outs which remained reasonably dry.

Two types of man-made feature would also be factors in the fighting. These were the 'sunken roads', where the local highways had been cut through the gentle rises of the plateau area, and the numerous quarries which the villagers had cut into the side of the nearest hill. Sunken roads and quarries provided good cover in this open area and often formed the basis of a defensive position.

The war had passed through this region in a matter of hours in the German advance of 1914, in fact the original British Expeditionary Force had marched through the southern part of this area in their retreat from Mons and Le Cateau to the Marne. For the next two years it had all been a German rear area until the British and French forced the Germans out of their strong defences farther west during the Battle of the Somme. The Germans had then constructed a strong new defensive line, running south-eastwards from Arras for seventy miles to a point near Soissons. After devastating the intervening area, the Germans slowly withdrew to this new line early in 1917. They named their new position the *Siegfried Stellung*; the Allies called it the Hindenburg Line. After following up the withdrawal and suffering many casualties from booby traps and the German rearguards, the British and French soldiers found themselves in possession of a 900-square-mile area in which not one building had been left standing, every bridge was demolished, every railway line removed, water wells blown in or poisoned, and even the fruit trees had been chopped down. And before them stood the seemingly impregnable defences of the Hindenburg Line.

The British had occupied the northern half of this devastated area, and two of their 1917 offensives made indentations into the Hindenburg Line. The southern part of the Battle of Arras left the British holding a small salient in the German lines at Bullecourt, and the tank attack at Cambrai in November 1917 left a much larger one farther south; this was sometimes called the Cambrai Salient but more often the Flesquières Salient. The area around this now contained many reminders of the Cambrai battle – the unburied corpses of infantrymen in No Man's Land, wrecked and abandoned tanks, cavalry horses which frequently had the flesh cut away from their rumps by soldiers who were not averse to roast horseflesh. One curious feature of the Flesquières Salient was the Canal du Nord, which had still been under construction when the war came and which existed now only in the form of a completely dry, brick-floored excavation; even the scaffolding left by the French workmen in 1914 remained – wooden poles set into earth-filled barrels. This dry canal ran

right through the battle lines and the two front lines consisted
of sandbag barriers fifty yards apart across the bed of it. The
opposing units here on 21 March would be the Saxons of the
53rd Reserve Division and a battalion of West Yorkshiremen
of the 17th (Northern) Division.

The British front line had extended only as far south as a
position four miles north of St Quentin in 1917, but they took
over two stretches of French-held line in January 1918 and
by the end of that month the British front extended to the
village of Barisis, five miles south of the River Oise. The
Germans had been intending to attack the junction of the
French and British armies, and this extension by the British
to the south had unwittingly made them the target for the
whole of the German attack.

The immediate front-line area contained only two towns of
note. On the Oise, near the southern limit of the British-held
front, was the German-held town of La Fère, through which
the river ran by way of many small streams. The British front
line was on the east bank of the Canal de l'Oise on the western
outskirts of the town. La Fère had been a garrison town since
the time of the Romans and the French Army had maintained
an important artillery barracks there since 1719. The town is
also reputed to have been the home of one of the Three
Musketeers – Athos, the Count of La Fère.

Thirteen miles farther north was the far larger and more
important town of St Quentin, again just within the German
lines. The main feature here was a massive, gaunt basilica
built in the sixteenth century. The roof had burned and
collapsed at some time since 1914 but the tower still stood
and was a valuable observation post for the German artillery.
Many German ex-soldiers have a strong affection for St
Quentin. Their front-line trenches ran along the fields only
just outside the town and were linked by communication
trenches to the nearest buildings. The French artillery had
been ordered not to bombard St Quentin – France had enough
devastated towns already. When the British took over this
front, the French passed on the request that St Quentin be
spared from shellfire, so the town still stood relatively undamaged right on the edge of No Man's Land. The French
civilians had all been removed when the Hindenburg Line had

been constructed, so the German soldiers could now shelter in comfort and safety in houses only a few yards from their front-line positions. Germans who served in St Quentin often refer to what they called the '*Kuhdenkmal*' – the 'Cow Memorial' in one of the town's squares. This was a fine statue of a bull harnessed to a plough which formed the main part of a monument dedicated to '*La Vie des Champs*' – the agricultural life of the area.*

One part of St Quentin that was not spared from shellfire, at least by the British after they took over, was the area of the main railway station.

Every evening between 6.0 and 8.0 p.m., the companies in the trenches each sent a party of twenty men back through the town to the square in front of the station to pick up the hot meal from our *Gulaschkanonen* – mobile field cookers. There was an English battery of four guns and it often fired four shells into the square hoping to catch us at the cookers. But these English were clever; the shells did not arrive every night and not at any set time so that we were always very nervous when we went back to the station for this hot food. (Gefreiter Carl Klemp, 211th Reserve Regiment)†

The German rear areas contained the towns of Cambrai and Le Cateau. The British had no towns near their front line. Bapaume, Péronne and Ham were a few miles to the rear but all had been destroyed by the Germans before they fell back in 1917. The whole region abounds with small villages; these are too numerous to mention here but many will be met later in the book. Where the villages did not form part of the front lines, they were used by both sides as rest billets, but there was a great difference between the villages on the two sides of the lines. The German-held villages had at least a proportion of the houses intact. The bleak ruins left to the British in the area devastated during the withdrawal provided no such comfort.

*

* The Cow Memorial survived both world wars but was demolished after 1945 to make way for a new building development.

† This and similar quotations are from interviews or correspondence with men who took part in the fighting on 21 March 1918. Christian names, instead of initials, will be used with German quotations because it is the German custom to do so. Appendix 1 will give translations for the German ranks used.

All forces on the Western Front had a chain of command which went up through 'division' and 'corps' to 'army', but the French and Germans had an extra level of command be.ween the army headquarters and General Headquarters that the British did not. This was the 'army group', which directed the operations of, usually, three armies. As the British Expeditionary Force contained only four armies, this 'army group' was not necessary.

The description of the German forces chosen to attack the British on 21 March can begin with two of these German 'army groups', both of which were commanded by royal princes. The whole of the attack front had originally been in the army group area commanded by Crown Prince Rupprecht of Bavaria. Prince Rupprecht had been in command of the German Sixth Army for the first three years of the war. He had handled many of the early offensive battles against the British at Ypres in 1914 and early 1915 and had then handled the German defence against many of the British offensives, particularly those at Neuve Chappelle, Arras and Passchendaele. Prince Rupprecht was an experienced commander who knew the British well. To the south of Prince Rupprecht's Army Group had lain that of the Kaiser's son, Crown Prince Wilhelm – the 'Little Willie' so often made fun of by British cartoonists. Crown Prince Wilhelm had also commanded an army from 1914 and had then become an army group commander, but most of his active service had been against the French and often on quieter sectors. It must be stressed that the role of the two princes, both earlier and in the coming battle, was the conduct of strategy rather than of battlefield tactics and their soldiering had all been carried out at comfortable headquarters well beyond the range of Allied guns.

Ludendorff decided not to give the entire offensive to Rupprecht, who until then had commanded the whole area of the coming battle, but to allocate the southern flank of it to Wilhelm. The ostensible reason for this change was that by dividing control in this way Ludendorff himself could keep greater control of the coming battle, but it is almost certain that jealousies between the two princes and the desire to give the Kaiser's son a share in the hoped-for final victory of the *Kaiserschlacht* were also factors. So the boundary of Crown

Prince Wilhelm's Army Group moved northwards and took in the southern one third of the attack front; by no more than a coincidence, this was the former French sector just taken over by the British.

Three armies from the two army groups were to carry out the attack. In the north and the centre, Rupprecht had General Otto von Below's Seventeenth Army and General Georg von der Marwitz's Second Army. These two formidable Prussians had excellent records. Von Below had served under Ludendorff at Tannenberg in 1914 and had had a string of successes to his credit since then, culminating in his most recent victory against the Italians at Caporetto in the previous October. Ludendorff fetched von Below to the Western Front and gave him a new army headquarters and a vital part to play in the coming offensive. Von der Marwitz, a cavalryman, had been a successful commander on the Western Front since 1914; he had a thorough knowledge of this sector and it was he who had planned and carried out the successful German counter-stroke at Cambrai. These two army commanders were given the main roles to play. Von Below's orders were to break through to Bapaume and von der Marwitz was to go for Péronne; their two armies would then wheel right and, shoulder to shoulder, roll up the British positions to the north.

Crown Prince Wilhelm had only one army in the coming attack. This was General Oskar von Hutier's Eighteenth Army, again a newly created command. Von Hutier was another of Ludendorff's Eastern Front protégés and had commanded in the great German success at Riga, which had been one of the final knock-out blows administered to the Russians in 1917. It is worth commenting that the failure of Russia at the end of 1917 had released not only large German forces for use in the West but also some of the finest talent in German generalship. Von Hutier's role was to break the British lines near St Quentin and push through to capture the town of Ham, but then, while the two German armies to the north wheeled right, von Hutier's was to form a flank guard to protect the rear of the other armies. The role of Crown Prince Wilhelm and von Hutier was thus more limited than that of Prince Rupprecht and his two armies, but it was a role

TO ALL AT HOME

vital to the success of the whole plan. The British defences will be described in the next chapter but it can be said here that this southern army was to attack the weakest of the British sectors. This British weakness and the ambitions of Crown Prince Wilhelm were to be major factors causing the Germans to depart from their original aim during the battle.

The fourteen German corps commanders who would pass on and help implement their superiors' orders will not play much part in this account and can be ignored. It is better that we jump across to examine the ordinary German front-line soldiers on whose skill and spirit the hopes of their leaders would ultimately depend.

*

The main characteristic of the German Army of 1918 is well known – tough, brave, disciplined, patriotic and skilful – the perfect material in fact for making soldiers. The German Army never cracked from start to finish in two world wars; nor did the British, their adversaries in the coming battle, but the British soldier, though patient and enduring, was slower to rouse and less aggressive.

The main characteristic, however, of the German Army of 1918 was that it was far more professional than the British. There were several reasons for this. Conscription for military service had been a feature of peacetime German life for over a century. At the age of twenty, every fit German male had been called up for at least two years' service and this had been followed by five years on the reserve with an annual period of retraining. Even after this, the German remained on the strength of his local *Landwehr* or *Landsturm* unit until reaching the age of forty-five. In 1914 Germany had been able to mobilise an army of 4,000,000 trained men in eighty-two Regular and Reserve Divisions, with enough reservists left over to form more divisions later. The German Army had allowed the enlistment of a certain number of untrained volunteers on the outbreak of war but these, nearly all youths below the age of conscription, had never represented more than a small proportion of the German Army. There had since then also been the annual call-up of classes of new recruits, but these had always been incorporated into seasoned units.

There were further factors. Because the Germans had been on the defensive for most of the last three years, and as the defenders had not suffered as heavily as the attackers, the average German division had been wasted away to a far lesser extent than the Allied divisions. (I am aware of the argument that the defenders lost at least as heavily as and possibly more than the attackers, but I cannot support this school of thought. Taking all Allied attacks from early 1915 to the end of 1917, my opinion is that attacking casualties usually exceeded those of the defenders.) Then, the German system of allocating divisions to a sector of front was a far more permanent one than that of the Allies. Once posted to a sector, a German division stayed there to attack, defend, or hold trenches for as long as possible before being moved. Many of the sectors of the Western Front had been dormant for well over a year and the German divisions here and those that had been in Russia had rarely been subjected to heavy fighting. Sixty-eight of the German divisions on the Western Front had missed the Battle of Passchendaele whereas only nine British divisions did not fight there. When the Germans started assembling their divisions for the *Kaiserschlacht*, many of them had not been involved in a major battle for well over a year.

For all these reasons the German divisions which were soon to attack the British contained a far higher quantity of pre-war, fully trained soldiers than did the British. It is difficult to be precise but maybe one third or a half of the members of the average German infantry platoon in early 1918 were pre-war soldiers while, for reasons which will be described in the next chapter, the average British platoon at this time would be fortunate if it contained more than one or two such veterans.

An interesting comparison between the German and British infantry units of early 1918 is to be found in their officer content. The average British infantry battalion contained about thirty-six commissioned officers, six with each of the four rifle companies and a dozen or so specialists or administrative officers on the strength of battalion headquarters. A large proportion of the British junior officers were men who had been commissioned less than a year, either straight from public school or as 'ranker' officers. The German battalion had an authorised establishment of about twenty-five officers, five with each company and five more at battalion head-quarters. But the Germans had refused to dilute the quality of their officer corps by the commissioning, even temporarily, of what they considered to be unsuitable men to replace officer casualties, and the average German battalion was now being run by only *seven* fully commissioned officers – a Hauptmann (captain) as battalion commander, an Oberleutnant as adjutant, a medical officer, and four Leutnants for company commanders. Very rarely was a German platoon commanded by an officer. This position was usually filled by warrant officers or senior non-commissioned officers – Feldwebels, Vizefeldwebels and Unteroffiziers – or by a Fähnrich (officer cadet) or an Offizier Stellvertreter (literally a 'substitute officer'). The handful of German officers left in each battalion were not encouraged to expose themselves to danger as freely as were the British. So, although the German officers were low in numbers and held lowly ranks compared to those of a British battalion, the average German infantry officer had accumulated a far greater depth of experience than had his British counterpart, and the platoons, commanded as they were by experienced and battle-hardened men, although not commissioned officers, often performed better on the battle-field than did the British platoons led by inexperienced boy officers, however valiant.

These were the factors which led to the German Army of 1918 being described as more professional than its enemy in the coming battle. They are important points that will need to be remembered when the fighting of the first day is examined.

*

It is difficult for an Englishman to describe the 'nationalities' within the German Army because of the subtle distinctions between the different states that had come together over a long period to make the modern nation of Germany. If it were left to a British front-line soldier of 1918, he would probably refer to the Saxons and the Bavarians, who were both favoured as opponents because they were easy-going and liked to have a quiet time when holding trenches, and to the Prussian Guards, who were 'a hard lot'. The rest of their enemies were just 'Gerries'. But there were other Germans and most were to be represented in the divisions that would attack on 21 March. There would be men from many of the old kingdoms and dukedoms which now formed Germany. There would be regiments* from Baden, Bavaria, Branden-burg, from Hamburg and the other Hansa towns of Bremen and Lübeck, from Hanover, Hesse, Pomerania, East and West Prussia, the Rhineland, the Saarland, Saxony, Schleswig-Holstein, Silesia, Westphalia and Württemberg.

The only units that retained any form of national identity were the Bavarian divisions which had served in their own Bavarian Corps for the first years of the war; but these corps had since been split up and their divisions now served piece-meal among German divisions. The Bavarians were regarded by the other Germans as 'good brave soldiers', although a thirty-five-year-old Bavarian who in peacetime had been a farm labourer deserted to the 16th (Irish) Division on 19 March and stated that his comrades were sick of the war, that it was only the Prussians who were still 'war-keen' and that, with the exception of the official classes, Bavarians resented their complete subordination to Prussia. 'This', it is recorded, 'was the one subject on which the prisoner showed signs of animation.'† Other Germans say that there were always fights with the Bavarians over the right of entry to their canteens. Bavaria, with its fine breweries, kept its units well supplied with high-quality beer which men from other units would have liked to buy, but they were rarely allowed into the Bavarian canteens. Adolf Hitler was serving as a corporal in a Bavarian division but not one of the three that would be in the attack on 21 March; Hitler was in the 16th Bavarian

---

* The regiment was the standard German infantry unit. Each regiment had three battalions and there were three regiments in a division. Appendix 2 will give the Order of Battle of the German divisions involved in the fighting of 21 March 1918.

† From 16th Division General Staff War Diary, Public Record Office WO 95/1956.

Reserve Regiment and his division would not come into the battle until the sixth day.

The British favourites were undoubtedly the Saxons, and the Germans agreed that their Saxon comrades were not regarded as the best of soldiers: 'we called them *Kaffeesaxons* because they were always drinking their own kind of thin, watery coffee.' One of the Saxon soldiers who would be in action on 21 March describes his attitude to the war although his is probably an extreme opinion.

Just before my call-up for military service, in May 1916, I had been handing out anti-war pamphlets in Leipzig. In February 1916 I was arrested for this but, in view of my call-up, I was not sent to prison like my friends. An amnesty promulgated by the King of Saxony saved me. After I became a soldier I was extremely careful not to fall foul of the strict discipline of the army and I cultivated the art of passive resistance. During the whole of the remainder of the war I managed to avoid shooting at anyone. Fortunately I never found myself in a situation where I had to do. (Gefreiter Herbert Müller, 107th Reserve Regiment)

The only non-Germans who would be taking part in the attack were a few Austrians – men from the country over whose arguments Germany had originally gone to war in 1914. The Austrians had mostly fought on the Eastern Front and in Italy and their failure to match the high standards of the Germans earned them the nickname of '*Kameraden Schnürschuh*' – 'laced-boot comrades'. This was an unkind reference to the distinctive laced boots of the Austrians which, said the Germans, helped the Austrians to run more quickly. But Austria had little desire to fight now on the Western Front and, although four of her infantry divisions were reluctantly sent there later in 1918, none had arrived at this time. The only Austrians who were to take part in the coming battle were the men of several motorised heavy artillery batteries, a contribution by Austria to the considerable force of artillery being collected.

Of the élite German units, there were to be seven Guard divisions in the coming battle. Two of these, the 3rd and the 4th Guard Divisions, had only recently been formed out of Guard Regiments that had been previously scattered throughout ordinary infantry divisions and were now reunited in these new divisions early in January 1918, 'a great thrill for us all' as one guardsman said. Most of the Guard officers were from the German nobility and the rank and file were all Prussians. Even after three years of war, the Imperial Guard had lost little of its pre-war eminence in the German Army, and the British soldiers were wise to be wary of its regiments.

Two of the Hanoverian regiments who were also to be in the battle had a unique link with the British Army. Hanoverian Fusiliers had fought alongside British soldiers against the French in the Siege of Gibraltar in 1779–83 and had worn the battle honour 'Gibraltar' as a ribbon sewn on the left sleeve of their uniforms ever since. The descendants of the Hanoverian units of Gibraltar were now the 73rd and 79th Infantry Regiments and the 10th *Jäger* Battalion and, when holding the line against British troops, they often used to shout the word 'Gibraltar' across No Man's Land to their enemies. The two infantry regiments, although not the *Jägers* as far as is known, were both to be prominent in the coming offensive.

Jägers were an unusual feature of the German Army. The word itself means 'hunter'. The Germans are true hunting and shooting enthusiasts and the *Jäger* battalions reflected this spirit. The nearest British equivalents were the rifle regiments but the English term 'rifleman' is not quite appropriate and the term '*Jäger*' is best left untranslated. Earlier in the war, the *Jäger* battalions had been kept for special work, but most had now been brought together. They fought as part of conventional infantry regiments, although they always maintained some of their original traditions and the green uniforms with leather patches on knees, elbows and trouser seats so beloved by German huntsmen. A complete division of *Jägers*, the 195th Division, would attack part of the British front just south of the Bullecourt Salient on 21 March.

A few of the *Jägers* had remained independent. These were the *Jägersturmbataillons*, of which there were at least two. They contained only the fittest and most athletic of young men, who were proud to belong to such élite units. They did no trench duty but spent their time practising a mixture of athletic and military activities – sprint races, grenade throwing, obstacle courses, jumping, trench fighting. There were competitions at which books by patriotic German authors were awarded to the prize-winners. The *Jägersturmbataillons* were used as assault infantry for special attacks and when an important 'snatch' of enemy prisoners had to be made in a night trench raid. A specially chosen group of *Jägers* carried out the raid and then, on returning to the German trenches, were whisked back to the rear with any prisoners they had taken before the inevitable enemy artillery retaliation arrived. For this and because they did not do ordinary trench duty and received special rations of meat, the *Jägers* were not popular with the ordinary German infantry. The *Jägersturmbataillons* were to have a special role in the coming offensive.

By contrast there were many humbler, wartime-raised divisions which would be in the attack. One of the three German Marine Divisions, the 3rd, had been sent down from its usual sector on the Belgian coast to take part. It would follow up the attack on the 9th (Scottish) Division holding part of the Flesquières Salient. There were many Reserve Divisions; most had been mobilised in 1914 with fully trained reservists but some were the product of the disastrous experiment of allowing enthusiastic youngsters to volunteer in 1914; with only a small leavening of trained men and the sketchiest of training, they were thrown into the fighting around Ypres within weeks of the formation of their divisions. The result had been the '*Kindermord*' or the 'Slaughter of the Innocents' before the rapid and accurate rifle fire of the British Expeditionary Force at the Battle of Langemarck in October 1914. Three of the *Kindermord* divisions, the 45th, 53rd and 54th Reserve Divisions, would fight on 21 March, but they had matured since 1914. Three more divisions which were to take part in the attack had been formed for little more than a year. The most junior of these was the 238th Division, which had been raised at Lockstedt army camp, north of Hamburg, early in 1917 and was formed mainly of young men born in 1898 and 1899 with a handful of recovered wounded and other experienced veterans. Because of the youth of most of its men, the division was popularly known as the 'Division of the First Communicants'. One of its three regiments. was from the Hansa towns, mainly Hamburg, another regiment drew its men from Hanover and the third from Schleswig between Hamburg and the Danish border. The division had been trained carefully, had fought twice in a defensive role in the Battle of Passchendaele and would soon be making its first attack from the southern outskirts of St Quentin against the 36th (Ulster) Division.

Several of the attack divisions had only recently come to the Western Front from the East. Ludendorff had ordered that the best of the Eastern Front divisions were to be selected, and sent west for the *Kaiserschlacht*. British soldiers who were later to see much of the Germans at close quarters knew all about the great influx of Germans from the East and claimed that they could always tell these men by the smart new uniforms which were such a contrast to the normal shabby outfits of the regular Western Front German. This is a misapprehension; when the Germans were asked about it, they stated that it was only new recruits from Germany who had the smarter uniforms; the old hands from Russia were usually as threadbare as the rest.

Several of the Germans who had come from Russia were asked to compare the two fronts. There was a world of difference between fighting conditions. In Russia, the two sides had usually kept at least two kilometres apart and there had been very little Russian artillery fire, which was all a pleasant contrast to the narrow No Man's Land and intense bombardments of the Western Front. Enemy attacks had been carried out with the Russian infantry reputedly getting well drunk beforehand and then coming on in a large number of massed waves – eighteen to nineteen waves are mentioned – all driven on by Cossacks with long whips (although the Cossack whips may well be an exaggeration). The Russians were reputed to have no knowledge of or respect for the Red Cross, and for a German to be wounded and left behind on the battlefield was considered a very poor fate. The Russians were not cruel but their medical services were not very efficient. When it was the Germans who had attacked, a brisk bombardment was often sufficient to get the Russians to leave their trenches and surrender. But such encounters with the Russians had been rare, and many Germans had found the

Eastern Front a great bore and were keen to get to France to see more action.

Another factor was food, because the German soldier of 1918 was hungry wherever he served, with meat and decent bread scarce everywhere; the slightest improvement was appreciated. The general opinion was that, bad though the rations were on the Western Front, they did at least appear regularly, and one man says that a pound of bread weighed 500 grammes in the West but only 400 in the East. A final factor was that the movement to the West had started in the summer of 1917 and every man who left was delighted to do so before another Russian winter arrived.

The Germans on the Western Front were pleased to have this reinforcement but many have disparaging comments to make on both the fighting qualities and morale of the new-comers. It was believed that they 'did not really understand the special conditions of the Western Front' and they were also suspected of being tainted by Bolshevism; they were *'ein bisschen rot'* – 'a little red' – and more prone to desertion than units which had been in the West for several years. All this was, of course, denied by the Easterners.

The Germans would have more than seventy infantry divisions available for their attack – the German Official History says seventy-six divisions and the British seventy-four divisions. Both sources agree that thirty-two divisions would be in the first wave of the attack; a force somewhere between thirty-two and twenty-eight divisions was available to follow up in the second and third waves of the attack and the remainder were positional divisions that would hold the German trenches until the attack commenced and then take over the duties of looking after prisoners-of-war and the many other tasks to be carried out in the rear of the assault divisions. There would be 1,700 batteries of guns, 3,532 trench mortars, eighty-two squadrons of aircraft, machine-gunners, pioneers, and all the other elements making up a 1918 army. No figures can be found for the total number of German soldiers to be involved in this great affair but it was probably well over one million!

*

What Ludendorff was hoping to achieve with his soldiers – to break clean through the British trench lines into the open country beyond and get away once and for all from trench warfare – had been the dream of every Western Front commander since the great battles of manoeuvre and movement had petered out at the end of 1914. Each attacking commander since then had varied the same old elements of the offensive. Artillery bombardments had been short or long. Infantry had been used in this formation or that, with limited objectives or deep ones. Aeroplanes and, more recently, tanks had been brought to the battlefield in an attempt to break the deadlock. And usually the cavalry had been brought up to stand patiently behind the attacking forces, hoping always that a way could somehow be opened for them through the barbed wire and trenches, allowing them to create havoc in the enemy rear.

But it had never happened. No commander had ever achieved a breakthrough on the Western Front. Now Ludendorff was to make his attempt. He brought together the best tactical thinkers in his army, regardless of their rank, and set them to work studying the mistakes and lessons of old battles and trying to devise a plan to break the stalemate. The result was a series of pamphlets, under the title of 'The Offensive Battle in Trench Warfare', and then a fresh plan based on these studies. It will be convenient here if this plan is broken down into the separate roles to be played by the major participants – the artillery and the infantry – and by their supporting arms.

The man who is remembered more than any other for the German success of 21 March 1918 was a certain artilleryman, Oberst Georg Bruchmüller. Godspeed's *Ludendorff* describes Bruchmüller as 'an unknown, middle-aged officer brought back from the retired list to the staff of a Landwehr Division', a man 'with a unique talent for divining exactly how much ammunition was needed to soften a position before an infantry assault'. Bruchmüller's 'unique talent' had been spotted just before the German attack on Verdun in 1916 while he was only an Oberstleutnant – a lieutenant-colonel. He had been promoted by just one rank and had been artillery adviser to the German supreme commander on the Western Front ever since. It was as though Haig had allowed an obscure Territorial Army colonel to prepare artillery plans for the lieutenant-general who was his General Officer Commanding, Royal Artillery.

The dilemma that had always faced artillery commanders was whether to disclose an impending offensive by openly registering their guns and then firing a long and thorough bombardment or whether to retain the element of surprise by firing a short, hurricane bombardment. Ludendorff and Bruchmüller decided upon the latter. A great force of artillery was to be assembled, most to be kept well back until the last moment, and then brought up to fire a bombardment lasting only five hours, all with little or no previous registration of targets. It was known as 'shooting by the map' and it would require all the skill of the officers in the German artillery batteries. When the bombardment eventually opened at 4.40 a.m.* Bruchmüller was to have the greatest force of artillery ever gathered at one place, just about half of the entire German artillery strength on the entire Western Front. The total number of guns was 6,473, made up of 3,965 field guns (7.7 and 10-centimetre), 2,435 heavies (mostly 15-centimetre, known as the 5.9-inch to the British) and 73 superheavies (21-centimetre and above). These guns would fire approximately 1,160,000 shells in the five-hour bombardment. This compares with the 1,437 British guns which had fired 1,500,000 shells in the seven-day bombardment for the opening of the Battle of the Somme in 1916 and, in a later war, with the 1,000 guns available to Montgomery in his famous opening bombardment at the Battle of El Alamein. In addition there were 3,532 mortars which could fire bombs of various weights up to 100 kilogrammes on short-range targets. This great force of guns was sometimes referred to as 'Ludendorff's Battering Train', a suitable term considering the siege-like conditions of trench warfare.

The exact programme of the German bombardment will be given in a later chapter, but it was to have several new features besides its brevity and intensity. The first of these

* Twenty-four-hour times were not used in 1918 and times will be written in this way to preserve the usage of that period. Conveniently for this story, the Germans and the British were using the same times on 21 March 1918.

was the extensive use of gas that was proposed. The very effective mustard gas (known as Yellow Cross because of the markings on the shells) was not to be used because this was a gas that did not dissipate in the air but affected the ground for several days. The more lethal phosgene (Green Cross) was the one upon which the Germans relied on this occasion. The British gas-masks were known to give protection against phosgene, so the Germans tried a new twist by mixing in with the phosgene barrage a new gas which would cause intense irritation to the eyes. The British masks did not give protection against this. This new 'lachrymatory' gas would, it was hoped, irritate the British soldiers so much that they would be forced to take off their masks and then inhale the deadly phosgene. Various combinations of gas shells or high-explosive shells were to be used in the preliminary bombardment, with the high-explosive doing its conventional task of blowing up barbed wire, trenches, machine-gun and artillery positions. The normal mixture for this barrage was half gas and half high-explosive, but for the British artillery positions Bruchmüller had a special mixture – four gas shells to every high-explosive. This, it was hoped, would keep the British guns silent during the German bombardment and the vital first hours of the German infantry attack.

Another new feature of the Bruchmüller plan was the depth to which the bombardment would reach. Not only were all the British defences to be shelled, but also crossroads, assembly areas, and headquarters well behind the British infantry and artillery positions. To achieve this, the German guns were to be brought up as close behind the German trenches as possible.

But it was acknowledged by the Germans that a five-hour bombardment on unregistered targets along a fifty-mile front could not hope to achieve the complete destruction of the British defences, and the German infantry commanders were told bluntly that their men must expect to fight their way through. Barbed wire would be blown away, trenches blown in and artillery neutralised, but the British infantry and machine-gunners in their underground dug-outs could not be put out of action completely. The best that could be hoped for was that the British infantry would be so shell-shocked and confused by the hurricane of fire that would fall upon them and so affected by the gas, or at least the necessity to wear gas-masks for several hours, that they would put up no effective resistance.

*

Novel plans were also being made for the infantry. Previous attacks had usually been made according to rigid timetables and fixed objectives. It had long been recognised on the Western Front that, if enough artillery was turned on to a single line of trenches, attacking infantry could usually capture it and hold it if their flanks were covered. Any attack more ambitious than this simple method had usually foundered against subsequent lines of trenches or because of part of the advance being held up; the 'flank in the air' and the subsequent enfilading fire or counter-attack of the enemy had been the downfall of many an infantry attack. But the Germans decided that they could do better than the 'limited-objective' attack and were prepared to try a more ambitious method based on new thinking, the product this time of an even more junior officer, one Hauptmann Geyer.

Where previous plans had been based on rigidity, conformity and confrontation, Geyer's relied upon fluidity, initiative and infiltration. Where previous attackers had been given the task of a steady advance, the capture of one line of enemy trenches at a time and a careful link being maintained with troops to right and left, the leading units in this attack would merely be given a direction of advance and were told to move on as fast and as deep as they could into the British lines *without regard to what was happening on the flanks*. To be more specific, a division would be given boundaries, the direction in which it was to attack, and then left to prepare its attack plan according to the above principles, each division making allowance for local conditions and the availability of special troops. These 'special troops' were men who would spearhead the advance, specially trained 'storm troops' whose task would be to create the initial breaches in the British front line and then lead the penetration deep into the rear. Once through the front line, the storm troops were ordered to ignore and by-pass British defensive positions, search instead for points where resistance was weaker, and simply keep going farther into the British rear. The storm troops would have the assistance of a *'Feuerwalz'* – a creeping artillery barrage that was timed to move forward at a rate of 200 metres every four minutes. Arrangements were made for rockets to be fired asking for the *Feuerwalz* to be moved on more quickly if the storm troops were doing well but, significantly, no plans were made for the *Feuerwalz* to be brought back if the leading troops were held up. The storm troops just had to keep going.

Behind the storm troops would come 'battle groups' of more orthodox infantry in battalion or regimental strength supported by machine-guns, mobile mortars and – another novelty – field artillery which would go into action with the infantry and directly under the orders of infantry commanders. The battle groups' role was to surround and destroy those British positions left behind by the storm troops. Behind the battle groups would come more infantry formations to provide a constant stream of fresh reinforcements or to take over completely from those ahead and keep up the momentum of the attack.

There was one factor to the Germans' advantage that would help this plan: on this occasion they had the men available to bring an almost overwhelming strength to bear on the line to be attacked. A good example of this can be seen in the situation that would exist on the sector of front near the German-held village of Quéant. A 2,000-yard line of front here was held by the British with the left half of their 6th Division, with three battalions in the front line, one and a half battalions in support, and then nothing but a few Pioneers and Royal Engineers near the divisional artillery lines. It must be stressed that this was not part of the front south of St Quentin which had recently been taken over from the French and which was notoriously weak. The Quéant sector was well to the north and was an average British-defended sector of long standing. Opposite this half-division of defenders the Germans assembled a complete corps with two divisions for the first wave of the attack, two more in immediate reserve and a fifth in distant reserve. The equivalent of five British battalions, with their nearest reserves almost six miles behind the front, were to face forty-five German battalions.

*

The artillery and the infantry were the main elements of any Western Front attack. If this had been a British plan, at least three other elements would have been brought into action – tanks to help the infantry forward, aircraft to give further close support to the infantry, to observe for the artillery, to bomb the enemy rear and to keep opposing aircraft from intervening in the battle, and, finally, cavalry to fan out and exploit the expected breakthrough. The Germans were to use aircraft on a large scale but they had only a handful of tanks and no significant force of cavalry. Even though the tank had been a feature of Allied attacks since 1916, the Germans had not taken to this new weapon. Only nine tanks would take part in the German attack, five captured British models which had been repaired and four made by a German factory. Ludendorff only saw his first tank, a captured British one, in February 1918. This failure by the Germans, surprising in view of their use of tanks in the Second World War, was partly due to a failure in German military thinking to appreciate the value of the new weapon and partly due to the strain on German industry. As for cavalry, the Germans had several cavalry divisions but most had been left behind in the East to garrison the Ukraine. The few German horsemen later seen by British soldiers were mounted staff officers, artillerymen, or small parties of cavalry attached to the infantry solely for scouting purposes. Historians, both Allied and German, were later to say that this was one occasion when fighting cavalry could have been used to great effect in a Western Front battle, but the Germans decided to do without them.

The German attack, following on the five-hour hurricane bombardment, was to be carried out on a fifty-mile front, much of it with the kind of superiority available on the Quéant sector. The infantry attack plan was novel, bold and ambitious. But it was also risky and would require all the skill and nerve of the German infantry. If by-passed British positions stood firm and if the British reserves were used with imagination, then large bodies of Germans could themselves be cut off in the British lines. But if the German plan succeeded, so much confusion would be created that the British positions could start to collapse and the whole British defensive plan disintegrate. The great initial hope of the Germans was to smash through the British front-line defences and capture the British artillery on the first day. If that could be achieved, then the dream of every commander on the Western Front since 1914 would be realised – the breakthrough, the end of trench warfare, and the commencement of a war of movement. In this, the professional Germans believed they could beat anyone.

*

The ordinary German soldier began to think that something big was being prepared at about the time of Christmas 1917. It was obvious to him that the German forces on the Western Front were being heavily reinforced from the East and vague talk began to circulate that his leaders would be going over to the offensive in the spring. This feeling hardened in the New Year as there accumulated the unmistakable evidence that the front-line soldier always recognises as the preliminaries to an offensive in which he will probably be involved. The first sign was when he found his division had been taken out of the line unexpectedly and assembled in billets well to the rear, not for just a few days' routine rest but for a long period of training and re-equipment. All armies contained divisions that were reliable and others that were not, those that could be trusted to do well in an attack and those which were best left as 'line-holders', preferably on quiet sectors. It was the men of the better German divisions who suddenly found themselves taken out of their trenches and settling down in the comparative luxury of a back-area village. Divisional commanders and staffs were sent off for special courses of instruction and returned to train their regiments and battalions in the new tactics. These moves took place behind the entire length of the Western Front. Some artillery units were particularly lucky in that they were sent right back to Germany to re-equip with new guns. Divisions on the Eastern Front often carried out their training in

Russia before moving west. This wide dispersal was partly a
matter of convenience and partly a means of concealing from
the Allies the location of the coming attack.

There were many changes of personnel. Most of the men
over the age of thirty-five were removed from the divisions
under training and sent to the garrison division's left behind
in the East. The younger men from these garrison divisions,
together with newly trained men from the depots in Germany,
were in turn sent to bring the attack divisions up to full
strength. This was the time-honoured 'fattening-up' of units
before an attack. A cynical front-line officer in a division
which had just come out of the line in Belgium describes some
of the strains these changes produced in his unit.

Soon after Christmas all home leave was cancelled in our division
and we came out of the line and went to a rest area. Rumours
started to circulate that a big event in the West was being prepared.
There were whispers about a mighty offensive towards Amiens
with the intention of splitting the British and the French apart,
driving the former out of France and Belgium and then rolling back
the French to the south. At last there would be an end to the nerve-
racking trench warfare.

We had a good rest that winter and our units were filled up.
The transport park was improved and enlarged with some fine
horse transport from Russia. There was a drive at home, under the
command of a particular general, to get out from staffs and
garrisons, hospitals and orderly rooms, all those who could be
spared for fighting duties. All these people who had managed to
keep well out of the way had now to leave their *Gulaschkanonen* and
learn to march, fight and shoot. So old General 'Heldenklau'* – for
that was what we called him – made several hundred thousand men
free for the front. Many of these immediately found mysterious
illnesses to suffer from, or had the wrong documents; others
suddenly received bad news from their families at home or their
grandmothers died. They had flat feet, lousy eyesight, bad
stomachs, etc., etc.

Then they emptied the hospitals, and many old soldiers who had
been wounded three or four times were sent back yet again but
these were all good comrades, ready to do their duty at the front
again. Many young recruits turned up – good lads who had

* This word is difficult to translate; literally it is 'hero-claw' – a man who
drags out rear-area 'heroes'.

brothers or friends at the front and wanted to be in on the final offensive. Also many officers who had '*Brustschmerzen*' – 'chest trouble'; they wanted to get some medals there before the war was over. There was always the saying, 'From the front comes the hail of bullets; from the rear the medal-seekers.' But now each of them had to prove that he was a man indeed, a patriot and a hero.

It wasn't easy to weld all these people together and prepare for emergencies. Men of different ages did not always get on well with each other and, also, there were certain tensions among the officers. The old front-line 'pigs', who had shared everything with their men through blood and lead-filled air, preferred to ignore the instructions of the communication-zone cowards concerning the preparation of the troops for the final struggle. The old team spirit and comradeship of the front finally won over the excessive discipline of the barrack square. (Leutnant Friedrich Wellhausen, 46th Reserve Regiment)

The German soldiers got down to hard training. Perhaps the hardest work was done by the storm troops, who had to perfect the technique of penetrating the British front-line defences. There was much emphasis on trench fighting and rapid movement, and that terrible weapon, the flame-thrower, was sometimes attached to the storm-troop units. It is commonly believed that every German attack was led by special storm troops, but there was no regular pattern to their allocation. Divisions known to be facing particularly tough defences were given the best of the *Jägersturmbataillons*; others had to provide their own storm troops by sending selected infantry men to the *Jägers* for instruction and then forming a divisional *Sturmbataillon*. Yet again, it is probable that other divisions managed without special storm troops and simply put their best battalions into the front wave of the attack, trusting them to perform the vital breakthrough function.

The majority of infantrymen had no part to play in these storm tactics, and when survivors were asked what special training they had for the attack, they seemed surprised at the question. They all knew that a war of movement was hoped for and it was this that was practised, but the tactics were not new; it was what all good soldiers had been trained in before trench warfare had intervened and it was more a refresher course than a learning of anything new, although there was always the emphasis on speed, on keeping up with the creeping barrage. There was more to learn for the officers and staffs – how to handle their units in the open, how to exploit success without concern for flanks, how to handle communications on the battlefield. The ordinary soldiers were hardly concerned with all this; they were merely turned out to take part in large-scale exercises and marched from one spot to another and on again while their superiors relearnt the art of mobile warfare. Many men do mention the lessons learnt at Cambrai – how vulnerable a tank was to a brave man who could push a bundle of grenades under the tank track or to the field gunner who could destroy a tank by staying at his gun and firing over open sights.

The artillery had their own training. All guns arriving from the Eastern Front had to be calibrated on a huge firing range – a process that lasted eight weeks, during which at least 1,000 guns were checked. The artillerymen had to practise moving their guns forward over torn-up ground representing a battlefield. It was a tough time with, as one man says, 'several accidents including a few lost fingers'.

There were new weapons to be mastered. In particular, a new light machine-gun had been introduced and a special platoon of these was being formed for each company. It would be the light machine-gunners who would accompany the attacking infantry; the old pattern machine-guns mounted on heavy sledges, that had caused such execution as defensive weapons throughout the war, would be left behind in this attack. A young Bavarian officer, earmarked for command of one of these new machine-gun platoons, describes his introduction to the weapon:

> While my division, the 1st Bavarian, was being trained for the attack, I was sent to an officers' course at the Small Arms School at Harocourt, near Charleville. Here, future L.M.G. platoon commanders were trained in the handling of the new weapon. There were about 100 officers and officer cadets on the course; most of them were Prussians and I was the only one from Bavaria. It was a great joy and satisfaction to me that I won the final firing competition. The Prussians nicknamed me the 'Bavarian Poacher'.
> (Leutnant Reinhold Spengler, 1st Bavarian Regiment)

Many of the survivors' memories about these few peaceful

weeks when they were out of the line are more of their living
conditions and leisure time than of their military duties. The
following quotations give a few glimpses.

We came once more into contact with civilians. It was a cottage
that had once been an *estaminet*; the sign was still over the door. In
the room for the former customers were four or five sets of bunks,
each having three beds one on top of the other. For the family there
were two rooms including the kitchen. The people were father,
mother and two daughters; their names, strangely enough, were
Maria and Marie, aged about eighteen and sixteen. They were all
very poor and had almost less to eat than ourselves. We got on
very well with them during the seven-week stay. The girls were
well guarded all the time by the parents. Father took them every
night to Granny; nobody knew where she lived. (Gefreiter Paul
Kretschmer, 28th Pioneer Battalion)

In the rest area behind the line, we officers stayed in French
villages, almost always in private houses. Our hostesses, recognis-
ing the tabs on our uniforms, often greeted us with the words,
'*Oh, je le sais; c'est la Garde Impériale.*' In general the saying was,
'*Malheur la guerre – pour nous, pour vous, pour tout le monde.*' We
were well looked. after. Our present hostess put a hot brick into our
beds every evening. Most of these women had next-of-kin on the
other side. In spite of everything, the French behind our front were
still convinced they would win the war.

From time to time our commander would arrange a drinking
party for the officers of all three batteries under his command. We
drank until 4 a.m. and finished with a cup of real coffee. Our
paymaster had somehow managed to buy this at tremendous cost
from a U-boat based in one of the Belgian ports. After less than two
hours sleep, the alarm was sounded for the early morning field
exercises, which gave us the opportunity to sober up in the thick
fog at dawn. (Leutnant Wolfram Lindner, 5th Guard Field
Artillery Regiment)

The thoughts of many men were devoted to food for,
although they had regular rations superior to those issued to
civilians at home, the German soldiers were always hungry.

We knew that the Tommies had in their dug-outs all the good
things we hadn't – chocolate, coffee, corned beef, wine, spirits,
cigars, cigarettes. How did we fare? In the morning, a hot brew
supposed to be coffee but tasting of swedes, midday a thin soup of
swedes or dried vegetables without any meat, sometimes a few

pieces of potato; evening a brew called tea tasting of swedes. The bread was good. My age group (1897–8) got an extra thick slice daily, which was most welcome as we were always hungry. The older men didn't mind; they understood. Jam was of very poor quality and so was the sausage, which we called rubber sausage. All the same, nobody starved to death. (Unteroffizier Friedrich Flohr, 77th Regiment)

One night my section and myself stole two sacks of potatoes from a store which contained about a thousand sacks. We broke open the doors and didn't shut them properly again. That was how some of the potatoes inside got frozen and that was how they got to know that someone had been in. The field police carried out a search and they found the full sacks in our room. All nine of us were charged by a proper court martial of officers from another unit. I was told, 'You are responsible for what your section has done.' It was possible that I might have been sentenced to capital punishment – to be shot – but that did not happen.

The funny thing is that the field police never took the potatoes away and we cooked and ate the lot. They were delicious. (Gefreiter Wilhelm Reinhard, 109th Leib Grenadier Regiment)

It is a fine time. Our battalion comes to Bonnecourt; it is still populated and our men get quarters. Rations are not luxurious though quite sufficient. The officers of the battalion meet in the evening in the Lion d'Or and enjoy the good burgundy. I had lodged at the château, the French butler asked me whether we would like to buy a few bottles of burgundy. He didn't want the non-fighting people to have them after we'd gone. (Leutnant Hermann Wedekind, 79th Regiment)

There were other attractions besides food and drink. An effort was made to see that the troops under training got a real rest from the strain of trench warfare. There was home leave for some units; there were band concerts and soldier-plays in makeshift theatres. It is recorded that there was even a series of 'patriotic instructions' in the form of lectures for all the men due to take part in the attack.

Each division's training period finished with a combined exercise of every unit in the division lasting for twenty-four hours – a full-dress rehearsal for the part the division was to play in the opening of the attack. Cavalry rode in front of the advancing infantry, the line of cavalry lances representing the creeping barrage. After this the divisions stood ready for orders to move. Fifty-six divisions in all had been through the full training course – a force almost exactly equivalent to the whole of the British Expeditionary Force. Seven divisions did not receive special training; either there was not enough time or they were considered skilled enough to manage without.

*

After all the miseries of trench warfare there is no doubt that the average German soldier was prepared to go into this battle willingly, if only to force a result one way or the other and get the war over, although those responsible for the training and morale of the German soldiers had done their work well and few men expected anything but success. It must be stressed that only a handful among the men of the German divisions knew any details of the coming battle, but all knew that something was looming. These are some of the views of the German soldiers who would shortly be marching up towards the front once more.

The months' long static trench warfare had loosened the discipline and obedience of the soldiers and made them more indifferent towards the outcome of the war. Nobody had believed any more in a happy and victorious end for Germany. But the German soldiers became more confident after the end of the war in the East. There came a hope that now a decisive outcome by means of a great offensive in the West could be achieved. Every soldier on the Western Front was convinced that the hour of decision over war and peace was imminent. Cheerfulness and confidence slowly returned. Off-duty cards were played and jokes told. Letters full of hope to families at home were written. Everyone executed orders gladly in the knowledge that in a few days the last battle would begin and would be won. Joy and even euphoria made their appearance among the soldiers. (Unteroffizier Hermann Jericho, 39th *Landwehr Fussartillerie Bataillon*)

Our personal view about the attack wasn't so much concerned with the English; what we had much more in mind was the booty – the provisions, stores, cigarettes, tinned meat, biscuits. We knew what we were after. We had learnt the value of these delicacies during the tank battle at Cambrai. (Feldwebel Hermann Gasser, 110th Grenadier Regiment)

It was obvious to us all what was coming and we were glad that the monotonous life in the trenches was over. Most of us were nineteen or twenty years old and we longed for victory and peace. We didn't hate the English and French, especially the English for whom we had some understanding, being of the same stock. Had they not come from Schleswig-Holstein near where I lived in Hamburg some 1,400 years earlier? This was the last desperate attempt to bring about a change in our fortunes. Maybe 20 to 30 per cent of our unit were keen because they hoped to find plenty of food and alcohol; they were mostly the young ones. But the rest of us weren't at all enthusiastic; we just wanted to get the war over and get home alive. (Leutnant Rudolf Hoffmann, 463rd Regiment)

We were all young men and were afraid but hopeful that we would survive all right. There were a lot of swear words used at that time that we didn't usually use. Given the choice I would have as soon been out of it but orders are orders and we didn't have a choice. We knew that this coming battle could be the end one way or the other. We all felt the same. (Jäger Hubert Schroeter, 3rd *Jägersturmbataillon*)

It was these war-weary veterans and young boys, these hungry, shabbily clothed, but skilful German soldiers, who might yet decide the outcome of the war.

3

The Defenders

The general situation on the Russian and Italian fronts, combined with the paucity of reinforcements which we are likely to receive will in all probability necessitate our adopting a defensive attitude for the next three months. We must be prepared to meet a strong and sustained hostile offensive. It is therefore of first importance that army commanders should give their immediate and personal attention to the organisation of the zones for defence and to the rest and training of their troops. (Field Marshal Sir Douglas Haig, to his four army commanders, 3 December 1917)*

After completing the takeover of the French sectors from St Quentin to the south in January 1918, the British Expeditionary Force held 126 miles of line on the Western Front. The Germans were planning to attack exactly half of this early in the spring. Haig held his line with four armies, and two of these – the Third and Fifth – were to face the German attack. The northern one third of the German attack would fall on part of the Third Army's frontage and the southern two thirds of the attack would embrace almost all of the Fifth Army's front. The commanders of these two British armies were to be important figures in the coming battle.

The commander of the Third Army was General Hon. Sir Julian Byng, who was, like Haig, a cavalry officer, his regiment having been the 10th Hussars. Byng had commanded a cavalry division in the original British Expeditionary Force and then the Cavalry Corps until August 1915. His first infantry command soon followed and his first major action was a success, when the corps he was commanding, the Canadian Corps, captured Vimy Ridge during the Battle of Arras. This was followed by promotion to the command of the Third Army in June 1917 after the previous commander, General Sir Edmund Allenby, had been sent to take command of the forces in Palestine. Byng had taken no part in the Battle of Passchendaele. He had, however, originated, planned and

* British Official History, page 37.

executed the brilliant tank attack at Cambrai, only to risk removal from command because of the German counter-attack which caught his army unawares and led to the loss of most of the earlier gains. Byng survived this crisis; a corps commander was sacked instead. A wiser general now for his hectic experiences of 1917, he and his army were to face the northern wing of the German attack.

There was a popular revue playing at the Alhambra Theatre in London called 'The Bing Boys on Broadway' and the term 'The Bing Boys' was often applied to Byng's troops. Men of the Third Army who were taken prisoner in the German offensive were often asked by the Germans whether they were 'Bing Boys'.

Byng's front extended from three miles north of Arras down to the southern edge of the Flesquières Salient. Haig had wanted Byng to withdraw from this salient, thus shortening the line by three miles, but Byng was unwilling to do this and Haig had not pressed the point. If the line had been straightened out in this way, a complete division could have been relieved from front-line duty and this would have been invaluable farther south. Perhaps Byng saw himself losing the division thus saved to another army, and this may have been the reason for his reluctance.

*

Byng of the Third Army was to survive the war with his reputation intact, but the same cannot be said for his neighbour to the south. General Sir Hubert Gough was the commander of the Fifth Army, which was to bear the brunt of the German attack from south of the Flesquières Salient right down to the river Oise at La Fère, a distance of thirty-one miles. Gough had been a controversial figure in the British Army even before the war. In 1914 he had been in command of a cavalry brigade at the Curragh, near Dublin. The Government in London was planning to introduce Home Rule for Ireland against the wishes of the Protestants in Ulster, who were almost in open rebellion. Gough and most of his officers offered to resign rather than use their troops against the Ulster Protestants. Gough was summoned to London and threatened but he held firm, and he and the other officers involved obtained a famous guarantee in the form of a written promise that they would not be forced to act against the Ulstermen. But Gough had created the first of several groups of enemies.

Hubert Gough came from a fine soldiering family; his father, his uncle and his brother had all won the Victoria Cross. As commander of his cavalry brigade in 1914, he had ordered the first shot to be fired by the British Expeditionary Force. His cavalryman's dash and his undoubted strength of character led to rapid promotion, and he progressed from command of a brigade to that of an army in just over a year. If the British infantry had broken through at the opening of the Battle of the Somme in July 1916, it would have been Gough with his Reserve Army – sometimes called 'Gough's Mobile Army' – that would have exploited the success; but it was not to be. The Reserve Army became the Fifth Army, and Gough handled the northern sectors of the British attacks on the Somme for the remainder of that year.

Gough's big year came in 1917. When Haig was planning the Ypres offensive in the second half of that year, he personally selected Gough and his Fifth Army staff to play the principal role in the main series of attacks. But Ypres and Passchendaele brought Gough a new reputation. The 'Thruster' of the earlier war years now became known as the 'Butcher', and his Fifth Army built up a reputation among the corps and divisions which came under its command – a reputation for ruthlessness in pressing attacks and subsequent high levels of casualties. Divisional commanders who were doubtful of their ability to 'deliver the goods' for Gough are reputed to have dreaded coming to the Fifth Army and several were sacked and sent home to England. These disgruntled generals joined with those politicians in London who were concerned over the heavy casualties and lack of success at Passchendaele and became a new group hostile to Gough.

Lloyd George called for Gough's removal from command at the end of the year but Robertson and Haig stood firm, although the Fifth Army headquarters organisation was pulled out from the Ypres front and rested for a time without an active role. Gough's Chief of Staff and personal friend, Major-General Neill Malcolm, had done much of the hardest

driving in his master's name. He left the Fifth Army, probably at Haig's insistence, to take over command of a division.
When Haig had to find a commander for the new sectors
recently taken over from the French in the south, it was
Gough and his Fifth Army Headquarters who were sent to
this forlorn front, which Haig did not expect to be the scene
of any major action. So another general much wiser for his
1917 experiences came down, not to a backwater, but to be
the main target for the *Kaiserschlacht*.

An 'army', and its subordinate, the 'corps', were no more
than command organisations which planned and directed the
operations of infantry divisions and provided a number of
administrative and support units. Infantry divisions came and
went, sometimes frequently if operations were intensive.
Because of this, front-line soldiers were rarely conscious of
being members of a corps, still less of an army, and these
senior commanders, Byng and Gough, were virtually unknown; at best they were mere shadows to the trench soldiers.
A few men remember meeting Gough in the areas behind the
Fifth Army's new front line. One soldier found him 'an earthy
man but one who seemed to be concerned about my comrades
in the ranks. He swore a great deal.' Another soldier met
Gough out on a lone horseback ride. 'We had a long chat in
the road. I was very impressed and feel that he was a real
Tommy's man.'

Lieutenant-Colonel M. V. B. Hill, commanding officer of
the 9th Royal Sussex, also remembers Gough.

He spent a day with our division and he came round with me
inspecting my battalion while they were training and he said they
were a good battalion. Division was very annoyed that Gough
lunched with brigade and not with them. He was a charming man
but I didn't think he had too many brains. When I told another
C.O. in my brigade this, he was furious. He was a cavalry officer
like Gough.

This was not the only comment about Gough's background
as a cavalry officer and, in a war in which there was criticism
that cavalry officers as a group were too often selected for
high rank, it is of interest that possibly the greatest infantry
battle of the war was to be handled on the British side by a

commander-in-chief and two army commanders who were all three cavalrymen!

*

The divisions allocated to the Fifth Army took over from the French by stages in January 1918. They found the quietest of conditions; the French policy had always been to keep activity and casualties to a minimum when no large-scale offensive was in hand, and the British soldiers who came to the new trenches north and south of St Quentin inherited this state of affairs. They were quite happy with this but less so with the state of the defences they took over from the French.

The new British line also contained a short, four-mile sector south of the River Oise. The British positions here were opposite the St Gobain forest, which was the nearest part of the German line to Paris, sixty miles away. It was from this forest that a long-range German gun started shelling Paris at the end of March. The British line ended where the ground rose abruptly to a rocky, forested area still manned by the French. A London Territorial division, the 58th, were neighbours with the French here and, on 21 March, No. 13 Platoon of D Company, 7th Londons, would be the right-hand unit of the British Expeditionary Force.

*

Immediately to the rear of the British lines lay the desolate area devastated by the Germans in their retreat to the Hindenburg Line the previous spring. The ruin of each village was marked with a carefully painted sign. Those villages nearer the front line provided some accommodation for men in cellars, but farther back the army had built extensive hutted camps near the village ruins and these were used by units that were out of the line. The countryside was particularly bleak with neglected farmland and all its trees except those in woods cut down. Often the only sign of civilisation was the lines of new telegraph poles erected by the army. Civilians were not allowed to live in this area and the repeated requests by the former French inhabitants for permission to return and cultivate the land were all refused, although at least one old lady in the area held by the 14th

(Light) Division was still there, living in a dug-out near her ruined home. The Germans had not budged her in the Franco-Prussian War and she wasn't going to move in this one. It is not known what became of her when the Germans advanced over this area on 21 March.

Farther back were Bapaume, Péronne and Ham, also ruined and parts of them still considered dangerous from possible German booby traps; and then, even farther back, was Albert, the famous town with the Golden Virgin leaning over from its shell-damaged church tower. The Virgin's statue had been chained to the tower and legend said that the war would end only when the statue fell. Albert had achieved a small revival since it had been a front-line town in 1916 and it was now the headquarters of Byng's Third Army. One man who was in Albert at this time remembers it as a place with 'a large number of rats and a ruined sewing-machine factory, the place littered with spare parts'. Seventeen miles behind Albert was the fine city of Amiens, the important communications centre for this whole region. When Gough first arrived to set up his headquarters in a village near Amiens, he noticed that some old defences guarding the city were being dismantled. This area was now thirty-eight miles behind the front and apparently quite safe. Gough ordered that the work be halted. This incident was near a little-known village called Villers-Brettoneux. Gough later moved his headquarters farther forward to Nesle.

*

General Gough was not the only one to be thinking more now of defence than of the offensive operations that had occupied the British generals for the past three years. Gough in particular had much to worry about. There are many descriptions of the weakness in the defences and the shortages of troops at this time, both becoming more serious the farther south one went. It must be stressed that it was not until a comparatively late date that British commanders could be sure that the German attack would fall in the south but it is important to examine why these southern sectors were left in such a weak state compared to the rest of the British Expeditionary Force's front.

The following table shows the forces that would be available to the four British armies, running from north to south, on the eve of the German offensive.

Army	Divisions	Miles of Front	Frontage per Effective Division
Second	12	23	1·92 miles
First	14	33	2·36 miles
Third	14	28	2·00 miles
Fifth	12 + 3 cavalry	42	3·23 miles

The cavalry divisions in the Fifth Army could only produce a tren~h-fighting strength equivalent to one infantry brigade each so Gough's forces were the equivalent of only thirteen infantry divisions. In addition to the divisions shown above, there were eight more infantry divisions in what was known as G.H.Q. Reserve; these were spread out evenly behind the four armies but could be committed to battle only if released by the commander-in-chief. It can be seen from the table that the German attack was to fall partly on one of the most strongly defended parts of the British line – on the front of the Third Army – but also on the Fifth Army, which was by far the weakest.

Haig's priorities were simple ones. He was determined to keep the British Expeditionary Force intact and to ensure both the security of its zone as a whole and the links between the front line and the Channel ports and, thus, with England. If Arras is taken as the centre of the British line – the city was actually just south of the half-way point – then the entire northern half of the British front line was within fifty miles of the coast. South of Arras the British front ran away to the south-east and the coastline receded to the south-west. St Quentin was seventy-five miles from the coast, La Fère ninety miles. If Haig allowed the Germans to break through in his north, the British Expeditionary Force might be cut off from home. If the Germans broke through in the centre, the British Expeditionary Force would be cut in two. It was for these sound reasons that Haig kept the main strength of the British infantry divisions in his north and the centre.

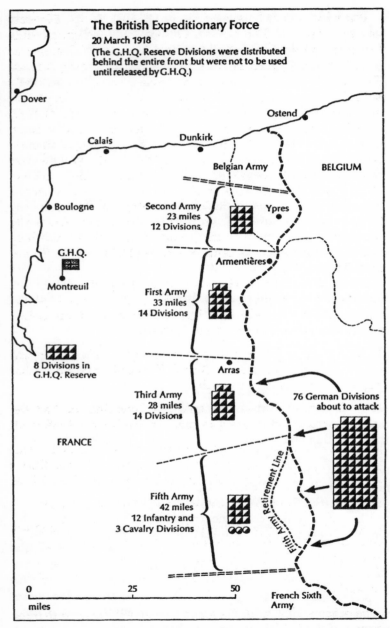

The British Expeditionary Force
20 March 1918
(The G.H.Q. Reserve Divisions were distributed
behind the entire front but were not to be used
until released by G.H.Q.)

Dover

Ostend

Calais

Dunkirk

Belgian Army

BELGIUM

Boulogne

Second Army
23 miles
12 Divisions

Ypres

G.H.Q.

Montreuil

Armentières

First Army
33 miles
14 Divisions

8 Divisions in
G.H.Q. Reserve

Arras

Third Army
28 miles
14 Divisions

76 German Divisions
about to attack

FRANCE

Fifth Army
42 miles
12 Infantry and
3 Cavalry Divisions

Fifth Army Retirement Line

| 0 | 25 | 50 |

miles

French Sixth
Army

Map 3

But what was to happen to the weak Fifth Army if it were heavily attacked? The policy here was again a simple one. Fifth Army was to stand and fight if it could. If Gough was forced to retire, then he was to conduct a fighting retreat. This would do little harm; there was nothing immediately behind his front that was vital to the Allied cause. Gough was informed of this in a precise written instruction from G.H.Q. on 9 February. He was given a final line to which he could fall back if necessary but instructed to keep a link at all costs with the Third Army to the north. While Gough was retiring, if forced to do so, the French would bring a force of at least six divisions into an assembly area behind Gough's final line. French and British together would then stop any further German advance, protect Amiens, and eventually counter-attack to recover the ground lost. This French help was the subject of an agreement between Haig and the French on 7 March.

These intentions of Haig are of vital significance to the historical judgements on the handling and outcome of the battle, and the reader might like to bear in mind four points which will all be relevant later in the book.

1. As a matter of deliberate policy, Gough's Fifth Army was left in a weakened state in a British Expeditionary Force that was itself well under strength.

2. If Gough was unable to hold his front line, he had the specific permission of Haig to conduct a fighting withdrawal.

3. The French had promised to provide an immediate reinforcement of six divisions, this in fulfilment of the conditions agreed when the British took over this part of the French line.

And the final factor was to concern the German plans:

4. The British were planning to hold in the north of the attack area, where the Germans wanted to break right through and manoeuvre in the British rear, but were prepared to give in the south where the German plan called only for a limited advance.

In other words, both Haig and Ludendorff realised that the centre of the British line around Arras was the vital area and that the south, where the forces of Crown Prince Wilhelm were to attack Gough's Fifth Army around St Quentin, was only subsidiary.

*

The British troops were not used to thinking defensively; as a matter of policy they had never been encouraged to do so. Many of the front-line positions they held now had not been chosen for their defensive value but represented the limits of previous offensives. There were few comprehensive defence plans and hardly any defences in depth. The zone occupied by the British Expeditionary Force at the end of 1917 was protected only by the thinnest crust of defence works. All this had to be changed.

It had always been anathema to British generals to give up any part of a front-line trench and many men had died over the years to uphold this principle. But experience had shown, as has been stated earlier, that there was no such thing as a completely impregnable position and that a determined enemy using sufficient force could always capture a single line of trenches, however strongly constructed and held. What was needed now was flexibility – 'elasticity' might be a better word – and throughout that winter a new defence philosophy was evolved. The front-line defence system was now to be classified as the 'Forward Zone' and was to be regarded only as an outpost line, held in sufficient strength to force the Germans to bombard it thoroughly and to commit an infantry attack upon it; then the defenders would inflict the maximum casualties on the Germans before withdrawing to the main defence – at least that was the theory.

The main defence was now to be in what was called the Battle Zone, a strong set of defences sited in the best possible tactical position and far enough back to escape the first German blow. The front of the Battle Zone would be 2,000–3,000 yards behind the outpost line and the Battle Zone itself would be the same distance wide; but there would be considerable variation to these distances depending on local ground conditions and fields of fire. The Germans would always have to approach the Battle Zone over ground exposed to British defensive fire. In normal times, that is before an attack developed, only the Forward Zone need be manned, battalions serving there on a rotation basis. The Battle Zone was only partially manned and most of its defenders could live in some degree of comfort in billets near by, resting, training, or working on the defences themselves, but always ready to take up position in the Battle Zone if an attack was thought imminent. Farther back stood the reserves, ready to counter-attack any part of the Battle Zone that might be captured by the enemy. Also planned was a 'Corps Line', which was a third set of defences behind the Battle Zone, but events moved too fast and little work on this line was ever done.

'Elasticity', or the readiness to give ground, was confined only to the Forward Zone; the Battle Zone had to be held at all costs. The great hope was that any German attack would expend most of its force on the Forward Zone and then break itself against the defences of the Battle Zone. This new concept represented a major move forward in British military thinking. It should be pointed out that this defence policy was common to the whole of the British Expeditionary Force front. The weak Fifth Army in the south also complied with it but General Gough had the special dispensation that he could retire to the fall-back line given to him by Haig until the French and British reserves came to his aid.

One aspect of the new defensive principles that occupied the attention of the British leaders was how to deal with tanks, for it was only a few weeks since British tanks had overrun the German positions at Cambrai. Much effort was now devoted by the British to see that the Germans did not achieve the same result. The front line was protected in many places by a primitive minefield made by laying 60-pound spherical trench-mortar bombs – known to the British soldiers as 'toffee apples' or 'rock apples' – just under the turf. A man's weight would not detonate these but that of a tank track would. A proportion of the 18-pounder field guns were detached from their batteries and sited well forward in concealed positions just behind the front line, to stay silent there until called upon to act as anti-tank guns in the event of a German attack. One artilleryman who saw some of his battery's guns posted in this way says, 'These guns and their

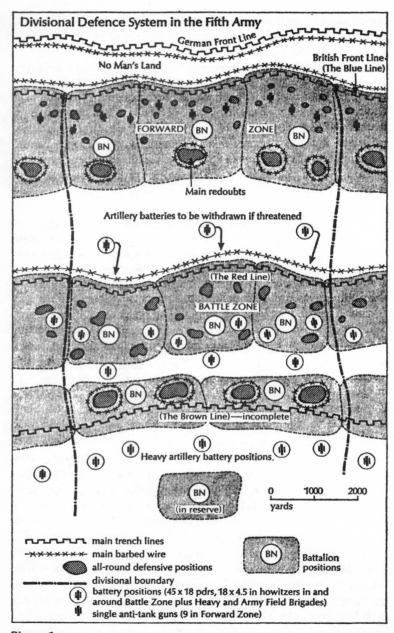

Diagram 1

crews were quietly regarded as expendable.' A further defence against tanks was the digging of many trenches in the Battle Zone to a width so great that a tank could not straddle the trench. These 'anti-tank trenches' were hated by the infantry who had to man them because they were so vulnerable to artillery fire. All these anti-tank preparations were a great novelty to the British soldiers. After what had happened at Cambrai, it was quite logical that the defensive planners should be concerned, but it was unfortunate that they were not able to ascertain that the Germans were not contemplating the use of tanks in any number; a considerable proportion of the limited labour available was wasted on a threat which never materialised.

It was one thing to produce fine schemes and draw impressive lines on maps; it was another to get the work done before the Germans came. It was a sad story. The Germans were successful in concealing the location of their attack until a late stage and the British had to spread their effort equally along their front. Much good work was done but the degree of priority diminished from north to south. Once again the Fifth Army was in a poor position because the French from whom they had taken over had done little work on defences. When it became obvious that the Germans were going to strike here, more labour units were sent to the Fifth Army, but because this area was the one devastated by the Germans the previous year, the new labour units had first to build camps for themselves before they could turn a single sod of earth in new defence works.

All down the Western Front men were digging and digging – Labour Companies of medically low-grade British, of Indians, Chinese, Italians, of German prisoners – but only well to the rear – Royal Engineers, Pioneers, and always the poor British infantry turned out of their billets to the ever-lasting 'working parties' (the word 'fatigue' had been officially abolished in 1915 owing to its 'unsavoury tone'). Unfortunately only a small proportion of this labour was actually digging defences. The British Official History records that the Fifth Army had 40,212 men in Labour Companies by mid-March but most of these were working on roads, rail-heads and all the other needs of an army in its rear; only one fifth were building defences. The majority of the work in the defences was achieved by infantry units which should have been training or resting.

For the men involved in this work there was not always a sense of urgency. Among those working in the Fifth Army were temporary pioneer battalions provided by the cavalry.

Just before the German attack on March 21st, 1918, the Cavalry Brigade in which I served moved to the area under Gough's command. From what billets we moved, after '50 years of blur and blot', escapes my memory, but I think it was from the neighbourhood of Amiens. It was unusual to me to find that the routine of 'one man to three horses' and the others up to the reserve lines, had changed to trench digging in the vicinity of the Crozat Canal, some ten miles or so south of St Quentin. Whether we were asked to volunteer for this or were 'told off', escapes my memory. And so I found myself in a mixed bunch of 'odds and sods', in quite good huts, French I imagine, near the Crozat Canal, which was spanned by an iron bridge. It was a desolate area and obviously had been fought over in the past. But discipline was easy in a mixed bunch such as we were and the line, though quite near, was uncannily quiet.

We crossed the iron bridge each day, dug our trenches, went back to quite good billets. The rations were good and so was the weather. I had the impression (quite mistaken in the light of things to come) that it was a sort of holiday atmosphere. Nobody queried why we dug these trenches and I don't remember giving it a thought. And so the days went by until March 21st. (Trooper A. W. Bradbury, 2nd Dragoons)

*

The progress achieved on these defence works before the Germans attacked can be summarised by splitting the attack front into three parts. In that part of the Third Army area from Arras to the northern edge of the Flesquières Salient, the British troops had been in residence for almost a year. The defences here were strong and the Battle Zone was almost complete, although the Corps Line behind it was not. Moreover there were sufficient troops here to man the front line at all points as well as to garrison the Battle Zone when required. The Flesquières Salient was a special case. Salients were always difficult to hold against a determined attack. Fire

C.O. (to sentry): 'Do you know the Defence
Scheme for this sector of the line, my man?'
TOMMY: 'Yes, sir.'
C.O.: 'Well, what is it, then?'
TOMMY: 'To stay 'ere an' fight like 'ell.'

Punch's cartoon of the Defence Scheme

came in from three sides and the base of the salient could be pinched out to cut off the garrison in the salient. It is probable that Haig again urged Byng to give up the Flesquières Salient but Byng was still reluctant to do so. On 10 March, G.H.Q. sent Byng a direct order that the Flesquières Salient was only to be held lightly as a 'false front' and was to be given up as soon as the Germans attacked. The Battle Zone here ran across the base of the salient and did not follow the bulge of it.

The twenty-five-mile front south of the Flesquières Salient – the entire front of the Fifth Army – never did achieve the status of a fully defended front. The British had come too late, the front was too long, there were not enough men. The front line was reasonably well protected by barbed wire but not by a continuous trench. The Battle Zone was not complete, especially in the extreme south, and the Corps Line in the rear was almost non-existent. Nor were there enough troops to man the defences fully if they had ever been built. Scattered outposts, sometimes manned by a platoon but often only by a section, watched the front, hoping to cover the empty ground between the posts with machine-gun fire. Scattered along the front-line area, usually just behind the true front but well in advance of the Battle Zone, was a series of 'redoubts' or 'keeps'. These were all-round defensive positions, sited on natural features dominating the surrounding ground. Like the smaller posts farther forward, they covered the gaps to the neighbouring redoubts with machine-gun fire but the redoubts were too distant from each other to give much mutual support. In the event of an attack, each would have to stand on its own. What would happen if the enemy attacked in the dark or in a fog or smoke screen and infiltrated between the outposts and redoubts did not bear thinking about.*

A typical Fifth Army brigade sector would be organised with one battalion in the Forward Zone, one battalion in the Battle Zone and one in reserve. Half of the Forward Zone battalion might have been split up among the smaller forward posts and half would be in the larger redoubts. Battalion

* Diagram 2, on page 264, shows the layout of a typical redoubt.

headquarters may have been in one of the redoubts, where it would be out of touch with the rest of the battalion, or it may have occupied a more central position but farther back. Whatever method was used, the degree of control that a battalion commander could exercise was limited, and much of the defence would depend on the resolution of company captains, platoon subalterns and, in the many smaller posts, sergeants and corporals. The story of the defence of the Fifth Army on 21 March is largely a story of the defence of these isolated forward positions. Many of the smaller ones never found a mention in official records but the larger redoubts did. They bore a variety of names – Chapel Hill, Vaucelette Farm, Malassise Farm, Malakoff Farm, Higson's Quarries, Fresnoy Redoubt, Enghien Redoubt, Ellis Redoubt, Manchester Hill, L'Epine de Dallon, Boadicea Redoubt, Race Course Redoubt, Jeanne d'Arc, Fort Vendeuil.

The British soldier likes to fight 'in line', with comrades at his right and left shoulder, and he fights well as long as this is so. Now, whether in company redoubt or corporal's post, the front-line defenders were not happy. No one explained to them that theirs were not intended to be permanent positions, that once the sting had been taken out of the German attack they might be allowed to withdraw. The authority to give such an order would be vested in an officer, probably a battalion commander, who was designated as 'Officer Commanding Front-Line System', and he could give such an order only when permitted to do so by his brigade commander. The realists could see for themselves that if the Germans attacked in strength and penetrated between the posts and redoubts then all was lost unless units from the Battle Zone counter-attacked. What the average junior officer and ordinary soldier were not told was that the new defensive policy did not include provision for counter-attacks to recover the Forward Zone. It would not be too dramatic a description to say that the infantry units which found themselves there when the Germans attacked were to be considered as expendable.

This section can close with the comments of a company commander in the Fifth Army.

We took over the right sub-section of the front line from the 6th Connaught Rangers. I was very worried about the scanty way the front line was held. The trenches were poor and shallow and the wiring in front consisted of a single strand of barbed wire held by screw-iron stakes here and there and, in stretches, this was on the ground forming no defence at all. All we had in the company front-line trench was a pair of sentries about every hundred yards on a long stretch of front. To impress the enemy of our great strength we had orders that the officer on trench duty was to take a Lewis-gunner with him and put the gun over the parapet and fire a few rounds every twenty-five yards or so. He would go one way and then travel back a few yards, fire again, and then move once again and repeat the performance. I do not think the enemy was very impressed. I complained bitterly of our weakness, but nothing could be done and we had to put up with it. We had practically no strength in reserve behind us. I then openly complained and stated that Jerry would come over one morning and walk through us. As a result of my forecast I was given a rough time by my seniors, who told me not to be so pessimistic.

My battalion received numerous orders and counter-orders relative to holding various lines. These were named after various colours and beautifully depicted on staff maps, but as a matter of fact were non-existent in some cases. There was a Green Line around Tincourt, but it had been merely split-locked; a Yellow Line on the outskirts of Ronssoy had not even got to that stage in its career. On one occasion the battalion received orders to hold the front with one company and to withdraw the remainder to this Yellow Line. The Commanding Officer pointed out that this line did not exist – I know because I tried to find it. Alarm and despondency was caused and a staff officer came up to see for himself! All available hands were now put on to dig, but defences were not complete when the curtain went up for the German thrust. This was the situation of the 16th (Irish) Division on the eve of the great battle. (Captain E. P. Hall, 2nd Leinsters)

*

Twenty-five British infantry divisions would face the first blows of the German offensive on 21 March. Of these, twenty-one divisions had been through the Battle of Passchendaele and one of the remainder had been badly mauled at Cambrai. Several divisions had fought in both battles. Thus, while no more than half of the German divisions which would be carrying out the attack had been in a major battle in recent months, all but three of the British divisions had been through such a battle. Moreover, while the German divisions had been brought up to full strength with reinforcements, the British had not.

When I wrote an earlier book about the First World War, I devoted a certain amount of space to what I called 'The Army of 1916', describing the background and character of the units and men who fought on the Somme in 1916. The nature of the British Expeditionary Force which went to France in 1914 started to change from the day it fought its first action. With expansion and with the replacement of casualties it continued to change with every month, and certainly with every battle, through to the end of the war. The 'Army' which went into action on 1 July 1916 represented just one stage in a process that ended only when the last shot was fired. The remainder of this chapter will attempt to do the same for what might be called 'The Army of 1918', or at least 'The Army of March 1918' because the divisions and battalions which fought in the summer and autumn of 1918 and were present when the Germans were finally beaten in November were certainly not of the same character as had faced the Germans in the spring of the year.

When I advertised for men who had been in action on 21 March 1918 to help me by sending personal accounts, each contributor received a questionnaire. One of the questions on this was 'When had you arrived on the Western Front?' The first hundred infantrymen's replies to this question were analysed in an attempt to establish the average content of the British infantry units in March 1918. There were:

two	1914 men
nineteen	1915 men
twenty-four	1916 men
fifty	1917 men
five	1918 men.

The average length of Western Front service of the hundred men on the eve of the German attack was just over fifteen months. It is realised that this random sampling is not scientific; in particular a sample of men who would write letters in 1975 is unlikely to contain a true proportion of the older men who had once formed part of the original British

Expeditionary Force. Because a simpler type of questionnaire was used for the Germans and because of the more
frequent transfer of their divisions to and from other fronts, it
was not possible to get comparable German figures; but the
statement in an earlier chapter that between one third and a
half of a German platoon was made up of pre-war trained
soldiers is probably accurate and is based on many conversations with German contributors during a research visit to
Germany.

Britain had not had any form of peacetime conscription and
her tiny professional army of 1914 had literally faded away
since then. The six infantry divisions of the original British
Expeditionary Force had grown to fifty-seven divisions by
March 1918. This expansion had been achieved mainly by
the great enlistment of civilian volunteers that had taken
place in 1914 and 1915 and then by conscription. Ten of the
British divisions were provided by the Empire but these
countries had started out with an even smaller proportion of
trained soldiers than had the United Kingdom. It is reasonable to assume that the average British platoon of March 1918
would be lucky to have a single pre-war soldier in its ranks.
Perhaps one third were early volunteers and two thirds were
conscripts. But the average rifleman was not a novice: he had
'been out' since the winter of 1916–17 and had almost
certainly been through Passchendaele and possibly Arras and
Cambrai as well. The reason for this relatively high average
of experience was, of course, Lloyd George's policy of
restricting the flow of reinforcements. The low number of
five men in the survey to have arrived in the first weeks of
1918 reflects this. The divisions which faced the German
offensive may have been low in men but the men they did
have were not completely inexperienced. Although their experience was mainly of offensive rather than defensive action,
it was a valuable quality to have.

*

The British infantry soldier's 'home' was his battalion – a
unit commanded by a lieutenant-colonel with a small headquarters, its fighting strength in four rifle companies commanded by captains, each company having four platoons

commanded by junior officers or sergeants. The total establishment of a battalion at this time was about thirty-six officers and 1,000 men. Because many men were always on leave or attending courses, or were 'left out of battle' at the battalion transport lines to provide a nucleus in case the battalion suffered disastrous losses, the battalion's 'trench strength' would be about twenty officers and 600 men. Strength returns for the Third and Fifth Armies dated 17 March 1918 show that the average battalion strength at this time was forty-two officers and 950 men. The reader may well ask how the British divisions can be described as being badly under strength because the casualties of 1917 had not been replaced at the same time as the average battalion had more officers than its establishment and was only fifty men short in its other ranks. The reason for this apparent anomaly was that the divisions of the British Expeditionary Force had just undergone a major reorganisation.

For most of the war a British infantry division had contained twelve battalions of fighting infantry and one Pioneer battalion. This well-tried organisation had served divisions well both in major battle and in routine trench warfare. But with all battalions badly under strength after Passchendaele, undue strains were being placed on surviving members, and the effectiveness of divisions whether in attack or defence was threatened. Haig had written to the War Office as early as November 1917 pointing out his shortages and suggesting that the best way to bring divisions up to strength was to reduce the number of divisions. He said that if five corps headquarters and fifteen infantry divisions were completely disbanded he could bring the remaining divisions up to full strength for the coming year's campaigns. This drastic solution would have reduced the apparent strength of the British Expeditionary Force by some 25 per cent – a reduction that would have been instantly pronounced unacceptable by Britain's allies. Haig had probably known this and this was probably why he suggested that particular solution.

London would have none of Haig's suggestion, but quite clearly something had to be done. Lloyd George still managed to avoid the obvious solution of sending out the trained men available in England and the War Office finally sent Haig instructions to reduce the number of fighting infantry battalions in some of his divisions by reducing each of the three brigades from four to three battalions. There was some hope that the Americans might replace the disbanded battalions; but the Americans were determined that their men should all serve together and under American leaders and this did not happen.

The proposed new three-battalion brigade was not all that unusual. Both the German and the French Armies had already taken the same step, the Germans to gain flexibility, the French because they had run short of men. But while the Germans had created extra divisions with their spare battalions and the French had progressively reduced their front by handing over sectors to the British, these same British were now expected to hold the same amount of front with the same number of divisions but with each division reduced in infantry establishment by one quarter! The order for the reduction was issued by the War Office on 10 January, but it was left to Haig to implement it.

The ten Empire divisions were receiving sufficient reinforcements to keep up to their original strength and it was decided to leave these alone. As for the rest of his divisions, Haig decided that half-measures were no good: every one of the forty-seven United Kingdom divisions would have to lose three battalions, making an overall loss of 141 battalions. The War Office complicated Haig's task further by laying down that no Regular or First-Line Territorial battalions were to be disbanded, so the cuts fell entirely on the New Army battalions formed after Kitchener's famous appeal for volunteers in 1914 and on the wartime-raised Second-Line Territorials. It was also decided that no Guards battalions were to be disbanded, but the Guards Division had to shed three of its battalions and these duly left to serve together as a brigade in the 31st Division, until then a humble North Country New Army formation.

So the weakest or most junior of the battalions under consideration, or perhaps those which were thought to have performed the least efficiently in recent battles, received orders to disband. The men from those battalions that had to disappear were at least all sent to other battalions of the same regiment, and when two battalions in a regiment had equal merits they were sometimes amalgamated to become one. This major process was carried out with remarkable speed, little warning being given to officers and none to other ranks.

My old battalion was the 17th Sherwood Foresters, 39th Division, and they told us we were going to the 2/5th Battalion. We felt that we were going to have a cushy time; the 2/5th had only just come over from Ireland. We heard that they had only gone over the top once [at Cambraï] and had come back straight-away and had had to be 'scotched up' by a Regular Battalion. It took us three days to find them – we were marching about from place to place – but we weren't very well received when we finally found them. We'd come from a unit where we'd had to get cleaned up as soon as we came out of the trenches; these people all had dirty buttons. Their C.O. came out and inspected us. He stared at us; I think he was a bit surprised that we were so clean. He didn't say much. The sergeant-major certainly had it in for us. Then they just split us up between their platoons and that was that. Afterwards we sometimes got together for a little chat and we always said how sorry we were to have to leave the old battalion. (Lance Corporal A. Bowler, 2/5th Sherwood Foresters)

It was like the breaking up of a happy family. The 9th Leicesters had been a happy battalion with a nice colonel – a gentleman. I was given a completely new platoon; none of our old companies or platoons were kept intact. It was very depressing. We didn't fancy the prospect of going to the 8th Battalion whose colonel was known to be very strict. Later, however, looking back on the March fighting, I think that the stricter discipline helped us through. (Second Lieutenant J. C. Farmer, 8th Leicesters)

On the day that the 1/7th Londons was disbanded, a fine midday meal was provided and then a mock funeral was held at which an empty coffin was buried. The grave was marked with a wooden cross topped by a steel helmet, the sign reading 'BURIAL PLACE OF 1/7TH LONDONS'. Part of the battalion then marched off to another London battalion near by that evening, played on their way by the band with 'Auld Lang Syne', and the remainder went to a battalion in another division the next morning. It had taken just thirty-six hours for all trace of a good battalion to disappear.

These details are taken from *The Long Carry*, written
by Private Frank Dunham who was a stretcher-bearer in the
battalion. Dunham then goes on to describe the great apprehension felt by the men who had earned for themselves by
long service in the old battalion the more comfortable little
jobs at company or battalion headquarters. Frank Dunham
managed to hang on to his job but many found themselves
back in a rifle platoon. And this is all it meant for most
soldiers – buttons to be cleaned or not, a bullying sergeant-
major or a stricter colonel, the loss of a 'cushy' job.

There was some regret among the survivors of the original
members of battalions which had come out to France years
before and had now to be disbanded. The 1/7th Sherwood
Foresters, originally composed of pre-war Territorials from
Nottingham, found that just eleven men were left of the 1,000
who had sailed from England in January 1915. In the 18th
Manchesters, a Kitchener's Pals battalion, six 'originals'
were found to be left in the rifle companies and a few more
with the transport, band and stores.

The process of reorganisation commenced at the end of
January 1918 and was completed by 4 March. It was a
remarkably swift and efficient piece of work, carried out while
divisions continued to hold the line as normal. The smooth
completion was a credit to staff officers, who rarely picked up
praise for their work. 115 battalions had completely disappeared, thirty-eight more were amalgamated to make
nineteen new battalions, and seven more became pioneers.
In some cases a surplus of men was left and these were formed
into 'Entrenching Battalions', which would be engaged on
the digging of defences but were also to be 'first reinforcements' for battalions in action. There was also a surplus of
junior officers and a new order came out saying that any
officer with more than two years service might return to his
regiment in England for six months' rest. Some commanding
officers took this opportunity to get rid of the less satisfactory
of more recently arrived officers by sending them back to
England also.

It cannot be suggested that the reorganisation, smoothly
accomplished as it was, could enable divisions to perform as
well as before, at least as long as the length of front to be

held remained the same. Three battalions had now to do the same work as had been done for years by four, and either the front line would be more weakly held or the infantry would be rested less often. By no more than a coincidence, the Machine Gun Corps units in each division were also being reorganised at the same time. The three old independent companies were now joined by a fourth company fresh out from England and all four companies were amalgamated into a new unit known as the Machine Gun Battalion. This machine-gun reorganisation was not quite complete, but the new divisions that were emerging from all these changes contained more machine-guns, the same amount of artillery, but much less infantry than before. Firepower was to make up for manpower. All this had taken place just after Gough's Fifth Army had taken over a long section of line from the French and while the entire British Expeditionary Force was in the process of adopting a completely new defensive role. Haig's divisions bore all these changes remarkably well, but they must have affected the fighting ability of those divisions which, within seventeen days of the completion of the reorganisation, were to be fighting against the German offensive.

*

It is time to be more specific and to concentrate on the twenty-five infantry divisions of Byng's and Gough's armies which would be fully or partially involved in the first day of the coming battle. The British Expeditionary Force contained four main types of infantry division – Regular, Territorial, New Army and Empire. With the exception of a brigade of South Africans and another of Canadian cavalry, the Empire units can be left out of this summary. Although their men, particularly the Australians and New Zealanders, were to play a part in holding the German attack at a later date, none were involved on the first day. As the Guards Division was also absent, it can be said that the battle of 21 March 1918 was fought almost entirely by the county regiments of the British Army. The regions with a particular stake in the battle were London, Ireland and Scotland with two divisions of men each. The city outside London with the deepest involvement was to be Manchester, with seven battalions in the battle.*

It might be thought a little hollow to refer to the 'Regular divisions' because so few of the original peacetime-trained soldiers were now left in them, but tradition dies hard and something of the discipline and professionalism of the 'Old Army' had definitely survived. Any corps or army commander who found himself with Regular divisions under his command considered himself fortunate. But there had been so much interchanging of battalions between divisions during preceding years that, apart from the Guards, there was no such thing as a division with an entire complement of Regular battalions although the recent reorganisation had reduced the leavening of New Army battalions. Three Regular divisions would be involved on 21 March. These were the 2nd, 3rd and 6th Divisions, and General Byng was the fortunate commander because they were all in his Third Army.

Almost as long in service on the Western Front as the Regulars, and far more exclusive, were the divisions of the Territorial Force (later called the Territorial Army). These were originally the part-time, volunteer units raised locally in England, Scotland and Wales but not in politically sensitive Ireland. The First-Line Territorials had come to France in late 1914 and in 1915 and had provided an effective reinforcement for the Regulars, although the role of the Territorials had originally been planned as that of home defence. Each Territorial unit had immediately started to raise a 'Second Line' made up of wartime recruits, and some of these had come to the Western Front more recently. Although the recruitment of Territorials as a separate class of soldier had stopped in 1916 and the later men in these units were normal conscripts, the Territorial divisions in France had been allowed to remain intact and even after the recent reorganisation there were no Regular or New Army battalions in Territorial divisions.†

* Appendix 3 will give the Order of Battle of the infantry and cavalry divisions involved on the first day of the battle.

† The Territorial battalions were numbered after the Regulars. In a typical county regiment, the 1st and 2nd Battalions were Regulars, the 3rd Battalion would be a training unit at home, the 1/4th and 1/5th etc. would be First-Line Territorials, the 2/4th and 2/5th would be the Second-Line. Where First- and

The Territorials were to be heavily involved on 21 March with six of their divisions in action; there was a seventh, the 50th (Northumbrian), in G.H.Q. Reserve but it took no part in the first day's fighting. The senior of these was the 47th (London) Division holding part of the Flesquières Salient; the Chief of Staff in this division for the last four months of the war was to be Lieutenant-Colonel Bernard Montgomery. Then came the famous 51st (Highland) Division, its high reputation as a 'stormer' division dating from the attack and the capture of Beaumont Hamel during the closing stages of the Battle of the Somme. But the Highlanders may have been used too often since Beaumont Hamel; they had suffered many casualties and were suspected of having lost their fighting spirit. There was also some doubt whether the Highland nature was as suited to sitting out a bombardment and then defending against an infantry attack as it was to storming German trenches. The remaining four Territorial divisions were all Second-Liners, which meant that a high proportion of their earlier volunteer recruits had been sent to the First-Line battalions in France and replaced by conscripts. Their divisions had then come out to France themselves, and they became the least experienced part of the British Expeditionary Force. Their reputation was not high although their efficiency varied from unit to unit. They were somewhat derisively known as 'Conscript Divisions' and it is reputed that a British corps or army commander once said, 'God save me from the New Army and Second-Line Territorials.' The four divisions in this group were the 59th (North Midland) holding the Bullecourt Salient in the Third Army, and the 58th (London), 61st (South Midland) and 66th (East Lancs) in the Fifth Army.

The Second-Line Territorials were often aware of their reputation, and survivors display a likeable self-deprecatory attitude somewhat unusual in old soldiers. One man who had been in the 59th Division, which had not performed well against the German counter-attack at Cambrai, says that 'we

---

Second-Line battalions had recently amalgamated, the prefix was dropped so that the 1/5th and 2/5th Battalions became, if joined, simply the 5th. The New Army battalions had started numbering after the Territorials.

weren't taken very seriously. If they wanted anything special doing, they didn't send for us.' The 61st Division reckoned it had been unlucky at everything it had attempted so far and called itself the 'Sixty-worst'. Six of its battalions had been disbanded under the recent reorganisation and a complete brigade of Highland battalions from the 51st Division had arrived. The Highlanders did not like the idea of serving with the Second-Line division but the South Midland men were well pleased with the new arrivals. 'We felt they would probably stiffen us up a little.'*

The most junior division in France was the 66th (East Lancs), the men in whose battalions varied from miners from the Wigan area – 'marvellous soldiers, many of them couldn't write but they could see like cats in the dark and could certainly dig' – to clerks from the business houses of Manchester. The 66th Division had gained a new commander after Passchendaele, none other than Major-General Neill Malcolm, who had been Gough's Chief of Staff at Fifth Army and had been responsible for the hard driving, in his chief's name, of several reluctant corps commanders. Malcolm was just what the division needed at this time, but it is ironical that he was now under the command of Lieutenant-General Sir Herbert Watts of XIX Corps, who had been one of the commanders pushed so hard by Gough and Malcolm during Passchendaele.†

*

The greater part of the British forces that would oppose the German attack came from the New Army. These were the

---

* One of the brigade commanders in the 61st Division was a well-known character, Brigadier-General the Hon. Robert White, who had earlier achieved fame by being one of the leaders of the infamous and unofficial Jameson's Raid into the Transvaal in 1895, which ended with most of the 478 raiders being captured by the Boers. Jameson and five of his officers, including White, were returned by the Boers to London where they were charged under the Foreign Enlistment Act and sent to prison for several months. 'Bobby' White had then served in the Boer War and in 1914 had raised the 10th (Stockbrokers) Battalion, Royal Fusiliers, for the New Army. Now he was a brigade commander and very popular with the men under his command. He was to be wounded on the second day of the battle.

† Major-General Malcolm was to be badly wounded by shrapnel on the ninth day of the coming battle.

battalions and divisions raised directly as volunteers from the civilian population by Kitchener's famous appeal in the first few weeks of the war. Many of the original units had been intensely local in nature, particularly in the 'Pals battalions' of the industrial areas. The New Army had undoubtedly contained the most idealistic and patriotic men of the country, and the war for these had almost been a crusade, albeit tinged with a measure of search for adventure and excitement. This fine material, completely inexperienced in battle, had first been put to the test at Loos in late 1915, but their real commitment to the war had come on the Somme the following summer. But courage and spirit had not been enough and the New Army had suffered terrible casualties. There had not been enough volunteers to replace the losses and a large proportion of the men in these battalions were now conscripts, although sufficient of the original members and of local pride remained for the individuality of the New Army to survive.

Fifteen of the twenty-five divisions which would face the German attack were nominally of the New Army and, although their battalions had been the first to be disbanded in the recent cuts, 128 out of 250 battalions in these twenty-five divisions were still New Army ones. The New Army were spread right along the attack front – four divisions in the Third Army, nine in the Fifth Army and two in G.H.Q. Reserve. So evenly over the United Kingdom had the battalions in these New Army divisions been raised that it is difficult to highlight individual units here; many will be met in subsequent chapters. There were, however, two divisions to be heavily involved on 21 March on which it is worth spending a little time. These were the only two Irish divisions on the Western Front: the 16th, mainly Southern Irish, and the 36th, from Ulster.

There is no denying that generations of Irishmen had provided good soldiers for the British Army, and these men performed many heroic acts and suffered heavy casualties right through the First World War. Some of their feats, notably the attack of the Ulster Division at Thiepval, where one of the few successful advances of the first day of the Battle of the Somme was made, have justifiably become part of Irish, or at least Ulster, history. This pride over feats of arms in what was not really Ireland's war has sometimes, however, led to exaggeration. The whole of Ireland was still then legally part of the United Kingdom and was governed from London. In reality, the Catholic South of Ireland had long wanted their own government and had been promised it. Unfortunately, the Protestant majority in the northern Ulster counties had virtually been in rebellion in 1914 over this 'Home Rule' and had been ready with their own army, the Ulster Volunteer Force, to fight English or Southern Irish to avoid being thrust into an unwanted independence with the South. It was ironical that the Ulster Volunteer Force was persuaded by Kitchener to become a division of the New Army and that enough Southern Irish volunteers were also found to form the 16th Division. Now both Irish divisions were in the line, almost side by side, awaiting the German attack. A further irony was that General Gough's army career had nearly been broken just before the war when he had refused to turn out the Curragh garrison to fight the Ulster Volunteer Force. Both divisions were now in his Fifth Army.

The two Irish divisions had both lost more of their New Army flavour than had similar English divisions. There had been no conscription in Ireland, although many politicians and generals were urging that conscription should be imposed there, if only to ensure equality of sacrifice throughout the United Kingdom. Many Irishmen will say that there was no need for conscription in their country, that enough men were willing to volunteer. This is not borne out by the facts. Below are the relevant proportions of the male populations of the various countries in the United Kingdom who served as volunteers or conscripts in 1914–18:

England	24·02 per cent
Scotland	23·71 per cent
Wales	21·52 per cent
Ireland	6·14 per cent

This failure by the Irish to follow up their first rush of volunteering – let it be said, quite understandably so in the political circumstances of the time – dispels the myth that Ireland had no need for conscription. It had also affected the character of the two divisions in France. Only three New

THE NEED OF MEN

Mr Punch (to the Comber-out): 'More power to your elbow, sir. But when are you going to fill up that silly gap?'
Sir Auckland Geddes: 'Hush! Hush! We're waiting for the Millennium.'

A cartoon from *Punch*. Sir Auckland Geddes was Minister of National Service.

Army battalions were left in the 16th Division and only five
in the 36th, the remaining battalions now being all Regulars.
In some battalions perhaps as many as a third of the men were
not even Irish, because drafts from English regiments had
been needed to keep the Irish units up to strength. The
Germans had made great efforts to suborn the Irish troops at
the front, but with hardly any success. The men of both
divisions were regarded as 'happy-go-lucky, very friendly and
open-handed'. There was much military crime of a petty
nature but no organised resistance to British Army military
discipline, despite the fact that many of the Ulstermen and
the Southerners had once been or would later be legally,
at least in English eyes, in rebellion against the London
government.

*

Before we leave the New Army, there was a brigade of the
9th (Scottish) Division – the senior division in the New Army
– which contained the only representatives of the Empire to
be involved in the opening of the German offensive. This was
the South African Infantry Brigade, which had been formed in
June 1915, its first men coming from the force that had just
concluded the successful campaign against the Germans in
South West Africa. Four battalions (called regiments in this
case) were raised and made up of men from different parts of
the Union of South Africa as follows:

1st Regiment – Cape Province
2nd Regiment – Natal and the Cape Province Border
                 area
3rd Regiment – Transvaal
4th Regiment – South African Scottish

Men from the Orange Free State could join any of the
regiments; many Dutchmen seemed to fancy wearing the kilt
and joined the South African Scottish. A medical unit was
also formed.

The South Africans came to France and joined the 9th
Division just before the Battle of the Somme. They suffered
severe casualties in their first battle at Delville Wood, but
volunteers came from South Africa to replace the losses and

the brigade never had to make up with other troops, although a batch of Rhodesians were among the last group of reinforcements to reach the brigade before the March 1918 battle. Some of the South Africans were boys below the age of nineteen, a state of affairs no longer allowed in British divisions at the front. The 3rd Regiment had just been disbanded and the remainder of the brigade was now at full strength. One of the officers says that 'the morale of the troops was exceedingly high; everyone was on his toes and expecting great things.' But another, less jingoistically, states that 'it was noticeable that the very high standard of the original brigade had fallen off due to war weariness and a severe winter in France, but morale was still good and discipline satisfactory.'

There were also a few United States troops serving with the British. Although the U.S. Army was determined to bring their divisions into action concentrated under United States command, it had answered British calls for help in several ways. Many front-line British units now had American Army doctors as their medical officers and there were some American surgical units and nurses at Casualty Clearing Stations just behind the front. There were also three United States Engineer Regiments – the 6th, 12th and 14th – working in the Fifth Army. General Gough describes in his book how he met these men, finding them 'a fine body of tall, strong, active men'. The Americans were building extra bridges over the River Somme behind the Fifth Army; within days of completing the work they would be blowing up the same bridges just before the Germans reached them.

There remains one last infantry division to bring into the picture. The 63rd (Naval) Division was in the Flesquières Salient, manning the vulnerable trenches at the extreme point of the bulge into the German lines. This division was a direct descendant of the naval and marine battalions that had been formed and dispatched so hurriedly to Ostend in August 1914 and which had then served in the Gallipoli campaign in 1915. For a time it had been fashionable for brilliant young men to find their way into the Naval Division as junior officers. The war poet Rupert Brooke was the best known of these. Now he was among the war dead and the division had lost many men as casualties and much of this earlier glamour. Only two brigades in the division were now composed of Naval or Marine battalions.

Finally there were the cavalry divisions, being relied upon now to make up for the shortage of infantry. When the Fifth Army took over the southern sectors of the British front, General Gough found that among the forces allocated to him were all five of the cavalry divisions in France. There were three British and two Indian divisions but the Indians would not be there on 21 March. The cavalrymen had had an easy war compared to the infantry. Their regiments had seen plenty of action in the opening months of the war but since then they had done little but come up for the opening of each British attack, only to be sent back to the rear when a break-through had not been achieved. Many of the regimental officers had left, the seniors to command infantry units, the juniors to join the Royal Flying Corps or the Tank Corps. During these years the cavalry had been almost useless to the Allied cause, and had consumed vast quantities of supplies, tied down a valuable reserve of trained soldiery and defied nearly all efforts to disband their units. Correspondence in the Public Record Office shows how the Army Council in London had been trying since May 1917 to disband a sizeable proportion of the cavalry in France; at least one full division was mentioned. The correspondence shows how Haig fought a long delaying action. In June 1917, just before Passchen-daele, he wrote:

I hold strongly that as the war develops a time will come, possibly at no very distant date, when the employment of cavalry in masses will be not only feasible, but urgently necessary in order to turn a favourable situation to full account. I consider it of such importance that the cavalry required for this purpose should be constantly available, and fully trained, that I am unable to concur either in any reduction of the five Cavalry Divisions now in France or in their constant readiness for action in masses being impaired by using any part of them as Divisional, Corps, or Army Cavalry, even as a temporary measure.*

The best that Haig could offer was the disbandment of just six of the twenty cavalry regiments – mostly Yeomanry – which were attached to infantry corps.

* Public Record Office WO 106/403.

Temporarily dismounted cavalry had sometimes manned trenches in the past, but only on quiet sectors. Now the cavalry divisions had left their horses in the rear again and been formed into makeshift infantry units, each cavalry division producing only the equivalent of one brigade of infantry. These dismounted cavalrymen were not in the front line but were held by Gough in the immediate rear as first reserves. One cavalry brigade was made up of Canadian regiments and these represented the only sizeable body of Empire troops besides the South African brigade to fight in the early stages of the German offensive.

*

This concludes the survey of the divisions which would defend the lines of the Third and Fifth Armies against the German attack. Each division had its usual complement of supporting arms and there were also corps and army units. There was plentiful artillery support with the divisional artillery to the fore with the 18-pounder field guns and 4.5-inch howitzers of the Royal Field Artillery. Behind these stood the Heavy and Siege Batteries of the Royal Garrison Artillery. Another artillery element, not present in earlier years, was the 'Army Field Brigades' made up of extra field batteries not committed to any particular division. The gunners of these liked to refer to their units as 'Flying Columns', believing that they were always sent to the scene of the most furious action, and there is some merit in this reputation, although each of the four British armies on the Western Front contained its share of such artillery. It is interesting to note that the men of the German mobile artillery batteries used exactly the same expression, *'fliegende Kolonnen'*. The total artillery available to the Third and Fifth Armies was 2,804 guns and howitzers, of which 2,491 were actually on the front that would be attacked.* The Germans had 6,473 guns directly supporting their attack.

The British units were similarly outnumbered in their trench-mortar strength, having approximately 1,400 mortars compared with the 3,522 mortars of the Germans. The British heavy trench mortars were manned by artillerymen

* The distribution of the British artillery is detailed in Appendix 4.

but the light mortars were still manned by officers and men detached from the infantry battalions of each brigade.

Generals Byng and Gough could also call on the services of the Tank Corps. The Third Army had four battalions – of thirty-six tanks each when up to full strength – and the Fifth Army three battalions. The tanks were to be brought up to positions immediately behind the Battle Zone and used in counter-attacks, with the infantry, to recapture parts of the Battle Zone captured by the Germans, but this type of work was all novel and the plans made were only of the sketchiest nature. Tanks, however, were the only weapon in which the defenders outnumbered the attackers.

The German attack was to come during the last days of the official existence of the Royal Flying Corps. This arm was to cease officially to belong to the Army on 1 April and the Royal Air Force would be born, although the squadrons in France would continue to operate under military orders as before. In the air the British were again outnumbered, but only by 730 German aircraft to 579 of their own.* For the squadrons which flew in support of the Third and Fifth Armies, the birth of the Royal Air Force would take place in the midst of hectic flying and fighting against the German offensive.†

*

It is not enough merely to count divisions and their strengths in men, and numbers of guns and tanks and aeroplanes, and then compare these with the German forces. It is true that the outcome of the battle would be decided largely by these factors but there were also others not so easy to measure: fighting spirit, perseverance, loyalty, and all those factors, almost indefinable, that come under the heading of morale. There have been many suggestions over the years that the morale of the British soldiers facing the Germans on 21 March 1918 was poor and that the Germans were able to profit accordingly.‡ The state of morale is never an easy

* The Royal Flying Corps Order of Battle is shown in Appendix 5.

† In anticipation of the creation of the Royal Air Force, Gamages of London were advertising complete new uniforms at a price of £9 2s. 6d.!

‡ For example, in *The Face of Battle*, a recent book by a Sandhurst lecturer, John Keegan, the following statement occurs: 'In March 1918 the British Fifth Army collapsed, as much morally as physically' (page 271).

subject to identify precisely, especially so many years later, but I was surprised to find that there was virtual unanimity among the men questioned on this subject and I am satisfied that what follows is an accurate description of the morale of the men who would soon be defending against the German attack. It should be stated before starting that, like their German counterparts, the ordinary British soldiers had no sure knowledge that there was going to be a German attack until a few hours before the battle began, so we are describing the situation during the first ten weeks or so of 1918.

On the face of it there was every reason for the morale of the British troops to be low at this time. In 1914 the war was going to be over by Christmas. In 1915 it would be over when the New Armies came. In 1916 the Somme was to be the 'Big Push' that would bring victory. All this optimism had died. 1917, with Arras, Passchendaele and Cambrai, had been a year of bitter disappointment. Arras and Cambrai could be borne, but the dreadful conditions of the final weeks at Passchendaele when men had been forced to exist and fight in a swampland of filth and slime, in cold and drenching rain, under constant German shellfire, had been the ultimate horror. When First World War survivors are questioned, they always mention Passchendaele first if they were there. They talk of the misery of 'the endless mud', not the casualties of this battle. For the Passchendaele men this resulted in the lowest point of their morale during the war. Because most of the British Expeditionary Force had been through Passchendaele and because there had been so few reinforcements since then, the army that would face the Germans on 21 March was virtually an army of Passchendaele survivors.

On the face of it there had been nothing in the events of the past winter to restore the spirits of the British soldiers. It was known that their Italian allies had been defeated at Caporetto and that the Russians had collapsed completely. It was known that the Germans facing them were being heavily reinforced. It was believed that the Germans were likely to attack somewhere, sometime, probably in the coming spring. It was obvious that the French could not be counted upon to win the war; the average Tommy's regard for the French had dropped steadily throughout recent years, and the Belgians had only a tiny army. The weakness of their own army was obvious in the drastic disbandment of so many battalions. There was vague talk of the Americans coming, but until they did come who would fight off the German attacks but poor old 'Tommy Atkins', who had already suffered so much?

A great deal, however, had happened since Passchendaele to restore morale. The sectors between Arras and the boundary with the French were heavenly dry compared to the Ypres Salient. A startling new British policy of keeping front-line activity to a minimum and avoiding casualties was much appreciated by the ordinary soldier. A great deal had been done to rebuild shattered battalions; lightly wounded had returned, some reinforcements had arrived, and the reorganisation of battalions had brought those battalions that were retained back to full strength. A battalion was now a crowded bustle of men once again, and the soldiers felt more at home here than in the scarecrow units that had marched out of Passchendaele. There was much difference between battalions, of course; one commanding officer who still survives says that 'a good battalion was like a good school, it absorbed new members without any loss of spirit.' A more junior officer says that 'there was a belief that a couple of bad shows behind a battalion strengthened rather than weakened it.'

The administrative services were also busy at this work of recovery. Unlike the Germans, the British were well and regularly fed, kept properly clothed, and lost or faulty equipment was replaced immediately. Home leave, always a boost to morale, was in full swing and would be kept that way as a deliberate matter of policy until the day the Germans attacked. 4,000 soldiers had been in arrears with their leave at the end of 1917 and much of this was made up in the first weeks of 1918. The records of one division show that at least 1,700 of its 10,000 infantry were away on leave on any one day and 700 more were attending various courses which gave some respite from front-line conditions.

Only a proportion of the infantry units were actually in the front line at any one time; the remainder lived in relative comfort in the hutted camps at the sites of the ruined villages behind the Battle Zone. Someone in authority at G.H.Q. had decided that the army should start growing some of its own food and fodder, and agricultural land behind the Battle Zone was being put under cultivation. The records of one division contain advice about the preparation of 'hot beds' for cabbage seeds as 'no young cabbage plants can be provided', and the Divisional Agricultural Officer ordered that every unit should submit map references of their agricultural plots and that the plots were to be handed over in the proper way to an incoming unit. The Highlanders of the 51st Division manured fifteen acres which were hoped to produce 'a fair crop of mixed hay', ploughed twenty acres for potatoes, and were farming 175 acres of land in all. It is unlikely that any of the British soldiers objected to these signs of a long and peaceful stay in this area.

There were some opportunities for leisure. Arthur Berhend was an artillery officer whose battery had come down from Ypres.

It was indeed a rest. One could with equal safety motor to Amiens to buy butter and vegetables for the mess or ride out on horseback to look for the front line. We could go and dine with our neighbours without hearing a shot fired; a hostile shell was an event. There were partridges to be hunted – with the brigade car (till the Colonel stopped it) because we had an old Belgian shotgun but no dogs – over the barren fields around our headquarters. I remember, too, how one of our planes, unable to establish contact with the battery for which it was conducting a shoot, landed in the battery position and asked the battery commander if all his wireless operators were on leave or only some of them . . . Since the Cambrai 'show', the whole brigade had suffered barely a dozen casualties. Indeed, since Christmas, life on the Bapaume front had been delightful – a succession of invigorating canters across the overgrown downs to the batteries, joy rides to Amiens through the snowy wastes of the Somme, early-morning partridge shoots over the fields around our headquarters.*

All these factors did much to rebuild the morale of the British units. There was, too, the absence of those signs which portray poor morale. A G.H.Q. report shows that there were only 1,921 absentees from the whole of the British Expeditionary Force in March 1918; this figure, representing

* *As from Kemmel Hill*, pages 41 and 53.

just one man for each battalion-sized unit, compares very well with Second World War levels of absentees from units which were under less strain than the 1918 men. Haig's own diary for 3 March shows his pride in the low number of his men in military prisons – nine men per thousand for the Australians (who had no capital punishment), fewer than two men per thousand for the other Empire troops, and one man per thousand for United Kingdom troops. 'Really, the absence of crime in this army is quite wonderful.'*

By the time the Germans attacked, there had been at least a partial recovery from the depth of Passchendaele's despairs. There would never again be the tight discipline and skill of the Old Army nor the crusading attitude of the Kitchener volunteers. There was not even any strong bond of comradeship now; the losses of preceding years and the 'endless dividing and subdividing' led to looser forms of friendship now. One man says 'there was still comradeship but not the homely comradeship of the past'. The British soldiers could only look forward to months and perhaps years of war with every prospect of hard fighting soon. There was an air of fatalism, of 'we're here for ever'. .

It was at this time that the British qualities of patience and endurance came into play. Some armies would not have stood what the British had stood and would not have faced the prospect now faced by the British. It might be that the different races in Britain would perform differently when the test càme. Would the Irish and the Scots, who were often so good in attack, be equally sound in defence? Would the New Army units, without the traditions and the nucleus of ex-perienced leaders that the Regular battalions still had, stand the strain? How would the Second-Line Territorials – the 'conscript divisions' – perform? There were many, from Haig downwards, asking these questions.

Although morale does not change abruptly at the boundary of one army with another, there was certainly cause for concern in Gough's command. When this new army front was formed at the end of 1917 and extended in January 1918, the armies to the north were forced to give up divisions for

Gough. The Fifth Army did not receive one of the strong Empire divisions, not one Regular division, and not one First-Line Territorial division. Gough's New Army and Second-Line Territorials were thinner per mile of front than any other army and were bolstered up with cavalry divisions whose performance as infantry was of unproved and doubtful value, his defence system was the least developed of all the British line, he had narrowly escaped being returned to England as a failure and he was certainly not in the best of favour with a commander-in-chief who, as a matter of deliberate policy, regarded the Fifth Army's front as expendable and of least priority if the Germans attacked.

Some officers will claim that the morale of their men was excellent and that 'they were spoiling for a fight', but this is nonsense. Morale was not 'excellent' anywhere in the British Expeditionary Force at this time, and the best that could be found between Arras and the junction with the French was a morale that was 'steady'. Let this chapter close with this quotation from one of Gough's humblest soldiers:

From the newspapers reaching us from home, we gathered that there was danger of a great enemy offensive. Millions of Germans were returning from the Russian Front, but we could not believe that the enemy would try to regain the 'Somme desert' given up by him in March 1917. *Our* worry was that there certainly would be a great *British* offensive in the spring, following the 1917 pattern, but even that was only mentioned in joking fashion. After the high hopes of 1917 and that year's cruel disappointments, my philosophy was that 'perhaps we shan't be in it, and if we are, perhaps my good luck will see me through.' We did not discuss it, but I am sure most men felt like that. (Private W. Greenhalgh, 2/6th Manchesters)

4

Before the Storm

The officers of the German General Staff had been busy all through the months of December and January developing the original plan for the *Kaiserschlacht* and overseeing the vast work of preparation required for it. One particularly important detail had soon been settled: the date for the opening of the offensive. Ludendorff had originally wanted it to start before the end of February in order to forestall any attack the Allies might be preparing. He need not have worried: the British and French were working hard on defence works and had no plans to attack the Germans anywhere on the Western Front. But the February date could not be met. The German divisions could not be trained and assembled in time. It was decided instead to allot the period to the end of February as the 'general period of preparation' and the first two weeks of March as the 'period of final preparation', with the attack to commence on 14 March. But even this was not enough time for Prince Rupprecht, whose army group was preparing two thirds of the attack. Rupprecht asked for an extra week, and the choice of date thus fell on 21 March. It was only because of this need by Rupprecht for more time that the battle was planned to start on the first day of spring. But 21 March was a very emotional day for the Germans: it was the anniversary of Bismarck's opening of the first *Reichstag* (parliament) of the German Empire in 1871, and Hitler would choose the same day in 1933 to open the *Reichstag* of his Third *Reich*.

Several major changes in the overall plan for the attack were still being considered as late as the first day of March. The Germans had been surprised to find that the British had taken over that part of the French line which ran from St Quentin to just south of the River Oise. But this development did not worry Ludendorff unduly. Instead of striking at the junction of the French and British Armies, as originally intended, a blow against the British right wing only would suit his purpose just as well. The terrain south of the Oise did not offer suitable conditions for an attack, and the destruction of the British Expeditionary Force had always been his main object. So the French, by a chance that they could not have foreseen, left the British to take the entire weight of the German blow.

Other changes that were considered by the Germans were a result of the wishes of their commanders on both flanks to extend the scope and weight of their attacks. On the German left, Crown Prince Wilhelm wanted to be free from the restraint imposed on him to halt and form a flank guard after the limited advance of his Eighteenth Army to the Crozat Canal, which was expected to take no more than three days. Wilhelm argued that the farther west he was allowed to advance the less likely the French were to come around from the south and help the British. He was prepared to find the extra divisions for this further effort from that part of his army group not engaged in the attack. It is not known how difficult it was for Ludendorff to refuse this request by the Kaiser's son and there was some merit in Wilhelm's proposals. They were accepted. This development would not affect the fighting on the first day but it was the first alteration to the balance and original aim of the German offensive. But a similar request by General von Below, commanding the right flank of the German attack, to extend the frontage of his attack to beyond Arras was refused.

The result of all these decisions was that the British were given an extra week's digging time in their defence works by the delay granted at Prince Rupprecht's request for more time, General Gough's Fifth Army was threatened with greater danger because Crown Prince Wilhelm had been allowed to add weight to his attack in the south, and the left of General Byng's Third Army in front of Arras – to be held on 21 March by the 3rd and 4th Regular Divisions and the 15th (Scottish) Division – was delivered from the threat of the attack that von Below wanted to extend to that sector.

A detailed timetable was drawn up for the assembly of the German units making the attack. A long stretch of front line which was only occupied by sufficient troops for normal trench-warfare conditions had to be transformed into an area full of the extra units and guns needed to launch a massive offensive. All this had to be done, if possible, without the British realising what was happening. This was the German timetable:

By the end of February: corps and divisional headquarters and headquarters of all artillery units to be in position.

1 March: period of final preparation begins.

1 to 5 March: advance parties from infantry and artillery units of attack divisions move up.

8 to 10 March: advance parties of air force, anti-aircraft artillery, pioneer and supply units move up.

9 to 12 March: air-force units move into airfields.

9 to 16 March: infantry units march by easy stages or come by rail to assembly areas ten to twenty kilometres behind the front.

10 to 14 March: artillery ammunition to be dumped at forward gun positions.

14 to 16 March: all artillery for which there are concealed emplacements to take up final positions.

15 to 19 March: corps commanders assume active command of their sectors.

16 to 18 March: infantry units march by night to villages nearer the front.

17 and 18 March: remaining artillery units move up, but those which have completely exposed firing positions will not be deployed until the evening before the attack.

17 to 20 March: pioneer and medical units move into final position.

18 March: advanced General Headquarters move from Spa, in Belgium, to Avesnes, sixty kilometres behind the front.

Night of 18–19 March: infantry units rest.

Night of 19–20 March: infantry units march to concealed positions in battle area.

20 March: infantry units rest in concealed positions. Noon of this day is the last time for postponement if weather is unsuitable.

21 March: 1.00 a.m., all attacking units to be in final positions;
　　　　　4.40 a.m., artillery bombardment commences;
　　　　　9.40 a.m., infantry attack commences.

We will follow this programme from 9 March, when a great influx began as nearly a million German soldiers started to converge on the battle area from rest and training areas deep behind the entire length of the Western Front. These early moves were carried out by day and usually by rail. The men were told nothing. Those of the 27th Division had trained and re-equipped at Colmar in Alsace. Their train took them north to Strasbourg and it was not until the train then turned west that they knew for certain that they were destined for the Western Front.

The German units assembled in dozens of villages behind the attack front. Every building was packed with men, every barn with horses; vehicles and guns were hidden under trees. Movement outside was forbidden during the day. Although the men were still told nothing of their future, they could have little doubt now that something was brewing, and excitement and tension started to build up. Most of these assembly areas were not troubled much by the British.

A great deal of unobtrusive work had been done in the forward area. Roads had been improved, bridges strengthened, airfields repaired. Many artillery battery positions had been surveyed and firing plans prepared for them by calculation from maps. As the Germans had once held all the ground that was to be attacked, they knew to the metre the position of roads, junctions, railheads, the main trenches and the likely positions of command posts. Shelters were dug for the final assembly of the attacking infantry. Thousands of wooden trench bridges were constructed and concealed; these would later be taken up behind the infantry and used to bridge captured British trenches so that artillery and supplies could get forward. As far as possible all the work was done by night, and daylight would find the area no more busy than at normal times. German pilots were ordered to fly over the area by day to ensure that no undue activity or any of the constructions were visible by day. A novelty observed by one officer who came into the forward area before the battle was that a large black ball was hung from an observation balloon at noon exactly on each day and hauled sharply up again ten minutes later. Every unit within visible distance could thus check their clocks and watches.

All this time the German front line was held only by the lower-grade divisions which would take no part in the attack and whose soldiers were told absolutely nothing about it in case they were taken prisoner in British raids. Offensive activity was kept to a minimum on most of the German front line. There was one exception to this. Between 10 and 16 March the Germans fired a steady bombardment of mustard-gas shells into the Flesquières Salient, possibly in the hope of forcing the British to withdraw from the awkward bulge in the German line. The British holding the trenches here suffered many casualties from this gas. Hardly a man in their 2nd Division was not affected and the whole division had to be withdrawn and replaced by a reserve division. Another division, the 63rd (Naval), suffered over 2,500 casualties in two nights of gas shelling but had to be left in the line. The British made no move to withdraw from the salient.

The Germans carried out the normal deception activities to prevent the Allies from identifying the exact area to be attacked. German army commanders on other parts of the Western Front were instructed to make preparations for an attack and each was encouraged to think that his area would be the eventual scene of the offensive. A particular effort was made on the front of the German armies which were facing the French between Reims and Verdun in the hope that the French could be convinced that it was they who were to be attacked. Several small but vigorous attacks were made on the French lines and 1,400 prisoners taken. A heavy bombard-ment was made on Verdun. A German observation balloon containing fake details of an attack on the French was allowed to blow into the French lines. Crown Prince Wilhelm attempted to produce confusion by announcing that he intended to be in Calais, which was behind the northern end of the British front, on 20 March and would be in Paris, behind the French front, on 15 April.

The Germans' ruses were successful. The French moved reserves to face several imaginary attacks on their front and no French reserves were placed near the British right wing as had been promised. Even the British had no sure know-ledge, until well into March, that they were to be attacked, and the last front of all to attract attention was the one on either side of St Quentin.

Haig's Intelligence section had been trying to establish the German intentions for many weeks. The first hint had come as early as 5 January, when two letters of sympathy signed by General von Hutier appeared in German local newspapers. This was the first sign that this well-known general had arrived from the Eastern Front. The letters were to the families of a senior officer, known by the British to have died on the St Quentin front, and of a young airmen who had died when his plane crashed in the Fifth Army's area. The British had to wait until early March for more information, but then General von Below, who was known to have been the successful German commander at Caporetto, was also reported opposite the Fifth Army. The news that two of Germany's most successful generals were facing the Fifth Army was significant, but sadly this knowledge was counterbalanced by the German deceptions elsewhere.

It was the pilots and observers of the Royal Flying Corps who brought in the next pieces of information. Part of the German deception plan was not to increase their own air activity over the area of the attack and they had to allow the British planes to fly over this normally. The British reconnaissance squadrons had been turned on to concentrated observation work on 24 February. They soon started reporting an increased level of German rail and road activity but most of the main German preparations remained undetected until 6 March, when the airmen spotted the ammunition dumps that the Germans were building up each night at the sites to which the German artillery would move at the last moment. The first dumps were seen in the area opposite the British VI Corps, at the extreme north of the attack front. This was probably an attempt by the Germans to keep attention from the south until the latest possible date and it was a further four days before similar dumps were seen in the St Quentin area. At first it was not known what these tarpaulin-covered objects, dumped quite openly in an otherwise empty landscape, could be.

11 March. The objects already referred to appear to have been largely increased during the past twenty-four hours. As many as 500 are now plainly seen. Each object is about 10' × 5'. It is

considered possible that they are mobile but rather too small for
tanks. They may be dummy dumps intended to deceive.

2 March. Objects bombarded. Further information reveals:
1. Study of track poiñts to the conclusion that they are mobile and
self-propelled.
2. 15' × 8' (lorry size).
3. Close to known battery positions.
4. Heavy explosion caused by a direct hit in a recent shoot.*

It had required some daring low-level photography by the
airmen flying the R.E.8 reconnaissance planes of 52 Squadron
to get the 'further information' referred to above. In another
British area, artillery fire was observed to set fire to eight
dumps and this tribute was paid to the Germans.

16 March. Our artillery set fire to eight dumps between 3 and
5 p.m. just north of Agache River about D.16, b1.9 [a local map
reference]. The enemy made great efforts to put out the fires and
showed great gallantry in remaining under our heavy and field
artillery fire. Some men were seen to be on fire.†

Another mysterious phenomenon was observed opposite
the area of 66 Division.

Some holes started appearing in No Man's Land, well in front of
the German wire. These were photographed from the air and there
was a big rumpus between the artillery and the trench mortars
about who was firing short. They both denied having done so and
there was much consultation about it, but no conclusions were
reached and the matter was forgotten, no action being taken. Later,
when I was a prisoner of war, I found that these were deep holes
dug out by the Germans and obviously used to shelter their assault
infantry, a sort of overflow from their trenches in an area unlikely
to be shelled by British artillery. On reflection afterwards, we
thought it was a damned clever idea. (Lieutenant A. A. Simpson,
197th Trench Mortar Battery)

All these signs were being reported to Haig's new Director
of Intelligence, Brigadier-General E. W. Cox. (Cox had
recently replaced the previous Director of Intelligence,
Lieutenant-General Sir Herbert Lawrence, who was now

* XVIII Corps General Staff War Diary, Public Record Office WO 95/953
† IV Corps General Staff War Diary, WO 95/717.

Haig's chief of staff.) The weekly summaries issued by Cox are of great interest. They reveal that G.H.Q. was expecting two major German attacks some time in March. One of these was expected to be against the British, between Arras and St Quentin, but the second major attack was expected to fall on the French. Only a 'minor offensive' was expected south of St Quentin, with a further diversion in the Bois Grenier–Neuve Chapelle sector in the British First Army area in the north. The intentions of the Germans in the attack expected in the Arras–St Quentin area were forecast as being the capture of the Flesquières Salient and the drawing in of the British reserves prior to a further attack elsewhere. Haig's personal assessment was that the total of the German attacks on all sectors could not exceed a length of thirty to forty miles because of the limited amount of the German artillery available. At the same time as he was privately making this forecast, Haig was telling Lloyd George that the Germans were about to attack the British on a fifty-mile front, but this was probably another attempt to get more men from England. This move by Haig to increase his strength was no more successful than others made during the winter and the British Expeditionary Force remained without significant reinforcement.

The German deception moves had thus been largely successful. Haig, as well as the French, believed that a major effort would fall on the French front and Haig's attention was still drawn to his north by the suspected German diversionary attack there. The width and extensive objectives of the German attack remained unsuspected and the southern half of Gough's Fifth Army was expected to be safe from major attack.

General Gough had first asked for help for his weak front as early as 1 February, when he pointed out the presence of von Hutier opposite him and asked for more labour units and an extra Royal Flying Corps reconnaissance squadron; but he did not request more infantry at that time. He did not press G.H.Q. for infantry reinforcements until 12 March when it was quite clear to him that a major blow was about to be struck against his army. The result of that late request will be described later, but an extract from Gough's book *The Fifth*

Army makes clear that he fully understood Haig's priorities and his own role in the coming battle.

Haig was absolutely sound in his judgement to keep his reserves in the north and to leave the Fifth Army to do the best it could with its divisions to hold up and perhaps exhaust the German forces. I understood this conception perfectly, and in my discussions with Haig it was clearly understood by both of us that the role I was to play was to retire gradually, and to delay and exhaust the enemy, without exposing my Army to annihilation.*

Gough had received additional strength in February when three divisions – the 18th, 20th and 66th – came down from the Ypres front, but these were probably the final moves to complete the Fifth Army after its recent extension of line rather than reinforcements to face the coming battle. Gough was annoyed, however, when he lost two of the five cavalry divisions that had formed part of his reserves. These were the 4th and 5th (Indian) Cavalry Divisions, which were sent to Palestine early in March. Gough did not blame Haig for originating this move, which was on orders from the War Cabinet in London, but he did feel that Haig could have persuaded London to delay the departure of the Indian cavalry until the end of the battle that was obviously coming. There was no crisis in Palestine, and this move caused Gough to lose the equivalent of two brigades of infantry at a vital moment. It was at exactly the same time that the French, because of the German deceptions, were moving their reserves away from the junction with the British to the French centre and right, where the reserves would be beyond immediate help to the British and where no attack would ever take place.

*

'Those first days of March 1918 were the quietest time I ever had in all my time in France.' There were many men who remember the peaceful days which persisted right up to the eve of the German offensive. The weather was fine, at least until the 18th of the month, and the fronts of the British Third and Fifth Armies were unusually quiet. Several men mention

* *The Fifth Army*, page 238.

that their battalions were left in the front line for longer periods than usual. The reason for this was that the dry weather and quiet conditions resulted in units requiring less frequent relief, and this in turn meant that the work of digging in the rear by units out of the line could be continued with less disruption. The question of divisional and brigade reliefs would become a matter, literally, of life and death for those who would finish up in the front line on the day of the German attack. But the British soldiers were not to know that and they took full advantage of the peaceful conditions. The following quotations come from the War Diary of an infantry battalion and from an artilleryman.

8 March (in the line). Most perfect weather for March or, for that matter, any time of the year. Nice frost at night, hot sun by day. More like a South African winter than a European March. The Bosche do not appear to be very interested in our doings – not so interested as we are in his.

11 March. We have been super busy perfecting our defences. 1 O.R. wounded.

13 March. Our artillery kept up a bombardment over any area where enemy might be assembling for attack.

16 March. Another uneventful day. A capital afternoon's ratting resulted in a bag of over fifty large rats being killed in the railway cutting where Bn H.Q. is located.

17 March. Nothing. Wind gone round to S.S.W. Still remarkable weather.

19 March. Having completed a tour of twelve full days in the front line, we were relieved by the 22nd Northumberland Fusiliers.*

Observation-post duty was a pleasant if uneventful break from the usual routine. We left the battery early, took the track to Templeux, then, following the valley road towards Hargicourt, we branched left up a sunken road to the crest of the ridge. The view eastwards was extensive, overlooking a section of the St Quentin Canal. Beyond the canal we scanned miles of rolling down-like country but it was surprising how little activity could be seen in view of the reputed evil intentions of our friends 'across the way'. The whole area was deathly still and complete lack of movement gave it a drab and mysterious appearance which was not lightened

* 1st East Lancs War Diary, Public Record Office WO 95/3061.

by our inability to interpret the situation with any degree of
certainty. After registering the guns, our orders were not to
indulge in more than minimal firing so that the Bosche might think
we were blissfully unaware of anything out of the ordinary. 'Live
and let live' seemed to be the slogan here.

As things turned out, this policy may not have been a prudent
one but I never heard anyone complain about it at the time! So
we sat in the pleasant sunshine day after day gazing over the lines
and speculating from time to time what really was going on in that
sinister landscape. (Bombadier H. J. Hewetson, 331st Brigade
R.F.A.)

Most of the men in the British units on the Arras–St
Quentin front now realised that a German attack was expected
sometime. Many men received letters from home saying that
newspapers there were freely discussing the probability of a
German offensive on the Western Front, and the obvious
concentration on defensive works and training made the
soldiers realise that their own commanders thought the same.
The prospect of being the defenders in a battle was a unique
one for every British soldier who had come out since early
1915. The Second Battle of Ypres, in the spring of that year
which now seemed a lifetime away, was the last occasion on
which the Germans had attacked the British Expeditionary
Force in strength. Now, one man says, 'there was a general
feeling of expectancy of the attack and a certain amount of
curiosity because we had almost always been on the attacking
side before.' There was little immediate sense of expectation,
partly because of several false alarms and partly because it
was expected that any German attack would be preceded by a
bombardment lasting several days. Once again, quotations
from various men reveal their feelings at the prospect of
action.

'The knowledge of something big looming ahead did not impair
our morale in any way; in fact the coming event was perhaps
thought of very lightly. The 'toast' over a social drink was, 'They
shall not pass', taken from the French slogan at Verdun. And, as an
indication of the spirit among the younger officers particularly, a
spirit which permeated all ranks, the subalterns C Company,
having got hold of a terribly jingo record, 'March on to Berlin',
adopted it as their own company 'marching song'! (Second
Lieutenant G. Leighton, 4th South Africans)

For some weeks before the German attack on the 21st of March 1918, there was tension everywhere but chiefly among the forward troops. There was no doubt in their minds that an attack was coming. Troops in the front line counted the days until they were relieved and, as they marched back to the reserve positions, hoped that the attack would come before it was their turn to go back into the front line again. (Captain T. D. Morrison, 9th Royal Inniskilling Fusiliers)

My recollection of the three weeks before the 21st is that it was a happy period, quite a contrast with the Third Ypres battle. We enjoyed our sing-songs in the dug-outs. Our cockney gunners used to have penny song-sheets sent out to them which had been bought in the East End market places.

On the offensive side we became aware of the German firepower one evening when Very S.O.S. lights went up and we opened fire on our S.O.S. targets. The reply from the Germans was such that we all agreed 'Fritz has got some stuff over there.' Our position was plastered with shells for about fifteen minutes, the gunfire then dying down on both sides. We were made aware in that brief period that this quiet front was illusory. (Gunner W. W. Lugg, 83rd Brigade R.F.A.)

The artillerymen were the most active of the British soldiers and the guns were often in action as the date of the German attack drew nearer. The ammunition that the Germans were dumping for their guns was the cause of great embarrassment to the Germans. As more and more of these dumps were spotted by the British, so the British artillery did their best to destroy them. One 4.5-inch howitzer battery in the 51st Division caused an estimated 100 dumps of ammunition to explode during a ninety-minute bombardment. It was also noted that, whenever counter-battery 'shoots' were fired at known German gun positions, the explosion of considerable quantities of ammunition was always seen. The Fifth Army had also ordered that road and railway bridges behind the German lines were to be bombarded, but not until after 14 March so that the Germans would not have time to rebuild the bridges.

The infantry of both sides were particularly quiet during these days. When the 1st South Africans went into the line at Gauche Wood, they were able to patrol well out into No Man's Land in the thick mist of early morning. They found

the bodies of some British soldiers who had been killed in the
Battle of Cambrai and were able to give them a decent burial.
In the same division, however, a German soldier in a party
repairing their barbed wire at night shouted across to the
front line of the 5th Cameron Highlanders, 'We are coming
for you, Jock.' Several parties of German officers with maps
were seen examining the British line just north of St Quentin
with binoculars, and soldiers of the 2/2nd Londons, manning
the thinly held British line on the banks of the Canal de l'Oise
near La Fère, could even hear the sound of Germans digging
a tunnel under the canal.

British commanders ordered raids to be carried out with
the traditional purpose of taking prisoners for interrogation
and identification of their units. This hated task was undertaken on many sectors and on many nights. But the raiding
parties found it very difficult to find any Germans to take
prisoner. The German policy seems to have been to scuttle to
the rear as soon as a British raiding party was detected and
leave the front line empty. Mortar, shell and machine-gun
fire was then turned on the raiders and there were many
British casualties. The 1st Leicesters made two raids. On the
first night two officers and fifty men found the German
trenches empty but brought back ten copies of a French-
language newspaper, *La Gazette des Ardennes*, published by
the Germans, and also the propaganda balloon that would
have released the newspapers over the British zone when the
wind next blew in a favourable direction. The second raid of
the Leicesters was on a German position known as Magpies
Nest Post but this was also a failure, the artillery being
blamed for opening fire one and a half minutes early. A few
prisoners were brought in from other raids but most were
like the Bavarian from a line-holding division who 'knew of
no impending attack and expected the British to attack'.

The following exploit is probably typical of the difficulties
encountered by a small raiding party.

The Battalion Scouting Officer, Lieutenant Neave, was ordered
to make an identification raid. The C.O. said that if we could get
a prisoner we should get a day out in Amiens. Lieutenant Neave
took one sergeant and five men and we tried one night but met a
German patrol so we had to give up. Next day Lieutenant Neave

came to my dug-out and said that we had to go out again that night. My friend, Ted Smart from Grimsby, asked if he could come and the officer said he could come and another man could stand down.

We crept across to the German wire, making for a gap that Neave said he knew was there, but we couldn't find it. He told us to hang on while he started to cut a way through the wire but after a couple of snips there was an explosion right in front of us. I don't know whether it was a Gerry throwing bombs or whether there was an ammonal charge in the wire which was booby-trapped. We all jumped up and made a scramble back for our trenches. Half way across someone put a hand on my shoulder and asked me who I was. It was Lieutenant Neave and he had blood all over his face and couldn't see. I told him to take hold of the entrenching tool handle hanging from my belt and I led him back to our trenches. Then I couldn't find the gap in our wire. I caught my rifle sling in the wire and started tugging away, getting quite excited. Lieutenant Neave calmed me down, 'Take your time. You'll do it all right.' And then I found the gap easily. I put him on top of the parapet and pushed him in because there were machine-guns firing and I wanted to get in myself. We had lost one man killed – Ted Smart my friend – and had three wounded but no German prisoner. I took Lieutenant Neave along to the M.O.'s dug-out. He thanked me, said 'Cheerio', and I didn't hear of him again until after the next war, when I heard that he had died in Singapore.* (Private B. Pepper, 4th Lincolns)

Several German soldiers deserted to the British lines during the first weeks in March. They disclosed details of the coming attack and gave several dates but these all turned out to be false. It is not suggested that the Germans deliberately 'planted' this misleading information, but it was certainly responsible for several false alarms. The British soldiers regarded the Staff as being 'very panicky' at this time. There were many nights when units in the rear were ordered to sleep ready to move at a moment's notice and many wasted marches to and from the Battle Zone. A 'wind clock' painted on a ruined wall at Ronssoy showed a permanent state of

* Private Joseph Edwin Smart, died 15 March 1918, has no known grave and is commemorated on the Arras Memorial for the Missing. Captain John Richard Neave, M.C., Malayan Civil Service but attached to the Army as a liaison officer, died on 22 January 1942 and is buried at Kranji War Cemetery in Singapore.

'wind vertical'. One battalion, in its morning report to
brigade, recorded facetiously, 'Patrols report all clear.
G.H.Q. can stand down.'

＊

It was not all work. St Patrick's Day, Sunday 17 March, was
a particularly important event for the two Irish divisions.
There were a few hard feelings, particularly among the
Southern Irish, that they had not been relieved from holding
the line before this great Irish feast day and several com-
plaints to that effect appeared as painted slogans on walls in
the ruined villages in the 16th Division's area. The battalions
holding the front line when the great day came had little
chance to celebrate, but those in support could. The recent
reorganisation of divisions had brought the 1st and 2nd
Battalions of the Royal Irish Rifles together and the two
battalions were united, for the first time since 1854, at a
Mass which was celebrated by a chaplain, Father F. Gill,
D.S.O., M.C. In the afternoon there was a football match
which the 1st Battalion won 2–1. The 1st and 2nd Battalions
of the Royal Inniskilling Fusiliers also met on this day and,
after shamrock had been issued to the men, the rest of the day
was spent in inter-battalion sports. Every event seems to
have been won by the 2nd Battalion, whose commander was
Lieutenant-Colonel Lord Farnham. But in the 16th Division,
the 6th Connaught Rangers had been ordered out to man the
Battle Zone early that morning and then had to stay out
working on the defences. They missed Mass and returned to
their billets to a special dinner which, it is recorded, 'they
were too tired to enjoy.' That night, the 1st Royal Dublin
Fusiliers were ordered to carry out a large raid, sixty men
strong, to obtain a prisoner from a suspected new German
division. The raid failed. One man was killed and five were
wounded owing to their own artillery support falling short.
Some St Patrick's Day!

The 20th Division, which was completely out of the line
resting at this time, arranged a sports meeting and an
officer's steeplechase on that Sunday. General Gough attended
and entered his horses in two races. In one of these he finished
fourth out of 120 starters. Gough later recorded his great

enjoyment of this day's sport and compared it to the way the Duke of Wellington showed his calmness the night before Waterloo by attending a ball in Brussels. 'I felt I had a good precedent for thus spending my Sunday afternoon.'*

Three days earlier, Gough had paid a visit to the headquarters of the 16th (Irish) Division to settle a dispute. The trouble was over the manning of the front line. One brigade of the division was in corps reserve, of the six remaining battalions five were in the front line, leaving only one for the Battle Zone. This unusual disposition had been thought necessary because the Germans had an excellent concealed assembly area just behind their front line in the form of the cutting through which the St Quentin Canal flowed, and the corps commander had insisted that the front line be strongly held. The division's newly appointed commander, Major-General Hull, had objected. It was a typical example of the stress produced by the shortage of troops in the Fifth Army. Major K. S. Mason, the Divisional Machine-Gun Officer, describes General Gough's visit:

> I was present in the Divisional Mess at lunch when General Hull told General Gough that he was unhappy about his dispositions. He wanted only one brigade in the front line. General Gough would not agree to this and said, 'I wouldn't dream of such a thing. The Germans are not going to break my line.' I saw quite a lot of General Gough during his visit and came to the conclusion that he was a very arrogant, conceited and pompous man. He said once, 'Lady Gough is having a very unfortunate time in London with the bombing. She's going to move out into the country.' Can you imagine anything more annoying than having to listen to this sort of thing when the Germans were about to wipe his army off the map?

*

The German units who were destined to take part in the attack had remained for several days in their assembly areas well behind the front. The big march forward from here commenced in the evening of Saturday, 16 March.

The whole regiment was paraded in Cambrai and the commander spoke to us. He told us we were going to take part in a big attack,

* *The Fifth Army*, page 255.

that this would be the last big battle, and that it would be decisive. We trusted our generals then and believed what he said. Our morale was very high. I thought of my parents and I prayed that God would bring me out of this safely. (Feldwebel Max Schulz, 46th Regiment)

From a great arc, possibly eighty miles wide, hundreds of thousands of German soldiers tramped off into the night towards the battle front. Signs on vehicles were covered over and shoulder straps with regimental numbers were rolled up so that units could not be identified. The 'normal singing and music' was forbidden and the wheels of vehicles and guns and the hooves of horses were muffled with sacking and straw so that the inhabitants in the French villages would not hear the passing of so many units.

We did not know where we were bound for. One memory of that march is still very fresh in my mind. We kept meeting other infantry and artillery regiments and, as we passed them, we always called out the names of our towns and villages. We heard about many friends and news from home in this way. This had a strangely depressing effect because so often the news of friends was bad news. We all knew too that we were off into battle again and to the slaughterhouse. That we were going to attack and attempt to retake ground we had given up the previous year, that we did not know. (Gefreiter Max Brenner, 123rd Grenadier Regiment)

The German author Ernst Jünger, whose wartime experiences are described in his book *Storm of Steel*, was a junior officer in the 73rd Infantry Regiment, which was one of the Hanoverian regiments with the 'Gibraltar' battle honour.

Towards dusk, we left the quarters to which we had now become very much attached and marched to Brunecourt. All the roads were crowded with columns on the march, eagerly pressing forward, with countless guns and endless transport. Nevertheless, everything went according to plans worked out by the general staff. Woe betide any unit whose movements were not up to scheduled time! They were ruthlessly relegated to the ditch and had to wait hours before they found a gap into which they could squeeze. Once we were caught in the scrum and Hauptmann von Brixen's charger was pierced by an iron-tipped wagon-pole and killed.*

---

* *Storm of Steel*, page 243.

This great march forward was to last for two nights, with the German units sheltering and resting in villages *en route* during the intervening day. There was no marching on the third night, that of 18–19 March; this was to give the German soldiers a full thirty-six-hour pause at places about ten kilometres behind the line to rest and make their final preparations.

Also on the move were Field Marshal Hindenburg and General Ludendorff. On Monday 18 March, they motored from their main headquarters at Spa in Belgium to the temporary forward headquarters that had been established for them at Avesnes just over the French border and sixty kilometres behind the attack front. Their 180-mile drive took them through the hills and woods of the Ardennes. The weather was fine and warm for most of their journey and the German commanders must have wondered whether these perfect conditions would hold for the next few days. Unfortunately there was a thunderstorm as they arrived at Avesnes and this brought a sharp change in the weather with much rain and strong winds. If that type of weather continued, there would be problems about the German attack, especially over the use of gas, upon which the plan for the bombardment was based.

It was the first time that Hindenburg had been in France since he had been there as a young officer in the Franco-Prussian war, over forty years earlier. Ludendorff's biographer, Godspeed, records that, 'in spite of the blustery weather, Hindenburg went out daily for his walk and looked around Avesnes with benign interest, speaking to people on the streets and patting children on the head.' The Kaiser also came to Avesnes; he arrived in his special train on 19 March. He tried not to get in the way of the two military leaders and 'whenever he found himself bored he steamed away to visit one of his armies.' Naturally, he chose to visit Crown Prince Wilhelm's headquarters first.*

*

On the night of St Patrick's Day two German soldiers quietly

---

* These details and quotations are from *Ludendorff*, page 196.

left a trench just south of St Quentin, crossed No Man's Land, and gave themselves up to the Ulstermen of the 36th Division who were holding the British trenches here. The deserters were men from the disputed province of Alsace, and they had decided that their loyalty to Germany was not strong enough to see out the coming battle. They were taken quickly back to the headquarters of XVIII Corps at Ham. The Alsatians talked freely. They revealed that they were from the 414th *Minenwerfer Kompanie* which had been detached from a cavalry division to take part in an attack. There were at least 100 mortars on the frontage of the German 36th Division and the duty of these was to blow away the British barbed wire before the German infantry attack. There would be a six-hour bombardment in which prussic-acid gas shells would be used. The deserters could not give the exact day of the attack. Although XVIII Corps decided that only 'a raid on a large scale' was about to be carried out on their front, full details of the deserters' statement were rushed to Fifth Army Headquarters.

This was the most reliable of a variety of reports that were coming into General Gough's headquarters at this time. Several German prisoners had been taken in trench raids and a German pilot had survived the crash of his plane into the British lines. Most of the Germans had given fragments of information. The recent bad weather had limited the amount of reconnaissance that the Royal Flying Corps had been able to carry out but a few reports had come through showing that the Germans were still dumping ammunition at forward positions and also that many field guns, some of them in the open, had appeared very close behind the German front line. The Fifth Army sent these reports to G.H.Q., where they were added to others, although not so numerous, that had come from the Third Army. By the morning of the 19th the Intelligence staff at G.H.Q. had an almost complete picture of the position. They knew that the German back areas were full of troops, that the Germans in the forward zone were working hard carrying ammunition, that there was no great number of German tanks, and that a new type of German gas-mask had been issued. It was concluded that the British Third and Fifth Armies were to be attacked on the 20th or the 21st after a short bombardment using a high proportion of gas shells, but the exact boundaries of the front to be attacked were not known.

When the British units were told by G.H.Q. that the attack was expected, full credence was not always given to the warning; there had been a similar warning earlier in the month but nothing had come of that. A general order did go out that the artillery was to go over to full 'counter-preparation fire' at night, and the infantry raids on the German trenches continued. The result of this was that the last few nights became noisier but the days continued to be extremely quiet. The latest information brought urgency to one British front-line operation. For several weeks three companies of the Special Brigade, Royal Engineers, had been planning a major operation against the German-held front-line town of St Quentin which was now probably full of German troops. 3,000 projectors and their drums of poison chlorine gas had been ready for firing since the night of the 14th but the wind had not been favourable. If the Germans had spotted the projectors and shelled the area, it would have been a catastrophe for the British, but the equipment was well camouflaged and the Germans suspected nothing. On the evening of 19 March the wind was at last favourable – west-south-west at six miles per hour – and at 10.0 p.m. the projectors were fired. There were only forty-one misfires. Observers could hear the clatter as the gas drums fell on the roofs of St Quentin. The Germans did not retaliate in any way and the British hoped that the operation had been successful, even that it might cause the Germans to postpone their attack for several days.

The gas attack had caught the Germans completely unawares. St Quentin had been full of troops, as the British had hoped. This type of concentrated gas attack produced such an intensity of gas that masks were frequently of no use; there was not enough oxygen left in the air to get through the filters. The Germans made several mistakes which made matters worse. Many of their soldiers had been asleep when they were awakened by the clanging of the empty shell cases sounding the gas alarm. Thinking that this was a warning of a British attack, they grabbed their equipment and ran into

the open without their masks on. An infantry unit outside of
the town was not stopped and it marched into the town and
into the gas without warning. A German pioneer who had
been working outside the town when the gas attack had
occurred describes the scene when he returned to St Quentin.

We made sure by sight and by smell that the gas was gone
before removing our masks and then we returned to our cellar in
the town. On the way we saw terrible sights. Here and there were
men from other units who had been surprised by the gas. They sat
or lay and vomited pieces of their corroded lungs. Horrible, this
death! And, much as they implored us, nobody dared to give them
the *coup de grâce*. We were badly shaken by it all. (Pioneer Georg
Zobel, 353rd Pioneer Company)

*

Some British units ignored the warnings issued about the
German attack, and leave parties continued to go away as
normal. In one battalion seventy-two men including the
commanding officer went on leave as late as 20 March. Senior
officers, too, continued to take their leave and the German
attack would catch several divisions and brigades under the
temporary command of more junior officers. Other British
units were warned by their officers that the German attack
was imminent and some were definitely told that a retirement
was contemplated, a most unusual move in the British Army.
The commander of an Irish battalion told a group of his
officers and N.C.O.s about the retirement which was to be
made 'in an orderly fashion, covered by artillery.' At the end
of the talk one sergeant spoke out: 'I fought at Mons, the
Somme and in other battles, and now after over four years of
active service all you can offer us is a plan to retire.'

There was, however, more talk of holding out than of
retirement. A company of infantry who were working on the
defences in their Battle Zone received an unexpected visit and
talk by General Gough.

He told us, 'This is going to be a very serious and important
battle. I expect you to hold your positions to the last man and to
the last round of ammunition and if you have to die there then I
expect you to do that.' I felt that this was the wrong note; we were
looking over our shoulders from then onwards. It would have been

better to promise us all the help he could even though he might not have had any help to offer. It was a very uneasy 'show', that one. (Captain E. Hakewill Smith, 2nd Royal Scots Fusiliers)*

Just opposite St Quentin, the 16th Manchesters – the 1st Manchester Pals – were due to go into the front line. Lieutenant-Colonel Wilfrith Elstob was one of the battalion's original New Army officers who had survived all their battles and was now in command. Before the battalion left its billets, Elstob had outlined the positions that his men were to occupy and the scheme of defence. Three companies would be split up in small posts in the front line and the remaining company and Elstob's headquarters were to occupy a large redoubt, appropriately named Manchester Hill. Elstob probably knew that there could be no counter-attacks from the Battle Zone to relieve forward posts like his if they were surrounded, and he concluded his talk by pointing to Manchester Hill on a wall map. 'Here we fight and here we die!' The battalion then marched off to the front, on the way holding a singing competition between companies and platoons. This was judged by the divisional commander but it is not recorded who sang best.

*

One man who had just returned from leave was Sir Douglas Haig, who had been absent from France for ten days. One of the reasons Haig took leave at this time was that Lady Haig was expecting the birth of their third child. Haig was now fifty-seven and dearly wanted a son; one was duly born on 15 March. Many of the front-line soldiers were later very bitter about Haig's taking of leave at such a vital time and for this reason, but Haig had been ordered home by the War Office because he was wanted at a meeting of the Supreme War Council being held in London, instead of Versailles, and he was back in France four days before the Germans attacked.

While Haig had been absent, Lieutenant-General Sir Herbert Lawrence, the Chief of Staff, had been in charge and it was he who answered General Gough's letter of 12 March,

* Major-General Hakewill Smith commanded the 52nd (Lowland) Division in the Second World War.

asking if more men could be spared for the Fifth Army, with this bleak reply:

It is considered that it should be possible for you to effect the necessary relief from the resources at present at your disposal which have been increased recently by the addition of one division.*

Gough stood one rank higher than Lawrence but the haughty Lawrence, although Chief of Staff for only eight weeks, spoke for the Commander-in-Chief and also knew that Gough was not in great favour at this time. It might justifiably be said that Lawrence was on the way up while Gough's star was travelling in the opposite direction. Gough moved his own slender reserves nearer the front and asked for permission to move the two G.H.Q. reserve divisions – the 20th and 50th – farther forward. The 50th Division was twenty miles back across the River Somme. Although Haig had returned by the time Gough put this request to G.H.Q., by telephone on the evening of 19 March, it was again answered by Lawrence. He gave Gough a little lecture on the principles of moving reserves, criticised the moves Gough had already made and refused permission for the two G.H.Q. divisions to be moved. Gough did not press to speak to Haig but closed the conversation testily. 'I shall fight them in my Battle Zone as long as we can hold them there. Good night. Good night.'†

Haig's Intelligence section was fully aware of what was about to break but Haig made not one last-minute change in his dispositions. He was obviously quite satisfied to let his previous plans stand. He was not yet prepared to weaken his front in the north. He would fight in the south with what forces were already there, however weak those forces were. Haig had planned and executed many Western Front attacks and he probably did not credit the Germans with the ability to make progress any faster than he had been able to do in the past.

What is more difficult to understand is the way in which several high-level command changes were allowed to be made at this time. Gough, who had earlier lost his Chief of Staff and had not been allowed the replacement he wanted, was

* Fifth Army General Staff War Diary, Public Record Office WO 95/521.
† *Goughie*, page 271.

now, within four days of the German attack, deprived of his Assistant Quartermaster General and his head of Intelligence. And, in the last week before the battle, one divisional and two brigade commanders were sent home in this way for reasons of age or unsuitability, and all had to be replaced by men in other commands.

The removal of one brigade commander was at the instigation of the new commander of the 66th Division, Major-General Neill Malcolm, Gough's former Chief of Staff. It is described by the brigade major in the brigade concerned.

I think it was on the night of the 16th. He was relieved at one hour's notice. I think the divisional commander thought he was too old for the coming battle but the way of it was very bad. He looked very silent and glum at supper and afterwards he took me aside and said, 'I've been kicked out like a housemaid at one hour's notice. The G.S.O.1 rang me up just before supper and told me I was being relieved immediately by the C.R.E. [Commander Royal Engineers] who would arrive in a couple of hours. They don't even trust me to look after the brigade for the night.'

In my view the decent course would have been to have called him in several days earlier to see the divisional commander and be told of the decision to relieve him. But this was rather typical of the army at that time. It must also be remembered that Malcolm had not been very long in the division and it was probably only late in the day that he had the opportunity of realising what a tired and ageing man our brigadier was and that, with the German attack imminent, he felt it essential to make the change without delay. (Captain R. L. Bond, 199th Infantry Brigade H.Q.)

Another unit, the 39th Division, had other problems. Major-General E. Feetham was away on leave when the division's artillery commander, Brigadier-General G.A.S. Cape, who had been left in charge, was killed by a German shell on 18 March during a tactical exercise. One of the brigade commanders had to take temporary command of the division and, as another was also on leave, this division had to go into the battle short of one major-general and two of its four brigadier-generals.*

Examples can be found in the study of any battle of staff officers who continued to send out orders which can be seen

---

* Major-General Feetham was himself killed by a German shell on 29 March.

later to have been comical or ridiculous in the circumstances, and the last days before this German attack were no exception. On 17 March, the Fifth Army's A and Q Branch informed all units that the Army Agricultural Officer would shortly inform them when they could draw young pigs for fattening from the Services Agricoles at Péronne. The 11th Hampshires, the Pioneer battalion in the 16th (Irish) Division, decided that 18 March was a good day to commence the ploughing of its agricultural plots, and on 20 March the 1st Cavalry Division's routine orders included an appeal by Lieutenant Brown of the 16th Lancers.

LOST. A red lurcher greyhound . . . Broken tail, orange eyes, large scar between eyes. Answers to 'Jack'. Last seen Péronne on 17 March. Reward – 50 francs.*

*

The British Expeditionary Force had an important visitor on 19 March. With his flair for choosing the right time and place to be at historic moments, Winston Churchill, Minister of Munitions, arrived to meet Haig and some of his staff officers to discuss the tank-building programme. He lunched with Haig, talking of the 4,000 tanks he was planning to build and of his hope that, in the British Army, machines could gradually take over from massed soldiery. Churchill then asked for Haig's views on the possibility of making peace. For once, Haig gave his opinion that Britain should be prepared to compromise in her demands. He feared that Britain's strength and influence, now at a high point, could only diminish if peace did not come soon and that the United States would take Britain's place in world affairs. It was a shrewd answer.

Churchill was due at a conference on chemical warfare at St Omer on the 21st and he decided to spend the intervening two days with the 9th (Scottish) Division, in which he had commanded a battalion earlier in the war. He motored to the divisional headquarters at Nurlu, which was only five miles behind the front line.

* Public Record Office WO 95/1100.

5

The Last Day of Trench Warfare

The German soldiers had passed the day of 19 March in the last village billets behind the front. Although the great mass of ordinary soldiers had not been told that their next march would take them up to the front and into battle, most realised that a major attack could not be far off now. They spent the day resting, gossiping, and attending to their equipment. Only very few were allowed out of doors. It was a day of miserable weather, with a succession of heavy showers. There was dismay in at least one village when a British plane flew over and dropped some hastily printed leaflets bearing this message: *'Viel Glück zur Offensive am 21. März'* ('Best of luck for your attack on 21 March'). Late in the afternoon junior officers received their orders and this was followed by much activity. A few last items of equipment were issued: ammunition, which for some men included a little bag of twenty steel-cored bullets for use against tanks, grenades, and the special gas-mask filter to give protection against the lachrymatory gas that was going to be used in the opening bombardment. A good hot meal was provided, which for once contained plenty of meat.

The move forward began as soon as it grew dark. The plan was for the first wave of attacking troops to march right into the front-line area and take cover there in a variety of shelters – dug-outs, cellars of ruined houses, special assembly shelters which had been dug just behind the German front line. The assault troops would have to spend the whole of the following day, the 20th, packed into these places. If the attack received the final go-ahead, they would then deploy to their jumping-off positions during the second night. This plan depended upon hundreds of units keeping to an elaborate timetable, and if the first move was not completed before dawn of the 20th, those Germans units not then under cover would be left exposed to the full view of the British artillery observers.

The heavily laden German soldiers paraded and marched off, the men of one machine-gun crew all smoking the cigars that one of their number had stolen from an Austrian artillery battery the previous day. They soon left the roads and were taken by guides across tracks through the wilderness of the front-line area. There was little cheerful banter now, only whispered orders, curses as men slipped in the mud, tripped over obstacles or tumbled into shell holes. Guides took the wrong turning and columns of men got lost, turned back again, became mixed up with other columns. It rained steadily. The British artillery fired steadily.

Leutnant Ernst Jünger was leading his company of Hanoverians into position.

When we got as far as the second line, where we were to be quartered, it turned out that the guides had lost their way. Now began a chase to and fro over the dim and sodden shell-hole area and a questioning of innumerable troops, who knew as little of where they were as we did. To prevent the complete exhaustion of the men, I called a halt and sent out the guides in all directions.

Sections piled arms and crowded into a gigantic crater, while Leutnant Sprenger and I sat on the edge of a smaller one. There had been single shells falling about 100 metres in front of us for some while. Then there was one nearer; the splinters struck the sides of the shell hole. One of the men cried out and said he was hit in the foot. I shouted to the men to scatter among the surrounding shell holes, and meanwhile I examined the man's boot to see if there was a hole. Then the whistle of another shell high in the air. Everybody had that clutching feeling, 'It's coming over!' There was a terrific, stupefying crash. The shell had burst in the midst of us.

I picked myself up half unconscious. The machine-gun ammunition in the large shell hole, set alight by the explosion, was burning with an intense pink glow. It illuminated the rising fumes of the shell burst, in which there writhed a heap of black bodies and the shadowy forms of the survivors who were rushing from the scene in all directions. At the same time rose a multitudinous tumult of pain and cries for help.

I will make no secret of it that, after a moment's blank horror, I took to my heels like the rest and ran aimlessly into the night. It was not till I had fallen head-over-heels into a small shell hole that I understood what had happened . . . I have often observed in myself and others that an officer's sense of responsibility drowns his personal fears. There is a sticking place, something to occupy the thoughts. So I forced myself back to the ghastly spot . . . The wounded men never ceased to utter their fearful cries. Some came creeping to me when they heard my voice and whimpered, 'Sir . . . Sir!' One of my favourite recruits, Jasinski, whose leg was broken by a splinter, caught hold of me round the knees. Cursing my impotence to help, I vainly clapped him on the shoulder. Such moments can never be forgotten.*

Twenty men were killed and more than sixty wounded in Leutnant Jünger's company but it should be stated that this was not typical of the experience of the majority of German units which were on the move that night. The British artillery scored successes like this here and there but most of the German soldiers managed to reach their shelters in safety, although some fell behind time and were still in the open when daylight came.

The rain continued into the morning of the 20th but then the weather changed, the clouds cleared, and the sun shone. Several hundreds of thousands of German soldiers had to spend the whole of this day within range of British shellfire. They could do no more than huddle in their shelters, packed so tight that there was no room to lie down and sleep. Some were in open trenches or sitting on the steps of dug-outs. They chatted, played cards, dozed, grumbled, smoked, cracked jokes or spent long periods sitting silently with their thoughts.

The following account is typical of the experiences of many German soldiers on this day.

There was a platoon of us, about twenty-five men I should say, under a Feldwebel. We were in a small underground shelter but only just below ground level. It was a very frightening time; we couldn't leave. We tried to sleep but most of the day we were just talking nonsense, arguing a bit – not real arguments just rude jokes on each other – or just getting plain bored, but always hoping that a shell wouldn't come through that thin roof. Toilet? You did it on a spade and then went up the steps and threw it outside. The other things we had tins for and, if you were careless, you got the contents of this back when you threw them out the top of the steps. (Gefreiter Willy Adams, Lehr Infantry Regiment)

* *Storm of Steel*, pages 244–6.

Many miles away from the front, Ludendorff consulted
Leutnant Doktor Schmaus, his meteorological officer. The
wind was the main problem. If it blew strongly from the west,
the gas from the German bombardment would come back into
the faces of the attacking German soldiers. The recent squally
weather would have been very dangerous, and Ludendorff had
been prepared to order a postponement if no better prospects
could be found, even though the attacking divisions had all
moved into the front line. But the wind dropped almost to
nothing with the passing of the rains and Doktor Schmaus
was able to forecast that the calm would continue well into
the following day. Ludendorff made the final decision at noon:
everything was to proceed according to plan. Whatever
happened to the weather now, the bombardment would open
at 4.40 a.m. on the following day and the infantry attack
would follow five hours later.

*

The British front-line units had 'stood to' as normal before
dawn on the 20th but when no attack developed they were
able to relax and resume their routine tasks, many men no
doubt wondering whether the Germans really were going to
attack or whether the whole thing was an extreme example
of 'wind up' by their superiors. But this was the beginning of
what one British soldier later described as 'the last day of
trench warfare as we knew it'.

Most of the front was perfectly quiet for the entire day.
The 2/6th Manchesters paraded for pay in their camp near
the Battle Zone. Lieutenant E. T. Hollins was the paying-out
officer; he survived the next day's fighting but is believed to
have been a prisoner-of-war twenty-four hours after his pay
parade. The 11th Royal Sussex sent an officer and fifty men
to form a guard of honour at Brigadier-General Cape's
funeral at Péronne. A trench-mortar man in the 30th Division
was surprised to see newly erected signs pointing the way to
prisoner-of-war cages – such optimism! The staff of the 1st
Cavalry Division tested out their movement orders in the
event of a German attack by going out on a staff ride. The
2nd Wiltshires, holding the Forward Zone facing St Quentin,
ordered a proportion of men in all companies to go back to

the rear 'to maintain a nucleus if things went too badly'. The 1st West Yorks did the same, but someone in the rear countermanded the order and the 'nucleus' went back into the line that night with the ration party. The commanding officer of the 6/7th Royal Scots, the 59th Division's Pioneer battalion, took every officer and man to complete the digging of a new trench in the division's Battle Zone.

There were no large-scale infantry reliefs during the day, but many of the artillery forward observation officers changed around.

Persistent rumours were abroad that the enemy were going to launch an attack at dawn on the 21st and it so happened that it was the turn of my battery to man the forward Observation Post in our front-line trench on the 20th. The officer detailed to this duty came to me, begging me to take the duty for him, he having explained that, as he was a married man, his first thoughts were for his wife and his safe return to her after the war. I, being much younger and a bachelor, made up my mind at once and agreed to his request. This proved to be my undoing for I was taken prisoner next day. Since then I have often thought that I was a bit of a mutt. After all, he had become an officer and he should have expected to take his turn in the proper way. I suppose I was a bit soft. (Lieutenant C. H. Mapp, 327th Siege Battery)

German activity was very light. There was some ominous artillery registration of British battery positions, but the firing stopped as soon as the correct range had been established. The London battalions holding the short sector from the River Oise to the junction with the French line found that their forward posts were being registered upon by German trench mortars; again the firing ceasing immediately a direct hit was registered. This was almost certainly a deception to persuade the British that this sector was about to be attacked. In the 34th Division area, fifty miles to the north, a Lewis-gunner describes his afternoon.

It was warm, sunny and quiet, and for several hours there had been absolutely nothing doing. I took the opportunity of cleaning my Lewis gun and seeing that all the panniers were loaded, they each held sixty rounds of ·303. Others were busy with boxes of Mills bombs which they were fusing. The only eventful thing that happened was during the afternoon when a Bosche plane came in at about 500 feet, nosing round and generally making a nuisance of himself. I decided to try and move him on. There was an A.A. post at the end of a forward sap between the front line and the support line and I made my way there. He was still flying around when I mounted my Lewis gun on a cartwheel attached to a post – Heath Robinson, but it worked. As he came over the sap, within range, I let off a burst at him and he dropped a red flare. I fired again but, before I could let off another burst, a high-velocity low-trajectory shell hit the top of the sap about twenty yards away from me. This was followed by three more equally close. However, there was no more firing and the plane had left. I made my way back and then was accused of waking everybody up and starting a row. That was the only activity and firing that I can recall in that otherwise strangely quiet day. (Corporal H. J. Smith, 9th Northumberland Fusiliers)

In the trenches of the 51st (Highland) Division, an officer and N.C.O. of the Royal Engineers were ordered to take newly painted signs to be attached to the dug-outs in the entire divisional trench system. From one front-line trench, the officer could see many German soldiers walking over the open behind the German front line but he failed to persuade two near-by artillery observation officers to turn their guns upon the Germans. The 51st Division's records tell of a scout who had gone well out into No Man's Land the previous night; he remained out all day in a concealed position and watched between 6,000 and 7,000 men enter the German trenches during the afternoon!

There was a great number and variety of rumours passing between various units over the possibility of the Germans attacking the next day.

During the day of the 20th my battery commander hacked over to 19th Corps H.Q. and visited the C.R.A.'s office where he was told that, from information obtained from German prisoners, the attack was due on the 21st. But on his way back he called at 66th Lancs Div H.Q. who pooh-poohed the idea. When he got back to us he told us that he thought that his information from higher up was more likely to be right and we ought to be prepared, and the battery did so without orders from above. The O.P. [Observation Post] at Le Verguier was warned. Two thirds of all shells in the position were fused, the wagon lines alerted and everything in the position was made ready for instant action. (Lieutenant L. Rushforth Ward, 113th Heavy Battery)

This quotation really typifies the position all along the British front. The German deceptions, the previous false alarms, optimism, realism or pessimism, had all led to a complete state of confusion in the minds of British commanders and there was no comprehensive direction to the last-minute preparations for the battle. The '66th Lancs Div H.Q.' which had 'pooh-poohed' the idea of a German attack in the morning was that of Major-General Neill Malcolm, Gough's old chief of staff. A report written after the battle – and after Malcolm had been wounded and left the division – states:

The general deduction drawn from all the evidence was that the weight of the attack would probably fall upon the Third Army and that only the fringe of it would extend sufficiently far south to involve the 66th Division.*

The attack next morning would extend for twenty-two miles to the south of Malcolm's positions! The line of his division was to be held with three battalions in the Forward Zone and six battalions in the Battle Zone. Malcolm insisted that three of the Battle Zone battalions should remain at rest in the rear so that half of his Battle Zone was fully manned and half held only by 'caretaker parties'. He refused the request of at least one brigade commander that the resting battalions should be got into the Battle Zone that evening before any German artillery bombardment began. This situation also highlights the difficulties of the recent reorganisation of divisions. A four-battalion brigade could have manned all its defences and still had one battalion out at rest.

General Gough spent most of this day motoring around the headquarters of his four corps commanders. He does not record what he said to them; there was little he could do but exhort them to do their best. He had moved up all his reserves to positions immediately behind the front and, if the Fifth Army got into serious trouble, help could only come from outside. He had already written to his wife. 'Everyone is calm and very confident. All is ready.'

* Public Record Office WO 95/3121.

At his headquarters at Montreuil Haig also wrote to his wife, telling her that he had decided to postpone for a week a further period of leave that he had intended taking on the 22nd. Haig was obviously devoted to his wife and delighted with the recent birth of his son. 'The cook is making some soup for you and I am arranging to send it by King's Messenger.' Whether a further statement to Lady Haig that 'everyone is in good spirits and only anxious that the enemy should attack'* truly represented the view of all the men under Haig's command is very much to be doubted.

*

As soon as it was dark, the area immediately behind the German front line became a mass of moving men. It was a fine, dry, moonlit night but a ground mist was developing in some places. First on the move was the artillery; many of the German guns had not yet moved into their exposed battery positions. One infantry officer, who had earlier moved up in the advance party for his regiment, has described the sight of these positions before the guns moved in.

On my way to the front the numerous well-camouflaged ammunition dumps caught my eye. Under every bush and in the open lay ammunition of all calibres in large numbers. Not a single gun was present – small yellow wooden stakes stuck in the ground instead, hundreds of them, under every bush and in the open. Two stood in line for the wheels of a gun, a bigger post behind for the trail. Every gun position was fixed geometrically. It was a most peculiar scene. (Leutnant Kurt Fischer, 464th Regiment)

The German batteries prepared to march.

Before we moved off on that last evening, we were paraded and an order from our divisional commander, Major-General von Roeder, was read out to us. I can remember that it ended with the words, '*Auf den Höhen von Rocquigny sehen wir uns wieder*' – 'We will meet again on the heights of Rocquigny'. Every battery had its own timetable from billets to firing positions, down to the last detail, and it ran just like a railway timetable. We didn't have much trouble on our way up. One thing I do remember was passing heaps of wooden bridges built by our pioneers ready for trench

---

* *The Private Papers of Douglas Haig*, page 294.

crossings. There seemed to be thousands of them. (Unteroffizier Otto Jaffé, 2nd Guard *Fussartillerie* Regiment)

Major-General von Roeder's meeting place 'on the heights of Rocquigny' was eight miles behind the British front line and, if his Guards Division reached there, then any British troops left in the Flesquières Salient would be half-encircled.

One place that was packed with artillery was St Quentin. The Rue de Paris is described as being 'one gun behind the other, all down the middle of the road'. An Austrian motorised howitzer battery was in position at the 'Cow Memorial' and many guns had moved into the shells of the houses on the western outskirts of the town. These were less than one mile from the British front-line trenches.

So the thousands of German guns that would take part in the opening bombardment eventually came up; the gunners found the numbered post that denoted each gun's position and its own pile of ammunition. They heaved their guns into place, the gun-position officers received the latest '*Balta-Sekunden*', which was the meteorological data that they would need to make their final firing calculations. The German gunners settled down then to wait for the opening of the bombardment at 4.40 a.m. A few guns never made it. The British artillery was firing on many of the approach roads and inflicted casualties but the great majority of the German artillery was in position in good time.

The German infantry did not have so far to go. When it had become dark they had been brought food, sometimes hot but more often cold, and two flasks of tea or coffee mixed with rum for each man. They were told to make this drink last as long as possible because no one knew when they would get any more. Some men refused to eat their food, being afraid of being wounded in the stomach. The German infantry who had been in temporary shelters could now stretch their legs as they moved up to their attack trenches. It was with amazement that they saw the field guns that would accompany the infantry advance standing just behind the trenches; this was a novelty.

The German front-line trenches for fifty miles from the village of Cherisy down to La Fère were packed with infantrymen, trench-mortar men and machine-gunners. So too were the support and reserve trenches and any shell hole or other type of shelter. Behind the front-line trench system stood the main strength of the German artillery, the pioneers, the medical units. Then were to be found the second-wave divisions in ruined villages, farms and woods. Behind these, again, stood the reserve divisions.

One million men. Ten thousand guns and mortars. They all waited.

*

On the British side of No Man's Land it was a mixture of routine and action, again depending on how seriously local commanders viewed the situation. Despite the many reports of abnormal German behaviour, there was as yet no sure information that the attack was to start in a few hours, and neither the Third nor the Fifth Army sent out a specific warning order. XIX Corps, on the Fifth Army's front, even sent out orders that night to No. 1 Special Company Royal Engineers to prepare another large-scale gas operation, saying that they had four days to complete their preparations!

A brigade of the 47th (London) Division completed the relief of part of the front line of the Flesquières Salient from the 2nd Division. The relief was carried out with only a little German shelling and was completed by midnight, but the opening of the German bombardment would find the London men in strange trenches that they had never seen in daylight. At least two battalions, the 1st Kings Shropshire Light Infantry and the 7th Royal Fusiliers, had received large drafts of a hundred or more reinforcements during the day, and these new men all went up into the front line that night.

Two miles north of St Quentin, the commander of XVIII Corps had ordered the 61st (South Midland) Division to send out a strong raiding force to enter the German front line and take prisoners. A and C Companies of the 2/6th Royal Warwicks were selected and the raid took place at 10 p.m. Because the division became so involved in the great battle that started a few hours later, hardly any details exist of a brave venture. The name of the officer leading the raid is not known, nor the plan used. What is known is that the raiding party returned to the British trenches with a German machine-gun and twelve German prisoners. (Other reports say thirteen or fifteen prisoners.) The casualties of the raiding party were one man killed and four wounded. The prisoners talked readily, revealing that they came from three regiments in two separate divisions (the 40th Regiment and 110th Grenadier Regiment from the 28th Division, and the 426th Reserve Regiment from the 88th Division), that they were assault infantry, and that the artillery bombardment was due to start at 4.40 a.m. They were anxious to be taken to the rear.

This was the most reliable piece of information that the British had yet obtained. They had at least five hours' notice of the German intentions but, sadly, little was done with this priceless asset. Some gas cylinders were activated in the 61st Division's front line and some attempt was made to warn neighbouring units. The corps artillery was ordered to bombard the German trenches from 2.30 a.m. to 4.07 a.m. – it is not known why that odd time was chosen to end the artillery fire. But 'Man Battle Stations', the order that would have got resting infantry battalions into the Battle Zone before the German bombardment, was not given. Perhaps the information given by the German prisoners was not really believed.

The British artillery were active on other sectors. Many of the batteries were firing steadily on suspected German assembly positions and approach roads. The entire 36th (Ulster) Division's artillery fired a fierce bombardment during the evening and then most of it was pulled back to new positions. There were many movements of guns like this that night. Some were moves from a position considered to be known to the Germans to another position near by which it was hoped was unsuspected, but most of the moves were to positions well back, as in the case of the guns of the Ulster Division. British front-line infantry who saw, or later heard of, the movement of the guns to the rear were convinced that the artillery had deliberately moved to safety, leaving the infantry to be sacrificed. This feeling is strongly held by many of the survivors to this day. What was happening, of course, was that the guns were being pulled back into the

Battle Zone according to the defence plan, but no one ever explained this to the infantrymen.

It was a quiet night apart from this British artillery fire. There was a complete absence of German gunfire, and many men remember this night as being without the flares of which the Germans normally made much use; the Germans had no wish to draw attention to their activities. Many British patrols were sent out into No Man's Land. Some returned to say that all was quiet, some discovered that gaps had been made in the German barbed wire or heard the rumbling of vehicles and guns being moved. Some met large bodies of Germans out in No Man's Land and managed to creep away quietly to return with the news. But nothing was seen again of a complete platoon of the 2nd Wiltshires which went out on patrol, and, of two patrols provided by men of a Royal Engineers Field Company because the divisional infantry were 'short-handed', one came back and reported 'abnormal quiet' and the other never returned.

There were undoubtedly a lot of apprehensive men in the British front-line positions.

I had been in a little disgrace because I had gone straight to the Colonel with a request for leave instead of going through the battery commander. Because of this, I was told that I would be sent up to the O.P. when the German offensive was expected. I went up the evening before the attack and spent a very hectic night being asked by brigade what was going on. I kept telling them that there was nothing going on that I could see but that there was much tension. There were three telephonists and an anti-tank officer from one of the 18-pounder batteries. I remember that we spent much of the time talking about what might happen. (Second Lieutenant W. H. Crowder, 256th Brigade R.F.A.)

It was worse for the infantry. Many men undoubtedly knew what was coming; they knew too, if they were in the south, that their own positions were weak. R. C. Sherriff's well-known play *Journey's End* is set in a company officer's dug-out on the St Quentin front on the eve of the German attack. Sherriff portrays the hard-drinking, war-weary company captain and his mixed batch of platoon officers. Higher-ups insist on a raid in which a popular officer, 'Uncle', is killed, and the remainder nervously pass the last few hours before the German attack. Sherriff did not write this from his own experience; at that time he was recovering from a wound received at Passchendaele. But his old battalion, the 9th East Surreys, was in the line just north of St Quentin and *Journey's End* was later judged to be completely realistic by others who were in the front line at that time. Some retired generals wrote that there could not have been so much drinking by officers in the front line, but ex-infantry officers replied to these criticisms by asking how the generals could know; they had never been seen in the front line!

These accounts tell of how the eve of battle was spent by some of the British soldiers.

We were in dug-outs in the third line of trenches and were definitely expecting the attack next morning. After tea, the canteen which was just outside our dug-out entrance was thrown open to us. There were barrels of porter from Belfast, whisky, cigarettes, biscuits etc. All was quiet. But there was an air of uncertainty about tomorrow; we were all in high spirits and, like the poem, 'there was a sound of revelry by night'. We had a bit of a concert and, for the first time and the last time in my life, I sang by myself – I always remember the song, 'Little Brown Jug'. We kept drinking steadily and, in the end, the C.Q.M.S. said that we could help ourselves and, by about midnight, the drink was all gone. We certainly had some fun that night. No one went to sleep; we just sat and talked then for the rest of the night. (Rifleman J. Potts, 16th Royal Irish Rifles)

The ground in front of our battle position was quite flat so we had quite a fine view of a considerable area up to the front line. 'When the Bosche comes, we'll let him have it' was the cheery reply to 'How will we face up to it when it comes?' So, with everyone full of confidence, we ended what was to be the last day of peace for us. I had been on leave and had been back about a fortnight, feeling on top of the world that night as I had received a parcel from a girl I had met on a train returning from Liverpool to London. It had socks, cakes, sweets, a couple of books and, believe it or not, a love letter of twelve pages – that after about three hours on the train! So I kept on reading this letter till long after lights out. (Private W. J. Yendall, 17th Kings Liverpool)

We set about getting as much ammunition as handy as possible, filling all our spare belts, getting extra cans of water for cooling the machine-guns, putting up bits of camouflage and, generally speaking, getting ready. Personally I wondered what it would be like. I think I imagined that the Germans would stumble unwittingly up to our guns and that we would shoot them all down and then resume our previous pattern of life. I felt that nothing would hit me; I felt I was fireproof. (Private F. Plimmer, 24th Machine Gun Battalion)

All of us were full of anticipation – but of what? It was at this point that my pal and I made a pact that, whichever one was lost, the other would do his utmost to look for, or find out what happened to, the other. Many such pacts must have been made at this period. (Private R. Gibson, 7th Lincolns)

It was my turn for sentry duty about 1 o'clock on the morning of the 21st. As I stood on the fire-step I could hear sounds coming over from the German lines; they were of the movement of the wheels of transport wagons and occasionally I heard voices. When the platoon officer came round about 3 a.m. I reported these facts to him. He seemed rather concerned and said that other posts along the line were making similar reports.

By the way, this visit of the platoon officer was the only contact we had with anyone after stand down the previous morning and no one came up with the rations. (Private R. T. Smith, 2/6th South Staffords)

*

Most of the German soldiers had reached their final positions by 1 a.m., the appointed time for the final deployment. They had three hours and forty minutes to wait before the artillery bombardment opened. One man remembers the 'intense stillness with no wind'. In some places the earlier ground mist had turned into thick fog. If this persisted and became more widespread, then there would be complications for both attackers and defenders. In some units a message was distributed: 'His Majesty the Kaiser and Field-Marshal von Hindenburg are at the scene of operations.'

Closely packed in a dug-out, we waited for the start of our artillery barrage. Tense with expectation, I had all sorts of visions, not having taken part in an attack before, and I was very nervous. In the past, I had been in dangerous situations in the trenches; now it would be different. Would we be mown down by machine-guns or have to fight man against man? Would I be wounded? I didn't mind a minor wound and being sent to hospital in Germany; this was the hope of so many. I was certainly not keen to be hit by a large splinter in the chest or belly or to lose a limb. I would prefer to die a 'hero's death'. To pray doesn't help, I know from experience. In the end I gave up my gloomy thoughts and trusted to luck. The war had gone on too long already.

We felt fairly secure in our dug-out in spite of the lively fire from artillery and mortars. The enemy was aware of our plan. Suddenly a terrific bang and blast. A heavy shell had partly demolished the entrance of the dug-out. We cleared it in no time with spades and shovels. (Schütze Karl Brunotte, 465th Regiment)

I didn't sleep much – too many things on my mind. I wasn't the only one. We thought of our next-of-kin, parents, wife or fiancée. I was not engaged to get married, I hadn't even a sweetheart. I was only twenty and hadn't ever been with a woman. I wanted to survive to have that experience. (Musketier Willi Raschkow, 230th Regiment)

By early morning the stars were sparkling cold and clear in the sky. Nearly 4 o'clock. The crews stand at the guns. The roads absolutely deserted. Not a sound. It must be the same picture all along the front. Wherever there is room for a gun there is one, the gunners around it dead silent. The infantry of the storm division lie in cellars, combat packs ready – a cartridge belt, two bags with hand grenades, gas-mask, steel helmet and rifle.

Nobody wants to talk, the strain is too severe. How will it go? Because of all the preparations, down to the smallest detail, none of us had earlier had any doubts concerning the High Command but now, with everybody idle and waiting, the tension was almost unbearable. Nagging doubts overcame us. There was no artillery fire from the enemy. Not even a single rifle from the trenches could be heard, only the flares from the trenches to illuminate the ground, rising high into the air, burning themselves out quickly. (Unteroffizier Erich Kubatzki, 20th *Fussartillerie* Regiment)

6

All Hell Let Loose

During the night we had helped to push this great 28-centimetre gun into position. It had all been done very carefully and quietly. The gun stood in the open but just behind a small rise and just over the rise were our trenches. The shells for it were already there. We stood around then and waited for the bombardment to open. We wanted to see the first shot fired and were only two or three metres from the gun.

Someone shouted '*Feuer frei*' and then the gun went off with a great crash. We all fell over on our backs and the gunners laughed at us. The gun settled down to fire steadily after that – about one shell a minute I would say – but we didn't stay long. We went back to our trench. (Gefreiter Wilhelm Reinhard, 109th Leib Grenadier Regiment)

This was just one of several thousand guns and mortars that opened fire at 4.40 a.m. on 21 March.* In some sectors it is said that a single heavy gun fired the first round giving the signal to the other batteries to open fire. At St Quentin a large white rocket fired into the air was the signal to open fire. One of the great battles of the First World War had started.

Along fifty miles of front line, it was as though the most violent of storms was raging with the thousands of gun flashes and one continuous roll of thunder. The firing of individual guns could not be heard; conversation was impossible. The earth trembled as though there were an earthquake. When each gun fired, a flash of flame burned up the fog and lit up the surrounding ground – but only for a fraction of a second; then the darkness and the fog closed back in again, only to be swept away once more when the next shell was fired. Handling the heavy shells and cordite charges was hard physical work for the gunners, with the roar of the explosions all the time deafening and stupefying

* In a further effort to mislead the British, the Germans did not commence their bombardment north of the Flesquières Salient until 5.05 a.m. This does not affect the general description of the bombardment in this chapter.

them. Soon the foul-smelling fumes and smoke from the burnt cordite polluted the air, mixing with the fog around the gun positions. There was hardly any wind to carry it away. The blast of the discharges of the heavier guns was sometimes so great that the roofs and walls of near-by cottages collapsed under the shock waves. The barrels of the guns became too hot to be touched and too hot also for the accurate firing of the gun. Wet sacking had to be wrapped round the barrels and constantly doused with more water. Many infantrymen were pleased to help by carrying buckets of water from near-by shell holes. There was nothing an infantry soldier liked better than to see his own artillery blasting away before an attack.

This infantry officer describes the sensation created by the bombardment.

We could see the flashes of guns behind us but could see little in front because of the thick fog. If you put your hands over your ears and then drum your fingers vigorously on the back of your head, then you get some idea of what the drumfire sounded like to us. (Leutnant Rudolf Hoffmann, 463rd Regiment)

This artillery observer was in the attic of a house in St Quentin.

Within seconds of the bombardment opening, we could see sparks and columns of fire in the enemy trenches and their rear area. A terrific roar, an immense noise greeted the young morning. The unbearable tension eased. We were ourselves again and knew that it had come off all right. In the past the French and the Tommies had bombarded us for seven days without a pause; we would now do it in five hours. We laughed and looked happily at each other. Words were useless; the hell of the inferno outside saw to that. There was only lightning and noise.

We went down to the battery but we couldn't use our old way there because, from every window, just above ground level, and from every doorway, a field gun spewed death and destruction. The air became heavier and heavier. Our own gas and the cordite fumes from the guns poisoned the air. We had to wear our gas-masks; it was impossible to breathe otherwise. Making a detour, we arrived at the gun site. The gun crews also had their masks on. We felt sorry for them – rapid fire with 42-kilo shells, gas-masks on; it needs the heaviest physical effort. Still, every man gladly does his best. Round after round roars into the dark. The barrel is hot, sparks from the cordite wads rush through the stinking air. Pale and colourless dawn struggles to overcome the fog. (Unteroffizier Erich Kubatzki, 20th *Fussartillerie* Regiment)

There were seven separate phases in Oberst Bruchmüller's artillery bombardment plan. For the first twenty minutes every gun and mortar in the bombardment force of artillery (this excluded the field guns attached to the infantry units) was to fire in what the Germans called 'general surprise fire'. After this the mortars dropped out of the bombardment temporarily, saving themselves for a later phase and leaving the guns and howitzers to continue the shelling.

The main bombardment would be fired for five hours.

*

It happened during my turn 'on duty' in the company positions. The captain and the other subalterns would be asleep. I was going round inspecting the posts and just happened to be standing on the fire-step, with my head just over the parapet, looking out over No Man's Land. Then I saw this colossal flash of light. As far as I could see from left to right was lit up by it. I heard nothing for a few seconds and, for a moment, I wondered what it was. I think I just managed to hear the gunfire itself before the explosions as the shells arrived all around us.

The shells, I should think they were five-point-nines, were exploding in a line at intervals of fifteen yards or so, but they were just a little short. We sat down in the bottom of the trench and, for some time, we were between a succession of shells which continued to fall in the same places either side of us. We were quite safe between the two bursts and didn't suffer any casualties, but we were soon covered with mud. (Second Lieutenant H. V. Crees, 22nd Northumberland Fusiliers)

I was impressed by the way it came down with one big crash. We had known of the coming attack – but not the exact day. I had only been out since November 1917 and this was my first big do. I had always thought that the bombardment would develop gradually but the full force was almost instantaneous. Our section were making their way back to Company Headquarters after being on duty manning a trench. One moment we were walking along as normal, the next there were shells bursting all about us. We all ran like mad for cover. (Private E. F. Harrison, 8th Queens)

These two quotations describe how the German bombardment first fell on the British front-line positions. But the German plan resulted in shells falling on many different places, from the front line right back to locations many miles in the rear. It is impossible for a narrative such as this to follow every detail of the Bruchmüller plan, with its constantly changing emphasis. Instead, the effect of the bombardment will be described by stages, starting from the British front line, working by stages to the farthest extent of the bombardment in the rear, and then returning to the front line again for the final phase.*

The soldiers in the British trenches took what shelter they could. The lucky ones were able to get down into dug-outs where they were safe from anything but a direct hit by a heavy shell. The walls of the dug-out appeared to rock with the explosion of the nearest shells and vibrate steadily with the shock waves travelling through the earth from the more distant ones. Fine, dry earth kept trickling through the joints in the roof timbers and candles were always blowing out. But many of the front-line infantrymen had to remain in open trenches, huddled tight into corners or little scrape holes in the wall of the trench or down in the floor of it. The shells crashed all around them, the sound like 'hundreds of glass-houses cracking all around' or 'millions of saucepans all boiling together'. Many British survivors use exactly the same words when describing the bombardment: 'All hell was let loose.'

Great hot lumps of jagged metal did fearful things to men's bodies. Trench sides were blown in and men buried beneath a tangled mess of splintered timbers, sandbags and earth. The air was full of smoke, dust, fog, gas and burnt explosives. This was when a man's sense of duty and discipline was under the severest test – the officer or sergeant who had to visit his posts and give comfort to his men, the sentry with body flattened against the parapet, crouched down so that he could just see to the front beneath his steel helmet, the stretcher-bearer, the company runner given a message for battalion headquarters because the telephone wire was

* Details of the bombardment plan are in Appendix 6.

already broken. Most ordinary soldiers could do little at this stage except protect themselves as best they could and keep their weapons clean and close to hand. Most men had been under shellfire before but the endurance of all would be tested by this prolonged and intense bombardment. No man could be sure that the next moment would not be his last, let alone that he would still be alive when the Germans decided to send over their infantry. The British tensed themselves to see out the bombardment.

I had thought that I might as well be ready if an attack started that morning and had decided to have an early shave. I was just in the middle of shaving when the shelling started and on went my gas-mask. I kept lifting my respirator and shaving a little bit more and, eventually, I got it all finished. It was just as well because I had my gas-mask on for the next five hours. There was a mixture of gas and high explosive. It was damned uncomfortable but there were no casualties in my little lot. (Second Lieutenant J. C. Farmer, 8th Leicesters)

I noticed that there was no answering fire by our guns. I sent a runner back with a message to this effect but I got no reply. It was the first time I had been in an attack and I was surprised at how few men were being killed although many were being wounded. We sent these down to the dug-outs. There wasn't much I could do as an officer except walk up and down. (Lieutenant W. D. Scott, 6th Somerset Light Infantry)

We had been fast asleep, with our equipment off and boots off, in small shelters in the side of a railway embankment a few hundred yards behind the front line. We woke up, of course, and the sergeant ordered us to get ready to move up to the front line along a communication trench. We lost all touch with each other. With the fog and wearing a gas-mask, you couldn't see six yards in front of you. I was dazed by explosions all around and partly stunned by a blow on the head by a piece of shrapnel which actually pierced my steel helmet though, fortunately, lifting it from my head. I found myself completely alone and recall very vividly the strange, dream-like feeling of a world apparently empty except for the hell of bursting shells. (Private L. Straugheir, 12/13th Northumberland Fusiliers)

I was in charge of two chaps in a little dug-out in the side of the sunken road. On the ground near by was a steel plate which some former tenant had left there and which saved our lives. We thought the world had blown up, explosions and screams of shells smashing everything. We lay flat on our backs and put this steel plate on end and kept it up with our feet and the shrapnel kept crashing against it. It seemed to go on for hours. (Lance Corporal T. Quinn, 4th East Lancs)

This Vickers machine-gunner, less than a month in France, had just gone on duty with a friend when the bombardment started. Each man was alone in an exposed machine-gun post.

Then it happened. It seemed as though the bowels of the earth had erupted, while beyond the ridge there was one long and continuous yellow flash. It was the suddenness of the thing that struck me most, there being no preliminary shelling but just one vast momentary upheaval. I do not recall being particularly concerned about my own safety although it was the first time I had ever heard a shell fired. I suppose I thought I would be safe enough crouching in the trench but not so the guns, for both my mate and myself realised that they could be damaged by the shellfire. So we both, separately and independently, got them down into the trench. If I had any particular worry at the moment it was the fact that I had no watch and would not be able to report the time at which the bombardment commenced.

By now, things were at their worst. I just crouched there, listening to the shells bursting and to those screaming over, which fortunately most of them did. I was beginning to feel that I could not possibly get away with it much longer and that I would most assuredly collect one of those shells all to myself. I wondered how my mate was getting along. Then I heard someone shouting. The shouting came nearer. I looked up to see it was the sergeant half-way down the slope. He was yelling, 'Come in. Bring the gun.' My mate and myself must have acted on the same impulse for we both scrambled out of our respective trenches lugging the guns with us and, of course, making great haste to get to safety. When we got to the top of the rise, I noticed that the sergeant had sort of fallen in behind us as though he was shepherding us to safety. We had only brought the guns back; the tripods and the ammunition were left behind. How the three of us got up that rise without being hit can only be put down to the fortunes of war. There was stuff exploding all around. I expected to be blown out of this world. (Private F. Plimmer, 24th Machine Gun Battalion)

This Royal Army Medical Corps man was in a forward dressing post.

It was impossible to see beyond a few yards outside as the misty fog was now thick and the cascade of screaming shells, explosions, and vivid flashes everywhere was something one just endured and waited for it to go – but it didn't. The two transport motor drivers now scrambled in and reported both ambulances knocked out. This was a real blow as, instead of having them to ferry down the line and back to us as anticipated, it meant we must do the job on Shanks's Pony, a round trip of a couple of miles a time. Now the wounded commenced to arrive – not in big numbers but sufficient to keep us busy in the Dressing Dug-out and all bearers at our post carrying stretcher cases down the line to the next post.

The first journey was really mind-bending. One couldn't see a couple of yards around and shells seemed to be landing under our feet and whistling past our heads. We knew the way down the winding trench to the next post – quite a distance with a heavy man on a stretcher – but we were glad of the protection that the trench gave us and were not collecting too many casualties as a result. Subsequent journeys were made in a sort of bemused, half-awake state which stifled fear and kept us going like automatons. (Private A. H. Flindt, 27th Field Ambulance)

A high proportion of the shells being fired into the area behind the British front line were gas shells. The fighting soldiers of both sides had long ago become used to taking precautions against gas. Every dug-out had its impregnated anti-gas blankets ready to drop over the dug-out entrance. Every man always had his gas-mask near by. The gas-mask was actually a gas helmet, with a mouth-piece and a clip for the nostrils. Gas was really a harassing weapon, forcing men to wear gas-masks for long periods. The poor eye-pieces restricted visibility and the laboured breathing through the filter sapped a man's physical energy. Gas was not normally lethal unless a man inhaled a large dose of it, but if it did come, death by gas was a terrible thing with the victim coughing his lungs out. Those men who inhaled only a small amount were not badly affected at the time but many would find themselves suffering from chronic bronchitis in later years.

On this morning the Germans were mostly using chlorine, with its normal distinctive smell, and phosgene, 'a filthy gas' which smelt like 'corpses or rotten fish'. Lachrymatory gas shells were also being used on a large scale. These had a smell 'like pineapples' and its effect was similar to that of modern tear gas. Many British accounts describe encountering it. It caused much irritation to the nose and eyes but it does not seem to have had the widespread success that the Germans had hoped for in forcing men to take off their gas-masks and inhale the more deadly gases. The gas shells came over with a curious warbling or wobbling sound, believed to be caused by the liquid gas inside, then burst with a subdued 'pop' as a small charge blew off the nose-cap and then the liquid inside vaporised into a small cloud of gas.

Most British soldiers in the bombardment area had to wear their gas-masks for many hours that morning. Men who suffered from claustrophobia had a frightening time and their friends had to keep them from tearing off their masks. Many men took a short 'breather' with the nose-clip off for a few moments and paid the penalty by vomiting into their masks a few minutes later. Horses also had masks and often panicked because of this. All these effects of gas were designed to help 'soften up' the defenders before the German infantry attack.

The Germans fired another type of gas into the British positions in the Flesquières Salient. This was mustard, which had a longer-lasting effect than other gases. The units in the salient were subjected to a long mustard-gas bombardment and there were many casualties. This man was one of them.

A party of us, four or five, were in a shallow dug-out about ten feet square and two feet below ground. The entrance had no curtain. We had been asleep and awoke with daylight. By then gas from gas shelling that had been going on had seeped into the dug-out and I had absorbed a certain amount. Somehow the others were not affected. The way it took me was at both ends at the same time – diarrhoea and vomiting. As shelling was still going on, one did not go outside but one's pals advised using one's groundsheet, which could be cleaned later, for a lavatory. Of course we had effective gas-masks, and, if we had been awake we would have just put them on, but the gas got us before we could take counter-measures. (Private A. L. Robins, 15th Londons)*

This mustard-gas shelling of the Flesquières Salient should

* The Civil Service Rifles.

have told the British commanders that the Germans had no intention of making an infantry attack directly on the salient.

One of the principal targets for the German bombardment was the British artillery. Many an infantry attack had in the past been broken up by the defending artillery, and much of the German gunners' efforts were now devoted to knocking out their British counterparts. This again was a time when discipline and duty were under test as the British artillerymen manned their guns to fire on the prearranged 'S.O.S. targets', often under a hail of bursting high-explosive and gas shells.

There had been one great roar of fire to start with. It wasn't the explosions we heard but the unmistakable firing of an enormous number of guns – as artillerymen we could tell the difference. Almost at once, the explosions of the shells themselves could be heard and then the two sounds merged together to become one continuous mixture of a rumble and many crashes. We had been sleeping in good dug-outs with a 'Stand To' bell and I rang this. Our dug-outs were almost alongside the guns and we got the first rounds away in ten to twelve seconds without orders. We fired on the pre-set lines we had been given. It was something like two rounds a minute with our 4·5-inch howitzers.

One or two random shells fell but nothing much for about two hours. Then we came under really heavy fire. It felt like a whole battery and we got fifty shells or so in half an hour. We hadn't had a round fired at us before that day but it was obvious that our positions were well known. Their fire was very accurate. Either two or three guns were hit but my own gun only got a near miss and we continued firing. The men in my detachment were very cool but I was ducking my head as each German shell exploded. The noise was enormous and I think my ears had become very tired over the months. One of the gunners shouted, 'For Christ's sake, stop ducking your bloody head.' I said 'Sorry gunner.' It was the only time I ever apologised to a gunner. (Sergeant J. Sellars, 295th Brigade R.F.A.)

The gun detachment were all old hands compared with myself and needed no urging to do their best. At the height of the shelling, I remember feeling a kind of relief after previous days of apprehension and I also remember that the words of a ridiculous song, heard weeks before at the 21st Divisional Concert Party, 'The Soarers', kept going through my head to the rhythm of the gun fire and shell bursts.* It was the comic female impersonator who used to bewail a certain faithless Mr McPherson, ending with the immortal words 'Oh Mr McPherson, you said you'd love me true. Come back, tickle me back, the same as you used to do.'

It was lucky for us that we had no direct hit with an H.E. shell which could have knocked us all out, but a gas shell, landing right in the gun-pit, mortally wounded Bombardier Bond – a splendid, cheery chap who had been brewing tea for us all during a short lull half an hour before – and putting two other men out of action with wounds and gassing, but we were able to keep the gun in action until, I think, about ten in the morning, when the breech jammed and we were unable to put it right. (Second Lieutenant G. K. Thornton, 108th Army Field Brigade)

*

A definite object of the German bombardment was the shelling of the headquarters and command posts of the British fighting units. Many of these were well dug in and did not suffer seriously from the shelling, but those which were above ground were very vulnerable. Some of the German shelling was extremely accurate. The very first shell fired at the headquarters of the 36th Machine Gun Battalion killed three men and wounded ten more, and the first shell to fall into the area occupied by the 16th Rifle Brigade, which was in a reserve position, hit the battalion Signals Office, killing the Signals Sergeant and many of the signallers. The following quotations by a brigade major and by an artillery brigade adjutant describe further incidents.

Brigade H.Q. was in huts about a mile and a half behind the front line. The previous division hadn't done much work and we had only just started digging some deep dug-outs. Most of the officers were having breakfast when the shelling started. One heavy shell fell alongside the hut in which the brigade commander and myself were sitting but we weren't hurt. About a hundred yards further forward was the hut which was used as our Battle H.Q. This was hit and five officers were wounded – the Staff Captain, his assistant, the Intelligence Officer, the Signals Officer and a G 'learner' we had with us. They were all evacuated and we fought the rest of the

* The Soarers Concert Party was named after the commander of the 21st Division, Major-General 'Soarer' Campbell, who had won the Grand National in 1896 as a subaltern in the 9th Lancers on his horse Soarer.

day with just the brigade commander and myself running the brigade. (Captain R. L. Bond, 199th Infantry Brigade H.Q.)

I was almost blown off my bunk by a concussion like an earthquake. I thought a shell must have hit us but the concussion went on. There was no doubt about it, this was *der Tag*. Salvoes of high-velocity shells were passing just over us and bursting in Grand Seraucourt. I then went to the telephone pit and told the signaller to get me on to each battery in turn. The bombardment could not have been going on for much more than a minute, yet every line was cut. And the telephone lines had all been buried *six feet deep*!

It was impossible to find out what was happening. At about 6.00 a.m., Achilles, the Brigade Signals Officer, and Jessop went out to try and get some information. They returned at about 8.00 a.m. Achilles had gone out a boy and he returned almost an old man, and quite unstrung. They brought back little information except that shells were falling everywhere. Poor old Achilles! He never really recovered from that shaking up. For months he couldn't speak except in a whisper. He was very young and had served in France since early in the war. Until his breakdown, he was keen and efficient and quite fearless, but his usefulness as a soldier in that war ended on the 21st March 1918. He stuck it out for another month, then he went quite off his head and had to be sent away. (Captain F. N. Broome, 173rd Brigade R.F.A.)

There were many headquarters, like those of this artillery brigade, which soon found themselves cut off from direct communication with their units. Main telephone cables had all been buried six feet deep but many were cut by German heavy shells. From that time on, commanders had to rely on such methods as runners or pigeons to get information, although a few units had wireless transmitters. The result of all this – the effective shelling of headquarters and the cutting of communications – was, together with the thick fog, often to cause a state of uncertainty and confusion that contributed considerably to events later in the day.

Another feature of the German bombardment was the distance into the British rear that was reached by the shelling. Again, the German knowledge of the location of targets well behind the Battle Zone was sound, and accurate shellfire started to fall at many places – the billets of reserve battalions, divisional and corps headquarters, railheads, tank parks (called 'tankodromes' in those days), airfields, and, most importantly, road junctions. Bapaume and Péronne, six and a half and eleven miles behind the line, were both shelled by long-range guns. The accuracy of much of this shelling was admired by many British soldiers. But this was a region once held by the Germans and shooting 'by the map' was an art that had been well mastered in this fourth year of war.

The petrol and ammunition dump for three battalions of tanks was blown up and most of the officers in the headquarters of one of the battalions were wounded. One German heavy gun was firing down the side of the main Cambrai–Bapaume road where many administrative units were positioned. This gun was gradually lengthening its range and its shells reached a forward dressing station. Shells fell into this for fifteen minutes until the fire moved on again. The airfield at Mons-en-Chaussée, ten miles behind the front, was shelled for several hours. In the middle of this, two ludicrous events occurred. A Royal Engineer's steamroller, which had been working on a road at the airfield for the past few days, commenced work as normal, its elderly driver ignoring the falling shells. Then the ground staff of No. 5 (Naval) Squadron, who were hurriedly loading their stores into lorries, were interrupted by a telephone call from a distant headquarters enquiring about the progress of vegetable planting on the airfield! Not one casualty was caused by the prolonged shelling on this airfield.

A complete reserve infantry brigade was encamped around the railhead at Achiet-le-Grand. One of the first shells here hit the Medical Hut of the 1st Wiltshires and killed nine men, but subsequent shelling killed only one man in the rest of the brigade. In this village stood a pair of smart, newly built civilian houses still occupied by French families. These were completely destroyed by one heavy shell and a near-by infantryman comments, 'I don't know the fate of the occupants but remember thinking that their optimism had deserved a better reward.'

This extensive spread of shelling did not cause serious casualties but it did cause some of the confusion that the Germans intended among headquarters and supporting units in the rear. The men here had rarely before been under serious shellfire. There was a certain amount of panic and the attention of such men was often diverted from their duty by the instinct for self-preservation. It was an ominous sign and a portent of what was to come later.

*

Having reached the limits of the German long-range gunfire, it is time for this survey of the bombardment to move back towards the front lines. Apart from the men already in the trenches, the most important British soldiers were those of the units which were to man the Battle Zone defences. Most of these had still been in their billets when the bombardment started. Because of the earlier false alarms, their commanders had almost all failed to act on the latest intelligence warnings and get their men into the defences beforehand.

We were literally caught with our trousers down. It was pitch black and, if you can picture sixteen men with full equipment packed into a bell tent with heavy shells falling all around, you can imagine the chaos which existed. We awoke to grab at our trousers only to find often enough that we had one leg in our own and the other in someone else's. Eventually someone found matches and when a couple of candles had been lit a little order came out of the confusion.

Considering the intensity of the bombardment the casualties were very light. A bell tent does not offer a lot of protection against flying shrapnel. (Private J. Crimmins, 9th East Surreys)

Many units were in hutted camps where 'the intensity of the bombardment could be judged by the fact that huts literally bounced up and down and the sides shook and seemed to be on the point of collapse'. Much damage was done to these flimsy camps, and men there often comment particularly on the destruction of cookhouses and latrines – essential places in their memories. Men had to get dressed, gather up equipment and stand by ready to move when ordered. One man realised that 'Fritz's offensive had begun and I seemed to realise even then that it was going to be a historic event.' A young infantry officer remembers 'getting up by the light of a guttering candle, the cold, a barely tepid cup of tea, and the realisation that this was at last *it*. It all made a depressing start to the day.'

It was not long before the order came down through
division and brigade: 'Man Battle Stations.' Some men had
been lucky enough to get a hot breakfast, but these were a
minority. In at least one battalion, it was suspected that gas
shelling had contaminated the food and an otherwise good
hot breakfast for several hundred men was tipped away into a
hole. Last-minute orders were issued and then the platoons
of men moved off into the darkness. This moment marked a
watershed in the lives of all these men. The winding country
lanes out of the camps could lead only to wounding, death,
a prisoner-of-war camp, or constant fighting and movement
for the next sixteen days.

We marched up the hill from Montigny towards Hervilly with
some distances between platoons, No. 13 – mine – leading. Randle
and I were at the rear of the platoon, the last two men. I recall our
conversation, which illustrates our complete lack of anxiety about
the morning's events so far. We agreed that it was going to be a
hungry morning. Randle said, 'As soon as we get back to Montigny,
the first job for you is to make a mess-tin of burgoo' (porridge) – I
regarded myself as an expert at making oatmeal porridge. The
general idea in the ranks seemed to be that the Germans were just
trying to make themselves 'a bloody nuisance'.
   Faces, generally wearing gas-masks, peered at us from the high
bank at the right of the road. I suppose there were battery
positions there. We donned our masks two or three times. In
about twenty minutes we turned right into a field near Hervilly
village. The village was under very heavy shellfire, much of it 5·9
overhead shrapnel. In isolation, we should have heard such shells
coming well before they burst, but that morning they merged into
a continuous roar. As the bursts were becoming uncomfortably
near, our platoon was moved across the shallow valley to the side
of Hervilly Wood. There we lay down to await further orders.
(Private W. Greenhalgh, 2/6th Manchesters)

We had been in a hutted camp at Heudicourt but we were shelled
out of there pretty quickly with a few casualties. We had often
practised this move, to the Liéramont Sunken Road position, but
this time it was pandemonium; everyone was left to fend for
themselves. There was more shelling and we made our own way
there in no sort of order. When we got there we even found that
some of the recently arrived batch of reinforcements had not brought
their rifles with them and several of the more experienced men had

to go all the way back to fetch them. The rest of us set to to dig in. We hadn't reached the sunken road. (Rifleman H. Griffiths, 16th Rifle Brigade)

The seventy or eighty battalions moving to their Battle Zone positions often suffered serious casualties – casualties that would not have been incurred if commanders had acted on the warnings of the day before and put their units into position the previous evening. Several battalions lost more than fifty men killed or wounded in this way, a serious depletion of their fighting strength. Even when they arrived at their allotted positions, platoons and companies often found the defence works incomplete and had to dig hard under further shellfire. Some units moved into positions they had never seen before. They occupied the trenches, set up their weapons and peered out through the barbed-wire entanglements without any idea of what lay beyond the wall of thick fog a few yards away. But despite the confusion, the casualties and other setbacks, the British Battle Zone was fully manned well before the German infantry attack commenced.

*

Although the emphasis of the five-hour bombardment changed many times, the German shelling was never far away from the positions held by the British infantry. Sketches reproduced in a book written by Oberst Bruchmüller after the war show that the Germans knew the exact location of the three lines of British defences – the outpost and support or redoubt line of the Forward Zone and then the Battle Zone. The outpost trenches were the targets of the German mortars, short-range howitzers and light field guns; the support trenches and redoubts were the responsibility of the heavy howitzers, and the Battle Zone positions further back of the medium and heavy field guns. Sometimes the Germans would lift their fire from the British trenches for a few minutes in order to give the impression that the bombardment had finished and draw the British infantry up from their dug-outs. Sometimes the German guns would sweep the open ground between the British defensive lines to catch isolated posts or any unit moving up as reinforcements. But always the shell and mortar fire returned to the British trenches, posts and redoubts and, as the bombardment period progressed, with steadily increasing intensity.

The men who give the following descriptions of the bombardment were all in the Forward Zone or the Battle Zone. They describe their experiences and emotions during those five hours of shelling. They did not know at the time that the shelling would cease at 9.40 a.m., but they did know that if they survived the shelling they would almost certainly have to man what was left of their trenches and fight for their lives against the German infantry attack. Such moments were the ultimate test in a soldier's life. It was in this way that the governments of so-called civilised nations attempted to impose their will on others and it was this experience that God was called upon to bless by the churchmen of both sides.

I was the company commander's batman. I asked him if I should put up the S.O.S. flare, a 'white-over-white' one fired by rifle grenades. The officer said that one had already gone up but there had been no response. I think that the German artillery had already knocked our guns out. The officer then told me to go along the trench telling all platoons to come off the fire-step and lie in the bottom of the trench. He went one way; I went the other and I never saw him again. I heard that he was taken prisoner. I met another officer though, with his gas-mask on. He was shell-shocked and making a horrid noise. I've never seen anybody before or after make that noise. He was sent down into the dug-out and I never saw him again either. (Private J. Jolly, 9th Norfolks)

Artillery was the great leveller. Nobody could stand more than three hours of sustained shelling before they start falling sleepy and numb. You're hammered after three hours and you're there for the picking when he comes over. It's a bit like being under an anaesthetic; you can't put a lot of resistance up. The first to be affected were the young ones who'd just come out. They would go to one of the older ones – older in service that is – and maybe even cuddle up to him and start crying. An old soldier could be a great comfort to a young one. On the other fronts that I had been on, there had been so much of our artillery that, whenever Gerry opened up like that, our artillery retaliated and gradually quietened him down but there was no retaliation this time. He had a free do at us. I think we were sacrificed.

Then a shell must have burst in our trench but I don't remember it. I woke up with just my head free, the rest of me was buried in sandbags and muck. I was completely stunned. I don't know how long it was before this fellow from the Durhams pulled me out. My helmet and gas-mask had disappeared. I saw my corporal – his head was blown off – and all the rest of the section must have been buried. I think it was being up on the fire-step as look-out that had saved me, but I found out later that I had been wounded by a bit of shell that had cut right through the muscle in my shoulder. (Private E. Atkinson, 1st West Yorks)

The mud bank at the end of the trench began to slide down, causing the mud level to rise nearly to our knees. I expected the soft walls of the trench to collapse and engulf us but they held. After a while my brain felt as if it would burst through my ears and I was still fighting the urge to vomit because of the gas. We had fixed bayonets and made a token 'stand-to', but we spent most of the time crouched against the side, each man isolated behind his gas-mask with his own private thoughts and fears. Never at any time, then or later, did I think I might be killed, but I *was* afraid of being buried alive if the walls caved in.

The sense of isolation really got me now. We were trapped in a stinking mud hole filled with gas-laden fog, no adequate fire-step and no protecting wire. All we could do was crouch there in the mud and wait, stunned by noise and concussion. As time dragged on without any let-up in the bombardment, fear was replaced with weary exasperation. I recall thinking 'For Christ's sake, pack it up, Jerry. Come over and fight, you bastards'. At the same time I was sane enough to realise that while all those shells were falling we were safe from infantry attack. (Private T. C. H. Jacobs, 15th Londons)

We were in Epéhy village, in a position known as Roberts Post. It consisted of several ruined houses connected by a trench. We slept in the cellars. I was on gas sentry when the shelling started. Having roused the others to put their gas-masks on, I was in my post for four hours. For most of this time I had to put up with the bursting of shells, possibly from a five-point-nine, on one particular spot just ten yards away on open ground. I felt that one German gun was supposed to be firing on Roberts Post and was firing just a fraction short. I could hear the shell coming like a train rushing through the air and had to duck down every time, thinking it might be for me. (Private J. Wignall, 7th Leicesters)

The experts among us were trying hard to distinguish whether shells would land short, over, or on us. The whole of the Lewis-gun team were alert on the fire-step; one or two kept looking out in front. Suddenly we could hear a shell coming and could tell that it was going to be a hit. We crouched down and it burst in the parapet right in front of our position. The explosion threw us all into the bottom of the trench. When the dust and muck had settled, we sorted ourselves out. We found two of our men had been hit. One had his head blown off, the other an arm off. The blood had already drained out of his body into a big pool in the floor of the trench.

Then a company sergeant-major came along the trench. He'd got a fellow with him carrying loaves of bread and tins of bacon. The C.S.M. was breaking off chunks of bread and giving out the bacon. 'Get this down you, lads – you'll be needing this.' I reckon he was a hero and I often wonder what happened to him. We ate the food and, with our water bottles, felt quite refreshed. (Lance Corporal A. Wallace, 2/5th Sherwood Foresters)

The bombardment on our trenches started around dawn on the 21st March and was sheer hell – shells, trench mortars, the lot, gradually cutting down our platoon. During this time our lieutenant-colonel, the captain, and his runner came along the trenches to see how things were. At that time there were only about three or four of us alive but no order was given to draw back or pull out. While we were discussing what to do – there being nobody in charge – my pal was hit with a piece of shell which sliced his head completely off. You can imagine how I felt. All the rest were dead by now, mostly having lost their limbs, so I decided to go along the trenches to see if I could find anybody alive. This was not easy as parts of the trench were blown in . . . Giving up all hope of survival and feeling hopping mad, I waited with my Lewis gun for the enemy to come over the top. (Rifleman E. Chapman, 18th Londons)*

The German artillery plan ran the full course of its five-hour programme. There was one major setback. At dawn it had been intended that German artillery observers would correct the aim of some of the batteries that had been firing, by the map, on targets which should have become visible from the observation posts. But the thick fog that now lay over most of the battlefield, especially in the centre and the south, had prevented this and the German gunners had been forced to fire the whole programme blind. This type of firing depended very much on correct meteorological

* The London Irish Rifles.

information and was known as the 'Pulkowski method' after a certain Hauptmann Pulkowski, a Regular officer in the *Fussartillerie* who had perfected this method. It is sometimes contended that the German bombardment on 21 March 1918 was completely devastating and that this was the reason for various calamities suffered by the British later in the day. But Ludendorff's artillery was bombarding 150 square miles of British defences to say nothing of the long-range harassing fire in the British rear. This was too great a target for only five hours of shelling even with the 10,000 guns and mortars that were firing. The Germans knew this and had never expected that the bombardment would completely overwhelm the British defences. There are many reports of well-concealed British positions – both infantry and artillery – being overlooked completely by the bombardment and others, like the situation at Roberts Post in Epéhy, where the firing by the map just missed a target. No one will ever know the exact casualties caused by the shellfire among the British troops in the various defence positions but there is some evidence – which will be discussed in more detail later – that no more than about 2,500 men were killed and, possibly, 5,000–6,000 wounded. This loss was from a figure of approximately 100,000 troops who would be manning the British defences by the time the German infantry attack commenced.

What the Germans had achieved with the bombardment was the blowing-away of much of the British front-line barbed wire, the blowing-in of many of the front-line trenches, the partial destruction of trenches farther back, the neutralisation for several hours of part of the British artillery, and some confusion in the rear areas. There were also large numbers of British infantrymen and gunners who, while not actually wounded by the shelling, were stupefied by it and also suffering from the effects of gas. These men were in poor shape to face the German infantry attack.

*

The bombardment was the most heartening thing that the German soldiers could have witnessed at this time. After daylight came, those who were on higher ground or where the fog was not so thick could see a wall of smoke and dust over the British trenches which shuddered again and again with the glow of bursting shells. The deafening noise prevented normal speech and men shouted excitedly at each other but without being heard. It was easy for the German infantrymen to believe that the enemy defences would be crushed before they had to attack.

The German mortars had fired for only the first twenty minutes of the bombardment – the 'general surprise fire' phase – and had then fallen silent. Late in the bombardment (the exact time is not recorded), the mortars opened fire again, their target being the British front-line trenches and the barbed wire protecting the trenches. This Bavarian soldier was a messenger between a mortar battery and the observation post which was directing its fire.

The Leutnant stood next to me and spoke or probably shouted. I heard nothing. He drew my attention to the trajectory of the bombs fired from our six mortars. They were a metre long and were clearly visible climbing over the wall of smoke and, after having reached the apogee, tumbling down head-over-heels to explode on impact with a terrific force. The blast lifted the smoke over the battlefield considerably.

'One mortar is firing duds,' wrote the observer on his pad and ordered me to take the message to H.Q. On the way I came very close to death. At the end of the sap, two light mortars were firing at top speed. When I was near the entrance to their trench, a terrific blast hurled me back against the barbed wire. One of the mortars was a shambles; the bomb had exploded inside the barrel, killing the operator. His steel helmet and head looked as though they had been split with an axe.

I went on to find the mortar which was firing the duds. There was only one explanation; the safety pins to be removed from the fuse immediately before firing had been left in place, forgotten in the heat of battle. I showed every mortar captain the written message. No. 4 was just ready to fire. Off went its bomb to land as another dud. When the Gefreiter saw the message he could only scratch himself behind his ear. The observer never knew who had been the culprit. (Pioneer Johann-Baptist Hilmer, 302nd *Minenwerfer* Company)

But the shellfire was not all German. Some of the British batteries were able to carry out some counter-firing during this period. This German artillery officer's battery was bombarded by some guns in the area of the 16th (Irish) Division.

Now the enemy realised that the great day of the German attack had come. It was only a very weak barrage to start with but it soon became stronger. In particular the villages of Ossus, Vendhuile and Aubencheul came under very heavy fire. Our 1st Battery were badly hit in their position at Ossus. An enemy heavy battery, probably without knowing it, had the exact range. The very first salvo transformed my battery, which was all ready to march, into a chaos of bloody and dying men and horses. It was absolute hell – screams, moans, shouts, orders – all lost in the darkness and the smoke and gas clouds. The firing lasted for perhaps five minutes but the results of it were terrible. Those who hadn't been hit helped and comforted the casualties as best they could. We shot the wounded horses. My batman was killed with both of our horses. The 1st Battery was put completely out of action even before the advance began. At daybreak, the remaining gun crews went to other batteries of the regiment. I joined the infantry regiment we should have been supporting. (Leutnant Artur Seiffert, 63rd Reserve Field Regiment)

Another British shelling incident had an unusual outcome.

It was all over for me early in the morning. I was in command of a small section of men and we came to the jumping-off trench for the attack occupied by Bavarians. There was a dug-out there that I wanted for my men as a shelter. Actually it was a hand-grenade dump. We removed the cases and made ourselves as comfortable as possible. I sat outside in order to be on hand for further orders. A British artillery observer must have noticed what was going on and, seeing the cases, ordered his guns to fire and killed the whole section with a single shell. I was the only survivor, badly wounded in the chest and thigh.

After the war a British artillery officer had an appeal in my local paper asking for men who had taken part in the 21st March 1918 battle and who wore the 'Gibraltar' tape. I wrote to him. He came from Glasgow and his family name was Philip; he was taken prisoner later that day. He said that he had been the artillery observer who had nearly killed me. We exchanged about fifty letters until about 1960. (Gefreiter Walter Junk, 73rd Regiment)

A further danger experienced by the Germans on many sectors was exposure to their own gas. There was only the slightest of breezes blowing from the west but this was sufficient to carry some of the gas from the German shells bursting in the British trenches back to the German lines. The British were also firing gas shells in their counter bombardment. Because the gas was often mixed in with the thick fog which was so widespread and because smoke was also drifting from the British trenches, the German soldiers were often slow to realise the presence of the gas and they suffered many casualties from it.

The fog, which was present on much of the battlefield, was going to be a major factor in the German infantry attack which was to commence shortly. There have been many arguments as to which side benefited most from the presence of the fog. The ordinary soldiers of both sides, experiencing at first hand as they did the confusion and difficulties caused by the fog but not seeing the difficulties of their enemy, usually say that it was more help to the other side than to their own. It is certain that, in this early stage of the action, the fog was a definite help to the German infantry, enabling them to complete the removal of their own barbed-wire defences and deploy their first waves of storm troops in the open spaces of No Man's Land without being seen or fired upon by the British. The German artillery, on the other hand, was still firing completely blindly although it was now well past dawn. The big question which officers and ordinary soldiers alike were now asking was how would the fog affect the outcome of an infantry attack which had been planned to take place in broad daylight, but was about to be launched in conditions of extremely limited visibility.

*

The last phase of the German bombardment began at 9.35 a.m. All the guns and mortars started firing a final hurricane bombardment on the British front line lasting five minutes and using only high-explosive shells. All the German infantry had moved to their final positions. They stood in packed trenches or lay out in the open, waiting for the bombardment to lift and the order to advance. It is impossible to generalise about the thoughts of soldiers at such a moment. Emotions will vary between young men and older ones, between officer and private soldier, between married men and single ones, between the timid man and the brave. Let a few of the German soldiers speak for themselves.

Feelings before the battle? Can I describe them after so many years? The older men couldn't care less, only to be out of the shit. The younger ones of course are frightened and anyone who dares to deny it is a liar. But also the tension. How will it go? But at that time we were brought up through school and parental discipline in the spirit of the military empire of the Kaiser. (Musketier Wilhelm Boscheinen, 230th Reserve Regiment)

I looked once more at my men and noticed one who should not have been there. I asked him why he was not with his section at the transport. This man, named Baier, had been a Hauptmann at the beginning of the war, a regular officer with an infantry regiment. He had been court-martialled and reduced to the ranks in 1916 after coming home on leave without warning and shooting a strange man that he found in bed with his wife. He had gone back to the front as a private soldier.

We had become friends. He was a born soldier with an uncompromising idea of honour. My commander had told me in confidence about his past and I had to give my word of honour to keep my mouth shut. He hadn't worn any medals all the time I had known him. Now he was standing before me with his decorations — Iron Cross 1st Class and several other medals on the left breast and the Turkish Crescent on the right one. He carried no weapons but in his right hand he had large wire-cutters. He said he was well aware that he was not supposed to be where he was but, as a former officer, he owed it to his conscience and honour to be in the first line. We shook hands. (Vizefeldwebel Wilhelm Prosch, 463rd Regiment)

A time like this was bound to create a certain anxiety. Having been under fire again and again in the past, it wasn't too bad for me. The call of duty and the iron discipline worked all right. One thinks about home and the family and God. Didn't all people expect help from Him? Hadn't they been told they were fighting for a just cause? Didn't they all pray for victory and peace? How often has His name been misused to start a war, not in the interests of the people, but in the interests of ambitious and greedy rulers of the land and the church? (Musketier Adolf Vogelsang, 394th Regiment)

In spite of everybody's awareness that there were untold thousands of men in front of us and to the right and left all with the same tensed readiness, each of us had to rely on himself and make himself ready to face death. How far will we advance today? Shall we achieve the great breakthrough? Will our section, bound in year-long comradeship, stay together or be torn apart and, if so, who will catch it? I had thoughts of my parents, my sisters, my much-loved grandmother who had told us children about the 1870–1871 war which had brought tears rolling down her face and affected me deeply. How right she had been in her wisdom to condemn war! (Gefreiter Karl Pütz, 65th Reserve Regiment)

Just before the bombardment ended, the battalion commander, Major Scherer, started to sing '*Deutschland, Deutschland über Alles*' and the singing spread across to us and we all joined in. It was the first time that I had heard of our men singing the National Anthem since the autumn of 1914 when our young volunteers had been heard singing it in their attacks in Flanders. The spirit now wasn't the same as in 1914 but I think the battalion commander sang this to take our soldiers' minds off the coming battle. The men were quite happy – there was no English artillery fire and we thought that there were no English soldiers left alive. (Leutnant Hermann Wedekind, 79th Regiment)

Most of the men were very quiet, some made a few jokes. One, I remember, took out a letter and a photograph of his wife and looked at it. He didn't say anything; they were all thinking of home. Possibly half of the men went to a quiet part of the trench and said their prayers. I too. (Leutnant Rudolf Hoffmann, 463rd Regiment)

Because of the fog, I was overwhelmed with fear that I might be left alone or get lost in it somewhere. Shortly before the attack began I had to go again to the company commander who gave me exact instructions about what I had to watch out for and what I had to do with my No. 3 Platoon. Then he gave me his compass so that I could meet him just west of the sunken road near Benay. Then came instructions about my taking command of the company in case he was killed or wounded. It was too much for me and I started crying. Thank the Lord that the chief didn't object to my tears. The strain remained, though, and the fear too. I was emotionally finished and glad in my heart when, after the four-hour barrage, the signal 'Spring up' sounded. This ancient call blown by our trumpeter helped me to get rid of my tears but the fear still remained. (Fähnrich Alfred Bruntsch, 145th *Königs* Regiment)

7

The Fight for the Forward Zone

Du Sauerei, die Artilleristen, uns einige brockt haben; müssen wir jetzt auslä̈ffeln – Those pigs in the artillery have stirred things up for us; now its our turn to face the music. (German infantryman)

The first waves of the German attackers, usually storm troops with a few pioneers, had crept well out into No Man's Land during the last minutes of the bombardment. It was important for these men to get as close as possible to the British barbed wire so that they could deal with any wire not blown away by the shellfire and then rush the British front-line trenches before the defenders could come up from their dug-outs. This was the vital moment for the first phase of the infantry attack. If the barbed wire could not be forced quickly and if the British defenders who had survived the bombardment could get into position and set up their weapons, then the initial attack could easily turn into a bloody failure. The first casualties suffered were those Germans hit by their own shells and mortar bombs falling short, but that was a hazard that had to be accepted. At 9.40 a.m. the bombardment of the British front line ceased.* There were a few moments of silence as thousands of German gunlayers adjusted their sights, and then the guns opened fire again on their next targets. German company, platoon, and section commanders sprang up, shouted to their men 'Raus, raus', and dashed forward. The pioneers carried their tubes of explosive; the infantrymen mostly had their rifles slung across their backs, the long-handled 'stick' grenades carried in each hand were more useful at this time. Every man wore his long overcoat, the usual belts, straps and packs, and his unwieldy 'coal-scuttle' type steel helmet.

* In the extreme south of the attack front, the Germans had started attacking at 6.15 a.m. so that they could build footbridges and then cross the Canal de l'Oise under cover of darkness. This will not affect the main story.

Many also had to wear their gas-masks. A grey-clad host rushed through the fog at the shell-tossed remnants of the British front line. The German orders had stated that the attack was to be launched 'without hurrahs'.

I wait with another man – Skorczyk his name was, of Polish extraction. Between us we have to carry this long tube of explosive. The infantry commander shouts, '*Drauf!*', and we rush forward. But where is the expected enemy fire? There is hardly any. His line is not so near as we thought and we had to run. I soon became out of breath and couldn't see out of the eye-piece of my gas-mask so I tore it off. After all, we thought that this was going to be our last day; there isn't going to be any escape for us. I never thought I would survive. But I only coughed a couple of times and my eyes watered a little. That was all that I was affected by the gas.

There was a little machine-gun fire and some of our chaps caught it. Leutnant Wiese was hit and the man who was carrying the explosive with me either fell over or was wounded, I don't know which. I carried on alone, still with that damned tube. We came to a minefield with trip-wires every five metres. The mines were covered with tufts of dry grass. Here and there there were explosions. Were they the mines or shell bursts? Fire from the enemy infantry is now almost non-existent.

Then we reached the barbed wire, our objective. But there is nothing for us to do. The wire is completely destroyed. There wasn't really any trench left, just craters and craters. Now I looked back the way we had come and saw the swarm of men following. I couldn't stop a lump coming to my throat. Only a few of the enemy had survived the storm; some were wounded. They stood with hands up. There was no need to tell them; they got the message – 'to the rear'. (Gefreiter Paul Kretschmer, 28th Pioneer Battalion)

Our front-line trench had been so badly damaged that, when the bombardment lifted, we were ordered to fall back to the support line about a hundred yards further back. We had to leave the platoon commander at the top of the dug-out steps; he was dead with both legs blown off. The company commander sat at the bottom of the steps still issuing orders but he was too badly wounded to move. The dug-out itself was full of men wounded by the shelling – they were all left behind.

As we fell back, we came to a side trench hurriedly blocked with a barricade of sandbags and earth. As I passed this I stood up and looked over and there, on the other side, was a German with a steel helmet on. He was only four or five feet away. We both got down quickly. I got out of the way fast because I thought he might throw a grenade over but I never heard one. Perhaps he was frightened too. (Corporal J. E. Osler, 9th Norfolks)

The experiences of these two opposing corporals were typical of the situation on much of the attack front. A large proportion of German accounts stress that there never was any kind of fight for the British front line. The German artillery and mortars had done their work well here. Most of the barbed wire had been blown away and what had once been a trench was now just a cratered ruin. Many of the Germans did not know that in the southern part of the British line they attacked there never had been a properly manned trench, only a series of posts. There is also no doubt that in many places the British had deliberately evacuated their front line, sometimes on orders from officers, sometimes on an 'every man for himself' basis. The few British soldiers who were left were either dead, wounded or so shocked and gassed by the bombardment that they were incapable of offering serious resistance. Some of the defenders had been slow to leave their dug-outs and could only come out to surrender. As one German says, 'They were brave soldiers but what else could they do?' Any man who was too slow to come out of his dug-out risked receiving the time-honoured trench-fighting treatment used by both sides – a grenade down the steps and no pity for the consequences.

It would not be an exaggeration to say that nine tenths of the British front-line trench or outposts fell without much of a fight. These further accounts describe incidents in these positions and the first meetings between enemies.

We had lost direction and come to a trench which should have been taken by another company. The last barbed-wire entanglement was completely undamaged. I was the only one who had a wire-cutter and managed to make a passage. Visibility was so bad that your outstretched hand couldn't be seen. When I had finished the job, I slung my rifle, the bayonet fixed. I had to carry two boxes of machine-gun ammunition. The chap originally detailed as carrier had been wounded. I was just going to enter the trench when a giant of an Englishman, fully armed, faced me. I dropped the boxes but was too late anyway as he stood there, rifle at the ready, bayonet fixed. Then a shell splinter tore the tip of his chin away and he dropped to the ground, holding on to my rifle. I had no desire to kill him. Being in a hurry to join my platoon, I stepped on his hands and left. Splinters kept coming. It was our guns which were firing. (Gefreiter Rudolf Loss, 210th Reserve Regiment)

We met some wounded Englishmen in No Man's Land. We believed that the English had left their front line empty as a decoy to attract our artillery, hoping that we would waste all our shells on that trench. I think that perhaps these poor fellows had been left behind in the trench as a *Scheinbesatzung* – 'a deception party'. My impression was that they had been ordered to keep up an appearance in this trench and then, because they could have no chance when we attacked, were allowed to surrender. They came out with their hands up – no weapons – only steel helmets. There were somewhere between six and ten of them but we had no time to look after them because we had to get on and our own artillery dropped a salvo of heavy shells among us at that moment and wounded some of my men. I think the artillery battery's watches were wrong. The English just kept going back to our lines and I never saw them again. We came to their front line then; it was completely destroyed and there was no one there at all – not alive or dead. We had expected to fight for the front line and were astonished and happy – more astonished than happy in fact – to find it empty. We went straight on and found it the same in the second trench. (Leutnant Hermann Wedekind, 79th Regiment)

I saw my first Englishman – dead, headless, in the British trench. In my mind I saw a map of England and Ireland and I thought that somewhere there there would be sadness. We had not been fired upon at all and our first realisation that we had reached the British front line was the sight of this dead man. We could hardly realise that this had once been a trench; it was difficult to see the line of it, it had been so heavily shelled by our artillery. That dead English soldier was the only Englishman I saw all day, dead or alive. We found a tin of sea biscuits there, very hard and yet most welcome. Then it was time for us to get on again. (Fuselier Waldemar Schmielau, 5th Guard Grenadier Regiment)

The bombardment stopped and we started loading ourselves up with rifles and ammunition to go up and man the trench. We waited just a little to make sure the shelling was over, no more than three minutes. Suddenly there was a Gerry at the top of the dug-out

with a rifle and bayonet pointing down the steps. He shouted
something at us. We'd had it; there was no argument about it. If
we'd been awkward, there would have been a bomb or a tube of
ammonal down; we'd heard plenty of stories about that. They
were so quick that we felt they had kept the shelling going on our
bit while they went through on both sides but that was only what
we were told later. We threw all our equipment off, came up and
were gathered together in a sunken road. I'll give them their due;
they were quite fair. That chap at the top of the dug-out could
have stuck a bayonet in us as we came out but an officer just
pointed to the rear and left us to it. (Lance Corporal B. Lambert,
7th Sherwood Foresters)

It was very foggy and I heard no firing at all. If I had been more
experienced, I would have known what was happening but the
first I knew that the Germans had attacked at all was when I went
round the traverse of our trench and walked into this horrible little
German with thick glasses on. It was the first German I had ever
seen. He put his bayonet at the centre of my stomach and said,
'*Kamerad*, yes or no?' I said, 'Yes'. (Lieutenant W. D. Scott, 6th
Somerset Light Infantry)

This incident is described by a soldier in the 51st
(Highland) Division who did not wish his name to be
mentioned.

There were no dug-outs in our front line; it was very thinly held
to prevent casualties. We had had to huddle up under the parapet
during the shelling; there was no other shelter. When the bombardment lifted, we were not attacked frontally. We were considerably shaken by the shelling. It was a moment of fear. 'What's
coming next out of the mist?' We fired our rifles blindly into the
mist then heard firing from our left and from the rear. We realised
that we were being outflanked. The men started to drift back until
we were left with only two men, myself and a sergeant.

The next thing I knew was that two Germans were coming up
the trench on our left; they were about ten yards away. The
sergeant had been at the rum for some time. I cleared off; I wasn't
going to get caught. The last I saw of the sergeant he was shaking
his fist at the Germans and using strong language. I saw him taken
prisoner.

In some places the German bombardment had not quite
got the range of the British trenches, and in others the

Germans had not spread their shelling or their infantry attack evenly along the British front. They often concentrated on punching holes in certain sectors and left the intervening British trenches to be dealt with later. There were thus several isolated British positions left intact after the bombardment. Some of these put up a good fight; some surrendered quickly. Some survivors managed to get back to the next line of British trenches; some did not. But none of these British positions was strong enough to stand for long and the end always came after a brief fight, usually with the appearance of Germans in their rear or bombing down the trenches on either side, or when the Germans brought up their mobile trench mortars and put a few bombs into the British trench. The battalion history of the 7th Sherwood Foresters records that this was the fate of one of their Lewis-gun teams who had actually gone out into a shell hole in No Man's Land to escape the bombardment. When the German infantry attacked, the Lewis gun opened fire with great effect until its crew were all killed by a single mortar bomb.

This German soldier was in front of a part of the British front line which had escaped the worst of the bombardment.

Going into the attack, two of my men held back and I never saw them again. I heard from them later – a letter from Berlin. I don't know whether they were wounded or whether they had said they were ill. I know they didn't like the war and I think they were only interested in survival and managed to get out. As for me, I was pleased to see the back of them. We couldn't have won the war with the likes of them.

The rest of the section was laid out about fifty metres in front of the British barbed wire. I didn't fire myself and my men neither. We were all Verdun veterans and it was probably the other sections who opened fire first. It was thick fog and we couldn't see anything to fire at. We were experienced soldiers and one didn't fire wildly in situations like that. The English couldn't have been any better because their bullets were flying well over our heads. We had managed to dig ourselves in a little, so we had no losses. This went on for some time until the fog lifted and then we could see that the English were retreating. I just saw the last one running away back up his trench about 200 metres away. I didn't shoot him though; the last one away was the bravest and I wasn't

going to shoot him in the back. (Gefreiter Michael Pitsch, 16th
Reserve *Jäger* Battalion)

This little action had been just in front of the village of
Lagnicourt. A British company commander was defending a
trench near here although he was not one of those who were
able to escape.

I don't remember the bombardment actually lifting. There was
shelling and rifle fire all around us although the shelling was
mostly over our heads on the supports. There were very few orders
issued; we just took up our positions and opened fire. There was
plenty of fire coming in, much of it from in front. The Germans had
taken cover in No Man's Land or they were still in their old front
line. They weren't making an assault just here; probably they were
relying on a penetration elsewhere. They weren't wasting men
attacking a well-defended position frontally. We'd fired back at
where we thought they were and even sent a report back: 'We have
beaten off the attack.'

Two incidents of that morning remain vividly in my memory.
As I stood on the fire-step, firing a rifle as rapidly as I could, doing
my little bit to add to the awful pandemonium of noise, a Tommy
standing near called out, 'Look at that bloody hare!' There, just in
front of us was a March hare, dashing backwards and forwards in
the barbed wire, not knowing where to go. I can see it now, ears
sticking straight up, eyes popping out of its head. I wonder if it
got away!

I stood on the fire-step firing to my front. Just behind me,
lying on the back of the trench, Lieutenant Patterson was firing at
the Germans who had broken through on our flank and were now
behind us and still advancing. He had a box of fifty Gold Flake
cigarettes in his tunic pocket (so had I) and was chain-smoking as
he fired (so was I). It must have been about 10 a.m. when a Tommy
came up to me and said, 'Mr Patterson's been killed, Sir. Can I
have his cigarettes?' Sounds pretty callous, doesn't it? It didn't
strike me that way at all. The poor chap was probably dying for a
cigarette and had been watching Pat enviously for some time.
Perhaps he thought that if he took the cigarettes without permission it would be robbing the dead but, if I said 'yes', it was all
right. I said 'yes'.*

* 'Patterson' was in fact Second Lieutenant Robert Paterson of Perth; he has
no known grave.

Shortly after this I was knocked out by a bullet which came in one cheek and out the other. It knocked all my teeth out. I was a hell of a mess. (Captain N. H. Beedham, 2nd Sherwood Foresters)

It was misty rather than foggy. We saw them at about 300 yards. Their grey uniforms didn't show up too well against the mist. There were thousands of them, a blanket of men coming straight at us. You hear about waiting for the orders to fire but there was none of that. Our sergeant called out to me, 'I'm a lieutenant, Taylor. You're a sergeant.' I think he was a little bit crazy at the time; who wouldn't be in those circumstances? Their numbers confronting us seemed to diminish. We were certainly hitting a lot of them but I think others had gone to ground. We didn't have a really good wire; the Germans had been blowing it away faster than we could put it up. Several of them got caught up in the wire. A few of them had great big wire-cutters. We were sniping them off as they were doing that. I found that our company commander, Captain Martin, had been killed, shot through the head, but his body was leaning against the back of the trench. I rested my rifle on his shoulder for five or ten minutes while I fired. One of our men wanted to get up and have a go at them but as soon as he got above the trench he was hit and fell back. I could have hit twenty or so Germans; I was certainly in a soft spot there.

There was no doubt about it that we held them in front of us to start with but they got in further along and came along our trench. We sent a pigeon back with a message asking for reinforcements but I don't know what the result was because we were soon marching towards Deutschland. The Germans were on our parapet; they'd got through the wire at last. The sergeant shouted, 'Bolts out and put your hands up.' We threw away our rifle bolts and did as he said. (Private S. S. Taylor, 1st Wiltshires)

When the attacking infantry reached our trench, the fog was still very dense. A shower of stick bombs forced us to leave the trench and we climbed out on to the back to maintain a line but beyond the range of their bombs. There I met one of our corporals who had got a German prisoner. The German had come in, with a revolver held in both hands, but deliberately looking for someone to take him prisoner. Not wanting to be loaded with a prisoner, I took his revolver away and pushed him back into the trench and, in turning round, I saw six or seven German officers or N.C.O.s in the open looking at a map. They were only three or four yards away so I automatically came up with the revolver I had acquired and that was the only occasion in which I can honestly say that I shot any Germans in two and a half years of front-line soldiering. I didn't wait to see how many.

After that I collected together about a dozen of my men and attempted to get back to Battalion H.Q. in Enghien Redoubt. I knew that I had to cross a certain sunken road near Fayet above which was a memorial to the Franco–Prussian War. I came to this road but could quite clearly hear Germans talking in it. I decided to cheer and yell and we ran down across the road and up the other side without being fired upon. We got going again in the fog and were fired upon by one of our own machine-guns; we could tell it was one of ours from the sound. By that time we were pretty lively at getting down when anything fired and none of us was hit. I shouted 'Second Fourth Oxfords' but this had no effect. One of my men shouted '*Kamerad*' and it stopped at once. We found the machine-gunner was as lost as we were and he came with us.

We never got through to Enghien Redoubt but eventually we reached Brigade H.Q. I was the only officer to get back from my battalion and they attached my little party to the 2/5th Gloucesters. (Second Lieutenant H. Jones, 2/4th Oxford and Bucks Light Infantry)*

Within less than an hour of the commencement of the German infantry attack, the British front line had disappeared for fifty miles from a point seven miles short of the northern boundary of the Third Army down to the River Oise at La Fère. The only exceptions were the positions in the front of the Flesquières Salient, which had not been seriously attacked, and a few isolated posts still holding out but so scattered and weak as to be of no further significance to the outcome of the day's fighting. Because of the effectiveness of the German bombardment, the fog, and the speed and skill of the German infantry assault, the British front line had been overwhelmed and its defenders had been able to do little in the way of inflicting serious casualties on the Germans or of holding up their further advance. The garrisons of most of the British positions were dead or prisoners. Very few, like Second Lieutenant Jones of the Oxford and Bucks, had been able to come back to fight again. But the British had never expected their front line to perform miracles. There still remained the support trenches, redoubts

---

* I visited Mr Jones's sunken road near Fayet in September 1976 and found that the memorial had collapsed but the great blocks of stone were still there.

and the smaller posts of the Forward Zone and then, well back, the new Battle Zone on which so many hopes rested.

*

The next phase of this battle was fought in what might be termed the main positions of the Forward Zone. It is an unfortunate complication for the narrative here that this meant different things in different places. However, it will be an acceptable expedient to say that north of the Flesquières Salient – on the sectors defended by the Third Army – these defences were the support and reserve trenches of the front-line system, while south of the salient, on the Fifth Army's sectors, they would be the line of redoubts and smaller supporting posts behind the outpost line. Both in the north and the south, there was an area of ground behind these positions which was largely empty of defences and which separated the rear of the Forward Zone from the front of the Battle Zone.

There was a far greater variety of weapons and men in the main Forward Zone positions than there had been in the front line. In addition to the infantrymen, always positioned around their main weapon, the Lewis gun, there were light trench-mortar and heavy machine-gun posts and the single 18-pounder field guns placed forward to act as anti-tank guns. There were also many observation posts with artillery observation officers and their telephonists and the command posts of all the infantry battalions in the Forward Zone. The highest ranking officers in this area were the battalion commanders – lieutenant-colonels, or majors if the regular commanding officer was on leave or sick.

The role of these positions in the British defence plan was a simple one. They were to absorb as much of the impetus of the German attack as possible, inflict the greatest number of casualties on the Germans, delay them for the longest possible time. These were the 'expendable' positions held by what the soldiers in them so often called 'sacrifice units' because there were little chance of counter-attack or re-inforcement from the Battle Zone. Already many of the forward battalions were out of touch with their brigade headquarters because telephone lines had been cut by the

German shelling. On the face of it, this was no great loss because the only orders a brigade commander could give were to hang on as long as possible, but broken communications induced a sense of uncertainty and isolation that would test the nerve and will to resist of those officers who were commanding defensive positions. Broken telephone lines were more of a setback for the artillery observation officers who were prevented from directing the fire of their batteries, although, as long as the thick fog lasted, they could hardly do anything useful even if they were in touch with the gun positions.

The reader may be able to visualise the roles of the various defensive positions, and the unfolding events of that morning in 1918 can be recreated to form an intelligible picture of the battle's progress, but it must be stressed that there was no such perception and clarity available to the men involved in that battle. Brigade, divisional, corps and army commanders had their maps and had issued their orders but they had little knowledge of what was actually happening out there in the fog. Even battalion commanders had little control over their dispersed companies. They had sometimes heard the sound of firing from their front line but such sounds had often been lost in the greater sound of the German bombardment that was still being fired. A few wounded men with garbled messages had come back, but very few.

The British battalions in the Forward Zone had degenerated into thousands of tiny groups of men, each in a trench bay, in part of a redoubt, and, in the south, in many an isolated post that was in touch with no other post. These groups had a few rifles and grenades, a Lewis gun, a Vickers, or a trench mortar. Many were commanded by young corporals or lance corporals. Many men say in their accounts of the battle that they never saw an officer after the German bombardment opened. It is true that every post and every man formed part of a carefully prepared scheme of defence and, if there had been good visibility, they could have performed their parts in that scheme with confidence. But there was no such visibility. The British soldiers could only crouch over their weapons and stare into the swirling fog outside their posts. Their ears could only try to make some sense out of the cacophony of noise assailing them – exploding shells, rifle and machine-gun fire, bursting grenades, distant shouts and screams. It was cold and dank. These men did not have warm breakfasts in their stomachs. They had not had a full night's sleep. They had suffered a four-hour artillery bombardment. There was some quiet resolution but also a great deal of looking-over of shoulders.

One point should be explained further. The Germans had often penetrated the front line so quickly that they were upon the main positions within minutes of the opening of the attack. The actions which are now going to be described often took place well before the fight for the front line was finished. It is only a literary expedient to separate the last part of the narrative, which described the fight for the front line, from this fight in the main positions of the Forward Zone.

*

The Germans were not without their own difficulties. The fog caused confusion among their infantry units as soon as their advance started and most could only find their way by compass. Groups of men met in the fog, their leaders compared maps, separated and moved on again. Battalion and regimental commanders lost touch with their units.* Gas was

---

* British survivors of the battle often mention the German bugle calls which could be heard that morning and they guessed, quite correctly, that this was a method by which the Germans could pass messages in the fog. Each German infantry company had a bugler who had to learn by heart twenty-four different calls. By adding a few special notes it was possible to address a call to a particular part of a unit. In this way, a battalion commander could send, for example, this order: 'No. 1 and No. 2 Companies, advance. No. 3 Company, stand fast. No. 4 Company, move to the right.'

Buglers of all armies help themselves to remember bugle calls by learning simple rhymes to say in their head in time with the call. When Germans who were on the battlefield on 21 March 1918 were asked about this, they all said that the call used most frequently that day was the one ordering units to advance. The usual bugler's rhyme for this call was:

Kartöffelsuppe. Kartöffelsuppe.	Potato soup. Potato soup.
Den gänzen Tag, Kartöffelsuppe.	All day long, potato soup.
Kartöffelsuppe.	Potato soup.

As a variation, the last line could be:

Und kēīn Flēisch ('And no meat').

Continued overleaf.

still a danger and British shells, fired blindly into suspected German approach areas, caused bursts of terror and casualties. Many German units, finding less opposition than expected, pushed on fast and found themselves under the shellfire of their own creeping barrage which actually jumped forward two, three or four hundred metres in one bound. No visual artillery observation was possible and the German barrage continued to roll on remorselessly irrespective of whether the German infantry were behind or ahead of it.

Despite all these hazards, the German tactics of that morning were well suited to the foggy conditions: Infiltrate. Avoid the defended positions. Push on fast. All this the Germans could do in some safety because the British infantry weapons that were supposed to cover the open spaces were blind. The storm troops were still leading, but the infantry of the battle groups with their machine-guns and mobile mortars were following up close behind. The dry-ground conditions were another advantage for the Germans, the legacy they had inherited from the dry winter. One of their infantry officers has described the ground over which he was advancing as consisting of 'old fields but no crops, dry underfoot, some short grass or simply bare earth with a few old weeds flat on the ground. It was only March and there was no new growth. It was mostly level ground and flat, a few new shell holes. My men kept putting up partridges and called out to each other excitedly, wanting to shoot them, but I wouldn't let them.'

The German advance was seldom at right angles to the British defence lines. At purely local level, the Germans tended to push their forces through in the lower ground, partly because it was more foggy here and there were good tactical reasons for doing so and partly because when heavily burdened men are trying to move fast across country

---

A *plattdeutsch* German would use:
Dor sitt noch watt. Dor sitt noch watt.
Dor sitt, dor sitt, dor sitt noch watt.
Sitt nöch wött.
A translation of this: 'There is still something about' or, more freely, 'There are still enemies to be dealt with.'

their feet automatically take the lower paths. But whole groups of German divisions had sometimes been given a line of advance that angled sharply away from the apparent centre line of the attack. This was especially so for several miles on either side of the Flesquières Salient where the Germans were attempting to complete a massive encircling movement the base of which was twenty miles across. These are some of the reasons that British troops in positions that had not yet experienced a frontal attack so often found Germans in their rear. But this experience, which was to prove so demoralising for the British soldiers throughout the day, had another cause: this was the fanning-out of German follow-up units after the storm troops had forced the initial passages through the British front line.

So the German units moved up to fight for what remained of the British Forward Zone.

When we came into the open, the air was filled to such an extent with gas, cordite smoke and probably natural fog that visibility was barely three metres. I had left my rifle at the entrance to the dug-out; the stock was shattered, probably by a shell splinter. I left the useless thing where it was. I still had my hand grenades in case it came to a sticky situation. Already some groaning men lay in the trench unable to stand on their feet, overcome by gas. We put our blinker signal equipment and combat pack on our backs and held on to the next man, making a chain to keep together. Then we tried to move forward in the fog. This wasn't so easy. The ground was torn by shells and most difficult to negotiate. The first enemy trenches were about 600 metres away. We had, therefore, to toil hard to get over this distance. After some ten minutes I was completely exhausted. I pulled off my mask and staggered on by holding fast to my friend, Weber, the man in front of me. During a short stop I screwed the reserve filter into the mask and I think I obtained some relief from this. The density of the gas apparently lessened as it was soon possible to take off the mask for a few seconds. (Gefreiter Walther Jachmann, 418th Regiment)

We were surrounded by acrid cordite smoke and dense fog and could see only a few metres. The main orientation was only possible through the whizzing of our shells and the noticeable direction of the fire. Watch in hand, I was able at first to follow the creeping barrage with my light machine-gun section but, because of the increasing noise of the battle, it became more difficult to rely on the right direction by ear. After about 500 metres, tall, thin soldiers with broad-rimmed, flat steel helmets emerged from the thick fog. We didn't know who they were, having always had the French as opponents before. These men were all pitiful young Englishmen. They had no weapons and their raised arms indicated their surrender. Coming closer, one could see that their faces were marked by the terrible events of the last hours. I felt sorry for them, told our medical orderly to dress one who was badly wounded, and sent the lot to the rear without escort. (Leutnant Reinhold Spengler, 1st Bavarian Regiment)

The first encounters between the British soldiers manning the main defences in the Forward Zone and the advancing Germans were often a surprise for both sides. The fog still persisted in all sectors except those in the very north, where it was now starting to thin a little. The German storm troops, pushing on fast, suddenly found themselves in front of barbed wire which had not always been cut by the bombardment. The British had often not received word from the front line that the German infantry attack had even commenced and were rarely expecting the arrival of German troops so quickly. The fog was the big factor. Because the British defences here were all chosen with open approaches and good fields of fire, the Germans would have been seen at a distance on a clear day and would have come under the fire of the infantry weapons. Instead, there was often only a hesitant outbreak of firing and then the Germans usually disappeared again into the fog. They were simply following their tactical instructions to avoid the defended localities and infiltrate between them. The fog could not have suited the Germans better at this stage of the battle.

It was the duty of the German 'battle groups', following up behind the storm troops, to deal with these British positions. Sometimes the battle groups mounted an immediate assault but because so many of the positions were strongly held and in the form of redoubts with all-round defence, this fighting usually developed into a series of small sieges with German infantry first surrounding the redoubt and then the heavier weapons – machine-guns, mortars and, later, the mobile field guns – being brought up to reduce the British positions. These engagements were not the small affairs that had characterised the fights for the front line. The British positions usually held at least a company of defending infantry, supported by machine-guns and sometimes by mortars, and they had often not been hit too hard by the bombardment.

Three men – a German and two Englishmen – describe their experiences in this fighting.

We get through the first trenches and behind them we are in the open – an eerie stillness. Suddenly we get heavy machine-gun fire from a trench we hadn't discovered. Our artillery has moved its fire on to the enemy rear, giving these machine-guns a free hand. I estimate a distance of 500 to 600 metres. We fling ourselves down. I scream to my men, 'Defend yourselves. Otherwise you will be killed like hares. Range 600.' I shake a man next to me and shout, 'Shoot.' He doesn't move. He is dead. I kneel, in order to observe the hits on the ground from an enemy machine-gun not far away. My left shoulder gets a hard blow. I have been hit; blood flows from the sleeve. One of my men tears my tunic open and tries first aid. I manage to reach the nearest trench behind. It is crammed with reserve troops. There I come across my regimental commander; he wished me a speedy recovery. (Leutnant Hermann Wedekind, 79th Regiment)

Herr Wedekind was fighting against either the 9th Norfolks or the 2nd Durham Light Infantry, and this British soldier could not have been far away:

We were ordered to man the fire-step and I was told to pass the order along. There was a Lewis-gun team and one man in it said he wasn't going up; he was afraid. Out of the line he ran a Crown and Anchor board and always had a lot to say for himself, but he wasn't so brave then – the officer let him stay down in the trench to fill the pans with ammunition. A little later they were all killed, except the corporal in charge; he was in tears.

I took up my position and I could see the Germans quite easily, coming over a bank in large numbers about 200 to 300 yards away. They had already taken our front line. We opened fire and there appeared to be hundreds being killed coming over that bank but they might have just been lying down. Their attack was certainly halted. One German, dressed differently to the others, his uniform was more blue than the normal grey, kept coming in short rushes, dropping every time we fired and lying quiet for a little before coming on again. I think I fired at him four times and others were firing too, but he wasn't hit. He got within about fifty yards of us and then turned and went back in exactly the same way again without being hit.

There was a German sniper in a shell hole about 100 yards out and we could see the smoke from his rifle. I fired at him but I must have been high because I saw the dirt fly up from the back of the shell hole. He lay down for a bit then started firing again. This went on for about an hour but I didn't see any of our men hit and I think we hit him in the end because he stopped firing.

A hare came along and, like hares do, stopped and sat up right in front of us. I had a shot at him but missed. I wonder whether anyone else remembers that hare.

Then an officer came and said that the Germans were getting around us but, before anybody could leave the trench, the wounded had to be got away. Myself and another man were told to take one wounded man out on a stretcher. We gave him a rough passage but he thanked us later. (Private J. Jolly, 9th Norfolks)

This artilleryman, a signaller from an 18-pounder battery, was manning an observation post in the trenches of the 5th North Staffords near Bullecourt.

I think my officer knew that the Germans had broken through; he told me later that we were a 'sacrifice unit' and we had to stay there so that the others could get away. He started burning maps and smashing up everything that could be useful to the Germans. I had always been keen to get into the line, so here was my chance. I grabbed a rusty old rifle and fifty rounds of ammunition in cloth bandoliers and told him I was going up with the infantry. He said, 'All right, look after yourself.'

When I reached the trench there were a lot of dead and much of it had been flattened. I found two privates of the North Staffs – they were on the parapet firing. I should have thought there would have been more but I think the rest had hopped it but I can't be sure. These two never said anything to me or even looked round; they just went on firing. I stepped up between the two of them and started firing with them. There were a lot of Germans advancing two or three hundred yards in front of us. We fired at random but I can't remember seeing any of them falling. I should think we carried on like this for another twenty minutes and I fired most of my fifty rounds but we were lucky and there wasn't much fire coming at us until a burst of fire suddenly swept the parapet of the trench and I was hit by three bullets in the left arm; one of them smashed the bone in the upper arm. The other two men were hit as well and I remember calling out, 'Are you hurt, chums?' But there was no answer. They had both been hit in the stomach; I had to crawl out from under one of them. (Gunner F. W. Woodward, 296th Brigade R.F.A.)*

Many of the British positions in the area in which the battle was now taking place were very small ones. There were all manner of posts which were intended to form links in the defence system but the fog had left them as isolated islands, their small garrisons knowing nothing of the progress of the battle. The clashes between such posts and the advancing Germans were usually sudden and violent.

All of a sudden a Gordon came in the end of our trench – the Gordon Highlanders were in our front line. He was covered in blood and his face was completely expressionless, I reckon from shock. He looked half dead as though he just wanted to go somewhere and pass out. He went straight down into the dug-out and that was the last I saw of him.

I was looking over the top and could see forms in the mist. I turned and said, 'Eh, sergeant. They're coming.' My mate said, 'Ach. They're the Gordons.' 'Not in them tin hats,' I said. 'Shove that belt in.' We fired a few rounds but it was too misty to see how many we hit. Sergeant Webb was looking over the top when a sniper got him straight through the back of his windpipe. He put his first-aid pad over it and I lost sight of him. I have often wondered whether he survived.† Then three Germans rushed us from the left. One of them hit my mate across the head with his rifle butt. He had his steel helmet on but it still sounded like a drum and I saw my mate fall. I never saw him again either. I realised it was all over and was trying to get the lock out of the machine-gun to throw away when a German officer with a beard and his left arm in a sling came into the post from the right. I would like to meet that officer again. He was fierce and so correct, but he was human, and I reckon he stopped his men finishing me off. (Private W. H. Ware, 61st Machine Gun Battalion)

Another man was an observer in a divisional observation post.

* The name of the artillery observation officer with Mr Woodward was Lieutenant G. H. Philip, son of a Glasgow vicar. Lieutenant Philip was also captured and was the artillery officer who later kept up a correspondence over many years with Walter Junk, the German soldier from Hanover (see page 166).

† Sergeant Webb did not die of this wound.

We watched over the top – no movement, no rifle or machine-gun fire – don't seem to be coming this morning. Got a fire going to brew up and fry the bacon. I stood on the fire-step with my canteen and bread and bacon and my back to the front line, watching the heavy gunfire on the back areas. Quite casually I turned round to face the front line. 'Christ almighty. The bloody Jerries.' About eighty yards away there was a loose bunch of sixty to eighty Germans advancing towards us. I noticed they were big blokes and that they all had new uniforms.

I opened fire. The rest of the section knew then that it wasn't a leg-pull, mounted the fire-step and opened up rapid fire. We just couldn't miss with the K.A.P. ammo going right through, sometimes hitting the bloke behind.* They advanced steadily but with the caution of seasoned troops, with the exception of a few eager ones who were brought down first. We managed to get them down on the ground after about thirty yards, well out of 'tater-masher' range.† The lance corporal on my right had still got his bread and bacon sticking out the side of his mouth; he spat it out during a lull in the firing. Corporal Jago sent two men with all the maps and a report to Brigade H.Q., leaving the rest of us to carry on, shooting at any movement at all to keep them down and out of bomb range. If it was a wounded chap trying to help himself, that was just his bad luck – it was like they had us on the Somme. One Jerry did get up on his feet with a 'tater-masher' but before he threw it he was hit about four times. We didn't go to a sniping school for nothing. He went down and the bomb exploded among them and that kept them quiet. This pattern was kept up for hours.

To tell you the truth, I didn't want to die but I thought we were going to. I didn't think we were going to see the sunset but I remember thinking that, whatever they did to us, we had at least earned our bob that day. Mind you, we had no fancy ideas about fighting to the last man. (Private G. H. Leedham, 1st Leicesters)

*

The British positions in the main part of the Forward Zone soon began to fall, just as the front-line positions had fallen. The bombardment, the isolation in the fog, the overwhelming German strength, the weakness of the British defences, and, in some places perhaps, a tendency by some of the defenders to fall back or surrender – all these factors led

* K.A.P. is Kynoch Armour Piercing, a special sniper's ammunition.

† A German stick grenade, named after the potato-mashers used by housewives at that time.

to the fall of the British positions. They began to crumble first in the south of the Fifth Army's front, where the defending units were particularly weak. The extreme south of the front attacked was held by the 2/2nd Londons of the 58th Division. This battalion was attempting to defend a 6,000-yard sector in front of La Fère and along the Canal de l'Oise. A record has survived of the messages sent by the battalion commander, Lieutenant-Colonel A. R. Richardson, who was in one of the company 'keeps'. The Germans here had attacked well before their normal Zero Hour after bridging the canal under cover of darkness. The forward posts had fought hard but had soon been overwhelmed. These are the messages that came back from Lieutenant-Colonel Richardson.

6.30: All Keeps badly lumped [shelled]. Considerable trench-mortar activity. Will the two trench mortars taken from line the other day be sent up? Visibility very poor. In touch with nobody, except by runner, not even guns.

7.30: (by Fuller key) Main Keep almost surrounded.

7.45: Am not able to ascertain what has happened. Patrols out.

7.50: (by runner) Cannot ascertain situation. O.K. here. Cannot see more than a few yards.

8.00: O.K. at Keep. Cannot ascertain situation. Bomb and machine-gun fire on left. Patrols not yet returned.

8.10: Please sweep my left flank with machine-gun fire.

8.20: (to 18-pounder gun near quarry) Sweep my north flank. Bosche in communication trench between Brickstack and Keep.

8.50: (to Upshot [another keep]) Main Keep still holding.

8.50: (to Uphill) Still O.K. at Keep. Bosche in communication trench and part of wire on east face – I don't think in strength but cannot see 10 yards. Patrols sent out to flanks have not returned.

9.30: Bosche now in old H.Q. but appear lost in small parties. I think a counter-attack would easily drive them back. My casualties very heavy.

There were no more messages and the battalion's rear headquarters then recorded:

10.15: The Adjutant, Captain G. C. Seers, M.C., and 40 O.R.s constitute the remnants of the battalion. Company Sergeant-Major

H. M. Boag and these men withdrew to defend the Battle Zone with the 2/4th Londons.*

Some of this battalion's smaller posts held on for a few more hours and one did not fall until the evening of the following day, but Lieutenant-Colonel Richardson and approximately 500 of his men became prisoners. Six N.C.O.s and fifty-five privates – but no officers – were killed. The end of this battalion and its casualty list, with a high proportion of men becoming prisoners-of-war, was typical of many of the units defending the Forward Zone.

German soldiers taking part in this attack often say that they had little difficulty capturing positions in the British Forward Zone. The village of Fayet, just north of St Quentin, was held by part of the 2/8th Worcesters and was captured by a company from a Karlsruhe regiment.

We followed up the creeping barrage quickly but, as soon as we appeared, the British threw away their weapons and surrendered. There was really no fight for Fayet. I think they were hoping for an opportunity to surrender. One of them even gave me his razor. I think he wanted to thank me because he had been taken prisoner and not killed. I still have that razor and use it every day. I could have sold it but it still gives a very good shave.† My meeting with this man was soon over. I waved him back with my hands. I didn't know any English so I told him, '*Tout suite! Zurück!*' I was a prisoner myself four days later. (Gefreiter Wilhelm Reinhard, 109th Leib Grenadier Regiment)

Another post held by the 2/8th Worcesters proved more difficult to take.

We moved on steadily, encouraged by the feeble opposition. Small parties of enemy soldiers – from three to seven men – surrendered. They gave us cigarettes for which we gave them a friendly pat on the shoulder and sent them off to the rear. Then we came under heavy fire from a strong point in the ruins of the château in Selency. The fog had lifted by then. Our creeping barrage had missed this and we had fallen behind the barrage. We attacked one post here without success and then I found a way round to get at it from the rear. We tried six times in all and at last

---

* Public Record Office WO 95/3001.

† Herr Reinhard fetched this razor from his bathroom while he was being interviewed. It was made by Thomas Turner and Company of Sheffield.

captured it and the English defenders. There was a captain and one other officer and fourteen men. The captain was wounded and I took him to our dressing station where our doctor, an affable gentleman with the rank of major, dressed his wound. They had quite a talk. The captain said, 'We English always say that there's not enough room in the world for both us and the Germans and, now, here I am sharing a hole only a metre wide with a wounded German grenadier!'

Back at the firing line, the company was still at the same place, under heavy machine-gun fire from the château. Heavy mortars were brought up and these did the job. The defenders surrendered. (Feldwebel Hermann Gasser, 110th Grenadier Regiment)

This German platoon commander describes his advance and the capture of a company position of the 1st King's Own Shropshire Light Infantry which was in the Quéant sector many miles to the north on the Third Army front.

Our orders were very simple: 'Always forward and keep right up with the creeping barrage.' I noticed a minefield, which we avoided easily, and, in their front-line trench, a heap of bloody slime rose up in front of me – an English soldier, his eyes imploring. I had my pistol ready to put him out of his misery but somehow I couldn't. He fell back into the mud. A terrible end for him in this cruel war.

We went on farther against only feeble resistance but then the fog lifted and we were fired on by a machine-gun post. I got several bullets through my jacket but I was not hit. We all took cover. A few hundred metres to the right I saw the commander of the 3rd Battalion, Hauptmann von Wulffen. It was good to see him there. His trumpeter was next to him and he sounded the signal 'advance'. Trumpeters left and right followed suit. It was a most heartening sound. In long, loose lines we moved forward, looking like a picture of the old battlefields. A platoon from another company joined me and between us we killed the six or seven men – every one of them – in the machine-gun post. I lost five or six men in my platoon; I don't know what the other platoon lost. The whole action had taken about thirty minutes. I was thirsty so I went to one of the dead Englishmen and took his water bottle. It contained tea, not hot but still warm. It was marvellous. It must have been good because I can still remember it so well.

I looked across to the right and there were British prisoners going back. I estimate that there were about 120 – a company perhaps. They were stooping down and hurrying back to avoid being hit. I think that English position had been covered by the nest that we had just wiped out and this much larger number of enemy decided that they had better surrender. (Vizefeldwebel Max Gerchow, 89th Grenadier Regiment)

The end for some of the British positions came unexpectedly.

We were in action for some time and I think we hit many Germans. Then it went quiet and I thought that we had stopped them. I was loading another belt into the gun when I felt a bump in the back. I turned round and there was a German officer with a revolver in my back. 'Come along, Tommy. You've done enough.' I turned round then and said, 'Thank you very much, sir.' I know what I would have done if I had been held up by a machine-gunner and had that revolver in my hand. I'd have finished him off. He must have been a real gentleman. It was twenty minutes past ten; I know to the minute because I looked at my watch. (Private J. Parkinson, 16th Machine Gun Battalion)

This section, dealing with the positions in the Forward Zone that fell in the first phase of the fighting, started with the story of the 2/2nd Londons at La Fère. It can finish with the story of another battalion, this time many miles to the north, near Bullecourt. The 7th Sherwood Foresters was a Nottingham Territorial unit that had just been formed from an amalgamation of the 1/7th and 2/7th Battalions. The 1/7th had been an unlucky battalion, having been smashed up twice – once at the Hohenzollern Redoubt in the Battle of Loos in 1915 and again at Gommecourt on the first day of the Battle of the Somme the following year. The 2/7th had been in France for a year and had been in action at the Battle of Cambrai. The new battalion was now holding a sector of the 59th (North Midland) Division's defences, but there was not even a village near by to give their battle a name.

It is not really correct to write of a 'battalion action' because no battalion fought as a complete unit in the Forward Zone on that day. But there must have been something about this Nottingham unit to make its men perform better than the units around them. Their front was attacked at 9.40 a.m. and very little is known about how the fight went except that it lasted little longer than an hour. Two wounded officers and twelve men found their way back before the battalion was surrounded. The Official History several times describes units as being 'overwhelmed' and this is just what happened to the 7th Sherwood Foresters. The registers of the Commonwealth War Graves Commission and the battalion's own history published after the war are in close agreement over the fact that twelve officers, forty N.C.O.s and 119 men were killed, leaving twelve officers and 470 men, many wounded, to become prisoners. The figure of 171 dead for this battalion is far higher than that of any other British battalion on that day.

*

So swift was the German advance that few men from many of the British forward units ever got back to the Battle Zone but there were exceptions. The garrisons of some of the smaller posts sometimes made off in good time, and there are several reports of leaderless bodies of men straggling through to the rear and German reports of positions found empty or, like the position captured in front of St Quentin, which contained 'only one rather drunk corporal, apparently from the stores. He had stayed behind too long and missed the bus.' The question of more substantial retirements by complete units from the Forward Zone is an interesting one. In theory there were the 'Officers Commanding Front-Line System' who had authority to order a retirement but, presumably, only on brigade orders. There were few brigade commanders who ever knew what was happening in their Forward Zones at this time, let alone who were prepared to permit a withdrawal before the battle was even two hours old. The retirements that did take place at this time were usually the result of spontaneous decisions by small bodies of men who had decided that the fight was as good as over in their sector and that the only alternatives were surrender or a dash to the rear.

We kept up a rapid fire as they advanced but there were so many of them and we seemed so pitifully few. In the heat of the attack I was nearly shot by my comrade on the left. He suddenly saw a party of Germans bombing their way from the right, swung his rifle round and fired, and the bullet burned my ear as it passed. But now we could do no more. A lot of our chaps put up their hands and surrendered but we decided to fall back to our reserve positions, a decision which I am afraid cost many of our men their lives because we were under shell and machine-gun fire as we fell back.

I particularly remember, as I passed one shell hole, seeing one of our lads, who was small of stature but was always most cheerful, lying there with both his legs shot through. Our sergeant, a tall Irishman, dropped into the shell hole beside him but I do not think he would have been able to do much for him. It is a tragedy to be badly wounded in a retreat because, naturally, the enemy attend to their own wounded first. Then I came across a lad of my own section. He had taken a burst of shrapnel in his legs and could not walk. With the help of another lad, we carried him out of the action. He wrote to me afterwards from a hospital in Liverpool thanking us for saving him. As he put it, he would never have got away and would have fallen into enemy hands. He had nineteen wounds in his legs. (Lance Corporal T. Fetch, 2/6th South Staffords)

The attitude to the question of retirement of two neighbouring battalion commanders in the Forward Zone of the 6th Division is perhaps typical of the difficulties encountered under the stress of the fierce German attack that morning and also reveals the reluctance by some officers to contemplate withdrawal. This story is made up by studying the War Diaries of the two battalions concerned and also the account of one ordinary soldier, a battalion runner, who took his own private decision to save himself. His testimony fits in well with the facts recorded in the War Diaries.

Lieutenant-Colonel A. St J. Blunt commanded the 2nd York and Lancasters. His front-line company had suffered heavily in the bombardment and only fifteen men came back from it. Then the two companies defending the right of the battalion's support positions were seen to surrender *en masse*. Lieutenant-Colonel Blunt later recorded that 'the garrison surrendered without fighting, being plainly visible leaving the trench with their hands up as the enemy approached. This left my left flank exposed.'* Blunt decided that he must retire with what was left of his battalion and sent a message

---

* The War Diaries of the two battalions are in the Public Record Office: 2nd York and Lancasters – WO 95/1610; 1st King's Shropshire Light Infantry – WO 95/1609. Despite their title, the York and Lancasters were a Yorkshire regiment only.

to the battalion on his left – the 1st King's Shropshire Light Infantry.

This battalion was commanded by Lieutenant-Colonel H. M. Smith, an officer who had already lost one eye in an earlier action. Private Thomas Link was one of his runners.

Another runner had come down from the York and Lancs to our relay post between the forward positions and battalion head-quarters and he told our colonel that the message was that we had to retreat. Colonel Smith said, 'There is no such damned word in the British Army as "retreat". I've lost one eye for one medal and I'll lose the other for the V.C.' Then he told me to come with him. He led the way with a revolver in each hand. I followed him down this trench and then we reached the junction with a trench from the left which Gerry had covered. As we went past the opening of this, a bullet came 'ping' in between us. The Colonel said, 'That's bad aim on your part, Gerry.' I let him go on a few more yards down the trench towards where we could plainly hear the fighting. I didn't say a word to him but turned back. I knew I might be shot as a deserter but I would have been shot or taken prisoner if I had gone on. I went back to where I had started from but the others there had gone. I was left on my own but I caught them up later.

The Shropshire's War Diary states:

The great majority of the battalion under Lieutenant-Colonel H. M. Smith, D.S.O., were surrounded and decided to fight it out to the last.

Lieutenant-Colonel Smith and over 400 men of his battalion became prisoners; thirty-three men were killed. The York and Lancaster casualties were ninety-nine men killed – mostly in a stand they made later in the day – and over 300 taken prisoner. The combined strength of the two battalions at the end of the day was 101 men.

*

The Shropshire and the York and Lancaster battalions were in the Third Army's line, well to the north of the Flesquières Salient. The area in which they fought had been held by the British for many months and the Forward Zone here was made up of the usual front-line, support and reserve trench systems that had served the British Expeditionary

Force well through three years of trench warfare. But the area south of the Flesquières Salient had been French until recently and was now only weakly held by the British. As described earlier, the Forward Zone here consisted of the outpost line, which had fallen at the first German rush, and then the line of redoubts or keeps. The German advance had soon reached these positions but the storm troops had usually swung away into the empty spaces between and had carried on towards the Battle Zone leaving the follow-up units to deal with the by-passed positions. The remainder of this chapter will describe the situation in the larger of the redoubts during the first phase of the battle. There were also many smaller posts holding out and some of these will be looked at, but records about the experiences of these small posts are not usually available, and even if they were there would not be space to deal with them all here.

The reader may care to remember two things that were common to all these actions. Firstly, they were all on the southern part of the battle area, where the fog was thickest and most persistent. More important, though, is the fact that the British Expeditionary Force had never before fought a defensive battle in defences such as these and was never to do so again. Fighting on in isolated positions with no hope of relief was an entirely new experience for the British soldiers involved. These men were all in units of General Gough's Fifth Army.

Fifth Army's sector started on the southern edge of the Flesquières Salient. The division in the line here was the 9th (Scottish), but it was only the South African Infantry Brigade, holding the right of the divisional front, that was seriously attacked. Gauche Wood, held by a company of the 2nd South Africans, was the first position to be assaulted, and no more need be said about the fight here than that the South Africans fought hard until pushed out of the wood about midday, with only forty out of the 130 men who had formed the South African garrison not having been killed or wounded. The Germans did not press any further.

To the south of the South Africans was the sector held by the 21st Division, which had two strong natural defensive positions: Chapel Hill on the left and the village of Epéhy on

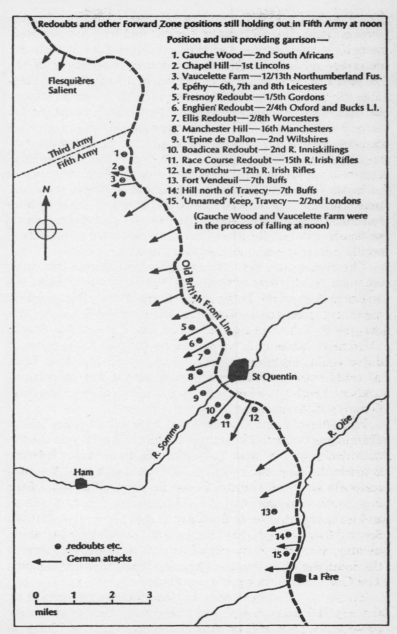

Redoubts and other Forward Zone positions still holding out in Fifth Army at noon

Position and unit providing garrison—

1. Gauche Wood—2nd South Africans
2. Chapel Hill—1st Lincolns
3. Vaucelette Farm—12/13th Northumberland Fus.
4. Epéhy—6th, 7th and 8th Leicesters
5. Fresnoy Redoubt—1/5th Gordons
6. Enghien Redoubt—2/4th Oxford and Bucks L.I.
7. Ellis Redoubt—2/8th Worcesters
8. Manchester Hill—16th Manchesters
9. L'Epine de Dallon—2nd Wiltshires
10. Boadicea Redoubt—2nd R. Inniskillings
11. Race Course Redoubt—15th R. Irish Rifles
12. Le Pontchu—12th R. Irish Rifles
13. Fort Vendeuil—7th Buffs
14. Hill north of Travecy—7th Buffs
15. 'Unnamed' Keep, Travecy—2/2nd Londons

(Gauche Wood and Vaucelette Farm were in the process of falling at noon)

Flesquières Salient

Third Army
Fifth Army

N

Old British Front Line

St Quentin

R. Somme

R. Oise

Ham

La Fère

● redoubts etc.
◄── German attacks

0   1   2   3
miles

Map 4

the right. Between these two positions was Vaucelette Farm, whose natural situation was not so favourable. This sector of the British defences was a particularly important one because it was through here that the Germans were intending to drive the southern arm of their encirclement of the Flesquières Salient. (Official maps will show that all three of these positions were supposed to be in the Battle Zone but this was a sector where the Forward Zone was almost non-existent – Vaucelette Farm, for example, was only 500 yards behind the front line – and these positions can be safely included in this description of redoubt fighting.)

Chapel Hill, held by the 1st Lincolns, was the scene of fierce fighting and the Germans gained part of the hill, but then the Lincolns were reinforced by the 4th South Africans – the South African Scottish – who came down from the north to help hold the remainder of this important position. This reinforcing move is the only example of a forward position receiving help in this way and it took place only because Chapel Hill was technically in the Battle Zone. The general rule that Forward Zone positions were not to be aided still held good.

Vaucelette Farm, held by part of the 12/13th Northumberland Fusiliers, was in a valley between Chapel Hill and Epéhy. The garrison held out for two hours, but the Germans were determined to push through this valley. They brought up mortars and eventually took the farm from the rear at about midday. The fog then lifted and the German units advancing up the valley became visible to the Lincolns and South Africans on Chapel Hill and to the garrison of Epéhy on the other side of the valley. Very heavy casualties were caused to the Germans advancing up the valley and their advance halted abruptly. This was exactly the type of defence for which redoubts were intended – the domination of the ground around them – but the timely lifting of the fog here was not repeated farther south.

The defence of Epéhy itself was one of the most important actions of the day. A sensible order by the divisional commander, Major-General 'Soarer' Campbell, had resulted in the front-line trenches being evacuated an hour before dawn and only small parties of men had been left there to keep watch. This man had been in one of these look-out posts but he had been able to get back to the main position.

Back on the fire-step with our company, we felt more secure. With a good trench and plenty of ammunition, we wondered, as we peered into the fog, what lay ahead. We hadn't long to wait. The fog became less dense, the sun broke through and almost at once the fog cleared, revealing an amazing sight. The foremost of the enemy infantry, completely disorganised by the fog, were trying to get sorted out. Not far behind them came several platoons of infantry, moving forward in solid blocks, four men abreast. Behind them were groups of cavalry [probably horse artillery and mounted officers] coming on at walking pace and, farther behind, about 600 yards away, were horse-drawn general service wagons and horse-drawn ambulances. It was like a panorama on huge canvas and we simply couldn't believe it.

The Germans were moving forward as if they expected no opposition. We opened fire. The Lewis guns got busy and the enemy groups scattered. They had very little cover and no chance of survival . . . After a while nothing was moving throughout the whole visible front except for a few riderless horses, terrified by the shooting. We could hear the screams of stricken horses; I was glad when they eventually galloped away from the scene. We watched, but there was no sign of any further attack and we wondered what had been going on on our right flank.

Looking to our right, we could see Jerry troops steadily making their way into territory we had been told was held by the 16th Irish Division. About half a mile to our right, we could see the Germans moving forward in single file and many were already well behind us. It was not yet midday. Jerry was moving as if there was no opposition and we reckoned we were in real trouble on the flank. (Lance Corporal S. T. North, 7th Leicesters)

This man's description sums up the position at Epéhy admirably. There were no fewer than three battalions, the 6th, 7th and 8th Leicesters, in and around Epéhy, and because of the decision to evacuate the front line early, casualties in the preliminary bombardment had not been heavy. Although the Germans had made a deep penetration on the right, Epéhy itself stood quite firm. German soldiers who fought here that morning tell a sorry story of various setbacks. The gas in the German bombardment had blown back in particularly heavy quantities here and had badly affected the German infantry. There was also much confusion caused by the fog and by the British counter-shelling, and this delayed the deployment of the attacking German units. These units had then been further confused by the empty British front line and, finally, the fog had lifted to expose them to the fire of three well-positioned battalions of infantry and to the view of the artillery observation officers in Epéhy.

Epéhy was unusual in that the fog had lifted early around an extremely strong position which the Germans failed to encircle. There was no such good fortune for any of the other Fifth Army redoubts, all of which were held by no more than half a battalion and around which the fog persisted long enough for the Germans to complete an encirclement before the defenders could do anything effective with their weapons.

The Irish units south of Epéhy had fared badly. It was here that the corps commander had ordered – against the wishes of the divisional commander – that a large proportion of the infantry battalions be posted in the Forward Zone defences. General Gough had backed the corps commander but this policy had played right into the hands of the Germans; the Irish battalions had suffered heavily from the initial bombardment and their positions had been quickly overrun. Only one redoubt, at Malassise Farm, had held for any time. Its garrison was provided by the 2nd Royal Munster Fusiliers under Lieutenant W. S. Kidd. The only account of what happened in the Forward Zone came from a report written by a brother officer while he was in a prison camp at Holzminden in Germany. This account was written on small sheets of cigarette paper and was somehow smuggled back to England. It told how Malassise Farm was overwhelmed about 11 a.m. with Lieutenant Kidd being severely wounded. He died later in the day.

There were few redoubts in the area of the next two divisions. No Man's Land was very narrow here and the Forward Zone defences were in the form of front, support and reserve trench lines. These positions were held by the Second-Line Territorial battalions of the 66th (East Lancs) Division and by the 24th Division. The front-line battalions did not last long – the headquarters of one, the 2/8th

Lancashire Fusiliers, near a position known as Malakoff Farm, was surprised and taken prisoner by the Germans before anyone there even knew that the German infantry attack had commenced!

Next there came a chain of redoubts which all experienced similar fortunes during the morning. They formed the backbone of the defences in the Forward Zone of five divisions over a distance of seventeen miles north and south of St Quentin. At least eleven redoubts can be identified as still holding out at midday. The names of these and of the battalions which provided their garrisons are: Fresnoy Redoubt (1/5th Gordon Highlanders), Enghien Redoubt (2/4th Oxford and Bucks Light Infantry), Ellis Redoubt (2/8th Worcesters), Manchester Hill (16th Manchesters), L'Epine de Dallon (2nd Wiltshires), Boadicea Redoubt (2nd Royal Inniskilling Fusiliers), Race Course Redoubt (15th Royal Irish Rifles), Le Pontchu (12th Royal Irish Rifles),* Fort Vendeuil and another position, unnamed, near by (7th Buffs), and an unnamed keep in Travecy held by part of the 2/2nd Londons. Most of these positions contained at least a company of men and the local battalion commander was usually in the redoubt also.

In every case the Germans had come through in the fog and encircled the redoubt but had been unwilling to mount serious attacks until the fog cleared and their mortars and light field guns had been brought up. There was nothing that the defenders of the redoubts could do in the interval but exchange a little fire with the Germans who were watching them. As long as the fog persisted, the British could do little to engage the masses of German infantry pushing on through the big gaps between neighbouring redoubts; the many smaller British posts in these gaps had been swept away long ago. It was just as though the redoubts were a line of sand-castles on a beach, with an incoming tide washing around them and on farther up the beach. But the tide would not turn here. There would only be more and more Germans and there could be no relieving attacks by the British from

* The 12th and 15th Royal Irish Rifles were originally the Central Antrim and the North Belfast Battalions of the Ulster Volunteer Force when that organisation became the 36th (Ulster) Division in Kitchener's New Army.

their main position because such attacks were not part of the British plan of defence.

These surviving redoubts, from Chapel Hill down to the keep with no name at Travecy, represented the only pockets of resistance left after the first ninety minutes of fighting in the Forward Zones of the Third and Fifth Armies. Their fate will be described in a later chapter.

8

Review at 11 a.m.

The time at which co-ordinated resistance by the British units in their Forward Zones ended is a convenient place to pause and leave the detailed description of the infantry battle. This will be the first of two 'review' chapters which will give a summary of the position at the end of a distinct phase of the battle and will also describe the activities of some of the less obvious of the participants in the battle. It must be stressed that this is a somewhat artificial means of bringing in certain material that would otherwise impede the smooth flow of the 'action' chapters. There were no such pauses in the fighting on that day in March 1918, nor were there such clear-cut phases in the battle. Not many men on the battlefield knew when the fight for the Forward Zone ended and that for the Battle Zone began. There was fighting in several parts of the Battle Zone well before 11 a.m. but, again for literary expediency, the full description of that can be given later.

*

This first summary of the battle's progress need not be a complicated or lengthy one. The German success in sweeping away the British front-line defences so completely and over such a long stretch of front was a unique achievement by First World War standards. For eleven miles, as the trench lines ran, north of the Flesquières Salient and for thirty-eight miles south of it, the British Forward Zone defences no longer existed, except for the stand made by the defenders at Chapel Hill and Epéhy and in the isolated redoubts and keeps in the south. There had been no initial success like this in any other battle on the Western Front since the trench lines had been formed at the end of the campaigns of movement late in 1914. It is true that the British defence had been considerably hindered by the widespread fog and that the British had never intended to make this their main line of defence, but this initial German success was still a major one.

The most important aspect of the German gains, however, would not become apparent until later. This was the extent of the loss to the British of fighting units. It is fairly easy to calculate the proportion of General Byng's and General Gough's forces that were no longer available. Because the German advance had been so swift and because so few of the British front-line defenders had been able to get back, the British Third and Fifth Armies had lost approximately forty-seven battalions of their infantry. The proportion of the men in these battalions who had been killed was not high; most were prisoners or were tied down in the positions that still held out, but all were as good as completely lost to the British commanders. This loss was the equivalent of almost one fifth of the total fighting strength of the British divisions facing the German attack. The position in Gough's Fifth Army was particularly serious. He had lost thirty-two battalions in the front line and six and a half more battalions had become isolated south of the River Oise. These would have to retreat with the French and would not rejoin their parent division until this battle was over. Even counting in that part of the cavalry divisions which would fight as infantry, Gough had lost thirty per cent of his effective infantry in the first hour and a half of a battle that would rage for sixteen days! If these huge losses had occurred during the course of a prolonged fight in the Forward Zone with the infliction of a great number of casualties on the Germans and the breaking-up of the momentum of the attack, then the loss might not have been too serious to the British cause. But nothing of this sort had happened. The German units were still largely intact and were sweeping on to the next line of British defences. This clear advantage in casualties in favour of the Germans was the main result of the first phase of the day's fighting.

There was one part of the British line which stood like an island while the defences on either side of it were being overrun. The Germans had made no serious assault against the eleven miles of trenches in the Flesquières Salient, hoping to capture the entire salient and its garrison by a wide encircling movement. The salient had been heavily bombarded and gassed and then there had been several

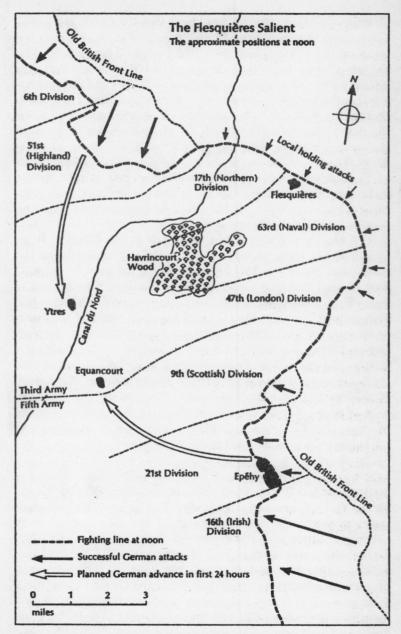

The Flesquières Salient
The approximate positions at noon

Old British Front Line

6th Division

51st (Highland) Division

17th (Northern) Division

Local holding attacks

Flesquières

63rd (Naval) Division

Havrincourt Wood

47th (London) Division

Ytres

Canal du Nord

Equancourt

9th (Scottish) Division

Third Army
Fifth Army

21st Division

Epéhy

Old British Front Line

16th (Irish) Division

- - - - Fighting line at noon

⬅ Successful German attacks

⇦ Planned German advance in first 24 hours

0   1   2   3
miles

Map 5

German holding attacks on the salient's front line. The Germans had got into the British trenches at some points but were mostly evicted, and the attacks were all being held. The British troops here thought they had done well and had beaten off a major German attack. What they did not know – nor did the German soldiers who fought and died here – was that these attacks were all part of a gigantic bluff. The Germans did not want to push the British troops back out of the salient but neither did they want the British to withdraw. The attacks were pressed with just the correct amount of persistence to keep the British engaged, although the inclusion of mustard-gas shells in the preliminary bombardment should have told the British commanders that no serious attack was contemplated here.

The reader will recall that Haig had urged General Byng to withdraw from the Flesquières Salient well before the battle, but that Byng had been unwilling to give up ground won at heavy cost by his army in the Battle of Cambrai. The defending troops were still manning a position that had always been an unfavourable and exposed one and was now becoming progressively more so as each hour passed. General Byng was still making no move to pull his units out of the salient. The German plan was to complete the encirclement within the first twenty-four hours of the battle. If this ambitious plan succeeded, there were the makings here of a humiliating setback for the British with the prospect of three full divisions and elements of two more being cut off behind the German advance.

*

As long as the fog stopped most of the Royal Flying Corps planes from operating effectively, the various British headquarters were completely dependent for information upon messages filtering back from the fighting area and then finding their way up the chain of command. The big problem at this time was that few reliable messages had reached brigade headquarters from the Forward Zone; their War Diaries contain many references to their difficulties. A few fortunate brigades still had uncut telephone lines to their forward battalions and some even had wireless links, but most had to rely upon an occasional message coming in by carrier pigeon or runner, or a report given by a lightly wounded officer who had managed to come back from the front line. But brigade and divisional staffs on the Western Front were used to dealing with such confused situations, and the information that was being passed back to corps and army had soon started to make sense.

General Byng never wrote a book and had no books written about him. There is thus little record of what transpired in his headquarters in Albert other than a few brief entries in his General Staff's War Diary.

General Gough's day, however, is well documented. At his headquarters at Nesle, fifteen miles behind the front, Gough had been woken by the distant roar of the German bombardment and he realised that 'it was so sustained and steady that it at once gave me the impression of some crushing, smashing power'.* Reports had soon come in to say that the entire length of his army north of the River Oise and also part of the Third Army were being bombarded. The extent of the German attack was a shock to Gough, as it was to other British commanders. For Gough it meant that virtually the whole of his weak army was in action and that he could not 'thin out' any safe sector to help others. Support could only come from outside.

Gough went back to sleep for an hour, then got up, had breakfast and prepared to handle the greatest battle of his career. He had brought all of his own reserves well forward before the battle; all that remained at hand were the two G.H.Q. reserve divisions behind his front. To Gough's relief, G.H.Q. immediately released these for use. One, the 20th (Light) Division, was close behind the front and would be in action before the day was out but the second, the 50th (Northumbrian), was twenty-five miles back. This was the division that Gough had previously asked G.H.Q. to move nearer the front, but the request had been refused by Haig's Chief of Staff, General Sir Herbert Lawrence. But there must have been some swift staff work now because the 50th Division moved at once and, although it had to cross the narrow bridges over the River Somme to reach the front, the

* These quotations and details are from *The Fifth Army*, pages 260–62.

division would be fully deployed for action by 8 a.m. the next morning.

When Gough had rung G.H.Q. to ask for these two reserve divisions, he had spoken not to Haig, who was being briefed by Lawrence, but to Major-General J. H. Davidson, head of the Operations Section. Gough pointed out that even with the two reserve divisions the position of his army would still be extremely vulnerable and he asked when he might expect to receive further troops from the two strong armies to the north, neither of which was under attack. Davidson replied that five divisions were being moved *but that the first four of these had been allocated to the Third Army and Gough's first reinforcement would not arrive until three days later!* Here was Haig sticking rigidly to his policy of holding his north and centre at all costs and deliberately risking his south. It remained to be seen whether the French, on Gough's immediate right, would fulfil their promise to support the Fifth Army now that the Germans had attacked.

Gough fretted at his headquarters for the rest of the morning. He nearly set out for a tour of his four corps head-quarters but it was too early for this so he stayed put, working with his staff on plans to scrape up makeshift fighting units from reinforcement camps and administrative units of the Fifth Army. Reports came in from the corps commanders telling of heavy fighting in the Forward Zone. Gough would soon find out that the Forward Zone defences had not delayed the Germans long.

In his office in the French army barracks at Montreuil, a quiet little town near the coast, Sir Douglas Haig also studied the first reports of the fighting. For all his long experience in command, this was the first defensive battle that Haig had handled since he had been a corps commander in the retreat from Mons in 1914. His diary entries for this day are scant and formal. He reveals nothing whatever of his thoughts during that morning. From the decisions taken that day at G.H.Q., it is probable that Haig's attitude was a mixture of calmness and complacency. It is unlikely that he had any conception of the huge loss of men suffered by the forward battalions of both of his armies that were under attack or that the Germans were coming on so fast. None of Haig's

1. Sir Douglas Haig, Commander-in-Chief of the British Expeditionary Force.
2. Sir Hubert Gough, Commander of the British Fifth Army.
3. The German High Command. Field Marshal von Hindenburg, Kaiser Wilhelm and General von Ludendorff. The Kaiser was half British by birth and was a cousin of King George V. Ludendorff was the brains and driving force behind the *Kaiserschlacht* battles.

4. St Quentin, the front-line town. This photograph, taken by the crew of an R.E.8 plane of No. 52 Squadron on 9 March 1918, shows the comparatively undamaged town with the cathedral top left. The German front-line trench can be seen only a few yards in front of the outskirts of the town. The road in No Man's Land, bottom centre, ran into the British lines held by the 30th Division.

5. This picture, taken on 15 March, also by No. 52 Squadron, shows, on the left, the new and curious shapes that perplexed the British. They were the dumps of ammunition left in readiness for the German guns that would be brought up just before the battle commenced. The well-dug German reserve trench down the centre of the picture is a good example of a First World War trench.

6. German transport and troops in the streets of St Quentin.
7. One of the five captured British Mark IV tanks, used by the Germans in the attack on 21 March, seen in St Quentin before the battle.

8. German storm troops. It is unfortunate that the Germans do not seem to have sent up any official cameramen to photograph their great attack on 21 March. This picture was taken later in 1918 but shows typical storm troops advancing to the attack with grenades in their hands and rifles slung.

9. The German caption to this photograph says that the Scottish and the German soldier have both died by poison gas. Someone has taken the good quality boots of the Scottish soldier.

10. Battlefield scene near Savy on 22 March. The British 18-pounder field guns were probably dragged out of their gun-pits (left) during the previous day's action to allow their crews to handle their guns more freely. Behind the German stretcher party is Holnon Wood, and the guns had belonged to either the 30th or the 61st (South Midland) Division. The dry, firm ground that helped the German advance is clearly visible.
11. British, and possibly German, dead in a captured British trench. Also to be seen are a British rifle, a Lewis gun, circular 'pans' of Lewis-gun ammunition and the camouflage netting that had concealed this typical Battle Zone trench from aerial observation.

12. A column of captured British soldiers, probably in St Quentin. The long column, four men wide and disappearing into the mist, gives an idea of the large number of unwounded British soldiers taken prisoner.

13. A completely shelterless collecting 'cage' where the British prisoners had to spend the first few nights of captivity.

14. A mixed party of British prisoners being fed by the Germans. These men were probably from Third Army units; the caption says they were captured in front of Bapaume. The curious headwear seen on some men are the 'liners' of steel helmets, the helmets having been removed to serve as dishes for the German stew. The woollen headwear seen on other men are 'cap-comforters'.

15. German prisoners. The best the British could muster for their cameraman; note the 'coal-scuttle' type helmets.

16. Walking wounded. Two men of the 66th (East Lancs) Division.
17. Lightly wounded British soldiers in a special ambulance train brought into service to clear large numbers of such wounded from the Casualty Clearing Stations back to the Base Hospitals. The train has stopped just outside Amiens for refreshments to be distributed.

18. Casualty Clearing Station. It was at medical units such as this, just beyond the range
of German guns, that seriously wounded men received their first surgical attention.
Some C.C.S.s specialised in certain types of wound and many of the men here seem to be
head wound cases; they are now awaiting evacuation. These are mostly men from Third
Army units at a C.C.S. near Bapaume on 22 March.

19. The remnants of a battalion. King George V inspects the few men of the 7th Sherwood
Foresters who survived the battle. 630 men had gone into action on 21 March. 171 were
killed – the highest battalion loss of the day; only fourteen men remained unwounded at
the end of the day. Just behind the King are Lt-Col R. B. Rickman and Capt. W. Foster,
officers who were not present at the 21 March battle and who later rebuilt the battalion.

20. The 'Golden Virgin' of Albert basilica, probably photographed by the Germans immediately after they captured the town on 26 March.

21. The tower of the basilica, deliberately destroyed by British guns to prevent the Germans using it as an observation position. It had been a legend among Allied soldiers that the war would end only when the statue of the Virgin fell.

W9573—GD1900 11,000 2/19 HWV(P898) H8064

WAR OFFICE,

LONDON, S.W.1.

April 1919

/Arty C/1598 A.G.3 (P.W.)

The Secretary of the War Office presents his compliments

to   2nd Lieutenant W. H. Crowder

Royal Field Artillery

and begs to state that he is commanded by the Army Council to

inform him that his statement regarding the circumstances of

his capture by the enemy having been investigated, the Council

considers that no blame attaches to him in the matter.

The investigation was carried out by a Standing Committee

of Enquiry composed as follows :—

Major-General L. A. E. PRICE-DAVIES, V.C., C.M.G., D.S.O.

Brigadier-General C. R. J. GRIFFITH, C.B., C.M.G., D.S.O.

Brevet-Lieut.-Col. E. L. CHALLENOR, C.B., C.M.G., D.S.O.

22. Every captured British officer had to explain the circumstances of his capture when he returned to England after the war. 2nd Lt Crowder was an artillery Forward Observation Officer captured in the trenches of the 51st (Highland) Division on 21 March 1918. The three officers on the Standing Committee had all served as brigade commanders on the Western Front during the war.

23. Vadencourt British Cemetery, a typical War Graves Commission cemetery in the battle area. This had been in the Battle Zone positions of the 9th East Surreys, 24th Division, on 21 March. Very few of the March 1918 men have proper graves, although that of Lt-Col Dimmer, V.C., killed near here leading a counter-attack on horseback, is in this cemetery.

24. The Arras Memorial to the Missing. The memorials to the men of the Third and Fifth Armies who have no known grave were both placed inside existing British war cemeteries because the French Government were concerned that too many special memorials were being erected on the battlefields. The panels of this memorial list the names of 34,924 British soldiers who were killed around Arras, mostly with the Third Army, in the years 1916–18. The names nearest the camera are from the 63rd (Naval) Division.

previous attacks, on much smaller frontages and after longer bombardments, had ever been able to develop so quickly.

Winston Churchill, according to his memoirs, had woken at the headquarters of the 9th (Scottish) Division behind the Flesquières Salient just before the German bombardment had opened. One German gun, nicknamed 'Percy' by the divisional staff, steadily dropped heavy shells only 100 yards from the headquarters dug-outs, but Britain's Second World War leader was not hurt. Churchill realised that he was in the way and left by car at 10 a.m. He called briefly at G.H.Q. but wisely decided that he could do no good here either and thus passes from this story.

*

The artillery was the most important of the various arms supporting the British infantry, and many of the gunners had been in hectic action. The most forward artillerymen were the gunners manning the 18-pounder guns posted for anti-tank purposes in the Forward Zone and the officers and signallers who were in observation posts near the British front line, attempting to direct the fire of the main batteries farther back.

Few records have survived of the fate of the anti-tank guns. There is no record at all of any encounter between these guns and the handful of German tanks being used. The 18-pounders and their crews had little chance in the thick fog and most of them were quickly overwhelmed. There were examples of the gun crews briefly engaging infantry with small-arms fire and in one or two places the fog was thin enough for the guns to be fired at close range at the advancing Germans. It is recorded that one such gun in the 16th (Irish) Division fired 175 of the 200 rounds of ammunition with the gun and were seen stood ready to fire the last twenty-five rounds when the Germans came again. Nothing further was heard of this gun. But such resistance was usually brief and the gunners had soon been killed or captured. The view taken before the battle that these guns and their crews were expendable was a correct one. Approximately 100 guns – nine per division – were lost in this way.

A good artillery observation officer could cause heavy

casualties to be inflicted by gunfire if he could see clearly to direct that fire, if his telephone line to the gun position remained intact, and if the infantry in the trenches around his Observation Post could defend their positions. Very few artillery observers in the British front line had any of these benefits that morning and they had been unable to contribute anything useful to the battle. Some of the more experienced of them had realised this and abandoned their O.P.s, a few were killed and many became prisoners-of-war. Here are the experiences of two of the observation officers.

I had only left Bristol Grammar School O.T.C. the previous May and I joined my 4·5-inch howitzer battery opposite St Quentin on 1st March, a very raw subaltern just 19 years old. Until 21st March I barely heard an enemy gun fired. I was sharing an O.P. with a heavy artillery officer and our signallers. The 'Heavy' and I took turns to watch, the other resting below. I was sleeping there when, at about 5.20, the 'Heavy' came down to rouse me as there was heavy firing. I went up and joined him. Then he disappeared downstairs, came up with his belongings, and said he was off!

My line to the battery was cut, there was some mist, and a smell of gas. Not knowing the way back through the wire and ingenuously assuming this to be an ordinary shelling and that I should stay on duty the full 24 hours and try to get my telephone line repaired in due course, I stayed put.

When the bombardment ceased I ventured up into the narrow, shallow trench and came face to face with a Jerry who had just arrived on the edge of the trench. I was unarmed, my revolver being in my valise at the battery, so little did my C.O. prepare me for what might be coming! He dropped on his knee and fired at my head from about four feet. I sensed the bullet skim my helmet and saw the spurt of mud as it buried itself in the trench side a few inches before my eyes. Instinctively I ducked and, being on the top step of the staircase, skidded to the bottom. I am not brave and confess that I was 'windy' lest a grenade be thrown down. But this did not happen.

One of the Tommies suggested there could be a counter-attack to save us and, in my inexperience, I accepted this as a brilliant idea. So we lay doggo. Then there was shouting and the sound of a machine-gun and, eventually, an apparently inebriated Jerry came down the staircase waving a pistol. There was nothing for it but to surrender. (Second Lieutenant G. K. Stanley, 307th Brigade R.F.A.)

I had always imagined that I should see some sort of fight in front of us with our men fighting the Germans but it was so misty and I had to wear one of those horrible gas-masks that I saw nothing – just an occasional figure. I kept bobbing up and observing and then bobbing down and reporting. I could just see a few figures in the mist but couldn't tell which side they were on. Then machine-gun bullets came over our heads and I reported this.

After some time there were signs of visitors in the trench above us. I could hear rifle bolts and rifles being fired, but in the wrong direction, so we reported this to brigade. 'They're here,' we told them. This was most valuable to them for they knew exactly where the Germans were – in Gosling O.P. Brigade ordered us to hang on as long as possible and keep reporting and to cut the wire at the last moment. We carried on like this for about ten minutes – we could hear the Germans talking up top. I had a last look and could see them and went down to give the last report – 'They're coming over in thousands.' The weather was clear by then.

Then there was a loud bang on the steps; the Germans had thrown a stick bomb down. We'd had enough by then and the young subaltern who had been sent up to help me could talk a little German so I told him to shout up and tell them we were surrendering. I felt ghastly at this stage, that I had let the side down. For days afterwards I kept worrying about what I could have done but I eventually came to realise that we couldn't have done much more. I remember saying to the men that we were like rats in a trap. (Second Lieutenant W. H. Crowder, 256th Brigade R.F.A.)

The War Diary of Second Lieutenant Crowder's artillery brigade gives details of all of his messages. The first Germans appeared in the trench above, held by the 51st (Highland) Division, at 9.53 a.m. and the last message was received at 10 a.m., only twenty minutes after the start of the German infantry attack. Crowder's story was published in the national press in England before the week was out – 'the officer who stuck to his O.P. and phoned that the Bosche had passed him'. Nearly two years later he was awarded the D.S.O. for sending these messages.

The assistance given to the British infantry by the many batteries of artillery covering the front line was severely hampered during this first phase of the battle by the inability to lay down accurate, observed fire on the German attackers. Not only were the forward observers unable to help but few of the Royal Flying Corps artillery observation planes had been able to take off and the rockets fired by the British infantry requesting fire on the pre-planned 'S.O.S. targets' were rarely seen in the fog despite the provision of 'repeating stations' behind the front line. It was these factors, rather than the German counter-battery fire, that really hampered the British artillery. Many of the British batteries, either because their 'silent' positions, had never been detected by the Germans or because so many batteries had moved to new positions the night before, were not under German shellfire and would have been capable of providing effective support for the infantry but for the influence of the fog. The best they could do was to engage the 'counter-preparation' targets behind the old German front line. So little supporting shell-fire did he see that the average British infantryman who survived this battle was convinced that the artillery had been deliberately withdrawn to safety leaving the front-line infantry to be sacrificed. In fact hundreds of guns in and around the Battle Zone were in action and some of these fired huge quantities of shells, but these shells could only be fired blindly on distant targets where the gunners could be sure that there were no British troops and the marvellous targets of massed German infantry moving forward in the open could rarely be touched.

The conditions under which the British artillery were operating could change dramatically in the next phase of the fighting. The fog was already clearing, especially in the north, giving place to bright, warm weather. The Germans now advancing towards the Battle Zone would soon be in view of the artillery observers there and to the observers of the Royal Flying Corps whose aircraft would soon be up in this better flying weather.

There were other supporting units – tanks, medical units, the dismounted cavalry who were really infantry now. Only the medical units had been involved in the first phase of the action, but there had not been a flood of cases arriving for their attention. The swift advance of the Germans had prevented most of the British wounded being evacuated to the rear and it was the German medical services that would have to cope with most of the thousands of wounded men on the battlefield.

*

There were many British soldiers who suddenly found themselves in the situation of being prisoners-of-war, a condition for which they were entirely unprepared. They had often seen German prisoners in the past, but the British Expeditionary Force had not lost many men as prisoners since the campaigns of 1914 and little was known by the average Tommy of what it was like to be captured by the Germans. Newspaper propaganda at home had portrayed the German soldier as a callous and brutal man who ill-treated prisoners, and the British military code had always taught that it was a shameful thing for a soldier to surrender. Now several thousand British soldiers were seeing for themselves what it was like to be a prisoner-of-war.

An examination of the experience of the British soldiers taken prisoner that morning reveals a general pattern to which there were few exceptions. The actual moment of capture could be very dangerous, especially if a British position had put up a good fight and caused many casualties among the German attackers, but such moments of anger usually passed quickly, often to be replaced by the sympathy for a beaten enemy that is to be found among the front-line soldiers of many armies.

There were a few parties of English in scattered positions who didn't fight very hard. They threw away their rifles and wanted to surrender but none of us spoke English and we left them for the following waves. There were a few dead and wounded, casualties of our shellfire, and we told the wounded to wait for our Red Cross men. I remember the face of one who had a leg wound. He was only a young chap, about nineteen years old. He crawled towards some bushes. He must have thought I was going to kill him. He certainly looked frightened; I was probably the first German soldier he had seen. I made a sign with my hands to him that I wouldn't harm him but we had to get on then and I left him. (Fusilier Willy Adams, Lehr Infantry Regiment)

The captives soon found that they were not going to be shot out of hand, as many had feared, although there were the usual grenades thrown into dug-outs known to contain wounded men, but this casual practice was often a matter of course adopted by both sides to whom badly wounded prisoners on the battlefield were an embarrassment. There were many Germans who were keen to show off their command of the English language with this type of greeting – 'Hello, Tommies. You're going to my country now, a great country, and we shall be marching down Oxford Street in a fortnight.' There were only the briefest of searches or interrogations and the prisoners were then collected up and sent off towards the German rear, often without any escort.

The following descriptions of the moment of capture come from some of the British soldiers taken prisoner in the first hour or so of the battle.

When the Germans got right on top of us, Colonel Toller called out, 'Surrender, boys. Surrender.' Our wounded and dead were covering the sunken road that the battalion was holding and the Germans were through on both sides of us. We had certainly caused them many casualties because we saw their bodies on the battlefield afterwards.

It was such a terrible shock becoming a prisoner that you can't really describe how it felt. Many a time you had seen their prisoners coming back and shown them sympathy; now you expected a bit of sympathy from them but we didn't get it. One or two of the Germans turned their rifles round, held them by the muzzles, and were hitting us with the butts. They weren't all the same; I expect they had too much rum but I think there was a bit of revenge in it for the casualties we had caused. (Bugler H. Waldram, 7th Sherwood Foresters)

I set off back to the support line, holding my wounded arm. It felt as though it was going to fall off. I was happy to think that I was going home to England and I wondered which hospital I would be sent to. At the support trench I expected to find the troops I had seen there earlier but they must have gone and the trench was full of Germans. I had a shock when I saw them. I turned and bolted back to the dead fellows I had left. About a dozen of the Germans followed me. I couldn't put my arms up to surrender but I knew it was all over.

They searched me and were very interested in the photographs I had of several girls in Tewkesbury who had given me their photographs. I remember they said '*viel Fräulein*'. I found out later that this meant 'a lot of girls'. They gave me them back and all the girls got their photographs back after the war stamped with the German censor's mark. (Gunner F. W. Woodward, 296th Brigade R.F.A.)

Battalion H.Q. was in three or four dug-outs. Runners had been sent up to the forward companies but had not been able to find anybody. Then, when the fog lifted, one of our men spotted hordes of Germans coming across open ground about half a mile away. There were hundreds and hundreds, not marching but advancing in large groups; there were even tanks with them. The Germans stretched to left and right as far as the eye could see. What went through the Colonel's mind I don't know but my pal and I knew we'd had it and there was no chance of getting back. He had an invalid mother and I knew this worried him. The Colonel told us he would surrender. I was thinking about my parents as well and I remember thinking that we would have to hope for the best. I went down to the dug-out for my greatcoat – it came in very useful that night. We broke up the typewriter and anything else that was useful and burnt a lot of papers. When the Germans came quite near we all got out of the trench and the Colonel tied a white rag or a towel to a stick and waved it. I can remember German officers coming and there was much saluting and conversation. (Rifleman A. J. Murcott, 8th King's Royal Rifle Corps)

Four of the few German tanks used were with their XVIII Corps which was attacking here, south of St Quentin. Official records show that only two men from this battalion escaped from the Forward Zone.

We clambered out, they lined us up on the top and searched us. As I got out, I had picked up a packet of butter and a packet of biscuits – one of those penny-a-packet lot of arrowroot biscuits you could buy in the canteen – and when this German searched my pocket he stuck his hands into the butter. He was annoyed and wiped his hand down my face. I managed to slip my pay book, my photos and my letters down my trousers; it was a bit uncomfortable when I was walking but they were personal and I managed to keep them. We were amazed to see hundreds of other British troops going back as prisoners; it seemed as though the whole British Army had been taken prisoner. (Private W. H. Ware, 61st Machine Gun Battalion)

We were stood there with our hands up and a German who told us he had once been a waiter in Manchester said, 'You'll be all right, boys, plenty of grub where you're going to.' I told him about the wounded down one of the dug-outs. He took a stick grenade out, pulled the pin out and threw it down the dug-out. We heard the shrieks and were nauseated, but we were completely powerless.

But it was all a *mêlée* and we might have done the same in the circumstances. I saw a lot of German dead and wounded in No Man's Land and realised that we had inflicted far greater casualties than we had suffered. (Private S. S. Taylor, 2nd Wiltshires)

I was laid on a stretcher, wounded, when the trench suddenly filled up with German troops from behind. They rested against the side of the trench before moving on. I noticed that they were quite fresh. They hadn't been hard done by at all; their artillery had done all their work for them. They'd got smart new uniforms and were as fat as pigs; one of them told me they had come from Russia – '*Russland*,' he said. Their officer was a fine, blond young man, well set up. He hadn't been in the trenches long; everything on him shone. His revolver was still in the holster; I don't think he ever had it out that morning.

One of their soldiers – an ordinary man – came up to me, said '*Engländer*' and tipped me off the stretcher and nipped off with it somewhere. He must have had a pal somewhere who needed one. The rest of them moved off soon after and just left me there completely alone. If my legs hadn't been hurt I could have run all the way to England. (Private E. Atkinson, 1st West Yorks)

I started to tear up the map I had; we had always been told to do this. The Germans were marching over in columns of fours. They had dogs on leads, cameras, pigeons – it was as though they were all out on a picnic. There they came, column after column of them, so happy; they thought they had won the war. They took my 'British warm', my field glasses and compass. I wondered whether they would shoot us. We'd heard such tales of what they did with prisoners, putting bombs in pockets and such like, but fortunately for us they were Bavarians not Prussians. They told us the war would be over by Christmas but we laughed at that. (Second Lieutenant W. H. Crowder, 256th Brigade R.F.A.)

The Germans who threw grenades into the dug-out of the 2nd Wiltshires were Pomeranians from the 211th Reserve Infantry Regiment. Those from Russia who captured Private Atkinson were from the 20th (Hanoverian) Division. Second Lieutenant Crowder had fallen into the error of regarding all Germans as Prussians or Bavarians; his captors were men of the 119th Division, the regiments of which were recruited in Posen, formerly in eastern Germany, and now Poznan in Poland.

*

On the German side of the battle area, the scene now was everywhere one of movement. The follow-up divisions and all the supporting arms of a great army in attack had been piled up on roads and tracks for miles behind the assault troops. The units that had led the attack had made such a good start to their advance that those following up had soon been able to move off in their attempt to keep up. It was not easy. The fog and gas had caused many early difficulties. British shellfire was likely to fall at any place without warning. The roads were narrow, crumbling and often shell-damaged. Then trenches had to be bridged, barbed wire removed and shell-torn ground had to be negotiated. Hundreds of thousands of men, thousands of horses, guns and wagons lurched forward, following the sound of battle. Droves of British prisoners and of German walking wounded travelled in the opposite direction, most of such men being mightily thankful to be getting away from the fighting.

The first to move off had been the artillery batteries which were supporting the assault infantry. These guns – 7·7-centimetre field guns and 10·5-centimetre howitzers – had not taken any part in the preliminary bombardment but had waited just behind the German trenches with their ammunition limbers (ninety-six rounds per gun), all with horses harnessed ready to move. Soon after the assault infantry had attacked, these artillery batteries had followed. They were the élite of the German artillery. After years of trench warfare, these gunners were about to take up again the traditional role of the artillery on the battlefield of mobile warfare. But these batteries did not see much action in the first few hours of the attack. It took them so long to cross the battlefield that most were several hours catching up the infantry regiments they were supposed to support. The first of these guns into action were those that were called upon to engage the troublesome British redoubts that were still holding out in the Forward Zone.

Farther back, the bombardment batteries were gradually released from their hours of firing as the range of the creeping barrage started to become too great. With the news that the infantry attack had been successful, some of these batteries also received orders to advance.

Then came the glorious order, '*An die Pferde! Batterie auf-
gesessen!*' 'To your horses! Battery mount!' That was the order we
had been waiting for. Then the next one, '*Vorwärts!*' We didn't
get any fire from the enemy apart from a single shot, a shrapnel
shell which burst in the air in front of the battery just before we
moved forward. I can still see that shell-burst now, with the
shrapnel balls coming down like water out of a watering can. It
hit one of our young drivers. He slid from his horse, dead.

The move to the next firing position was uneventful. A pleasing
sight for us were the many groups of English soldiers going to the
rear as prisoners. For them it was all over. Apart from that one
casualty, the battery had no further losses on this memorable day.
(Unteroffizier Otto Jaffé, 2nd Guard *Fussartillerie* Regiment)

Our Leutnant Erlenkämper, proud and bold, led the 1st Battery.
We stood closely packed on the road and couldn't move; obstacles
had to be cleared and passages across the trenches made. Hot food,
bread and coffee were issued, everybody eating wherever he stood
or walked. In front of us we heard heavy shells exploding at
regular intervals. Tommy must still have artillery we hadn't
caught. Then came the first bad news. The 4th Battery had
received a direct hit by a heavy shell – nineteen men and twenty-one
horses killed. If only one could get a move on. As we were, a
direct hit would have had a terrible effect.

The first prisoners came by. They look fit and well, especially
well fed, some with quite a belly. Some carry a German casualty
pick-a-back; others, in fours, a stretcher with severely wounded
men, the poor chaps tormented by coughing from the gas. A
Tommy without a job had the haversacks of the guards to carry,
one in front, one at the back some forty-five to fifty kilos. It will do
no harm; they are well fed.

At last we can labour slowly forward. The air has meanwhile
become clearer and purer; the sun has broken through and reveals
a wild push to the fore. We have reached the exit of the town
[St Quentin] and have to stop again whilst our officers look for a
gun site. At the left of the road lies the first dead man, a driver
from one of the batteries accompanying the infantry. His greatcoat
on, he lies at my feet. Someone has bound up his chin with a red
handkerchief and now the eyes stare from the quiet face into the
sun. I had a good look at him and tried to understand his expression
– it seemed bitter and accusing. I only know that a dead soldier was
a terrible sight.

At last we move into our new firing position and open up again.
(Unteroffizier Erich Kubatzki, 20th *Fussartillerie* Regiment)

Divisional H.Q. decides to move to Riencourt. Shortly before they leave, I go on horseback. My charger, a new one and not well enough trained, is very unsettled and gets frightened by the noise. The sun is out now but there is little activity by planes. The roads are only tracks and more than full with traffic. Lorries can't use them yet. Pioneers work hard to improve the road. Twenty-five gunners try to haul a 21-centimetre howitzer stuck in the mud. Riencourt is just a heap of rubble. There is trouble at the divisional command post. Transport and guns tear the telephone lines to pieces and carry the ends away. What a job to find them! It is a most unpleasant situation.

H.Q. urges us on. Leutnant Goebel and myself do our utmost. In order to establish at least one connection, we install a blinker station. Radio has, as usual, let us down. The command post has its place about 300 metres north-west from Riencourt on the road to Cagnicourt. From a spot above the entrance of the dug-out I have an impressive view. In front is Rendecourt, completely destroyed. My billets were here in the spring of 1915 but the whole area is now a wild, torn, cratered landscape. There lie some dead men and horses; an old tank hangs in a sunken road, both drivers dead. (Leutnant Hans Baum, 6th Bavarian Divisional Signals)

Those British infantrymen who survived and who still believe that their own artillery had deserted them can take some consolation from the many German reports of casualties and disruption caused by British shellfire. It is true that this did not seriously affect the outcome of the battle but it did have a constant harassing effect among the German units moving along in the wake of the advance. The British gunners who were firing 'into the blue' and may have wondered whether their shells were doing any good were not wasting their time. One unknown British battery, firing from the area of either the 16th (Irish) or the 66th (East Lancs) Division scored this notable success.

Our divisional commander visited our battery in a farmyard. I can see him now, pulling on his gloves and shouting out to us, 'Boys. We are through. Better be dead than slaves. Get on! Get on!' Later we heard that he had been killed when his command post moved forward to a position near Hargicourt. He was hit in the head by a splinter from a heavy shell; the leather-covered spiked helmet he was wearing had not saved him. He was always very

popular and friendly in the division. He was buried on the battlefield. (Wachtmeister Bruno Lauritzen, 45th Field Artillery
Regiment)

This officer, Generalmajor Bloch von Blottnitz, commander
of the 18th Division, the regiments of which were recruited
in Schleswig, was the senior casualty of the day.

Supposed to accompany the attack were the nine tanks used
by the Germans on that day. These had all been allocated to
Crown Prince Wilhelm's forces around St Quentin – five
captured British tanks with the German XIX Corps and four
of German manufacture with XVII Corps. Unfortunately
none of the crew members of these tanks was among the
German contributors to this book but a machine-gunner saw
two of the captured British machines just north of St Quentin.

They were very slow, about 5 kilometres per hour, and they were
being guided by men outside the tanks knocking on the walls and
shouting directions. I don't know how they got on. We all got
mixed up and I missed them later. I remember a horsed artillery
battery coming through much faster and I shouldn't think the tanks
were fast enough to do anything useful. (Gefreiter August Bender,
36th *M.G. Scharfschützenabteilung*)

In fact the tanks were intended to be used in the reduction of
any British posts that still held out after being by-passed and
several British soldiers in such positions did see them in
action.

Another type of German unit following the battle were the
balloon platoons, of which there were fifteen with each of the
three German armies. Each platoon had one observation
balloon with a crew of an observer and a telephonist in the
balloon basket and twenty-four men on the ground to man-
handle the balloon forward by means of a complicated net-
work of ropes. It was hard going over the rough ground.

The move forward didn't work out as laid down in orders. A
high-tension cable lay across our route and had to be negotiated, a
difficult job. It was assumed that the cable was not live. We were
ordered to take up our respective stations. This meant that we had
to get ropes over the cable while the balloon hovered about 800
metres high, a job we had often practised. Whilst some of my pals
held the ropes, the catch-lines weighted with lead were thrown

over the cable. It was my job to catch a line on the other side. My neighbour, who apparently had become exhausted, gave me his rope. He wished to take my line, a somewhat easier job. Suddenly a gust of wind pushed the balloon back and the line my neighbour had taken over from me touched the cable. Nobody had expected that that cable was fully charged. My pal died at once. As he fell down he tried to give me his hand. But I had to keep hold of the balloon and I knew that I could not help him. His death touched me deeply. 'Rest in eternal life, my good comrade.' Two cyclists were sent to the transformer to switch off the electricity. The incident cost us two hours. (Luftschiffer Edmund Lange, 148th Balloon Platoon)

Our destination for that day was the village of Lagnicourt but we didn't quite get there. We did move forward and were kept very busy directing the fire of one of our 15-centimetre batteries. I was a signaller and was kept fully occupied delivering messages and mending telephone wires. I made much use of the English wires that were lying about in such quantity. They were so much better than ours. They had rubber covering; ours only had tarred paper.

When I recollect today what sort of thoughts I had as an eighteen-year-old that day, they were basically two-fold. I was glad not to be in a crowd but to be on my own and to be able to move freely. And I was particularly curious about the completely changed landscape of the battlefield, though hoping to come out of it and to breathe again the fragrance of undestroyed nature. I was a proper romantic! (Luftschiffer Ludwig Reineking, 117th Balloon Platoon)

The vast majority of the men who were marching forward behind the German attack were the infantrymen of the thirty or so divisions following up ready to reinforce the leading divisions or to take over from them completely. This man's unit was following up the attack on the 51st (Highland) Division north of the Flesquières Salient.

The scene was one of movement, not of noise. The whole front was in motion, all going one way. It was a silent march, just the occasional order to stop and lie down or to move on again. We heard no shooting. Where was the British artillery? Our artillery was silent too because they had started to move forward also. Our infantry ahead didn't seem to be fighting at all either. We didn't speak much; the exertion was too much for that. We thought that the English had withdrawn and concentrated all their reserves well back. We kept asking where the English were but no one knew. We believed that we had at last broken right through the English front and that the moment we had awaited all through the war had arrived. Now we could finish it off. It was a thrilling moment. (Unteroffizier Wernher Eberbach, 126th Regiment)

There was a particular encouragement for German soldiers near St Quentin.

We ceased firing soon after the infantry had started the attack. By 11 a.m., a message had come through by telephone and was passed on to the gun crews in a loud voice by the battery commander: 'His Majesty the Kaiser and Field Marshal von Hindenburg are in this area.' We looked around and saw a few motor cars on the road. The men near by shouted, 'Hurrah' and 'Hello'. (Unteroffizier Karl Heimgartner, 13th *Fussartillerie* Regiment)

9

The Fight for the Battle Zone

It was upon the defence of the Battle Zone that the main hopes of the British commanders rested. The defences here consisted first of a strong, continuous trench line – known as the Red Line – well protected with barbed wire and commanding good fields of fire over the open ground across which the Germans, who had earlier swept through the Forward Zone, had to advance. In the area behind the Red Line were many independent infantry positions, heavy machine-gun and trench-mortar posts, and artillery positions. At the rear of the Battle Zone was a second continuous trench – the Brown Line – about 2,000 yards behind the front of this defence zone. That last line of trenches represented the final substantial defence work between the Germans and the open ground which extended to the coast sixty or seventy miles away. There was supposed to be a further line – the Corps, or Green, Line – but hardly any work had been done on this. Even the Brown Line was not complete in the Fifth Army area.

The British garrison in the Battle Zone positions represented about half of the strength of the forward divisions. The remaining units in these divisions had either been in the Forward Zone or were behind the Battle Zone forming part of the slender reserves available to the local corps commanders. The remainder of the corps reserves were made up of the few reserve infantry divisions available, the dismounted cavalry and a few tank battalions. It was vitally important for the British to hold on to the Battle Zone and these reserves were to be used to counter-attack any part of the defences taken by the Germans or to fill any gaps appearing in the defences. Behind the reserves were only the many vulnerable administrative units found behind every fighting army.

The units holding the Battle Zone had all been able to man their positions before the preliminary bombardment ended but the German storm troops had swept through the front-line defences so quickly that, where the Battle Zone lay close behind, the Germans arrived within twenty minutes of the opening of their infantry attack. These early encounters with the Battle Zone defences usually took place before the dense fog cleared. The earliest fighting in the Battle Zone was on the high ground, near Ronssoy, which was held by the 7/8th Royal Inniskilling Fusiliers, 16th Division, and on the Louveral Ridge, held by parts of the 6th and 7th Black Watch, 51st Division. Thus, parts of the Battle Zones of both the Fifth and the Third Armies were being attacked, and breached, by 10 a.m., and many other parts of it were under attack within the next hour.

It must be stressed again that action in the two zones was often taking place at the same time but, while the Forward Zone soon succumbed in most sectors, the fight for the Battle Zone grew in intensity and it was to dominate the remainder of the daylight hours. It must also be stressed again that the description of this fighting will not be a blow-by-blow, unit-by-unit, hour-by-hour account. Such a story is well told in the British Official History. This is a less formal description, concentrating on the nature of the fighting and on the experiences of the men involved.

*

The area immediately in front of the Battle Zone was not completely empty of British troops. There were several artillery battery positions that had not been evacuated, small communications or engineer detachments and more artillery observation posts. All these would be surprised by the speed of the German advance. One artillery observation officer near Urvillers, just south of St Quentin, remained in his post despite the fact that his telephone wires were cut. After the German creeping barrage passed over his position, he saw this unusual evidence of the advance of the German infantry in the fog.

At 10.30 the bombardment again commenced to move forward. The enemy were using pear-shaped balloons about three feet long and flying about fifty feet, apparently to keep his infantry in touch. I saw two of these about 200 yards apart and about 200 yards in front of the O.P. They were clearly visible above the ground mist . . . I destroyed my papers and log book at the O.P. and left. (Lieutenant L. P. G. Bremner, 137th Heavy Brigade)*

German soldiers were often surprised to capture British positions so easily in this area.

We came upon a position for four field guns, 18-pounders I think you call them, like our 7·5-centimetre gun. It was just behind a railway embankment. Each gun had sandbag walls and camouflage netting but there were no barbed wire, no machine-guns and no infantry near by to give them protection. The infantry had all gone, leaving the artillery on their own. They gave up quietly, forty or fifty men including some officers. None of them had been killed at all. We found some mules there and we took two of these to pull our machine-gun cart. (Gefreiter August Bender, 36th *M.G. Scharfschützenabteilung*)

This British soldier was manning a small wireless station in a quarry in front of the Battle Zone near Savy.

One of our number, new to the life, came back from the top saying that we must have taken a lot of prisoners as they were marching along the road. Another one, more experienced, went up to confirm and returned to say they were all carrying bayonets!

We sent the 'forced to dismantle' signal, 'z z z', and set about breaking up our instruments. In our young training days we had often dreamt of sending z z z and breaking up instruments but were never permitted to rehearse either. A rifle butt made short work of the W/T set and amplifier but the power buzzer resisted all attacks we made on it and we had no grenades.

Shortly before noon a white terrier dog arrived in the quarry, took one look at our sentry, returned to the road and barked at some passing Germans who came to the sap and formally took us prisoners, i.e. removed our arms. Then, to our surprise, they joined us in the sap. There were three of them; one carried a Mauser automatic pistol which fired the same ammunition as their service rifles. They had maps in the cuffs of their greatcoats, marked with the objectives of the attack. The village of Ham was the objective for the first day. So far they had made five miles of the thirteen miles from St Quentin to Ham. (Sapper H. E. Hopthrow, 30th Divisional Signal Company)

Roles were reversed here later in the day when a British counter-attack released these men.

* War Diary, C.R.A. III Corps, Public Record Office WO 95/693.

Also in this area were parties of British infantry who had escaped from the Forward Zone and were now mixed up with the advancing Germans. This officer was with part of a battalion whose commander had ordered his men to fall back to the Battle Zone.

The mist was now lifting rapidly and, on glancing back, we could see hordes of Bosche passing over our old positions. Messages were being continually passed up from the rear for us to 'double up in front'. We were moving as quickly as possible but doubtless the presence of large numbers of the enemy, almost on the heels of those behind, literally gave them wings.

The trench by which we retired crossed a ridge which was about 600 yards from the Battle Zone line. A battery of our guns was situated a few yards behind the Battle Zone position and the gunners quickly grasped the state of affairs as they saw us retreating towards them. They waited until the first enemy waves were well in view and then opened rapid fire into them with devastating results. We arrived in the new position in time to enjoy the latter part of this spectacle and, after the Hun had made a few ineffectual attempts to push on, he saw the futility of these methods and halted on the side of the ridge opposite to us. (Lieutenant J. W. Randall, 8th Royal Berkshires)

All of the above incidents occurred on the St Quentin sector where the gap between the Forward Zone and the Battle Zone was a wide one. This incident also took place here.

While we were waiting for the German attack to develop, we were sent out on small forays to keep the approaches clear of Germans. We came upon two comparatively elderly Germans who had somehow slipped through, or possibly they had broken off from a larger party on one of our flanks. They were looking for someone to surrender to and were very pleased to give themselves up to us. They were sent back but I heard later that they were both killed by their own shelling. (Private S. G. Cane, 7th Queens)*

*

Because liaison with their artillery was still difficult, most of the early German attacks on the Battle Zone had to wait for their creeping barrage to move on before they could com-

* The Royal West Surrey Regiment.

mence. German infantry commanders knew roughly where the British defences were but their approach was usually a cautious one, preceded by a screen of scouts searching for any weak or undefended places in the British line. There were dramatic scenes in some places where the fog had lifted early, with field-grey companies of German infantrymen tramping across the open ground, mounted officers, batteries of horse-drawn artillery, an occasional tank, aeroplanes wheeling overhead – a great kaleidoscope of men and movement quite remarkable for the First World War. But in many places there was still fog, and most British soldiers, peering over the edge of their trenches, could see nothing of this greater scene.

For the average soldier, the fight for the Battle Zone opened as a series of tiny engagements. The following descriptions are all from men who were at the front of the Battle Zone.

While it was still misty, a German attack was made on our trench, led by an officer with a revolver; he was mounted on a horse and waving his men on. After two years of trench warfare, with rarely a chance of seeing a German, let alone fire at one, this was an opportunity too good to miss. So I took a careful aim and squeezed the trigger and had the satisfaction of seeing him fall from his horse, which then turned back and galloped off into the mist, followed by his men at the double. As my section were also all firing at the same time, I cannot be certain that it was my bullet which brought about the end of the attack. In a curious way, I quite enjoyed the battle. I expect it was because I had not previously been in a position to engage the enemy at close quarters and, at my age, then twenty-two, I was thoroughly enjoying myself, with no thought of the consequences. I think the same could be said of most of my comrades. (Sergeant W. Donoghue, 478th Field Company)*

I'm not sure how long it was before an alarm was given by our sergeant running down the steps of the dug-out. I know that, when I rushed up those stairs, I never dreamed I wouldn't be going back. I left my overcoat there; I went right through the rest of that campaign – the retreat – without that overcoat. My first sight as

* Many of the Royal Engineer field companies were helping to man the Battle Zone. The incident of the mounted officer leading the German attack at this point is confirmed in the British Official History.

we came up into the open was of one of our own men lying face downwards at the far side of a shallow bowl-shaped depression. I had been out in France since November 1917 and in the trenches since the New Year and had never seen a dead man in the battalion before. It was a mystery as to how he died; possibly he was a sentry.

My attention was soon taken up by the Germans. They were about fifty yards away to our left. We opened fire where we stood, in the open. It was the first time I had fired my rifle at the enemy, I don't know what the others did but I just aimed in the general direction of those Germans. You will gather that I wasn't a hardened soldier. (Private E. F. Harrison, 8th Queens)

I was on the edge of a sunken road, on top of the tin roof of a temporary cookhouse with a Lewis gun. The first German I saw was putting his machine-gun up in front of us. One of the men with me said, 'Look at that cheeky devil!'; then he shot him, clean as a whistle. After that, they came over in large numbers but crawling and making short rushes. We opened fire whenever we saw them.

There were only three of us and although the Germans were firing at us, on and off, with machine-guns and also with trench mortars – light mortars – I think they were in such a muddle that they couldn't concentrate on one object and none of us were hit. We must have been in action for some time. We had forty-eight drums of ammunition and I fired the lot off. (Lance Corporal A. Bowler, 2/5th Sherwood Foresters)

I suddenly saw small groups of Germans coming through on the high ground to the right of the Hirondelle Valley. We had lost our Lewis gun in the shelling and only had rifles. We opened fire. We undoubtedly hit some but this was the whole point of their tactics. As soon as one party was fired on, the others came on and round. They were looking for our weak spots. Whenever one of these parties got established, they opened up on us with a machine-gun but I don't remember any of my little group being hit. In *our* previous attacks, a platoon had gone over in a line and they made a good target; we found this new tactic of the Germans interesting.

We were probably a little relieved that there weren't more of them because we were so weak ourselves, although we were being joined by stragglers from the front line who seemed quite pleased to join us. We were having single shots at individual targets and it all depended on two things – whether you were a good shot and whether you had the range right. I think we opened fire too early,

900 to 1,000 yards, but at 500 or so we started hitting them. I don't think we hit many but it was one of only two occasions in the war when I am sure I hit a German. My diary entry for that day read, 'Had good pot shooting'. After an hour, or maybe a little more, a message was passed along that the company was withdrawing. I made the bad mistake of accepting it without verification – probably it was what I wanted most in the world – and we started to go back. (Lieutenant E. Foster Hall, 1st Buffs)

The Germans soon broke into the Battle Zone in many places. The defences were not always strong enough and the defending units were sometimes too weak. Close-quarter fighting developed.

After some time, Gerry had a bomber squad coming down the communication trench and dropped some 'tato'-mashers a dozen yards in front of us, whereupon Captain Case told off the first six men to go up the trench and shift Gerry. I was lying next to the trench entrance, so became second thrower. A Lance Corporal Lane of the 7th Sherwoods was No. 1. So off we went, No. 1 putting his head carefully round each bend and I looking over his shoulder. After about thirty or forty yards we found one another – Gerry popping his head round at the same time as Lance Corporal Lane. When their heads almost met, Lane jumped up, nearly knocking me over. All the rest did the same and ran like hell down the trench towards the sunken road. When we got to the end another officer, a lieutenant now, turned round and said, 'You will have to go back', which we did, but we could not find Gerry. He had run farther afield, so we set to to build the barricade. What a laugh we had when we talked about it in the prison camp. (Private L. Hencliffe, 2/5th Sherwood Foresters)

The defenders of the Battle Zone had been battered by two bombardments – the preliminary one and the creeping barrage that preceded the German infantry. They were sometimes manning trenches which they had never seen before and which were often incomplete. They were fighting against a determined and skilful enemy who were always superior in numbers and whose morale was high following the easy capture of the British Forward Zone. Although the British usually fought hard, far more so than had been possible in the Forward Zone positions, their Battle Zone defences began to break in some places. The following examples describe how the Germans penetrated the Battle Zone in three separate places – two defended by Second-Line Territorial battalions and the third by New Army battalions. The selection of these stories does not imply that other battalions all held their positions. These three examples are typical of what happened at many places in the Battle Zone that day.

> 11 a.m.: Casualties up to now slight. Second Lieutenant G. Carmichael killed. Enemy reported in wire on Red Line.
> 11.15 a.m.: Enemy reported entered Red Line between A and C Companies and, owing to the mist, were able to surround both companies. Battalion H.Q. formed defensive line in Cote Wood.

Thus reads the War Diary of the 2/6th Manchesters.* Private C. H. Martin was a Lewis gunner in one of the surrounded Manchester companies.

> As soon as the barrage eased off a bit, we stood on the fire-step and opened up. I had two or three men filling magazines and I kept pegging away at the Germans. I think there were thirty rounds in a magazine and you could fire one off in five seconds. We kept this up until my Lewis gun refused to continue. The lance corporal shouted at me to get it going again. I tried all the official 'stoppages' without result and then stripped the gun down. I discovered that the barrel was choked with carbon deposits. I got a rod with a bit of four-by-two and, after a quick clean, it agreed to resume work.
>
> But, by this time, the Germans had got very close and I saw, a little distance away, a sergeant and some men climb out of the trench with their hands up. I tried to escape along the trench but the way through was blocked by dead bodies. Among these was a corporal who had put me on a charge two weeks earlier. He had been hit in the middle of the forehead and both his eyeballs were hanging down over his cheeks. When I turned in the opposite direction, I saw two German soldiers approaching, spraying the trench ahead with liquid fire. One held the nozzle and the other had the cylinder on his back.
>
> There was often talk among the lads that, to be captured with a Lewis gun, you didn't stand a chance. You'd be finished off at once. So I dumped it into a water-filled shell hole and put my hands up. I was sorry to lose that gun; it was nearly new and I had become very fond of it.

* Public Record Office WO 95/3144.

Sergeant J. Fitzpatrick was a platoon commander here.

I was on the top of the trench behind my Lewis-gun team. I gave orders to concentrate fire on a gap in the communication trench. Suddenly, I was hit with a bullet through three fingers; I fell forward and my face hit the ground. I drew my hand from under me and rolled into the trench. One of the lads bandaged my hand – with a dab of iodine of course. Then we blazed away again at Jerry, for we could see him in masses on our left, coming through just like herds of sheep. You couldn't miss them. How many did I hit? I couldn't take the Lewis gun off the communication trench and was using a rifle. I probably shot off going on for a hundred rounds and I reckon at least 80 per cent scored hits. You couldn't miss. In fact my rifle was white hot, so I kept picking up others to keep the fire going. I don't think the Germans realised they were getting hit from the side.

They passed through eventually and things quietened down. I sat on the top of the trench and saw that some of them had come in behind us to take us in the rear. Then, about twenty yards in front of us, was a Jerry officer stood up in front of our wire and he shouted to us to come out. It was hopeless. We'd had it. I dropped my equipment to the ground and walked up to him. I'm very pleased that I never put my hands up. The officer stuck his revolver in my guts and pointed to his watch. I thought I had had my chips. I was lucky it was him, though. If it had been someone else he would have squeezed the trigger.

I went forward and then I saw so many of our battalion men and a sergeant, of another company, putting them into some sort of marching order. I thought, 'Bloody hell-fire! What resistance have they put up?' It seemed incredible. I felt ashamed. The other sergeant asked me, 'Give us a hand, Fitz, to put them in order.' I refused. 'Not bloody likely. Let the Germans put them in order.'

The British Official History's brief comment on this action is:

North of the Grand Priel Woods, the enemy was detained for some time by the 2/6th Manchesters about Fervaque Farm in the front line of the Battle Zone, opposite Villeret. Several attacks were beaten off and it was not until 1.30 p.m. that the British resistance was overcome by the aid of liquid fire. The enemy then pushed on again . . .*

* British Official History, page 188.

The battalion's War Diary states:

Remnants of the battalion returned to a line joining Carpeza Copse. Strength of the battalion now 12 officers and 150 other ranks.

*

Many miles to the north, the 59th (North Midland) Division was holding the small Bullecourt Salient with one brigade of Sherwood Foresters battalions and one of Staffordshire battalions, its third brigade being in reserve. The four battalions who had held the front line had been overwhelmed in the first hour. The Battle Zone was held by the 2/5th Sherwood Foresters – recruited in the city of Derby – around the village of Noreuil, and by the 2/6th North Staffords – from the Burton-on-Trent area – holding the village of Ecoust and a near-by railway embankment. The positions of both battalions were soon surrounded. The Sherwood Foresters were soon reduced to 150 men in and around the ruins of Noreuil and they held out there until 3 p.m., but then it was all over. Only four men from this battalion escaped to the rear.

The North Staffords held a little longer; the railway embankment provided a particularly good defensive position. The Germans attacking here were the 73rd Infantry Regiment – the Hanoverian Fusiliers. Leutnant Ernst Jünger was taking part in the German attack.

Half left of us, the great railway embankment in the line Ecoust–Croisilles, which we had to cross, rose out of the mist. From loopholes and dug-out windows built into the side of it, rifles and machine-guns were rattling merrily . . . We must have spent a long while running to and fro among the shell holes and engaging one target after another. At last I found myself at the foot of the embankment and I saw a dug-out window quite close to me covered with a sandbag, from which I could see they were firing. I shot through the cloth. A man near me tore it down and threw in a bomb. A shock and a cloud of smoke welling out showed the result. Two other men ran along the bank and dealt with the other loopholes in the same way. I raised my hand to warn the men behind, for their bullets at very short range were whistling past our ears. They nodded back, delighted. After that, we clambered with hundreds more at one rush up the bank. For the first time in the war I saw large bodies of men in hand-to-hand fighting. The English held two terraced trenches on the rear slope. Shots were exchanged and bombs lobbed down at a range of a few metres.

I jumped into the first trench. Stumbling round the first traverse, I collided with an English officer with an open tunic and his tie hanging loose. I did without my revolver and, seizing him by the throat, flung him against the sandbags where he collapsed. Behind me the head of an old major appeared. He was shouting to me, 'Shoot the hound dead'. I left this to those behind me and turned to the lower trench. It seethed with English. I fired off my cartridges so fiercely that I pressed the trigger ten times at least after the last shot. A man next to me threw bombs among them as they scrambled to get away. A dish-shaped helmet was sent spinning high in the air.*

The commanding officer of the Staffords, Lieutenant-Colonel T. B. H. Thorne, had been hit in the head and killed while directing the defence of Ecoust, and the battalion's positions were gradually reduced. Private F. Beardsell's account of this fighting includes the type of minor and unusual incident which is often all that the ordinary soldier remembers of such an action.

There seemed to be thousands of Jerries swarming down the slopes behind us and we retired to a refuge behind a barricade of sandbags. I've not the slightest idea whether I was hitting anything. I certainly never saw anyone fall. I'd been in France ten months and this was the first time I'd fired at the enemy. I wasn't frightened; it seemed to be something that was happening outside of me.

I was lying there with my friend, Private Sykes Dobson, with whom I had enlisted, firing away, when we saw a mouse come out of a hole and sit up between us. I immediately moved to hit it with the butt of my rifle but Dobson said, 'Don't do that, leave the little bugger alone. It's better off than us.' The mouse scooted off.

The young second lieutenant who appeared to be in charge of us ordered us to move out towards another position. I told him I wanted to stay with Dobson, who was wounded, but he refused to let me and threatened to blow my brains out if I didn't come. I resented this but I had to do as I was told. That officer was certainly wound up a bit.

The space for rifle fire in this next position was rather restricted so, after having a rifle discharged in my ear, I suggested that I

* *Storm of Steel*, pages 256–8.

should fire whilst my companion loaded. After having two rifles shot from my hands, I turned to speak and found the only British person visible disappearing into a small tunnel under the embankment. Following, I found the tunnel full of our wounded, many of whom greeted me. At the other end I found Major Keatinge. He said, 'Beardsell, climb up that embankment and see what is going on over the top'. I climbed, making a ripping target. When about half-way, I turned for some unknown reason and immediately felt as if my right arm had received a severe electric shock. I'd caught it, and pretty badly. The thought passed through my mind, 'Thank God. It's all over now'.

The party of men in this tunnel under Major O. J. F. Keatinge was the last remnant of the 2/6th North Staffords. They surrendered at about 4.30 p.m.

The fighting in the Bullecourt Salient was probably more severe than at any other part of the front. The casualties of the 59th Division were heavier than any other British division that day. Only one officer returned from the three Staffordshire battalions in the 176th Brigade to report to brigade headquarters! Of the known German regimental casualties, the Hanoverians of the 73rd Infantry Regiment, with twelve officers and 132 men killed, and the East Prussians of the 41st Infantry Regiment, with three officers and 132 men killed, were the third and fifth highest during the day.*

*

On the immediate left flank of the 59th Division was a sector held by a brigade of the 34th Division. The three battalions in this brigade were the 22nd, 23rd and 25th Northumberland Fusiliers, which had originally been Tyneside Scottish and Tyneside Irish battalions of the New Army. The sector they were holding was the northern limit of the main German attack. The two front-line battalions had been

* The German follow-up division which took over the attack on this sector later in the day was the 2nd Guard Reserve Division. For three of the battalions in the 59th Division, this was a meeting with old adversaries. Many of the men in the 5th North Staffords, the 7th Sherwood Foresters and the 4th Lincolns had come from the 46th (North Midland) Division under the recent reorganisation. This division had attacked the German-held Gommecourt Salient on the first day of the Battle of the Somme in 1916 and suffered heavy casualties there. It was the German 2nd Guard Reserve Division who had defended Gommecourt on that day.

pressed hard all morning, but the Germans do not seem to have advanced far at this point and the battalion in the Battle Zone did not suffer a frontal assault. The best witness available here is an unusual one. Captain H. H. Davies was the Brigade Intelligence Officer and had started the day at brigade headquarters.

The battalions normally sent in situation reports before breakfast but we had heard nothing that morning. We stood around Brigade H.Q. in a sunken road; it was foggy and noisy and we had no idea what was happening. We had a little conference and the brigadier decided that someone ought to go up to the front, see what was happening, and report back. I, as Intelligence Officer, was chosen to go. I and my groom set off on horseback. I don't know how we ever got there. I had a wonderful horse and he cleared barbed wire and empty trenches – he was taking me, I wasn't taking him. We never saw a soul.

We managed to get almost to the three Battalion H.Q.s, which were all together, when a shell landed just a few yards away and I was hit by a piece of shell in my shoulder. They bandaged me up at one of the Battalion H.Q.s; everyone was on the alert waiting for the Bosche to present themselves. We expected them at any moment. They realised that I wasn't in a fit state to go back, so they sent another officer on my horse. I heard later that the horse was killed under him, the officer was thrown into a shell hole and very badly gassed. I wasn't wounded seriously, in fact I was just numb and I didn't really know I had been injured.

I went up to the front line then – it was the old German Hindenburg Line – and I spent the next few hours helping to carry wounded and dead down into the palatial dug-outs that the Germans had built. The slaughter had been terrific, all caused by shellfire. By afternoon, the weather was fine; the fog had lifted and we were waiting for something to happen, perhaps the Germans to attack from the front or our own supporting troops to come up from the rear.

While we were looking to the rear with our field glasses, watching some troops approaching, thinking it was our supports, we saw to our astonishment that they were Germans, coming quite steadily in the open towards us. Those of our men who could do anything were getting fewer and fewer – we had been under shellfire all the time – so we collected all the arms we could, mostly Mills bombs, and concentrated ourselves into what we called a strongpoint in those days, so that we could make a last bid for it.

We held on for about two hours. The Germans simply surrounded us and outnumbered us and, when all our bombs and
ammunition had gone, we could do no more.

The Germans who had attacked Captain Davies's position
from the rear were from units that had successfully broken
the defence of the 59th Division and then turned north to
attack the 34th Division from the flank. In the greater scheme
of things, this was the start of the rolling-up of the British
lines from the northern flank of the main German attack. But,
because of the prolonged defence put up in their Battle Zone
by the 59th Division and then by the Northumberland
Fusiliers, the Germans did not make much progress northwards on this day.

There had been a minor drama at the place where the
battalion headquarters of the three Northumberland Fusilier
battalions had been sited close to each other in some dug-
outs in a reserve trench called Bunhill Row. The German
advance from the flank soon surrounded Bunhill Row and,
after burning all their papers, the battalion commanders and
their staffs defended this position against fierce attack. At
5 p.m., Lieutenant-Colonel Spencer Acklom, of the 22nd
Northumberlands, decided that he would attempt to fight his
way out with the men of his headquarters. Colonel Acklom
has been described as 'a small, slight, dapper, sandy-haired
Scotsman, a typical Regular officer who stood out as a fault-
less soldier in our New Army battalion. I don't know how
he put up with us'. Acklom's bid did not succeed and he was
killed, although some of his men did manage to escape. At
5.30 p.m. the Germans delivered an ultimatum to the other
two battalion commanders: if they did not surrender within
three minutes, fire would be opened with some heavy
mortars that had been brought up. As Bunhill Row now
contained many wounded men, the other two lieutenant-
colonels decided that they had no option but to surrender.

The War Diary of the 34th Division contains the following
forlorn entry about the activities of this brigade of
Northumberland Fusiliers.

Message. 9.5 p.m., by telephone from 101st Infantry Brigade:
Assistant Adjutant 22nd Northumberland Fusiliers says Colonel

Acklom killed. Two Battalion H.Q.s captured. Apart from a few stragglers, none of the 22nd left. Two other battalions cut off. Three companies of 25th Northumberland Fusiliers made a counter-attack; not heard of since.*

•

The British artillery batteries in the Battle Zone often found themselves under threat of direct attack by the German infantry. Some were allowed to pull back to less dangerous positions, but others were too late and there were many incidents where guns engaged German infantry over open sights and spare gunners took up Lewis guns and rifles to man the trenches dug for just this eventuality. British gunners had never been this close to their enemy since the campaigns of 1914.

It would be about noon when we observed 18-pounder batteries of the 16th Division on our left retiring at the trot and taking up new positions on our left flank. This looked ominous and seemed to indicate a German advance of some depth. We could hear the infantry battle raging ahead, but nothing much happened at the guns until machine-gun bullets began falling sporadically among us. They appeared to come from the direction of an overgrown copse on our northern flank and were probably the result of haphazard indirect firing which, fortunately, did no harm. However, in circumstances such as these, one prepares for the worst and Lieutenant E. C. Monson, a brave and popular officer who had not been long with us, set up the only Lewis gun we possessed and appeared game to fight it out to the end.† Two or three gunners had been given the few rifles we had and they manned the trench behind the guns which was now being used as a Command Post and First Aid Station. It was a slender force with which to repel the enemy storm troopers should they reach the guns, but it was a moral gesture of defiance which encouraged the men and we regretted there were not more weapons to hand.

Myself and another signaller were detailed to make a reconnaissance and for some time we sent messages back by signal lamp. We were soon recalled and, as we approached the position, we noticed that the guns, which earlier had been dragged from

* Public Record Office WO 95/2436.
† Lieutenant E. C. S. Monson, M.C., died of wounds on 15 June 1918 after being hit by German shellfire during a minor British operation to straighten the line in the Béthune sector.

their pits to give a broader switch of fire, appeared to be firing over open sights at a range of just about twelve hundred yards. To see our lads fighting back in the open with the coolness of veterans, and doing it with drill-book precision as though on manoeuvres at home, was an unforgettable experience, though one that was repeated often enough in the days that lay ahead. (Bombadier H. J. Hewetson, 331st Brigade R.F.A.)

The outcome of the engagements between the German infantry and the British guns were, in many cases, much closer than this and ended only when the British gunners surrendered or withdrew, leaving the Germans as the proud captors of the guns.

The ground rose slightly and we reached the top of a small rise together with our first line of men, almost without opposition from English infantry and with no casualties. Suddenly, we were fired on by a battery with shrapnel at close range and had to throw ourselves to the ground. Closely packed, we found cover behind a low railway embankment. The shots passed over our heads like hail, bouncing off the sleepers and rails. *Verdammte Scheisse!* So far all had gone so well. We had advanced seven to eight kilometres as the crow flies and now lay in front of a medium-calibre battery, under direct fire. The report from the guns and the explosion of the shells were simultaneous. A frontal attack against this made no sense. We made ourselves as flat as pancakes, faces against the ground. In one of the short intervals, I took a glance to the right and left to see whether my comrades were still alive.

As suddenly as it had started it stopped; we could breathe again. We rose up and were able to advance to the abandoned battery. The barrels of the guns were still hot. We saw some of the gunners running away. (Gefreiter Karl Pütz, 65th Reserve Regiment)

It was not only field-gun positions that became involved in the close fighting. This man was in a 4·5-inch howitzer position.

We were actually bombarded by German artillery three times in the morning and, by midday, the three other guns had all been knocked out and mine was the only one still in action. It had fired about a thousand rounds. It was the only time I ever used water to cool an overheated four-point-five. Several times the breach-block jammed and several of us got minor burns.

On one occasion my section officer called up to me, 'Come and look at this', and I crawled up to the top of the gun-pit. I could see one of our defensive lines of barbed wire about 800 yards away and could see German troops converging on two gaps in the wire. They were coming in from extended line into column and presenting highly desirable targets. Someone else was firing on them and the Germans were falling and scattering. We could not fire over open sights, being howitzers, but worked out the positions from the map and opened fire at reduced charge to get the shortest range. The margin of error isn't very big at that range so we got half a dozen effective rounds on to them straight away but they came under our guard, as it were, and we could no longer engage them at the shorter range.

All available rifles were collected and all ranks ordered to take cover behind the roofs of the gun-pits, signals shelter, etc. The Number Ones of gun crews were instructed to remove the dial sight from abandoned guns. My limber gunner went one better and took off the dial-sight carrier as well. Nobody was going to use my gun with any accuracy. The number of rounds we'd fired made a new calibration necessary anyway. Then we were given instructions to 'make a run for it' to a trench line some 100–200 yards behind through a gap in the wire which almost surrounded our position. We were on no account to stop to pick up casualties. This proved to be a wise order but it was heart-breaking to leave several good men hit, mostly in legs and feet, by machine-guns trained on the gap. (Sergeant J. Sellars, 295th Brigade R.F.A.)

*

The fighting in the Battle Zone resulted in many fresh batches of prisoners for the Germans, but the circumstances of the captures here were different from the earlier ones in the front line, where so many British soldiers, dazed from the recent bombardment, had become prisoners within minutes of the start of the German attack. The German troops who had made those earlier captures had been able to spend little time with their prisoners before moving on again. By contrast, the Battle Zone prisoners were usually taken after more prolonged fighting and by German soldiers who were often content to linger for some time in the positions they had captured.

These two British soldiers had both been wounded in the

fighting around Noreuil and Ecoust, which has recently been described, and they awaited their captors.

The stretcher-bearers had bandaged me up and taken me down into a dug-out. Then the Germans came along and threw a stick grenade down one entrance. It seemed a big explosion to me and the dug-out was full of dust and smoke and earth coming down from the roof but we weren't hurt. Then, from another entrance, a German officer appeared. He had a revolver in his hand and was shouting. I can see him now. He had a thin, narrow face and big glasses, and his helmet came down right over his ears. He looked like death warmed up. He was only a little man but he had a revolver and I didn't, so that made him bigger than me. The stretcher-bearers wanted me to go out first because I was wounded and less likely to be shot. I crawled out and the German spun me round, looked at my back and said something which I took to mean 'wounded'. He sent the two stretcher-bearers off and I didn't see them again. He left me down in the dug-out.

I gathered together several tins of 'bully' and some biscuits into my haversack so that I should have something to eat later. Many more wounded were sent down until the dug-out was full of wounded. The man next to me was moaning a lot; he had his leg off. My little store of food was taken by the Germans. (Lance Corporal A. Wallace, 2/5th Sherwood Foresters)

During the period of waiting, my feelings were rather mixed. Whilst my physical condition made me feel indifferent to what may happen, I had the wind up terribly lest the first Jerry who came along should stick his bayonet through me. Eventually they came, a fearful-looking lot of chaps with rifles slung over their backs, many eating biscuits from our ration bags. My fears were soon dispelled, their interest in us ceasing on finding we were wounded and unarmed.

The first officer to arrive, a big Prussian, finding I was only wounded in the arm, told me to clear out and go up to their lines. I didn't waste any time in clearing out but only went as far as our Officers' Mess. Two Jerries were leaning against the door post, looking very harmless, so I turned in and, to my surprise, found Sykes Dobson laid on a bed, having been carried in by the two Jerries at the door. After mutual enquiries as to wounds, I scrounged around and found half a tot of cold coffee and a little Johnnie Walker whisky. I drank them and then lay down. (Private F. Beardsell, 2/6th North Staffords)

Their first inspection of the British positions was of great interest for the German soldiers. After many months of trench warfare or of defending against Allied attacks, this was for most Germans their first real view of their enemy and his positions and equipment, and of living conditions in the British trenches. Even allowing for the mellowing of time and the desire of German contributors not to offend an Englishman, it is probable that the many expressions of regard for the fighting qualities and fair nature of the British soldiers and the sympathy for their dead and wounded are genuine. One German rifleman says: 'I would like to mention that I had already appreciated the courage of the English at Arras and in Flanders. Our captives gave us many cigarettes; it was like meeting old friends.' And again: 'More than once I was impressed at seeing wounded and dead English soldiers with their wallets in front of them, family photographs laid out.' Another German met a British officer standing by a wounded man. 'I suppose he was his batman. The officer refused to go to the rear without the man. He would only go if the man could be taken to the rear with him. I don't know what happened in the end; we had to move on. All honour to him for such loyalty.'

There were many Germans and British who were willing to try conversations in the other's language.

We met a troop of English prisoners coming towards us. One of them said, in German, that he was very thirsty and asked for a drink. I asked him about his very good knowledge of German. He told me that he had been an actor in Hamburg for a long time. He emptied my canteen full of coffee in a single go. He was most grateful. I don't know what his rank was; perhaps he was an officer, because he came first and the others seemed to be under his command. We exchanged addresses on a piece of paper. I wanted to talk to him a bit longer but one of our officers was sending the prisoners back quickly. I lost my piece of paper and I never heard from the Englishman. I wonder if he is still alive and might remember this if he reads it. (Feldwebel Max Schulz, 46th Regiment)

This wounded German soldier became, temporarily, a prisoner in a post held by men of the 36th (Ulster) Division.

After I had dressed the wound, using my first-aid pack, I walked to the rear and soon came to a quiet area where we had earlier by-passed an English machine-gun position. Actually, I wasn't aware of this until someone called out. I was right in front of the position. I put my hands up and clambered into the trench. They were very friendly and gave me a drink and a cigarette. There were about twenty of them, under a young officer. We could not understand each other in English, because of their dialect I think. The officer asked, *'Parlez-vous français?'*, I replied, *'Oui, monsieur'*, and then we had a short conversation. He asked where my company was. I pointed out the place where I had been hit and told him that our troops were through on both sides. He asked me whether they were now cut off. I lied to him. I knew that they were not yet cut off but, if he knew that, I think they would have got out. I don't know whether they would have left me there or taken me back as their prisoner.

About an hour later, a German officer approached with a white flag. I think he was a Hauptmann. He spoke in French with the English officer. He told the Englishman that they were cut off and the English officer said, 'Yes. Our prisoner has said the same.' Within no more than two minutes, the English had surrendered. They left for our rear, unarmed of course. The German officer said to me, 'Comrade, you may go home now.' (Musketier Adolf Schoen, 464th Regiment)

One company of German infantry, advancing in an open area between two sets of defences held by the 30th Division, which contained many Liverpool and Manchester troops, was amazed to find a football pitch laid out. 'The English, they always were sportsmen.' Elsewhere, a German rifleman went into a dug-out captured from a battalion in the 16th (Irish) Division. 'I operated the telephone by turning the handle. Someone spoke to me in English which I didn't understand. I just said, *"sabble di dot"*, an old Hamburg phrase meaning "talk till you are dead".'

This German artillery officer had earlier lost his horse, which had been killed by British shelling. He now found a replacement, again somewhere in the 16th Division's defences.

At about midday I found a magnificent English thoroughbred horse with silver-plated bridle. It stood beside its dead rider and five other dead men in the garden of a cottage ruined by shell-fire. I believed that it must have been a high-ranking officer's horse because it had such rich trappings. The dead man was an N.C.O.

with stripes on his arm. I think that he had been sent up with the five men to find out what the position was in the fighting area.

I kept that fine horse right to the end of the war but had to give it up when I left the regiment at Bonn. The regiment took it right back to Berlin but I don't know what happened to it after that. I think it was sold off when the regiment was demobilised. (Leutnant Artur Seiffert, 63rd Reserve Field Regiment)

But it was food, drink and booty that the German soldiers were really looking for in the captured trenches, particularly in the dug-outs of British officers. They fell with delight upon stocks of food and alcohol, the like of which they had not seen for years, and on fancy toilet goods. Old, worn boots were exchanged for good, sound British ones; the sleeveless leather jerkins that many British soldiers had were all requisitioned. One British prisoner watched his captors plundering a battalion headquarters dug-out. 'They were thoroughly enjoying themselves. There was no reason why they shouldn't, of course. After all, they'd captured it.'

There was hesitancy by some of the Germans because they thought that the British might have poisoned the food and drink that they had left behind. When the battalion head-quarters of the 2/5th Sherwood Foresters was captured, two officers' batmen – one a teetotaller – were forced at gun point to take a drink out of every bottle, a process which so affected the two men that, when some German reinforce-ments came down the trench, the two were slow to move aside and were forced up the side of the trench 'with a vicious kick up the backside'.

Men from a Bavarian regiment following the main attack ransacked a supply of captured provisions before coming into action.

We took as much as we could carry, even the champagne. When, late in the evening, we went into action and had to use our machine-gun, I was compelled to fill it with champagne because our water supply was giving out. Unfortunately, I had forgotten that only clean water should be used and, when we resumed firing again, the smell soon became unbearable when the champagne became hot. One of my gunners came off the best; he was putting one piece of *Gruyère* cheese after another into his mouth. (Unteroffizier Max Strobel, 7th Bavarian Regiment)

There were several important results of this plundering by the Germans of captured stores and equipment. Some German officers found it difficult to get their men to move on again and continue the fighting, and the capture of stores, especially drink, undoubtedly slowed down the German advance. The morale of the German soldiers was badly affected when they saw the ordinary daily fare of the British soldiers and realised how poor were their own rations and equipment. In his book Leutnant Ernst Jünger describes his own delight and that of his men when they ransacked a captured artillery officer's dug-out near Ecoust, but then he went on to compare what they found there with the normal life-style of his own men who 'for four long years, in torn coats, and worse fed than a Chinese coolie, had been hurried from one battlefield to the next'.*

*

It was by no means all success for the Germans. The Battle Zone defences were at least 2,000 and sometimes 3,000 yards deep and a successful attack against the front of the Battle Zone and the capture of positions within the zone were not enough for complete success. There were several sectors where the Battle Zone held for a considerable time and where the Germans could achieve only a shallow advance into it before nightfall. A good example of this situation was in the area held by the 24th Division, in the Fifth Army, where the Battle Zone around the village of Le Verguier held out for several hours. A good witness here is a British trench-mortar officer who was supporting the infantry of the 8th Queens with two six-inch heavy mortars.

At 2 p.m. the enemy were in Apple Tree Walk, about 150 or 200 of them. They were too far away for the infantry but, at 1,000 yards, just within our range. They were a 'good' target because I could see them well but they couldn't hit us. We opened fire, not rapid fire, just casually dropping them down the spout. I was in the 'O. Pip' – the observation post – about 150 yards from the mortars. The telephone line had been cut by the shelling earlier, so I signalled by hand to my corporal to lengthen or shorten the range. Our fire caught Gerry by surprise. It was probably the first time

* *Storm of Steel*, page 266.

he had been held up; he had probably come straight through the front line in the mist. I could see the white bursts of the mortar shells. The Germans hesitated and took cover, then retreated out of range to reorganise. I could still see them while they prepared to come again, not rushing but just the way we used to go over the top, steadily with rifles at the port. So we fired again, and again they took cover, but they didn't go back. We started being shelled then; probably a message had gone back to plaster our little area. This shelling continued for the rest of the action. I reckon it was battery fire of three or four rounds per gun at a time. Every time this happened, we ceased fire. It was pretty accurate stuff and throwing up great lumps of earth into our gun-pits but, fortunately, we didn't get anybody hit or any of the mortars hit. When it quietened down, we opened up again. I think he was firing by the map and couldn't alter his aim but I was firing on something I could see.

All this time the Germans kept taking cover but they made ground by little rushes of twenty-five yards. All the time there were more Germans coming from the rear to back them up. Before long, they came near enough for the Queens in Le Verguier to join in with Lewis and rifle fire. At about 5.30 p.m., Gerry got near enough to start firing pot shots at us and by 6.0 p.m. his persistence was rewarded – we were out of ammunition and he overran our forward site, capturing two gunners. We held on at the second site, using rifles against them, but they made no further attempt to rush us.

My casualties in all this action consisted of two men prisoners in the captured gun-pit, but no one was killed and none really wounded. We had many minor cuts and bruises from being blown about by the shelling but I've come off a rugger field in worse shape than that – but not as frightened! I think we had hit at least forty or fifty Germans; I could see that many bodies with binoculars and I hadn't counted the wounded who had cleared off. (Second Lieutenant S. Horscroft, 24th Heavy Trench Mortar Battery)

This trench-mortar action was just one small incident in the defence of the Battle Zone. There were many, many small actions like this one.*

* Among the German units attacking Le Verguier was the 93rd Reserve Regiment, part of the 4th Guard Division. Two officers in this regiment later became prominent personalities. They were Dietloff von Arnim, a company commander who was to become the last commander of the German Afrika Korps and who became a prisoner-of-war in Tunisia in May 1943, and Franz von Papen, a battalion commander who became a noted politician after the First World War and, as German Chancellor in 1933, was the man who formally handed power over to Adolf Hitler.

There was one substantial sector where the British units held their entire Battle Zone for the whole day. This was in the area held by the 30th and 61st (South Midland) Divisions of Lieutenant-General Maxse's XVIII Corps opposite St Quentin. Maxse was one of the soundest commanders in the British Expeditionary Force and had made his dispositions well. Only five battalions from these two divisions had been in the Forward Zone and remnants of four of these were still holding out in redoubts. What happened here was a good example of the new defensive plans working properly. The redoubts still holding out must have caused some disruption to the German advance, and it is significant that the open space between the Forward Zone and the Battle Zone was wider here – up to 4,000 yards – than at any other part of the British line that had been attacked. The mist had cleared by the time the Germans reached the front of the Battle Zone and they were forced to mount a frontal attack on well-sited, well-manned positions in conditions of clear visibility.

We saw him first of all at six or seven hundred yards, coming over open downland. We were on a high part and we could see them below us. We had no orders of any kind, so we opened fire independently. Where our officers had got to I don't know. You had it in your mind, 'If we don't hit those fellows, they're going to kill us.' We had plenty of ammunition and I must have shot off between two and three hundred rounds. I know my rifle was getting pretty warm. We checked them but they kept coming on. There were so many empty cartridge cases that we wondered what would happen if we wanted to surrender. Gerry would probably have shot us, seeing all those cartridge cases.

We were relieved at the end of the day – daft, silly and stunned after the earlier bombardment and then this long fight with the German infantry. (Private S. W. Foote, 2/5th Gloucesters)

Private Foote's experience is typical of the men in the battalions which held the front of General Maxse's Battle Zone – the 2nd Green Howards, the 2nd Bedfords, the 2/6th Royal Warwicks, the 2/5th Gloucesters, and then the 1/8th Argyll and Sutherland Highlanders who had to give a little ground to make a defensive flank because the Germans were through on their left.* The Green Howards also lost part of their position around the village of Roupy, but a counter-attack later restored the situation and the front of the Battle Zone on a six-mile sector right in the middle of the embattled Fifth Army was held all day.

It was a success for all arms. Every time the Germans formed up for an attack, they were engaged by artillery, mortars and heavy machine-guns and then, if they did advance, by the weapons of the infantry. The War Diary of the 30th Division gives these details of the activities of the division's heavy machine-guns during the day.

Twenty-four machine-guns were posted in the Battle Zone. Teams were provided with deep dug-outs or they fired from shafts . . . The guns came into action with great effect, breaking attack after attack. The Germans came to a standstill in the evening and the majority broke and ran to the cover of slopes in the rear. A quarry to the north-east of Roupy proved a fatal attraction. At one time, 1,000 men were in and around it. The machine-guns ripped through them with fatal effect, all guns firing at full rate. Two guns here fired 35,000 rounds, another 12,000 and a fourth a little less.†

The successful defence here could well have been achieved elsewhere if the conditions had been the same. The battalions holding the Battle Zone were not crack troops yet they held off four German divisions and parts of a fifth. The heaviest known German regimental casualties of the day were in the 66th Infantry Regiment – the 3rd Magdeburgs – with 182 men killed, 554 wounded and twenty-five missing. This regiment had attacked the 1st North Staffords in the Forward Zone in the morning and then had crossed over the boundary between the 24th and 61st Divisions to attack the Battle Zone

* One of this battalion's officers, Second Lieutenant John Buchan, had been wounded by the German bombardment but he stayed with his platoon all through the action of this day. For his leadership and his refusal to surrender when his post was almost surrounded, Buchan was later awarded a post-humous Victoria Cross. He was killed early on the following day. Appendix 7 will list all the V.C.s of 21 March.

The Argyll's commander, Lieutenant-Colonel James Macalpine-Downie, was also a casualty. He was not content to remain at his headquarters and was hit by shellfire and badly wounded while going round his men. He was a big man and it took four stretcher-bearers, instead of the normal two, to get him back to a dressing-station. He died of his wounds.

† Public Record Office WO 95/2313.

of the 1/8th Argyll and Sutherland Highlanders. The British defence was achieved with only modest losses. Four officers and 163 men were killed in the five battalions holding the Battle Zone; the number of wounded and the casualties of the supporting arms are not known. It is not known what the total German casualties from all the divisions attacking here were, but at least one of the first-wave German divisions, the 45th Reserve, had to be replaced by a second-wave German division at 3 p.m. because 'the original division was no longer up to it'. Unfortunately for the British, there were six more fresh German divisions available here to renew the attack the following morning, and the Germans were already well through on the right and partly so on the left. There was no other sector on the fronts held by either the Fifth or the Third Armies where the Germans were stopped on such a considerable frontage of the Battle Zone.

The outcome of this battle, like that of many another battle, would be largely decided by the number of reserve troops available to commanders and the way those reserves were handled. The Germans had committed approximately half of their available divisions to the attack and many of these still had plenty of life left in them yet. Almost three quarters of the available British divisions on the attack front had been in the line when the attack started. Large parts of these divisions had disappeared in the Forward Zone fighting and most of their remaining troops were now in action in the Battle Zone, leaving only a few battalions as divisional reserves. It was these divisional reserves, together with the few reserve divisions available to corps, that were now being drawn into the battle. Where the Battle Zone defences were clearly crumbling, where there were gaps appearing between defending units, where tired and shattered battalions were falling back – it was towards these places that the British reserves were being hurried. These men were all that stood between the Germans and the clear-cut success that the Germans hoped for on that first day of the battle.

Many of the reserve battalions had been shelled that morning in their hutted camps but their casualties had rarely been heavy. The later part of the morning had been spent waiting for orders, with the distant sound of battle the cause of much speculation. The 1/1st Hertfords, part of the 39th Division, was a typical reserve battalion which had been in camp at Aizecourt-le-Bas, six miles behind the embattled 16th (Irish) Division. Before the battle, their officers had often reconnoitred the roads to the front and met the Irish battalions they were covering. Lieutenant H. J. Knee was one of the Hertford platoon commanders.

News came through very slowly and only the vaguest idea could be formed of what was happening. And still we stood by. In the early afternoon, our camp was shelled and we moved to cover on the reverse side of a slope. I read aloud to my platoon from a light-humoured book to keep the men's mind off it. It passed the time away; there's nothing worse than boredom. If you've been sitting about all day doing nothing, then it's not easy to get the men on the move into action again.

Private W. H. Weller was also in this battalion.

At four o'clock in the afternoon, the bugle blew for tea. We did know what that meant. Such beautiful tea it was, in those big square dixies that we carried on our field cookers, nice and strong with plenty of sugar and the milk not put in until it had had time to draw nicely. Those of us who survived will always remember that tea. We never had a chance to drink it. The fall-in blew and off we went up the line.

We met a couple of pieces of medium artillery pulling out, which shows how far back we were when we started. We also met a single Irishman, who, contrary to the strict letter of the Army Act and the established custom of the Army in the field, replied 'Bloody awful' when we asked what it was like up there. Our humourist said he did not mind the language, but it was an offence to use words likely to cause despondency.

Lieutenant Knee again.

Then we met some more gunners, belonging to a battery of 6-inch howitzers, playing football – out of ammo, I suppose. The first wounded man passed us – a youngster with a gaping wound in his arm. We fell out for a rest and filled water bottles from an R.E. water point, and then carried on through Villers Faucon, which was being heavily shelled.

St Emilie had fallen! Our plans had to be revised and so we stopped short of a deep railway cutting on the left of the St Emilie road. There stood a heavy gun on rails – abandoned. It was a ridiculous place in which to stop and soon we moved again. Hereabouts there were a number of huts containing bodies of men who appeared to have been gassed.

We had no idea what the position was ahead; we weren't in touch with any other unit. We were very apprehensive. But when you are in company with many others, all in the same boat, one's own apprehensiveness tends to be dissipated. There was no singing or boisterousness. The men were very quiet and reserved but they weren't frightened. We were going up to do something but we didn't know what that something was.

The Hertfords eventually found a half-dug trench and they relieved there some Royal Engineers and Army Service Corps men who were 'glad to see us and happier still when they found that they were free to go back'.

There were many battalions like this one during the afternoon and early evening of 21 March, their anxious men pushed up into uncertain and dangerous situations. Some were immediately engulfed in fierce fighting; others – like the Hertfords in fact – would not have to fight until the morning. This platoon commander has recorded his experiences and the wistful thoughts that he had before going into action.

When we were given our orders to move up from Faillouel we were told to look for pockets of Bosche and to mop them up, but we did not see any. We met many of our gunners – heavy and field – streaming back in disorder and without arms, kit or officers. We collected them together and formed them into platoons and collected what rifles and ammunition we could find lying about and tried to restore order by turning them into infantry.

I well remember the wild anemones in the woods as we moved up and wondered if I would ever live to see them again in the woods around my home town of Tonbridge in Kent. (Second Lieutenant G. H. Gibbs, 11th Royal Fusiliers)

The arrival of the reserves in the Battle Zone was often the factor that prevented the Germans breaking right through the defences, and many of these troops were soon in action. This man was with a mixed party, including men from the 9th Royal Sussex who had come up from reserve and were now facing the German advance, near Jeancourt in the 24th Division's Battle Zone.

So there we were, just waiting for our first glimpse of the Germans. Then an incredible thing happened. Over the top of the ridge on our left came the first of the enemy. Not one, or two, or even a small detachment, but a whole line in extended order right across the whole of the ridge. This line of infantry advanced at a walking pace in fairly good order. Then, at an interval of probably twenty yards, a second wave appeared, and they kept on coming over the top of the ridge until we had the spectacle of several waves of German infantry advancing in extended order down the slope to Jeancourt. They were very tidy, just as though they were coming down Richmond Hill on parade.

I was very, very impatient about opening fire. I recall that one fellow in the Sussex opened fire early and he got badly chewed. I think it was a Sussex officer who was in charge and made us wait. When the first wave of the Germans was approaching a point where they would soon disappear out of view and into the hollow, we got the order. Everything in our position was brought to bear. Our machine-guns were firing, the Lewis guns of the Sussex were firing and everyone else with rifles. The Germans were about 300 yards away. I got five rounds or so off but can't say whether I hit anyone. You can't in an action like that.

I was unable to observe the effect of this firing because, almost immediately it started, two of our machine-guns were withdrawn and I was with one of them. (Private F. Plimmer, 24th Machine Gun Battalion)

One battalion sent up from the rear was the 2/4th Leicesters, which had only just come out of the line after twenty-four days of continuous trench duty. The battalion was now ordered to go up and reinforce the defenders of Ecoust. But Ecoust had already fallen and the Leicesters could get no farther than the rear of the Battle Zone, which may have been a fine line on the map but was no more than a marked-out trench with only the turf removed and having no barbed wire. It was completely exposed in the open. The battalion deployed in one extended line of men as far on either flank as it could reach. The men piled up in front of them the pieces of cut turf to give a little cover from the masses of German infantry seen advancing out of Ecoust. Some escaping field gunners, carrying the breech blocks of their guns, came through the Leicesters' line. Two aeroplanes had a dogfight overhead, which resulted in the

German plane crashing in flames. A Leicester officer, with a revolver in each hand, stood on the road from Ecoust, stopping stragglers and forcing them to take up position with the Leicesters. There was absolutely nothing between the advancing Germans and the open ground behind the Battle Zone except this single line of infantrymen in their makeshift positions. It must have been a dramatic scene.

Soldiers who were in that line tell of two men who did much to inspire them to stay and fight in this almost hopeless position. One was the battalion commander, Lieutenant-Colonel Sir Iain Colquhoun, who, as a captain in the 1st Scots Guards, had once been court-martialled for disobeying an order from Sir Douglas Haig, at Christmas 1915, not to repeat the informal truce and fraternisation held with the Germans in No Man's Land the previous Christmas. A real 'soldier's man', who was thought by his men to have turned down the command of a brigade to stay with the battalion, Sir Iain strode up and down behind the thin line of men, exhorting them to hold their position. Doing exactly the same thing was Regimental Sergeant-Major Withers, known as 'African Joe' because of his Boer War medal ribbons. The R.S.M. was heard to be muttering repeatedly, 'Be British! Be British!' and, more lugubriously, 'You'll all be bloody prisoners by morning.'

When the Germans attacked, the Leicesters did hold and the Germans advanced no farther here this day. The battalion's casualties were modest – twelve men killed and eighteen wounded – and they were not prisoners in the morning.

*

When the reserve troops came up into the fighting area, they were sometimes called upon to mount counter-attacks on positions in the Battle Zone that had been captured by the Germans. Such attacks were an important part of the defence plan. The holding of the Battle Zone was considered vital, and reserves were definitely to be used in this way. But counter-attacks carried out in the middle of a fluid and confused situation, such as existed in many parts of the Battle Zone on that day, were most difficult minor tactical operations to carry out successfully. They required at least four favourable factors: good knowledge of the ground, careful preparation, a secure position from which to launch the attack and troops well trained in this role. The companies and battalions that were pushed into counter-attacks in the afternoon and early evening of this day had few of these factors in their favour. Orders had usually been issued at corps or divisional level and then passed down the chain of command. By the time the unit chosen to make the attack was ready to move, the situation had usually altered. Sometimes a cancellation order had been issued but had not arrived. The counter-attacking units marched up, often against an unnerving flow of wounded or panicky men falling back from the fighting ahead. Sudden firing broke out from positions that had been thought to be friendly. Platoon commanders tried to deploy their nervous men into attack formation, tried to find out exactly where the Germans were, tried to mount the attack. The result was almost always the same. Heavy casualties were sustained, leaders were hit, and men quickly looked for the nearest cover. It was easy, although sometimes necessary, for higher commanders to order such efforts, but the conditions in the Battle Zone made successful counter-attacks a rare event that day. The Battle Zone defence system had already crumbled too much and the German strength and momentum was too strong to be reversed.

There are two particularly interesting counter-attack incidents that can be described. The first was in the 61st (South Midland) Division and concerns the efforts of a battalion, the 2/4th Royal Berkshires, that was ordered up from divisional reserve to regain ground lost near the village of Maissemy. The battalion commander was Lieutenant-Colonel J. H. Dimmer, V.C., M.C., a 'blood and thunder' soldier from an old army family. His father and grandfather had both been regimental sergeant-majors in the 60th Rifles (King's Royal Rifle Corps) and he is reputed to have been the first 'ranker' commissioned into this regiment. The outbreak of the war had found Dimmer serving on detached duty with the West Africa Regiment in Sierra Leone. He caught the first boat for England and was with a battalion of his regiment in the First Battle of Ypres, when he won a Victoria Cross for staying with a machine-gun despite being wounded five times. Now he was commanding this Berkshire Territorial battalion and the men he commanded were proud to belong to 'Colonel Dimmer's Battalion'. He had also been married just one month earlier.

Dimmer decided not only to lead the counter-attack himself but to do so mounted on his horse – a move that he believed would give his men more confidence in this hazardous venture. At least one company commander begged him to dismount before coming into range of the German fire but Dimmer refused and rode on, his groom, also mounted, at his side. Two companies of the Berkshires were spread out on either side of their commander and a third company followed in support. Many British troops in near-by positions watched. A man of the 2/5th Gloucesters, in a trench on the edge of Holnon Wood, remembers, 'We were astonished; we just couldn't believe it. It was good riding country but not in those conditions.' And a Royal Engineer: 'We realised that the two horsemen were silhouetted against the skyline and we put up covering fire to protect them. But as soon as they reached the top, they were picked off and fell to the ground.' Colonel Dimmer's horse then ran back through the men following and they had to break ranks to let it pass.

The Germans had been much nearer than had been believed and had themselves been on the verge of attacking. A long line of German infantrymen now sprang up from the ground and, supported by machine-gun fire aimed at the Berkshires, came forward. Unnerved by the loss of their commander and by the sudden appearance of the German attack, the Berkshires fell back in confusion. The counter-attack was a complete failure. Lieutenant-Colonel Dimmer and about forty of his men were killed.*

The men involved in the second incident were from another Territorial battalion – the 2/5th Lincolns, 59th (North

* Lieutenant-Colonel Dimmer is one of the few British soldiers from this battle with an identifiable grave. His body rests in Vadencourt British Cemetery, near the place at which he was killed. His horse was taken over by Second Lieutenant, later Captain, H. Jones, 2/4th Oxford and Bucks Light Infantry (see page 178) who rode it until the end of the war.

Midland) Division. The Lincolns were ordered up to relieve a Sherwood Forester battalion believed to be still holding out in Noreuil, but the Germans had already all but surrounded and overwhelmed the defenders of that village. The Lincolns moved forward by platoons, knowing little of what was really happening ahead or on their flanks. The leading platoon did just reach Noreuil before the Germans completed the encirclement of the village and it was a soldier of the Noreuil garrison who described the platoon's arrival. The incident is confirmed by the Official History.

We managed to get into a communication trench a bit farther back but this was absolutely crammed with men from another battalion who were being sent up. There was a sergeant with them. He was pressing them forward and nearly pushed us out into the sunken road again. Then he told his men to get out up on top and shoot at the Germans. I knew they didn't stand a chance. They were frightened to death. One young chap did climb up and got shot right through the head; he fell back right on top of a badly wounded officer who was propped up in the bottom of the trench. The sergeant tried to order some more men up. I told them not to – 'Let him get up and set an example himself.' That was really the end of it. The Germans had come round the back of us and we had to surrender. (Lance Corporal A. Bowler, 2/5th Sherwood Foresters)

The remainder of the Lincolns were still coming up, unaware that the Germans had encircled Noreuil and were pushing on fast. It was an almost ludicrous position, with the two sides moving fast, parallel to each other but in opposite directions. For some time, neither British nor Germans bothered the other. The Germans were happy to keep pushing on, the British thought that the men they could see on either flank were the defenders of Noreuil streaming back. Eventually the Germans turned inwards and three companies of the Lincolns found themselves surrounded.

Then the officers realised what was happening behind. There was no one much firing at us and we couldn't see anyone to fire back at. We saw then that the Germans had come through on both sides of us and we could see that the men behind us were being taken prisoner. We were in this horseshoe with Germans on three sides. I didn't see many German infantry, just a sprinkling with rifles, but I vividly remember seeing several teams of German artillery. I remember one German artilleryman leading the front horse of one team, quite an old fellow and obviously used to horses. He had a little curved pipe with a knot at the bottom of the bowl. I thought he looked so unconcerned that he might have been ploughing his fields at home.

The Germans started shouting, '*Los! Los!*', telling us to surrender. One man was flabbergasted and a little slow to get his equipment off, and a German came for him. One of our chaps told him to hurry up. We really couldn't do anything; I doubt if one man ever fired a shot. Some of the men were excited but most of us took it quite calmly. The officers were a bit down at the mouth but there was nothing we could do about it. We never had a chance. (Lance Corporal J. Wortley, 2/5th Lincolns)

Only a few men, in the rearmost company, were able to put up any resistance. They found a half-dug trench, all that there was of the supposed Brown Line at the rear of the Battle Zone.

There were no more than twenty of us. We could see the Germans bobbing up and firing at us; we were just beyond hand-grenade range – it was all rifle fire. The volume of it was terrific. No one was giving orders; each man did what he thought was best. Our rifles were nearly red hot. I was stood, firing my rifle over one of our men's shoulder, and he suddenly turned round and swore at me for deafening him – 'I don't care if you are a corporal, go fire your bloody rifle somewhere else.' Men were going down. One of them was a Notts and Jocks fellow next to me and he got a bullet through his head.* There was a great hole in the back of his head and blood was pumping out.

There were only seven or eight of us left at the end. All of a sudden, a German officer stood on the parapet with a revolver in each hand, shouting, '*Raus Engländer! Raus!*' A long line of Germans swept right past us on each side. It's marvellous what you think of at times like that. Every man drew the bolt of his rifle and threw it away and then dug the barrel of the rifle into the trench bottom. It was only a gesture really.

The Germans pointed to the rear and told us to go. They wanted to get on farther forward. I suppose we were just a minor obstacle. (Corporal B. Whyers, 2/5th Lincolns)

* 'Notts and Jocks': Notts and Derbys, the old name for the Sherwood Foresters.

Three complete companies, all but forty-nine men who were killed, were soon marching back towards the German rear.

It is not known how many counter-attacks were attempted to recover lost positions in the Battle Zone – perhaps a dozen during the day. Few of these were completely successful. German accounts often describe how their advance was held up by the unexpected appearance of British reserves, but these setbacks were always the result of stands made by the British in static positions, rarely the result of counter-attacks.

*

In many places along the battlefront, British troops were on the move, not forwards but to the rear. 'Retreat' is not a word favoured by the British Army – 'withdrawal' is preferred – but the movement that commenced in small measure on the morning of 21 March and which accelerated during the afternoon and evening would not stop for many days and this battle would become known, unofficially, as 'The March Retreat'. It all started in a small way.

When the Jerries came towards our line in large numbers, they were firing from the hip and I thought, 'Tosh. Do what some of the others are doing. Hop it back.' So I did. I was not alone, I can assure you, otherwise I don't think I should be able to write this.

The man who wrote this nearly sixty years later was a private soldier in an ordinary infantry battalion. It is not suggested that the whole army ran away; the descriptions in preceding pages of stout defence on many parts of the battlefield give a more representative picture. But what started as panic-stricken flight by a few men like 'Tosh' sometimes turned into a more substantial movement. A study of official British reports, often compiled when officers returned from German prison camps after the war, all too often reveals references to Germans seen coming through on the flank because the neighbouring unit had either surrendered or fallen back without sufficient cause. Personal accounts, written more recently, often echo the same theme, although it is rarely the writer's own battalion that is blamed for failing to hold; another unit to right or left always gets the blame. The effect of such retreats was that, right from the beginning of this battle, there developed an attitude of uncertainty about flanks, a tendency for men in good defensive positions to be looking over their shoulders and wondering if they too ought not to be moving back.

The artillery were also falling back, although their withdrawal was dictated more by necessity than panic. It may be dramatic to describe a battery of guns fighting to the last round over open sights, but an army that loses its guns is in serious trouble and it was necessary for threatened batteries to withdraw. Their guns could not be pulled out without the horse teams.

I remember that, on the morning of the 21st March, our 4·5 howitzers had been in stationary positions for many months, but during the morning, all that was changed. For the first time that we had been on the Western Front, things were being done according to the book, i.e. gallop up to the guns, limber up and retire for half a mile, take horses back a further 100 yards and wait for orders to repeat the operation. This happened several times during the day – and many times subsequently during the following days – and I well remember our C.R.A. [Commander Royal Artillery], who was an old officer, in a state of great excitement. I don't suppose he ever expected to see that sort of thing again. (Driver L. E. Williamson, 513th Company R.A.S.C.)

But for some other drivers this drill did not always work so smoothly.

We completely failed to find the guns. At about 13.00, when visibility had improved a little, we saw an officer coming from the line and our officer went over to him. He was an Intelligence Officer and was able to tell us that Jerry was pretty near and to advise us to clear off as there was nothing we could do. We therefore formed into column of route to set off for the advanced wagon line, but then heard shouting in the distance. We were able to distinguish a number of men who were shouting and waving to us. These turned out to be the remaining gunners from our battery. They were carrying the major, who had a bullet in his knee.

We asked them where the guns were. They said Jerry had them. Of course that amused us, but we then asked for the truth, whereupon they asked us why the hell they were carrying the breech blocks with them if it wasn't to prevent Jerry from using the guns. The last two teams of horses, of which ours was one, had been held back to take the gunners who crowded on to the limbers or rode on the off horses, and we all set off back to the wagon line. (Driver E. Carrington, 177th Brigade R.F.A.)

The sight of artillerymen who had disabled their guns by removing breech blocks, and sometimes dial sights, retreating on foot and carrying these items, was a common one.

There were scathing comments on some of the withdrawals.

South of Grand Seraucourt was a wide, shallow valley. Throughout the morning, artillery gun limbers and ammunition wagons used this spot as a rendezvous. There was also a 12-inch howitzer in action there. To my certain knowledge, this valley never came under shellfire throughout the day. Yet, by 11.00 a.m., that 12-inch howitzer had been abandoned by its detachment on orders from the officer. I visited it several times that day. Round the gun stood a large number of 12-inch shells, all ready fused. No attempt had been made to disable the gun. Even the officers' kits and the mess stores, including an unopened case of whisky, had been abandoned. There was also a perfectly good motor bicycle. It was the most disgraceful instance of panic I ever came across. We collected all the evidence we could and later on sent in a report on the incident to H.Q. An inquiry was held and the officer concerned was exonerated, a thoroughly disgraceful end to a thoroughly disgraceful episode.

It was this tendency to come back rather than to fight to the last that contributed largely to the *débâcle* of the Fifth Army. No one felt confident that the people on his right and left would stand firm. As I said before, there was a lack of collective courage. (Captain F. N. Broome, 173rd Brigade, R.F.A.)

Captain Broome, a South African, wrote these harsh words in the 1920s, but when he sent these notes to me recently he had added this further comment:

It was only years later that I realised that this first impression was not entirely correct.

Others who were on the move were the personnel of brigade, divisional and, later, corps headquarters and of all the administrative and service units around those headquarters whose commanders had decided that the German advance was getting too close for comfort. These moves often took place in two stages, with the non-essential elements being ordered away first, but the effect on near-by fighting units of staff officers and their servants seen hurriedly loading personal possessions into lorries, while the Germans were still some distance away by an infantryman's standards, did not improve morale and was often a contributory factor in the retreat of the fighting units. Once an army starts to move back, it is very difficult to stop that movement. The War Diaries of some fighting units contain scathing references to headquarters which commandeered scarce lorries to move personal baggage at a time, when units such as medical stations could not find transport to evacuate wounded men, or when the artillery had to abandon guns for want of transport.

Farther back, again, there was an area of more calm but also of some unreality. One man who was in an Entrenching Battalion working for the Royal Engineers at Tincourt, seven miles behind the front, remembers that the noise of the shelling was thought to be associated with a British attack not a German one, and when a rumour was circulated that the Germans had broken through, 'it was greeted with much scorn'. It was so quiet behind the Flesquières Salient that, at Sorel-le-Grand, only four miles from the front, the 6th King's Own Scottish Borderers played an inter-company football tournament during the afternoon. Paul Maze was a French *sous-officier* who was attached to General Gough's headquarters and he has described a journey he made that afternoon.

I was struck by the absence of troops anywhere back of the line. Generally, at this juncture of a battle, reserve divisions are marching to the guns. Alas! None were to be seen, for the simple reason that there were none available beyond two divisions which the battle had already engulfed.*

---

* *A Frenchman in Khaki*, Heinemann, 1934, page 286.

10

The Fall of the Redoubts

The prolonged defence by commanding officers and reserve companies in the Forward Zone is one of the most heroic actions in the history of the British Army and undoubtedly delayed the enemy and inflicted very heavy losses on him. (General Staff War Diary of Lieutenant-General Sir Ivor Maxse's XVIII Corps)*

21 March 1918 was not one of the British Army's best days, and the defence of the redoubts and of the other positions still holding out after the German attack had swept through the Forward Zone provided at least something in which generals could later express pride. This pride was later shared by the regiments whose battalions were involved and by at least one city whose men formed a majority of the garrison in one redoubt. It was often suggested that these positions held out 'to the end', implying either that no man in the garrison remained who was not dead or seriously wounded or that no more ammunition was left. Much of the pride in these actions was well justified, but a certain amount of legend grew up which does not stand up to closer examination, especially when German accounts are studied and when accurate casualty figures are examined.

After the Germans had completed the capture of most of the British Forward Zone, within two hours of the opening of their attack, the only positions still holding out there were all in the Fifth Army area south of the Flesquières Salient. The officers commanding these positions knew that there was little chance of their receiving any help from the Battle Zone and that they were expected to hold out for as long as possible and inflict the maximum casualties and delay on the Germans. In General Maxse's corps, which had many such positions, it had been stated that the redoubts should attempt to hold out for up to forty-eight hours and then, presumably if the fighting in the Battle Zone had gone well, some relieving counter-attack might be possible.

* Public Record Office WO 95/953.

The redoubts and similar positions that were still holding out at noon on 21 March can be split into three groups. In the north were Chapel Hill and Epéhy, neither of which had been fully encircled by the Germans but which were separated from each other by a deep German advance. North and south of St Quentin were no fewer than seven and possibly eight redoubts still holding out, all in divisions of General Maxse's corps. In the extreme south there were at least three further, but smaller, positions. This description of the fortunes of the men in these positions can start with the story of the main group of redoubts in the centre, near St Quentin.

Eight battalions had been holding the Forward Zone here, and it is probable that all of these still had some men holding out at noon although they had been attacked by no fewer than six German divisions. It has been explained earlier that the smaller posts around these redoubts had all been swept away by the Germans advancing in the fog; it was doubtful, therefore, if the larger redoubts thus isolated could now hold out for the forty-eight hours previously expected of them. An important order was issued by General Maxse at 3.55 p.m.; it gave permission for the redoubt commanders to break out after dark and make their way back to the main British positions if they could do so.

This order came too late for three of the redoubts. Fresnoy Redoubt, held by the commanding officer and part of the 1/5th Gordon Highlanders, and the small hamlet of Le Pontchu, with the last remnant of the 12th Royal Irish Rifles, both surrendered during the early afternoon. Very little is known about these two actions, but there are more details available about the next position to fall. This was L'Epine de Dallon, a redoubt based on the ruined buildings of a hamlet on a small rise directly opposite St Quentin and held by part of the 2nd Wiltshires. The defence here had started well when a party of British troops under German escort seen passing in the fog had been rescued, the escorts, according to the battalion history, being 'settled forever'. The rescued men turned out to be the battalion cooks. More German troops, seen passing in the fog, were fired upon before the Germans turned their full attention on the Wiltshires and commenced a series of attacks in which a German aeroplane joined. By 2.30 p.m., the Germans had infiltrated among the ruined buildings. Lieutenant-Colonel A. V. P. Martin, the Wiltshires' commander, was blown into a shell hole, wounded and dazed. The rest of the garrison had to surrender.

It is not known how many of the five remaining redoubts in this area received General Maxse's order permitting them to break out that night. At least one was still in telephone contact with its brigade headquarters but it is probable that permission, granted in mid-afternoon, to break out after dark, four or five hours hence, was of little comfort to the hard-pressed defenders. Enghien Redoubt, defended by battalion headquarters and D Company of the 2/4th Oxford and Bucks Light Infantry, held out until 4 p.m., but then the garrison tried to fight their way out on their own initiative. It is possible that no more than one officer and two privates escaped successfully.

The defence of the next redoubt to fall became the best-known action of the day, although its importance at the time was no more than that of the other redoubts near St Quentin and its experiences were very little different from theirs. Manchester Hill was a typical redoubt, sited on a small, completely featureless hill, from the top of which a good view could be had right into St Quentin. There was a concrete artillery observation post on the crest. In the rear of the hill was a quarry, into the sides of which had been dug the living quarters of the men who were now manning the defence posts on and around the hill. By no more than a coincidence, the men who held it were D Company of the 16th Manchesters, originally the 1st Manchester Pals. The Germans had a name for the hill too; they called it *'Margarine Höhe'* – 'Margarine Hill', possibly after the French name for it. The Manchester battalion commander, Lieutenant-Colonel Wilfrith Elstob, was also here with his headquarters. Elstob, son of a Cheshire clergyman, a schoolmaster before joining the Manchester Pals of 1914, is described as a 'big burly chap, very firm, but very understanding'. It was he who had spoken to his battalion before the battle and had made the dramatic statement about Manchester Hill – 'Here we fight and here we die'. The number of Manchesters present when the hill became surrounded was eight officers and 160 men. There

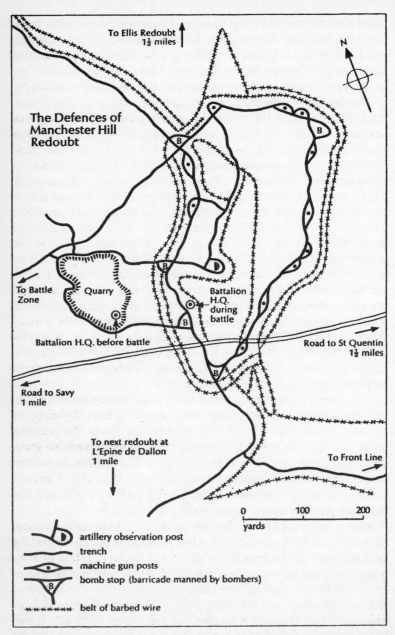

To Ellis Redoubt
1½ miles

N

**The Defences of
Manchester Hill
Redoubt**

B

B

B

D

To Battle
Zone

Quarry

B

Battalion
H.Q.
during
battle

B

Battalion H.Q. before battle

Road to St Quentin
1½ miles

B

Road to Savy
1 mile

To next redoubt at
L'Epine de Dallon
1 mile

To Front Line

0   100   200
yards

D   artillery observation post

trench

machine gun posts

B   bomb stop (barricade manned by bombers)

×××××××   belt of barbed wire

Diagram 2

were also mortars, heavy machine-guns and three men from the 11th South Lancashires who were operating a radio set, but it is believed that the artillery observation post was not manned. This was unfortunate, because a good telephone line to the rear remained intact almost to the end of the action.

The first sign of the Germans near the redoubt that morning had been when the scream of a sentry in an outer post was heard in the fog. He had been bayoneted. The Germans soon encircled the hill and some firing took place, but the first attacks were not pressed home. When the fog lifted later in the morning, the men on Manchester Hill could see platoons of German soldiers calmly trudging past the redoubt towards the Battle Zone. For some time these Germans took little notice of the Manchesters' positions – it was the old story of 'infiltrate and leave the defended positions to following-up troops'. The defenders had even been able to do some work on improving their trenches and Colonel Elstob visited most of his posts, distributing fresh ammunition and encouragement to his men. There was some excitement when a column of British soldiers was seen marching down a road from the Battle Zone, but these turned out to be prisoners under escort and the men on Manchester Hill realised, for the first time, how far the Germans had advanced past them and how serious their position was.

The Germans did not mount their main attack until 3 p.m., but then it took only ninety minutes of furious fighting to finish off Manchester Hill. The trench mortars in the redoubt soon ran out of ammunition and the Vickers machine-guns were knocked out, probably by the fire of a light howitzer battery that the Germans had brought up. The German infantry soon got a foothold in the trenches and posts of the hill and the defenders were gradually driven in.

Many men talk of the bravery of Lieutenant-Colonel Elstob, who took a leading part in the fighting. He refused a German call to surrender and spoke on the telephone to brigade headquarters. He reported that the Germans were in the redoubt and that his men were 'dead beat', but he assured the brigade commander that 'the Manchester Regiment will defend Manchester Hill to the last'. Returning to the fight, Elstob climbed out of his trench to throw grenades at the

Germans but was shot. His adjutant, Captain Norman Sharples, reached up to pull Elstob back but he, too, was hit. Both men died. The remnants of the garrison surrendered soon afterwards, although an officer in a British position a mile away claims that he heard a lone Lewis gun firing for an hour after all other sounds of action had subsided.

The Germans who had stormed what they called Margarine Hill were Westphalians of the 158th Infantry Regiment, part of the German 50th Division. Two battalions of the regiment had by-passed the hill and left it to the 2nd Battalion, under the command of Hauptmann Otto Gabcke, to take the hill. The final assault was carried out by the 8th Company under Leutnant Alsweh, a *Landwehr* officer. The German regimental history pays great tribute to the defenders, particularly to one post in the quarry behind the hill which refused to surrender and whose members all had to be killed by hand grenades; perhaps these men were with the lone Lewis gun heard firing after the main action finished. The German casualties are not known, although Leutnant Alsweh lost an arm and two platoon commanders were killed.

Lieutenant-Colonel Elstob received a well-merited posthumous Victoria Cross for his bravery, and the defence of Manchester Hill became a proud part of Manchester's history from that day onwards.*

*

* One of the 16th Manchesters men killed on this day was Private Hermann Schaefer, one of Manchester's large pre-war German population. When war broke out in August 1914, many of the Manchester Germans were holidaying in Germany and were conscripted into the German Army. Schaefer was one of those still in Manchester and he joined the Manchester Pals. The Manchesters' company commander on Manchester Hill, Lieutenant J. Clarke, died of pneumonia in a prison-camp hospital at Cologne in October 1918.

The German battalion commander, Hauptmann Otto Gabcke, became a Generalleutnant in the Second World War and commanded the 294th Infantry Division. He was killed on the Russian Front on 22 March 1942 and is buried at Kharkov in the Ukraine.

When I visited Manchester Hill outside St Quentin in 1976, I found the concrete and steel remains of the artillery observation post still on the top of the hill. The only other signs of the action here were a few lumps of chalk in the ploughed land on the hill, showing that deep trenches had once been dug here. There is no memorial to the stand made by Lieutenant-Colonel Elstob and his men. The quarry in the rear of the hill now has two uses. Part is a small nature reserve around a pond; part is a rubbish dump.

The three remaining redoubts near St Quentin all fell before dark. These were Ellis Redoubt, held by part of the 2/8th Worcesters, Boadicea Redoubt, held by the 2nd Royal Inniskilling Fusiliers, and Race Course Redoubt by the 15th Royal Irish Rifles. There are few details available of the fall of Ellis Redoubt but there are more of the two Ulster-defended positions.

Boadicea Redoubt was held by battalion headquarters and at least one company of the 2nd Royal Inniskilling Fusiliers. The battalion commander was Lieutenant-Colonel Lord Farnham, who only four days earlier had been refereeing the boxing competition between his battalion and the 1st Battalion in the sports on St Patrick's Day. Details of the fall of Boadicea Redoubt come from the history of the German 463rd Regiment, composed mainly of men from Hamburg, which was leading the attack of the 238th Division here. The redoubt had somehow been missed by the German bombardment and the German infantry were not keen to tackle this strong position, although they soon mopped up the smaller posts in the area. The 2nd Battalion of the German regiment was left to invest the redoubt and mobile guns were brought forward. So far, it was all a familiar pattern of events.

Then, Oberleutnant Prinz, a company commander, received a deputation from one of his junior officers and three privates who could all speak English, asking if they could approach the redoubt under a white flag and attempt to persuade its commander to surrender. Watched anxiously by German infantrymen who might soon have to carry out an assault, the deputation approached the redoubt. The defenders were told that unless they surrendered heavy artillery would bombard the redoubt. The German history describes how, a few minutes later, there filed out of the redoubt a lieutenant-colonel, carrying a small white dog, three captains, seven subalterns and 241 other men. Forty-one machine-guns and mortars were found in the redoubt. The British lieutenant-colonel asked for, and was given, a document stating that he had put up a good fight before surrendering. It is not known how many casualties the redoubt garrison had suffered; the total fatal casualties of the whole battalion − of which at least two and a half companies were not in Boadicea Redoubt

– were forty-seven men. No officers were among the killed. One badly wounded artillery officer was found in the redoubt and a German machine-gunner, Feldwebel Reckmann, dressed the wounds of this unknown officer and then helped him to write a 'good-bye letter' to his wife and children. The Germans also released two carrier pigeons which later turned up at the headquarters of the Ulster Division with written details of the fall of the redoubt.*

The other Ulster-held redoubt was the smaller Race Course Redoubt, which was on a railway embankment south of the village of Grugies. The commander was Second Lieutenant Edmund de Wind, a County Down man who had earlier in the war served as a private in a Canadian battalion. De Wind's post held out until after 6 p.m. and surrendered only after de Wind himself was killed. Like Lieutenant-Colonel Elstob, this officer received a posthumous Victoria Cross.

This completes the story of the eight redoubts around St Quentin. It had been hoped that they would be able to hold out for two days but none had managed to last for more than nine hours. No criticism is implied by this statement. The fog had enabled the Germans to mop up all the smaller posts forming part of the redoubt chain, and the ferocity and over-whelming strength of the German assaults could not be withstood. The vital weapon leading to the fall of the redoubts had been the mobile German mortars and the light howitzers, which had been brought up to safe positions within easy range and had then proceeded to send bombs or shells into the redoubts. There was no answer to this and the commanders who surrendered saved many lives. Of the eight officers commanding battalions in the Forward Zone here, one was killed, six became prisoners-of-war and one managed

* Lieutenant-Colonel Lord Farnham was possibly slightly wounded in this action. Earlier in the war, he had suffered a personal tragedy when two of his young sons died at the same time through a sudden illness at home. He had commanded the 10th Inniskillings until that battalion had been disbanded under the recent reorganisation, so had been with the 2nd Battalion for only a few weeks. He had always been very fond of dogs and the dog with him in Boadicea Redoubt was probably a local stray that he had befriended. His third son was killed at El Alamein in October 1942 while in command of the Middlesex Yeomanry, which was serving as a divisional signals regiment at that time.

to get back. This last was Lieutenant-Colonel H. E. de R. Wetherall, of the 2/4th Oxford and Bucks Light Infantry, who, after being captured by the Germans, managed to evade his escorts when they came under British shellfire and made his way to the Battle Zone that night.* The total number of men who managed to reach the Battle Zone from these eight battalions may have been no more than four officers and fifty men. The German Official History does not mention the resistance of any of the redoubts and it is probable that, despite the loss of life and what generals and regimental histories say, their defence did not materially affect the outcome of the fighting on 21 March 1918.

*

Nearly fifteen miles north of St Quentin, Chapel Hill and Epéhy were still holding out. The Germans tried many times to push the 1st Lincolns and the South African Scottish off Chapel Hill and they managed to do so towards nightfall, but the South Africans counter-attacked at once and retook the hill. The Germans had to give up for the day then. A member of the 123rd Grenadier Regiment, a famous Württemberg regiment with a high reputation, says that, that night, his company was back where it had started in the morning. 'For us grenadiers, it was a miserable situation. We felt ashamed and shattered.' Epéhy, with its strong garrison of three Leicester battalions, also held, helped by some Vickers machine-gunners who had come in from the 16th (Irish) Division which had fallen back on the right.

Why did Chapel Hill and Epéhy hold when so many apparently similar positions did not? The reason is probably that neither position was ever completely cut off. Chapel Hill always had a firm left flank attached to the positions in the Flesquières Salient that were not attacked. Epéhy, although the Germans were through on both sides, maintained its links to the rear. Men fight better when they know that there is still hope of relief or eventual withdrawal. Both of these

---

* Lieutenant-General Sir Edward Wetherall commanded the 11th (African) Division in Abyssinia in 1941 and then became General Officer Commanding in East Africa and, later, in Ceylon. He was still alive when this book was being prepared.

positions held out until beyond noon of the following day, but they had to be given up then as part of a general retirement that was taking place. German histories certainly mention Epéhy, and the defence here completely frustrated the German plan to cut off the British divisions in the Flesquières Salient during the first twenty-four hours of the battle. Epéhy, one German history says, was 'the flood-breaker'.

It had been a very good day for the Leicestershire Regiment. Their 6th, 7th and 8th Battalions had defended Epéhy successfully; the 2/4th Battalion had, as described in the last chapter, stopped the German advance by their stand in the half-dug trench at the rear of the 59th Division's Battle Zone, and the 1st Battalion had helped to hold the Battle Zone in the neighbouring 6th Division. Few regiments had upheld their reputation so well on this day.

*

There remained just three more positions still holding out. These were all right down at the southern end of the attack front, near La Fère. This was the extreme left flank of the German attack, where they were not planning to make any great advance on the first day. The most northerly of the three positions was Fort Vendeuil, a derelict but strong, brick-built French fort constructed in the 1870s. It had a deep, wide moat and contained eighty-six different compartments or positions, any one of which was capable of being turned into a strong defensive post. In this bizarre setting there was an unusual garrison made up of one platoon of the 7th Buffs (the East Kent Regiment), two platoons of men who were the 'bad marchers' and other misfits of their division, two trench-mortar teams, and an observation group of a Royal Engineers Field Survey Company who had been 'flash-spotting' and 'sound-ranging' on German guns. This motley garrison was commanded by Captain 'Flossie' Fine of the Buffs, an officer well known for his female impersonations in battalion concerts.*

---

* Fort Vendeuil was still standing in 1976 and was being used as a zoo and amusement park. It has some good photographs of French soldiers manning the fort during the First World War, but no sign remains of the short tenancy by British troops.

The other two positions that were holding out in this area had more conventional garrisons. Another platoon of the 7th Buffs was on a hill north of the village of Travecy, and in the village itself there was a 'keep' that never even had a name. This last position was held by a platoon of the 2/2nd Londons. The keep has been described by one of the men who was there: 'It had no wire, but had a first-class French dug-out with two entrances and, up top, just one good trench held by a good body of men under a good officer.' The 'good men' were mostly London 'East Enders', and the 'good officer' was Captain Maurice Harper from Stratford.

These three positions all suffered identical experiences. Because this was not an area vital to the German advance, the Germans made no effort to overcome the British positions. For their part, the defenders, who had plenty of ammunition, fired at any target that appeared – including on one occasion what appeared to be a group of German staff officers. If the British fire became too troublesome, the Germans sent along a gun and fired a few shells, but mostly there were just a few German infantrymen making sure that the British did not try to escape. This went on all through the 21st. The night following was quiet, but the firing and watching were resumed again on the 22nd. By the evening of that second day, food and ammunition were running out. The Londoners in Travecy had fired off 18,000 rounds of small-arms ammunition and 200 mortar bombs. All three posts surrendered that evening, the tired defenders reckoning that they could do no more.

11

The Second Review

The outcome of the first day of the battle was largely settled by the end of the afternoon, although the actual fighting was not quite finished. The map facing shows the progress made by the Germans during the seven hours since their infantry attack had commenced.

The British front that had been attacked can be split up and studied by sections. Parts of four divisions in General Byng's Third Army had opposed the main force of the German attack north of the Flesquières Salient. Two large wedges had been driven into the positions of these divisions. The right-hand brigade of the 34th Division and the whole of the 59th (North Midland) Division had been pushed right back to the rear edge of their Battle Zones, and, farther south, the 51st (Highland) Division was in a similar situation. Between these two wedges, the 6th Division was still fighting inside its Battle Zone but its troops were exposed on both flanks and would have to withdraw during the night to maintain a line with the units on either side. This type of move – falling back to keep in touch with flanking units – was the start of a constant and dismal process which would be repeated many times during the succeeding days of the battle. These four divisions had suffered heavy casualties, but General Byng had been able to bring up three fresh reserve divisions – the 19th (Western), 25th and 40th – and these were now coming into position to provide a strong line for the reopening of the battle in the morning. Even after using these reserves, Byng still had three more reserve divisions – the Guards, 2nd and 41st.

Next came the Flesquières Salient, which the Germans had still not attacked in any strength although the divisions holding it had suffered many casualties, mainly from mustard-gas shelling. The Germans now had little chance of encircling the salient in the first twenty-four hours of the battle, as they had hoped, but there had not yet been any decision by General

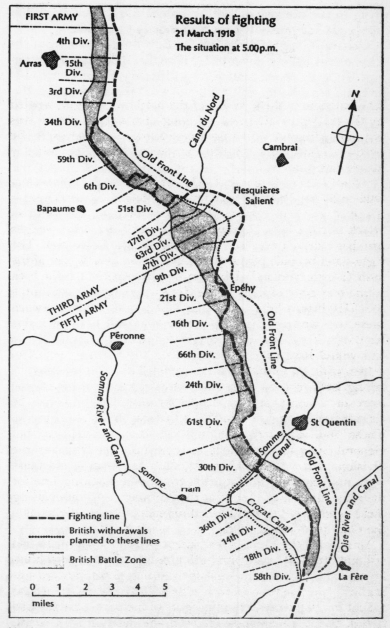

Results of Fighting
21 March 1918
The situation at 5.00 p.m.

FIRST ARMY

4th Div.

Arras

15th Div.

3rd Div.

34th Div.

Canal du Nord

Cambrai

N

59th Div.

Old Front Line

6th Div.

Bapaume

51st Div.

Flesquières Salient

17th Div.

63rd Div.

47th Div.

9th Div.

Epéhy

21st Div.

THIRD ARMY

FIFTH ARMY

16th Div.

Péronne

66th Div.

Old Front Line

24th Div.

Somme River and Canal

61st Div.

St Quentin

30th Div.

Somme Canal

Somme

Old Front Line

Ham

Oise River and Canal

Crozat Canal

36th Div.

14th Div.

18th Div.

58th Div.

La Fère

Fighting line

British withdrawals planned to these lines

British Battle Zone

0 1 2 3 4 5
miles

Map 6

Byng to pull his men out of this potential trap. Action on this important matter, however, was shortly to be taken.

General Gough's army, on its thirty-mile front from the Flesquières Salient down to La Fère, had taken a real battering. No army of the British Expeditionary Force ever had to face an assault on the scale or with the ferocity of that sustained by the Fifth Army on this day. Much would later be written and said about the fighting performance of the Fifth Army, but a study of the situation that evening shows that it had not acquitted itself badly. On the nineteen-mile stretch of front from the Flesquières Salient down to the Somme Canal in front of St Quentin – a frontage twice as long as that which had been attacked in the Third Army area – only one division, the 16th (Irish), had been pushed to the back of its Battle Zone defences. Five divisions and one brigade, nearly all New Army or Second-Line Territorials, were either still holding the front of their Battle Zone defences or had halted the German attacks within those defences. Whatever else might be said about the Fifth Army, this achievement should be remembered. The units that had achieved this successful defence were the South African Infantry Brigade and the 21st, 66th (East Lancs), 24th, 61st (South Midland) and 30th Divisions.

It was south of here that the real disaster had occurred – a disaster that was entirely foreseeable. Three divisions – 36th (Ulster), 14th (Light) and 18th (Eastern) – and one brigade of the 58th (London) Division had been thinly spread along the line taken over from the French only eight weeks earlier. Most of the troops had been pushed right out of their Battle Zone defences and large gaps often existed between the few battalions that still remained in the Battle Zone.

There was one big difference between the situation of Generals Byng and Gough. Byng had three reserve divisions still uncommitted and would soon be receiving the first of the new divisions being sent down by Haig from the north. Gough was in the process of committing all his reserves – the dismounted cavalry divisions and the 20th (Light) and 39th Divisions – and had only one completely fresh division remaining, the 50th (Northumbrian), which would arrive in the morning. It was these vital reserves, or lack of them, that would decide the outcome of the second and subsequent days' fighting.

•

Of the three senior British generals concerned in the battle, only two seemed to have been really active during the day. There is no evidence that Haig left G.H.Q. at Montreuil, which was more than fifty miles away from the nearest point of the battle. There was no reason why he should do so; it was better for him to remain at the end of a telephone and available to both of his army commanders. As has been stated earlier, neither Haig's diary nor the War Diaries of G.H.Q. contain much more than routine material for this period, and there is no way of knowing the state of the commander-in-chief's mind during this important day. Haig does make the occasional remark in his diary – 'Our men seem to be fighting magnificently' and, on the 22nd, 'All reports show that our men are in great spirits' – which are typical of his optimism in even the worst of situations. What is obvious is that when both General Byng and General Gough proposed major moves which would involve the voluntary giving-up of ground Haig gave his immediate permission and support for these proposals. This is an important point, and it cannot be said that Haig imposed rigid restrictions on the actions of his two army commanders when they were under pressure. It can be presumed that Haig spent most of the day in his office, receiving reports from the front and calmly sorting out which forces he could bring down from the north to feed into the battle – life or death decisions for many an unsuspecting infantryman then in quiet trenches near Ypres, Armentières or Lens. Haig sent messages to both Byng and Gough that night, congratulating their units on their fighting during the day.

General Byng had two problems to contend with – the situation of his divisions under attack in the Battle Zone and that in the Flesquières Salient. Because he had sufficient reserves, he was able to bolster up the units hit so hard during the day, and in some instances he was able to make preparations to relieve them: the 6th Division, for instance, would be taken out of the line for a complete rest twenty-four hours later. The day's fighting had left Byng's three divisions in the Flesquières Salient in a position even more exposed than before, yet he does not seem to have been over-concerned at the danger. It is probable that he had every confidence of holding future German attacks and he was still obviously reluctant, as he always had been, to give up voluntarily the ground his army had taken the previous autumn. It is not known whether Haig prodded him again during the afternoon, but early that evening, Byng finally decided that the men in the Flesquières Salient must be pulled back that night. Even then, the retirement he authorised was only a very limited one, of about 4,000 yards, and only by the units in the extreme front of the salient, not those on the flanks. This would still leave a sizeable bulge in the German lines as big as the original salient had been before the battle. The order for this retirement was issued by Lieutenant-General Sir Edward Fanshawe's V Corps at 6.5 p.m., and the opening words of the order give a hint of Fanshawe's reluctance to issue an order to give up ground and a disclaiming of responsibility for it! 'In accordance with Army orders . . .'*

Sir Hubert Gough was in deep trouble, and nothing that he had done or heard during the day could have given him much comfort. Air reconnaissance during the early afternoon had confirmed that the roads and tracks behind the German attack front were full of reserve divisions marching towards the battle. This information told Gough that the battle which had started that morning would be a prolonged one. General Humbert, commander of the French Third Army, had arrived just before lunch to discuss the help that could be given by French units. The promise of immediate French assistance in the event of an attack had been part of the bargain struck when the Fifth Army had taken over the French line south of St Quentin in January. But when the French and British generals met that morning, General Humbert made his famous remark, *'Je n'ai que mon fanion'* – 'I have only my pennant', a reference to the small flag on his motor-car standing outside Gough's headquarters. Humbert was not exaggerating: he had only his army headquarters

* Public Record Office WO 95/369.

staff – no corps headquarters, no heavy artillery, no divisions of fighting troops. The reason for this disappointing state of affairs was the successful deceptions achieved by the Germans on more distant parts of the French front before the battle.

So Gough was in the worst of all situations: the Germans driving his army back fast, without significant reserves of his own, with little chance of immediate reinforcements from the British armies in the north because of Haig's policy, and with no help at hand from the French to the south. In fact, the French moved surprisingly quickly. Once they had satisfied themselves that the Germans were not going to attack any part of the French front, their divisions started to move to Gough's help. The first division arrived on the following day, three more on the next day and then a continuing flow. But this help, valuable though it was, did not arrive fast enough to help Gough hold his positions, and it was not a substitute for the powerful central reserve that the British had imagined would be at hand when they agreed to take over this line from the French.

After lunch, Gough left Nesle by motor car to pay quick calls on his four corps commanders. His first visit was to Lieutenant-General Sir Richard Butler, who until recently had been Deputy Chief of Staff of G.H.Q. but was now in command of III Corps in that part of Gough's southern frontage that was in the worst situation. Gough met Butler at a hastily arranged rendezvous in the village of Beaumont-en-Beine to save driving the full distance to Butler's headquarters. This soldier, from the 20th (Light) Division which was in reserve here, was on sentry duty at the meeting place.

It was rather extraordinary that, during my two hours' stint immediately facing the arched entrance to a French farmyard, I should have had to turn out the guard five times in an increasing escalation, commencing with my company commander and finishing with Sir Hubert Gough, the Fifth Army commander. It was obvious that the guard had only hurriedly been mounted because the powers that be had been suddenly informed that the army commander would be holding a conference there. After I had turned out the guard for our divisional commander, Major-General Smith, a slim, elderly gentleman with grey hair and wearing a shabby 'mac', he dismissed the guard and told me to 'Carry on, sentry'. As I marched to the end of my post at the corner, the old boy wandered in that direction and, without looking at me directly, asked me if I would recognise the army commander's car if it came along. I told him that I would and, after telling me to turn out the guard as smartly as possible, he walked away without looking at me.

Gough's car arrived a few minutes later. I turned out the guard but poor little Gough – he was only a little fellow but very smart and quick in his movements – had more serious things on his mind. He gave us a quick salute as he hurried across the road towards the archway entrance to the farm, through which he disappeared surrounded by officers of various ranks. I only saw the back of his head. He did not even turn towards us as he hurriedly moved across the road in conversation with another general. (Lance Corporal E. I. Roberts, 61st Machine Gun Company)

The 'other general' was Lieutenant-General Butler, whom Gough found very despondent at losing so much ground and so many guns on the first day of his first battle as a field commander after his years as a staff officer.

Leaving Butler, Gough continued his tour and met the remaining corps commanders – Lieutenant-Generals Sir Ivor Maxse, Sir Herbert Watts and Sir Walter Congreve, V.C., all veterans in command on the Western Front and all in less trouble than Butler.

By the time he returned to his own headquarters, late in the afternoon, Gough had decided on his policy. The decision he made at this time was of the utmost importance to the troops under his command and would also affect the course of his own career. Gough decided that it was more important to keep together what was left of his battered divisions in the south than to hold ground. He sent orders to Lieutenant-General Butler that the whole of III Corps was to start pulling back from the rear edge of the Battle Zone, cross the Crozat Canal, and form a new line on the eastern bank for the following morning. The 36th (Ulster) Division, in Lieutenant-General Maxse's corps, was to pull back to conform, leaving the Somme Canal, which ran north-east into St Quentin at this point, to form a long southern flank for the rest of Maxse's corps.

There were plenty of good military reasons for this extensive withdrawal and the principle of it had been agreed with Haig before the battle, but it had never been envisaged that this ground would have to be given up before the battle was even twelve hours old. The decision was contrary to more than three years' tradition and philosophy of the Western Front, in which British generals simply did not give up ground. It is to Haig's credit that he fully concurred with Gough in this decision, but those who judged a battle's progress merely by studying the movement of lines on maps were being given ammunition for future criticism.

Gough's staff sent out the orders and the remnants of three divisions and one brigade were soon falling back to the bridges over the Crozat Canal. This was the last move that Gough was called upon to make in this first day of the battle. After dinner that night, he spoke again to G.H.Q. about the prospects for the next day's fighting. Again, it was Lawrence, the Chief of Staff, to whom Gough spoke. Lawrence gave his opinion that the Germans would not 'come on again' the next day; they would, he said, be too busy tending their wounded and reorganising their forces. Gough's heart must have sunk when he heard this and he wondered again whether anyone at G.H.Q. had any real idea of the danger the Fifth Army was already in and would be deeper into without reinforcements. He regretted that no one from G.H.Q. had seen fit to come and see the situation for himself. Haig did not visit Gough's headquarters at any time during the battle. Sir Herbert Lawrence came once, but not until the fourth day.

*

The day's fighting had been almost as severe a test for the Royal Flying Corps as it had been for the men on the ground, and the air effort devoted to supporting the ground soldiers had been considerable. Not only had all the operational squadrons of III and V Brigades – the R.F.C. units attached to the Third and Fifth Armies – flown to the limit of their ability, but so too had the Ninth Wing, a group of reserve squadrons sent by G.H.Q. to support the Fifth Army. In addition, many of the squadrons of II Brigade, which normally supported the Second Army north of Arras, had flown south and joined in the battle. This last support was a good example of the versatility of air power; the Second

Army planes were really the first reserves of any kind to arrive and join in the battle. It had taken them no more than the half-hour flying time from their own airfields to reach the battle area.

Not all of the squadrons' records for this period of the war have survived, but it is possible that as many as thirty-six squadrons were in action during the day or would be flying that night. These were made up as follows:

Fighters or 'scouts': nine squadrons of Sopwith Camels, seven squadrons of S.E.5a.s, four squadrons of Bristol Fighters, one squadron of Sopwith Dolphins, one squadron of Spads.

Reconnaissance and artillery spotting: six squadrons of R.E.8s, three squadrons of Armstrong Whitworth A W F K8s.

Day bombing: four squadrons of De Havilland D.H.4s.

Night bombing: one squadron of F.E.2b.s.

Two of these squadrons were from the Royal Naval Air Service and two from the Australian Flying Corps. It is not known how many flights were made by the aircraft of both sides, but, with the help given by the G.H.Q. and Second Army planes, the British air effort and that of the Germans was probably evenly matched.

Several of the Third Army planes had been able to take off soon after 6 a.m. Most had not been able to see much because of the thick fog on the ground, although Captain D. H. Oliver and his observer, Lieutenant W. H. Leighton, in an R.E.8, were able to see the German bombardment falling on the front line, and they dropped a few small bombs on the German trenches before a German shell passed clean through their plane, fortunately without exploding. Several control wires were cut and Captain Oliver had to return to his airfield. This was the first incident in a day full of incidents. As the visibility improved, more and more squadrons were able to take off and join in the action. The pilots and observers had the unique sensation of seeing below them a huge battle of movement taking place, and there were more targets for their bombs and machine-gun bullets than they could ever have imagined.

Set out below are a selection from the brief action reports written up by the men who flew sometimes two or three times during that day. They give a hint of the type of work done by the R.F.C. during the day's fighting, but they do not tell the full story. The reader must try and imagine these young men sitting in their cold, open cockpits in the slip-stream of a noisy engine, the ever-present danger of German fighters which might drop down on them out of the sun without warning, the danger of the low-flying work over the battlefield with perhaps hundreds of rifles and dozens of machine-guns firing at one plane, the fear of engine failure at low level, and the worst fear of all: fire and no parachute. And, when the flight was over, there were damaged planes to be landed back at airfields that were perhaps half obscured in mist.*

Observation impossible at commencement, owing to mist . . . Hostile aircraft opened fire on us. Observer returned fire.

The first patrol went up at 1.35 and found ample Huns doing contact patrol and also lots of enemy scouts at about 3,000 feet. The squadron started carrying bombs to-day and got some quite good results, although it rather interfered with the old spirit of shooting down the Huns.

Machine-gun fire very heavy from trenches. Crater at 20d [map reference] occupied by enemy gunners. Guns unlimbering and horses seen in vicinity of crater. Fifty rounds fired into crater and vicinity from 500 feet. Pilot wounded by machine-gun fire when over Louveral, flying at 500 feet.

11.30 onwards, enormous fire at W18c o.3. [map reference]. Column of white smoke 1,500 feet . . . Many E.A. (enemy aircraft) doing contact patrol and crossing our line.

Messages dropped on Corps H.Q. as follows: 'Enemy crossing via roads from Quéant and Pronville, especially at D21a and

* One of the best first-hand descriptions of a pilot's life at this time can be found in *Winged Victory* by Victor Yeates, who at that time was a lieutenant flying Sopwith Camel single-seater fighters with No. 46 Squadron from Le Hameau airfield just behind Arras. Yeates completed a seven-month spell of operational flying, which included the March Offensive, and made 163 operational flights totalling 248 hours. He crashed four times – twice shot down by German fire and twice accidentally. His book, nominally fiction, is recognised as being an authentic account of his time with No. 46 Squadron, and it vividly describes the strain of low-level flying over the battlefield and engaging German infantry with bombs and machine-guns during the course of the German spring offensive. Yeates died from tuberculosis, brought on by the strain of his wartime flying, in 1934, the year his book was first published.

D21b, in large numbers. Many e.a. scouts make it difficult to see position of line.' 'Masses of enemy troops at sunken road, J5c, 28 and 27b. No replies to any GF calls from our batteries.'

Lt Cowper saw a Rumpler at 1,500 feet and dived from a cloud to twenty yards range, firing fifty rounds. The e.a. dived steeply and gradually burst into flames. He crashed at 62B M36A.

Two bombs dropped on detraining point M.25.d. central. Reconnaissance of back areas – large westerly movement, transport seen on roads. Massed infantry observed M.2.3.4.8.9.and 10. Infantry also on roads running E out of Lesbain. 550 rounds fired along roads and into villages, also on troops.

Lt Richardson got separated in some indecisive scrapping and eventually surprised six Pfalz scouts from the sun while they were attacking some S.E.s. He fired one drum of Buckingham into one and he went vertically down with black smoke coming out in large quantities. Lt Richardson then attacked a Pfalz formation and fired 100 rounds at close range into one who went down into a sloppy spin.

100 rounds from Lewis gun fired on troops in open and wagons and horses from 600 feet. Line towards south quiet. Sunken roads south and south-west of Urvillers were packed with enemy troops. Machine heavily machined-gunned from ground.

Many abandoned British field-gun positions seen but guns gone. Much movement of transport at the trot westwards. There are enemy batteries in action along Benay-Urvillers road. Many dead enemy lying outside trench at G.12.b south of the road . . . Two message bags dropped on two batteries in G17a and G10d and handkerchief message bag on 60-pdr battery in G.8.b. – all were received.

Six pilots took off for low work. All returned, but Captain Smith forced landing B.28 C.7.8, 2/Lt McConnell forced landing near Vaux and 2/Lt Shorter forced landing at 59 Squadron.

Called for flares but no reply seen. Main trench Le Verguier held by us it is thought, but not certain . . . LL call sent on 1,500 infantry massed in A30S.o.9. answered by field guns only. Shells burst in trench . . . Flashes seen behind Bellenglise. 12 e.a. seen during patrol working in twos and threes. Maissemy being shelled.

Eight 25-lb bombs dropped on six cylinders sending over liquid fire. Silenced.

2/Lt Lunnon seen to land under control at Fluquières — probably shot down by e.a. Pilot seen to crawl out O.K.

2/Lt A. O. Lacey saw a balloon S.W. of Havrincourt Wood brought down in flames by e.a. and a parachute was seen to leave the balloon. The e.a. turned east and I dived from the sun, firing 100 rounds at 100 yards range. Several tracers were seen to enter the fuselage and the e.a. dived steeply under control into his own lines and appeared to be going to land. I followed the e.a. but lost it near the ground.

Eight 25-lb bombs dropped on two gun-teams coming west on road at M.2.D.8.5. causing confusion and six horses bolted back east.

Capt. J. A. Slater. Joined in a big fight just north-east of Bourlon Wood between e.a. and S.E.5a. Number of machines and types uncertain. Dived on a Fokker triplane, shooting from both guns at close range. After about twenty rounds, e.a. fell down 'out of control'. The attentions of other e.a. made observation of e.a.'s ultimate fate impossible but it was last seen about 5,000 feet below still falling, sideways, nose-diving, and upside down, completely out of control.

Bombs burst in village of Honnecourt close to canal. A.A. heavy and accurate. Seven e.a. manoeuvred for position but were beaten off. Attacked by about fifteen e.a. over target.

Lt Durrant reported many e.a. seen and engaged, one formation of fifteen. Fired about 100 rounds at an Albatross V-Strutter which spun and was last seen going down on its own back.

Two tanks seen stranded . . . Few of our men running along road E 22a . . . Observation impossible owing to heavy mist . . . Forced landing owing to mist.*

The last flying operations of the day were carried out by No. 101 Squadron with their F.E.2b night bombers flying from Catigny airfield. No fewer than thirty-four flights were made by the squadron, using all available aircraft in relays. The crews were given a 'roving commission' over the German lines opposite the south of the Fifth Army, and each aircraft dropped fourteen bombs, mostly 25-pounders, and

---

* These quotations come from the War Diaries of III Brigade, R.F.C., and Nos. 5 (Naval), 8, 24, 35, 46, 53, 56, 59, 82 and 84 Squadrons, which are in the Public Record Office under the following references: AIR 1/2242, 43, 1669, 172, 1399, 1427, 1818, 1911, 1781, 1436, and 1795.

opened fire with their machine-guns on villages or any lighted vehicles seen moving along roads. These flights had to stop at 11 p.m., when fog began to form over the airfield, and the last bomber landed safely at five minutes past midnight.

The efforts of the R.F.C. had met with varying success. There is no doubt that the bombing and machine-gunning of German ground positions and particularly of troops and vehicles on the march had caused casualties and some dislocation of timetables. The efforts of German planes to attack British troops had sometimes been frustrated but never as often as the British soldiers would have liked, although many British soldiers who were machine-gunned by German aeroplanes during the day report how ineffective these German attacks were as long as the soldiers were in a trench and not in the open. It was usually possible to duck down into the bottom of the trench or dodge round into the next trench bay. One British soldier, however, confessed that a machine-gunning German aeroplane had forced him to 'commit himself in his pants'. British commanders were very disappointed at what the Official Historian calls the 'complete failure' of the 'organisation for co-operation between the artillery and the Royal Flying Corps'.* Many plans had been made for such co-operation in the event of a German attack, but these just did not work under the strain of the German advance and the bad visibility. Both the artillery and the airmen had operated under conditions of static warfare for too long and new methods could not be learnt so quickly.

Claims and counter-claims in aerial fighting are usually difficult to reconcile. British pilots claimed fourteen German planes as 'crashed', two of which were 'in flames', and twenty-three more as driven down 'out of control', but it is not known what the exact German losses were. The German pilots claimed to have destroyed eleven British planes – five Camels, four S.E.5s and two Spads – and six observation balloons. In fact only four British planes – two Camels, one S.E.5 and one Armstrong Whitworth – and three balloons were shot down by German aircraft, a typical contradiction

* British Official History, pages 167–8.

which throws into doubt some of the 'victories' attributed to the 'aces' of both sides.

Fortunately, it is possible to be quite precise about the casualties among British planes on that day and also about the cause of those casualties.

Reason	Shot down	Crash landed and written off	Slightly damaged
Take-off accidents	–	1	2
German aircraft action	4	4	6
German ground fire	–	4	11
Landing accidents	–	3	10
Total	4	12	29

The sixteen planes shot down or not worth repairing after crashes were: five Sopwith Camels, four R.E.8s, three S.E.5a.s, three Armstrong Whitworths and one Bristol Fighter. Casualties among the crews had not been heavy. Only two British airmen were killed; three more became prisoners-of-war, and nine were wounded. Two ground-crew men were killed by shellfire and seven balloonists or balloon ground crew were wounded. Again, the German casualties are not known.*

*

* Several of the British and German pilots flying on that day were among the First World War 'aces' or achieved high rank in the Second World War. Among the aces were Second Lieutenant A. W. Beauchamp-Proctor, V.C., a South African in No. 84 Squadron, with fifty-four victories ('victories' included balloons destroyed and aircraft 'driven down out of control'), Lieutenant F. F. McCall, a Canadian in No. 13 Squadron, with thirty-seven victories (all but four with No. 41 Squadron), Lieutenant A. H. Cobby, No. 4 Australian Squadron with thirty-two victories, Flight Commander L. H. Rochford, No. 3 (Naval) Squadron, with twenty-eight victories, Captain J. A. Slater, No. 64 Squadron, with twenty-four victories, Captain G. E. Thomson, No. 46 Squadron, with twenty-three victories. All of these, except Thomson, survived the war.

German aces flying were Leutnant Erich Löwenhardt, with fifty-three victories, Leutnant Fritz Ritter von Roth, with twenty-eight victories, Leutnant Fritz Putter, with twenty-five victories, and Leutnant Fritz Friedrichs, with twenty-one victories. Löwenhardt, Putter and Friedrichs all died before the end of the war; von Roth committed suicide on New Year's Eve 1918. The greatest of the German aces, Baron Manfred von Richthofen, did not fly on 21 March 1918 because his airfield was affected by mist. He was killed exactly one month later.

Pilots flying during the day who later achieved high rank were: Second

The men who served in the British cavalry divisions were seeing more action than they had experienced for years. Records of the battle contain many references to parties of dismounted cavalrymen arriving in the rear of the Fifth Army's Battle Zone defences at vital moments and plugging gaps which were developing there, but most of these arrivals coincided with the petering out of the German attacks at these points. The cavalrymen would be fighting hard the next morning and on succeeding days, and their presence was certainly vital to Gough's reserve-starved army, but the few actions in which they became involved on the evening of 21 March do not, unfortunately, merit a large section in this description of the first day's fighting.

The only two cavalry incidents of interest that can be found do not involve men who went into the line that evening. Paul Maze, the Frenchman who was attached to General Gough's headquarters, tells the story of 'Georges', a French liaison officer attached to the 17th Lancers. Georges had never claimed to be an enthusiastic warrior and he had been waiting impatiently for a leave pass to visit his wife and newly born child. The pass came just as the Lancers were forming up to go into action on 21 March and Georges ran up to the commanding officer, leave pass in hand, and called out, 'Good-bye. I don't think much of the British Army if they can't keep the infantry in front of those bloody Germans, instead of dragging out the poor, miserable cavalry.'*

This British officer was in a regiment whose commanding

Lieutenant (later Air Marshal) Hugh Pughe-Lloyd, who flew an R.E.8 with No. 52 Squadron near St Quentin; he was the R.A.F. commander at Malta during the siege. Captain (later Air Vice-Marshal) Kenneth Leaske flew an S.E.5 with No. 84 Squadron and was commander of Nos. 24 and 40 Groups in the Second World War. Major (later Air Chief Marshal) Trafford Leigh-Mallory was in command of No. 8 Squadron but, like most squadron commanders at that time, did not fly regularly; he commanded No. 12 Group in the Battle of Britain and was later commander of all Allied Air Forces in the invasion of Europe. On the German side, Oberleutnant Robert Ritter von Greim was flying an Albatross DV with the Bavarian *Jagdstaffel* 34 and claimed a Sopwith Camel shot down during the day. His total victories in the First World War numbered twenty-five. In the Second World War he was a *Luftwaffe* general and commanded an Air Corps on the Russian Front. He committed suicide at the end of the war.

* *Frenchman in Khaki*, page 272.

officer was still hoping to see cavalry operating in its traditional role.

> We had been expecting, in this open country, at last to have the chance to operate in our traditional role as horsed cavalry and, at about 1 p.m., when the weather had cleared, we were moved forward with the rest of the 1st Cavalry Brigade to the vicinity of Bernes, nearer to the front.
>
> Our colonel, Algy Lawson, was in high spirits over the prospect of open warfare starting again. He left us near a crossroads, an unfortunate habit of his, and went to Brigade H.Q. Soon, we were ordered to send a dismounted party in support of the infantry at Vendelles. Then, long-range shells started to burst all around us and one of them broke the hind leg of my trusty and much-loved Arab charger and I had to put an end to him with my revolver. Our adjutant, Whitmore-Smith, wisely moved us back about half a mile, away from the continuing bombardment area, to the anger of Algy Lawson. When he returned, he immediately ordered us back to where we had been. Here we stayed until well after dark, seeing occasional small parties of infantry making their way back but learning little of what was happening in front. (Lieutenant W. R. Beddington, 2nd Dragoon Guards)

This was typical of cavalry experience during the years 1915 to 1918. The hope of mounted action did not materialise and the cavalry fought only as infantry in this battle.

*

The many British soldiers who had been taken prisoner had mostly started out on a long and arduous journey that would end only when they reached their permanent prison camps in Germany or the other destinations decided for them by their new masters. The experiences of those prisoners who had not been wounded in the recent fighting did not vary much. They were sent off towards the German rear with only the weakest of escorts. Many had thought of escaping and a few did so, but there were so many German troops moving up behind the battle that any British soldier seen going the wrong way would have been in trouble.

One party of captured Royal Engineers suffered a cruel experience.

> After we had been captured, they herded us into one of our own

trenches until the fighting was over. They didn't talk to us at all; they just treated us like dirt. Just as it was getting dark, they told us to get up on to the back of the trench, pointed to their rear and told us to go. We got started, but then they turned a machine-gun on us and opened fire. I don't know how many bursts; all I know was that the damn thing kept rattling and we kept running. I don't know for certain but I estimate that about half of us were hit. I only got hit in the ankle but several of our lads were killed. We were gathered together again by a fresh lot of Germans farther back. (Sapper T. Cass, 201st Field Company)

It must be said that such incidents were the exception and most prisoners were not ill-treated by the Germans.

If you want a bizarre touch, here it is. I asked, in my school German, what would happen to us now. The German officer replied, in French, '*Comme d'habitude*'. The pride of the German of those days, displaying his knowledge of the more civilised French language? Anyhow, he gave us a guide to the rear of the battle and we sauntered back, dodging an occasional bullet. Our guide was in none too much of a hurry, glad to be going back, evidently, and I had an astonishing view of the German army in action over a wide area.

There is perhaps one little redeeming feature to my inglorious story. We came across a British casualty, badly wounded and left neglected and like to die in a trench. I summoned up my school German once more, recollected the word for stretcher, and demanded one from some Jerries knocking around. This was at once produced out of the air and I was able to watch my men take the poor fellow to a nearby dressing station. The hours spent learning German at school were worth that moment!

None of this can be of much professional interest to you, but I am living my past as I write. Nothing will ever obliterate from my memory my boyish sensations of that day. (Second Lieutenant G. K. Stanley, 307th Brigade R.F.A.)

This fateful day in my life was to end with a further insight into the character of the Germans. They were most insistent that we should pick up the wounded, both English and German, and carry them to the nearest dressing station. The devastating shellfire had left the area littered with the dead and injured bodies of men of both sides. The sickening sight of mutilated human flesh was all around us and the Germans ordered us to pick up any bundle of remains that appeared to move.

Micky and I carried one poor British soldier on a duck-board held between our shoulders for about a mile and, sad to say, none of our own lads had the will to relieve us or lend a hand. The man's shoulder had been blown away and Micky pleaded for someone to lend his greatcoat as a covering, but nobody volunteered. Micky took off his own tunic and wrapped it round the lad. Fortunately, this was observed by one of our officers, a Captain Franks, who succeeded in getting a coat and detailed other men to take over the carrying. By this time, our shoulders were sore and black and blue with the bruising.

This pitiful incident was viewed with amazement by the German sentries standing by and it wasn't difficult to read their thoughts. Perhaps it best illustrates the utter collapse of the spirit and general feelings of the men on the realisation that they were completely in the hands of the enemy. While they had been war-weary for some time, they had continued, grudgingly, with the daily routines of trench warfare, never imagining their fate was to surrender. Now, all the old spirit of soldiering was gone, leaving only a sense of total loss and demoralisation. (Private A. V. Mason, 5th Border)

These examples of British prisoners being allowed to help British wounded were exceptional. The more general rule was that the prisoners were ordered to collect only wounded Germans and take them back from the battlefield as far as the field dressing stations. There were very few stretchers and most of the wounded Germans were carried in blankets or groundsheets — awkward loads to keep hold of and carry properly.

Another man and I were led to a wounded German who had been laid on a waterproof sheet which we made into a makeshift sling. As we got nearer to the dressing station, a battery of our heavy guns put a barrage down in front of us and, as splinters started to fly around, our escort decided that we should use a badly damaged communication trench. As we made our way along this, our casualty's leg, which was smashed and hanging out of the sling, knocked against the churned-up ground and, whenever that happened, he let out a squeal of agony. I felt that this was a sure way of upsetting his mate and was half expecting to get his bayonet in my backside, but he seemed unconcerned and, when we had gone a hundred yards or so, decided that we should sit down and rest. After he had had a drink, he passed his water bottle round. This kind of behaviour among front-line troops and their prisoners was not uncommon in the first war, a sort of *camaraderie* I suppose, and it was not until we came in contact with troops who lived in safe areas well away from the fighting that we received any rough treatment. We duly delivered our casualty and then had to carry another stretcher case into St Quentin. (Sapper F. E. Waldron, 30th Divisional Signal Company)

So the British prisoners made their way off the battlefield. The most dangerous time was when they crossed the old No Man's Land and what had been the German front line before the attack. British artillery was sometimes still firing on the German trenches, even though they were now empty, and the British soldiers had to run the gauntlet of this fire. Next came the German artillery positions from which German guns were still firing hard and the British soldiers were much impressed with the sight of the great force of artillery that had bombarded them that morning.

Many German infantry reinforcements were met, marching towards the battle.

We passed at least three battalions. I guarantee that none of the men were more than sixteen years old. They were singing away, and we were saying, 'Yes, you buggers. You'll soon stop singing when you get up there.' But they'd stopped us singing that morning. (Lance Corporal B. Lambert, 7th Sherwood Foresters)

We met quite a few infantry reinforcements coming up. They looked fresh and well equipped. They were shouting out to us; their chief question was, 'Are the *Amerikaners* on this front?' I think they were a little anxious about this but I couldn't tell whether they were keen to have a go at the Americans or whether they were scared of them. They also asked for cigarettes. We didn't answer much – we weren't really in the mood for conversation but several of our chaps gave them cigarettes. I met one German who was a much bigger man than me. He wanted my leather jerkin and he simply took it; I couldn't do anything about it. I was very cold that night. (Lance Corporal J. Wortley, 2/5th Lincolns)

Parties of prisoners gradually merged together to make longer columns and were given proper escorts of German soldiers, probably from the 'line-holding' divisions which had held the German front line for the weeks preceding the attack. It was at this time that the British prisoners realised the magnitude of the disaster that had overcome their front-line divisions that morning; many prisoners had, until then, thought that the Germans had been successful only on their own small sector. Some prisoners from the 2nd Wiltshires were annoyed to find that many soldiers of the Ulster Division, which had been fighting alongside them near St Quentin, were carrying haversacks packed with personal belongings and it was felt that these men had given up too easily. Another soldier was surprised to find a party of young British officers wearing soft hats; front-line prisoners usually wore steel helmets or were hatless.

A large number of British prisoners has been taken near St Quentin, and these men were collected together, marched into the town and then round the square 'umpteen times' to be photographed. These photographs of massed prisoners would be a fine tonic for the war-weary German civilian population when they appeared a few days later in German newspapers. Some of the prisoners at St Quentin also met Crown Prince Wilhelm, who had come forward to observe the success of his divisions. One British soldier remembers him. 'He spoke to us in good English and congratulated us on putting up such a good show and on our excellent rapid fire.' Other prisoners say that they met the Kaiser on this day but this meeting may have been one day later.

The prisoners in St Quentin spent that night in a large building in the town. One man was told that it had been a music college. These men were fortunate; in most other places, the British prisoners were herded into barbed-wire enclosures in open fields and had to spend the night there. Few received any food or drink that first night; the German supply organisation was at full stretch and there were no rations to spare yet for prisoners. It was the first night of a long, hard time for the British prisoners. There was a sharp frost, and in the morning several men were found to have died from exposure during the night.

12

The Evening

Heiss war der Tag und blutig die Schlacht,
Kühl war der Abend und ruhig die Nacht.

Hot was the day and bloody the battle,
Cool was the evening and calm the night.
(German infantryman)

Nightfall would not come until 7.50 p.m. but there would be few large-scale actions during these last hours of daylight. Most of the fighting was now of a minor nature; the outcome of this historic day's fighting was now well settled. One of the local actions during that evening involved the German soldier Baier, who had once been an officer but had been reduced to the ranks. The reader will remember that Baier had insisted on joining in the attack that morning although he could have stayed with the transport section of his regiment. A fellow N.C.O. describes Baier's activities that evening; these Germans were now deep into the defence of the 36th (Ulster) Division.

By early evening, we had taken the main positions but we paused a while at the foot of a slope, about ten metres high, near Contescourt. Our look-outs on top of the slope raised the alarm – a counter-attack! We fought this off and caused many casualties. The survivors crawled back to the nearest trench. The enemy fire stopped when our medical orderlies went forward to attend to the wounded. Their opposite numbers came out, too, which impressed us a lot.

Now came the chance for former Hauptmann Baier. As soon as the wounded had been removed, he hurried to the enemy, waving a white flag. They let him come. He told us later that he had convinced them that any further resistance was useless; our artillery had moved forward and would flatten the position. More than fifty men laid down their arms and came with Baier to us. He could speak English fluently. This brave action, by a single man, brought further opposition from the enemy to an abrupt end.

Baier was promoted to the rank of Offizier Stellvertreter, that is, a non-commissioned 'deputy-officer'. The divisional commander asked the High Command to have Baier reinstated as a regular officer. This was not allowed – only the Kaiser could permit this – but he was awarded the *Goldene Tapferkeitmedaille für Mann-schaften und Unteroffizier* – the highest medal awarded to an N.C.O. Unfortunately, Baier was killed in action several months later in the Chemin des Dames area. I was with him when he died. (Vizefeldwebel Wilhelm Prosch, 463rd Regiment)

Another British setback occurred that evening, but, fortunately, one without bloodshed. Two German soldiers have described the incident, and it is also quoted in a German regimental history. Somewhere in front of Holnon Wood, due west of St Quentin, German soldiers were amazed to see a company of British soldiers, headed by an officer on horse-back, marching down a sunken road straight into an area recently captured by the Germans. The British were obviously unaware of the enemy near by. The Germans allowed the British to come up the road until they were inside a perfect ambush. The astonished British gave in without a fight. The officer's horse was taken by Leutnant Kämpchen, a company commander in the 158th Regiment who had earlier in the day helped to capture Manchester Hill. Kämpchen kept the horse for the next few days but was then forced to part with it. One of the German witnesses to this incident says that after the surrender had been completed one of the British soldiers took out a mouth-organ and struck up a tune, and the captives marched off to the German rear. 'I think that they were quite pleased to be done with fighting.'

It has proved impossible to identify the battalion to which this company belonged. Many reserve units were on the move in this area during the evening and their War Diaries do not mention a detached company that disappeared without trace – a not uncommon incident in this battle. Regimental histories, compiled after the prisoners had returned home, perhaps did not care to record what might have seemed a humiliating or, at least, embarrassing episode.

The most extensive British action during the evening was a counter-attack made towards Doignies, a village in the Battle Zone previously held by the 51st (Highland) Division and now in German hands. The importance of Doignies was that the German advance here, if allowed to develop further, seriously threatened to come in behind the British troops still holding the Flesquières Salient. The order to retake Doignies had actually been issued by the commander of IV Corps, Lieutenant-General Sir Montague Harper, at 3.15 p.m. The battalions chosen for the counter-attack were the 8th Gloucesters and the 10th Worcesters, both from the 19th (Western) Division which had been in reserve all day. These men were to be supported by twelve tanks of the 8th Tank Battalion. The infantry and tanks had previously practised such a combined counter-attack but not over this ground.

It took nearly three and a half hours for the units involved to move up and deploy ready for the attack. At 6 p.m., the corps commander realised that it was getting too late for the attack to have a chance of success and he telephoned to the 19th Division, suggesting a cancellation. Typically, this release did not reach the attacking troops and, at 6.40 p.m., the attack started. The tanks advanced first, followed by two companies from each of the infantry battalions. The light was failing and a mist was again forming. Major E. D. Blackburn, a tank officer on foot, was providing the link between tanks and infantry. The infantry were under the command of their company commanders; the two battalion commanders stayed farther back, watching the situation and holding the remaining companies in reserve.

The War Diary of the 8th Tank Battalion states that their tanks caused heavy casualties among the Germans before they had to break off because of the darkness, and the presence of the tanks undoubtedly helped to achieve the limited success attained, although it must have been a difficult and frightening experience for the men inside these tanks, operating as they were in darkness and mist and over unknown ground. At least one tank was attacked by German infantrymen who clambered up and fired machine-guns through the tank's firing slits. One tank and its crew were never seen again; a second, 'Hotspur II', was knocked out, but its crew escaped with their Lewis gun and fought with the infantry.

Captain M. A. James, from Bristol, was commanding one of the Gloucester companies.

We were on the right and the Worcesters on the left. It was getting dark by the time we made a start down the slope towards Doignies. I don't think I was frightened; I think we considered it just one of those things to be taken in one's stride. Little did we know of the general situation at the time, as one does now – two battalions counter-attacking the German Army! We started over-running the forward posts that the Germans had put out for the night, and my company captured twenty-seven prisoners and two machine-guns, but then it got dark and the tanks had to go back. We lost touch with the Worcesters.

I had a conference with the commander of our other company, Captain 'Darkie' Bowles. We had reached our objective, the church in Doignies. The fighting was still going on and we were having to leave our casualties. The German machine-guns were firing at us all the time. One of my platoon commanders, Lieutenant Purton, had been hit in the leg – he lost it later – and I had been hit in the neck. We decided to go back a little and take up position in a trench we had passed. This had a few Seaforths in it – eight or nine men I should say, including an officer. They also had a Vickers. They seemed pretty cheerful. All this – the attack and the re-organisation – took until midnight. We got some of the wounded away and some more ammunition came up, but no reinforcements.

Thus ended the last big British action of the day. It is not known how many casualties were inflicted on the Germans, but the British infantry lost five officers and thirty-five men killed – mainly in the 10th Worcesters – and an unknown number wounded, and the tank men's casualties numbered nine missing, probably prisoners, and thirty-five wounded. The Gloucesters remained in the trench they had found and fought there for the next thirty-six hours. During this time, Captain James was wounded again, in the face by a piece of shell, and was then shot through the stomach. He was last seen by his men firing a machine-gun and was reported missing. After lying out on the battlefield for a further day, he was picked up and his wounds were treated by the Germans. He was awarded the Victoria Cross for the series of actions which commenced on the evening of 21 March and became a brigadier in the Second World War; unfortunately, he died while this book was being prepared.

❋

On many parts of the battlefield, British units were taking part in large-scale, organised withdrawals. The largest movement was in the extreme south, where parts of four divisions were trekking back along roads and tracks and over the open ground towards the Crozat Canal. A thick mist had descended but there was a bright moon. The routes for this withdrawal had been chosen before the battle and staff officers were busy contacting units and ordering them to move by a prearranged plan, although, to many of the ordinary soldiers taking part, it appeared little more than a rout.

As the sun began to decline and the mist to return, we could see what we took to be villages in flames, with volumes of smoke rising from them in the beams of the setting sun. Artillery began to pass us at the gallop, to the rear, and I found this disconcerting. As the night came down, I seem to remember a hazy moon shining through the mist, and it became cold.

A runner appeared and urged us to get on to the roadway, giving us the direction. Who he was and from where he came, I have never known. As I approached the road, I could hear the sound of what seemed to be thousands of men moving back to the canal line. It was a terrible experience to see these exhausted troops retiring. The various regiments kept no order and there were men with arm and shoulder wounds in blood-stained bandages, having to fend for themselves, survivors of the most savage and concerted bombardment in military history. I saw no ambulances. I was swept into the crowd and retired with them, still carrying my box of ammunition, which I did not dare to abandon.

As we passed a small, walled churchyard near a village, the name of which, Liserolles, sticks in my memory, we had to abandon the roadway because a battery of artillery had been caught in shellfire and had been annihilated. Dead men and horses were sprawled across the road and the stench of blood met us as we arrived. There was bright moonlight and the shadow of the churchyard wall lay across the scene in black relief.

And so to the bridge and over the canal. (Trooper A. W. Bradbury, 2nd Dragoons)

The Germans were slow to appreciate that the British in front of them were slipping away and there soon developed a large area of ground which was empty of any large bodies of troops. The march back to the canal continued all through the night, and the bridges over the canal were demolished after the last troops had crossed. There was a delay in demolishing three railway bridges near Jussy because the French engineer officer in charge had been arrested as a suspected spy by British soldiers before he could blow the bridges. The Royal Engineers only just managed to demolish these before the Germans arrived next morning. At another bridge, at Tugny, German soldiers following up the Ulster Division were actually on one end of the bridge when the time fuse failed. Second Lieutenant C. L. Knox, of the Royal Engineers, climbed down under the bridge and lit an instantaneous fuse which blew the charges at once. No one expected to see Knox alive again, but he was not hurt and survived to receive a Victoria Cross for this brave action.

No major British unit was left behind by the withdrawal, although many artillery guns were abandoned. There were, however, many British stragglers who were delayed or became lost and were left behind on the wrong side of the canal. Some of these met parties of German soldiers during the night. Two men – a British artilleryman and a German pioneer – tell of such meetings.

We set off in thick fog, our gun being last in the column of route. We kept stopping because of shellfire and, finally, we got stuck and bogged down in a morass. The scratch team of horses pulling my gun was two horses short and the others were not used to working together. The rest of the column moved on in the dark. We heaved and sweated to get the gun out but never made it. In the end, there was just me and two drivers; the rest of the gun crew had gone off to bring help from the battery. Infantry were streaming past us all the time but they were all fed up and wouldn't offer any assistance at all. We were fed up too; we'd been in action most of the day and were feeling sick because of cordite fumes and had had nothing to eat all day except a cake I had, left over from my birthday a few days earlier.

Then we saw some Germans in the fog; we identified them by their big helmets. They took our horses and put us under guard with a few more stragglers they had rounded up. We were so fed up with it all that we just couldn't care a damn what happened to us. Instead of sending us to the rear, as I would have expected, they took us with them as they went forward until we came to a ruined house with a yard behind it into which they put us. I estimate it was towards midnight then. There were twenty of us and I was the only N.C.O.

All at once, we heard a spattering of machine-gun fire and bullets were hitting the wall just above us. One or two of us kept bobbing our heads over the wall and we spotted men some distance away. By the shape of their helmets, we could see they were our chaps. We were off over the wall at that, and ran to join them. We found they were Royal Irish Rifles from the 36th Division. I found their officer and told him who I was and asked permission to move off and join our own battery. 'You bugger off,' he said. 'I don't want you.' Those were his exact words. We got over the bridge at St Simon just before it was blown up. (Bombardier J. P. Barker, 169th Army Field Brigade)

By 5 p.m. my company received orders to withdraw. We came across this small, ruined farm and went looking for something to eat. We had eaten our iron rations and the field kitchens hadn't caught us up. The company commander told us to be careful. 'You don't know who might be left.' There was a barn without a roof about fifty metres away from where my pals were. I forced the door open and there was this young Englishman standing there. He had a rifle and wore his full equipment – he was still at war. We were both surprised and I think we were both frightened. I overcame my fear first and knocked his rifle away. I said, 'Tommy, come on.' The Englishman replied but I didn't understand what he said. He was a nuisance to me, that prisoner, because I had to guard him and take him to where the prisoners were being collected. I didn't miss my dinner though, because the field kitchen never did come up that night. (Pioneer Wilhelm Niebuhr, 27th Pioneer Battalion)

Another large-scale withdrawal was being carried out farther north, where parts of four more divisions were falling back from the front line of the Flesquières Salient. This was only a limited withdrawal, averaging one and a half miles, to the next line of defences, and a large vulnerable bulge into the German line would still remain when the battle resumed the following morning. The men who gave up their positions at the front of the Flesquières Salient were very disappointed to receive their orders. They had held their positions all day and beaten off what they thought had been a full-strength German attack. They did not know that the British line had been pushed back so far on either side of them that they were in danger of being cut off. This R.A.M.C. man from the 9th (Scottish) Division probably sums up the general view.

As darkness came on, a despatch rider arrived from H.Q., ordering us to evacuate our post, pack up all medical supplies and instruments, and to proceed to the rear, because a general retreat had been ordered. This was a bit of a facer as we understood that our division was well on top and I heard later that there was almost a mutiny in the line, as our boys, far from retreating, were expecting to go over the top and finish the bloody-nose treatment they had given Jerry. It was only some weeks later that we understood the position, which had been caused by the collapse of the division who were supposed to support our right flank but who had simply disappeared in the day's confusion and left our flank hopelessly exposed. But the language from the front line must have taken years off Douglas Haig's life. The names he was called were the most ferocious and original that one Scot ever called another. (Private A. H. Flindt, 27th Field Ambulance)

This front-line company commander tells of how he received the order to retire.

It was customary for company commanders to send in a report of the day's events, so I went to a dug-out to write it and had a cup of cocoa. I must have been tired because I went to sleep but was wakened in a few minutes by a messenger. As I looked up, I saw a small mouse balanced on the rim of the cocoa mug, having a sip!

The message was to the effect that the enemy were behind us on the right and left and I was to retire as quickly as possible – to Havrincourt I think – destroying everything as I went. The first obvious thing to destroy was the dug-out, so I threw a phosphorous bomb into it in order to set fire to the timber stairway and the framework of the dug-out. As I did so, I thought, 'poor little mouse'. I didn't have time to see if the fire started. We formed the company up on a road and marched back to Havrincourt. It was a very orderly retreat – at least it was that night. (Captain P. Howe, 10th West Yorks)

As Captain Howe says, the withdrawal was carried out in good order, mainly because the Germans were not in a hurry to follow up in the dark over ground that they had so recently shelled with mustard gas.

There were other, less orderly withdrawals under way at many points behind the battle area. These were at places where, because rumours were rife or because officers had become casualties, small parties of men decided to pull back without orders. Such behaviour was all part of the pattern established on the first day of the battle and it would be seen again and again before the battle was over. This man, a good soldier with the Military Medal, had been a member of a makeshift party manning a trench but he had not been in direct action with the Germans during the day. It is significant that two of the three villages he believed to have been captured by the Germans were still in British hands at that time.

By late afternoon, our infantry were still holding on but the Germans had captured Epéhy, Ronssoy and Saulcourt, and they were now shelling St Emilie and the Brown Line which our scratch unit was still holding. After dark, our infantry fell back rapidly and, as they reached the Brown Line, we received the order to retire to Villers-Faucon. This was a perilous journey, owing to the artillery barrage on the roads. There did not appear to be any of our guns left to cover our retreat and it was now a case of every man for himself as, in the darkness, no one seemed to know just what was happening, but the essential thing was to get to Villers-Faucon or we should be surrounded and cut off. Order now seemed to have given way to panic; some men were running whilst others helped the wounded along, but the enemy was following us up rapidly and we were persistently harassed with machine-gun and rifle fire.

On arriving in Villers-Faucon, we resembled a flock of lost sheep returning to the fold in ones, twos and in clusters, tired, weary, hungry and dispirited. We were mustered together again and some attempt was made to restore order and confidence in the men. A start in the right direction was made by obtaining some food and drink for us. We happened to be in close proximity to a ration dump which, for some reason, had been abandoned by whoever should have been in charge of it and there was plenty of jam, bread and cheese available. So we gorged ourselves like a pack of hungry wolves, for we did not know when we could count on getting the next meal. There was no more time to waste and so, in the middle of the night, we continued our retreat. (Sapper G. Stewart, 16th Divisional Signal Company)

There were a few men in nearly every unit who had become, deliberately or accidentally, detached from their unit during the day and for whom flight to the safety of the rear was an obvious course of action. Every road from the front had its share of such men. Most would only get a few miles before being stopped by the Military Police, sorted out, and directed to return to their units. This man was probably typical of such soldiers.

After leaving the colonel, I met up with a machine-gun corporal; all his men had become casualties or gone. I stayed with him for the next few hours until it became dark. Then he took the barrel of the machine-gun and I carried the tripod and we went back to battalion H.Q., but they'd all gone. We went further back and found a Red Cap dead on his arse. I'd learnt to steal – they encouraged this whenever you'd lost anything – so I went through his pockets. We got 80 francs, his revolver, his wallet, and a leather belt. We divided it all between us.

Just before we left, there came a nice old string of fresh troops – there might have been a battalion. They were merry. I don't know whether they'd dosed them up with rum or what, but they didn't care about any Germans. I thought, 'You carry on. You'll soon see whether you care about them or not.' Next we came to a big dug-out that had been a headquarters – brigade or division, I should think. There was whisky, rum, cigarettes and cigars. We had a good drink from the bottles and it wasn't long before our water bottles were full of whisky so that we had a bit to go on with. We kept on going back all that night and finished up at Achiet le Grand the next day. (Private T. Link, 1st King's Shropshire Light Infantry)

All these examples of withdrawals, retreats or deliberate flight should not obscure the fact that there were thousands of men that evening who were still in the defensive positions they had manned for several hours. They were hoping for food, fresh ammunition, reinforcement, a little sleep, and, ideally, relief by a fresh unit. Most would be disappointed in these hopes. Lance Corporal S. T. North, of the 7th Leicesters at Epéhy, was only one of many thousands of British soldiers who still had their face towards the enemy.

I was ordered to take a party of six men out at dusk to fill in a gap in the barbed-wire entanglements in front of our trench. As we made our way towards the gap, each carrying a roll of barbed wire, several shots were fired at us. No one was hit in the poor light, but we were in no doubt that, out there on our right flank, someone was watching us closely. It was long after dark when we finished the job and returned to our trench.

As we tried to get a bit of rest at the close of an unbelievable day, all we knew of the situation was what we had seen for ourselves, and we realised that the longer we stayed in our present position the less chance we had of getting out of it. Our one topic of conversation was how soon would we get orders to withdraw. All was very quiet.

*

When the fighting died down at dusk, the German advance ceased and their tired soldiers prepared to settle down for the night. The battle was not over for these men; there was simply a pause for the hours of darkness. Most of the Germans would be called upon to fight again in the morning and they had to make the best of whatever location the flow of battle had haphazardly deposited them at when darkness fell. Their first thoughts were for food and drink, and then sleep. In many cases, fires could not be lit because British troops were not far away. Some of the more fortunate of the Germans received hot food from their *Gulaschkanonen*, if the cooks had been able to follow up quickly, but most fed off captured British rations. Here are a selection of German soldiers' experiences that evening.

After having made some sort of a trench, we entered the hut. What we found was a gold mine for hungry soldiers. I think it was a store room. There was corned beef, tins with cooked dinners that only had to be warmed, choice jams and marmalade and other foodstuffs – things we hadn't seen for years. What a difference from our food! We just stuffed ourselves. I found a tin with 100 cigarettes; they were the best I have ever smoked in my life. We opened every tin in sight because none of us could read English. I especially remember a tin with baked beans and pork. I enjoyed that very much.

The windows of the hut had sacking for curtains. There were twenty or so of us inside; we had all got candles and became a little careless. We were thoroughly enjoying ourselves when someone knocked over his candle and we had to get out quick. The whole hut burnt down. The adjoining room was full of ammunition. We expected a big explosion but there was none, just a loud crackle; it sounded like machine-gun fire. Some of our men near by thought that a counter-attack had started. Then an artillery observation officer came and wanted to know what was happening. He also thought that the English were attacking us. When he found what had happened, he only said, jokingly, 'Have you got a few good cigarettes for me, then?' The English were about 500 metres away and must have seen what was happening, but they didn't open fire. (Gefreiter Willy Adams, Lehr Infantry Regiment)

I wonder if the field kitchen will come? Yes, it's incredible! It has done very well for us and every man gets two litres of boiled beef and barley. The normal ration was one litre per man but we had so many casualties that there were double rations all round.

Soon after this meal, my friend August, from Hamburg, asked me, 'Waldemar, do you like pea soup?' I was insulted; there was nothing I wouldn't eat. I was always hungry – day or night. We had brought that hunger with us from Russia. He snatched my mess-tin and came back with his and mine filled up to the brim. It went down beautifully. This came from the artillery's cook. He could certainly compete with ours.

For once, we were really full. We pulled the tent sheets over our heads and the night came. We slept in turns and the night passed quickly. The delousing at Le Cateau, before we set off, had been more successful than on previous occasions. (Fusilier Waldemar Schmielau, 5th Guard Grenadier Regiment)

We managed to spend the night in a small ruined cottage. It was full of drink, food and stores. I took some underclothes – long underpants – and sent them back to my father because I knew that he hadn't got any. I found out later that he never wore them; they were too scratchy. There was some red wine in a barrel; probably the English had bought it from the French. One of our men, an ordinary rifleman, got really drunk. He took all his clothes off – every one. No one tried to stop him; everyone was busy looking after himself. There were no officers with us; we had lost them all as casualties that morning. The drunken man went off into the dark, shouting, 'I want to find an Englishman. I want to kill him.' He ran off towards the English positions and we never saw him again. (Gefreiter Adolf Renschler, 185th Regiment)*

It was often the humorous incidents that were remembered.

Most of the men in the 25th Infantry Regiment were from

---

* Herr Adams was north of the Cambrai–Bapaume road, in a position recently held by the 1st West Yorks, 6th Division; Herr Schmielau was near Brosse Wood, which had been held by the 2/7th Manchesters, 66th Division; and Herr Renschler was near Vadencourt, recently held by units of the British 24th Division.

Aachen and Cologne and were famous for their sense of humour, difficult for a 'cold' East Prussian like me to understand. They cracked jokes in even the most serious situations. There was a proper comedian from Cologne who was a company runner. When he returned from battalion H.Q., he said, 'The war's over. The artillery is auctioning off their guns.' He had passed a battery position and heard someone shouting, 'Seventeen hundred. Eighteen hundred. Twenty-two hundred.' Now we laughed. He had heard the orders for the range. (Musketier Gustav Schulz, 25th Regiment)

But this German officer found that he had lost a friend.

My feelings that night were not too happy. I was depressed, thinking of the losses we had suffered. Leutnant Dopheide, the commander of the 12th Company, was a good friend. We had been together for a year. He came from somewhere in the Ruhr. He had been shot in the heart and killed at once. It had happened near the village of Grand Seraucourt. We searched for him and found his body that evening near an English position with twelve or fifteen of our men. There were a few English dead, but not so many.

On the other hand we were very pleased with our progress and I was particularly pleased because, that night, I took command of the entire 12th Company. It was the first company that I had ever commanded. (Leutnant Rudolf Hoffmann, 463rd Regiment)

Herr Hoffman's regiment was in the 238th Division, which had been formed only the previous year, mainly of men from Hamburg and the neighbouring districts, and this had been their first attack. They had penetrated the positions held by the 36th (Ulster) Division and reached the edge of the village of Grand Seraucourt where their last effort had been beaten back by the 2nd Royal Irish Rifles, in the small action in which Leutnant Dopheide had been killed. But this advance, of four and a half miles from their starting position on the edge of St Quentin, represented the deepest advance of the Germans on that first day. It was probably the greatest advance by any unit on the Western Front since trench warfare had started late in 1914.

Where the battle had not gone so well for the Germans, their men did not feel so happy that night. Three signallers had become separated from their battalion in the fighting in front of Epéhy.

As it had grown dark, we discontinued our search for battalion H.Q. and decided to spend the night where we were. We found a hole in the ground, about two metres deep, and settled in as well as we could. We heated a tin from our iron rations with solid spirit. That was the only food I had this day. Then we lay down and tried to sleep. We weren't very successful, in spite of being dog-tired. Firstly, the night was frightfully cold and foggy. We hadn't sufficient clothing; many of our things had to be handed in before the attack. Secondly, Tommy started very brisk shelling again during the night. The three of us changed places from time to time so that each could lie in the middle. The two on the outside couldn't sleep – too cold and too wet. Our morale, until then of a confident nature, had now gone completely to pieces. We considered the offensive a failure. (Gefreiter Walther Jachmann, 418th Regiment)

And this sensitive young soldier, only eighteen years old and in his first battle, had followed the infantry with the crew of an observation balloon.

For hardship and incident, it had been a catastrophic day. Everywhere there were dead men, pieces of bodies blown off, hastily treated wounded, men bleeding and running about with torn uniforms. Because of all these things, one felt like bursting with anger. One asked oneself, 'What is a human being worth in wartime?' Born in pain by a mother, looked after and cared for during many years, and then shot to pieces on the battlefield! Oh, you poor nation! This is how you settle your politics.

I had many more terrible days before the war was over, but this one was the worst. I tried not to think about the battle that night but I didn't sleep very well. I was far too upset and the scenes of the day behind me were still vivid in my mind. I had seen too many dead men. (Luftschiffer Karl Löffelholz, 148th Balloon Platoon)

There was no rest for some of the German soldiers. Most of the storm-troop and *Jäger* battalions were pulled out of the battle that evening. These specially trained troops were not to be used up in the succeeding days of the battle but were being kept intact for the next big offensive. In the Seventeenth Army, the most northern of the three German armies involved in the attacks, many of the artillery units that had been in action during the preliminary bombardment were also withdrawn that evening in order to prepare for the next big German offensive, the *Mars* attack against Arras which would take place on 28 March. It is an interesting example of the speed with which Ludendorff was planning to strike the British again and also of the slenderness of his artillery resources. The *Mars* attack was not to be a success.

While the German infantrymen ate and slept, with their satisfactions or their sorrows, many of the German artillerymen were straining to get their guns forward across the recently captured ground, to be ready for the reopening of the battle next morning. They were helped by hard-working pioneers, who bridged trenches, cleared obstacles, and generally expended a great deal of effort.

There was never any rest for us. Some of the artillery horses had been killed by shellfire and we received orders to help get these guns forward before morning. We had no meal. The artillerymen had no meal. We were all fed up with this lousy job and there was a great deal of swearing between us before the night was over. (Pioneer Wilhelm Niebuhr, 27th Pioneer Battalion)

*

Not far away in the darkness, the British soldiers were also settling down – weary, sad at the loss of comrades, anxious about the battle that would probably be resumed in a few hours' time. They stretched out in trenches, shell holes, or in the open and tried to sleep. It was a cold night, with a frost. One soldier remembers that 'it was so cold that we had to get up from time to time in order to stretch our legs. Again and again, men who had gone astray came and asked for their units.' An officer describes the verdict of his seniors on the events of the day.

Most of the brigade was killed or captured and, by nightfall, there were only several small groups gathered together and under the command of colonels and majors. We had a meeting of the remaining officers and all that the colonels and majors had to say about the day was that it had been 'a bugger'. (Second Lieutenant C. C. H. Greaves, 4th Lincolns)

Officers sat down and attempted to write up the day's events in the War Diaries of their units. The diaries of the Forward Zone battalions that had been overwhelmed never would be properly written, but at the headquarters of the 1st

Buffs, which had been in reserve until the afternoon, an anonymous officer struggled to record the part played by his battalion in the battle. His pencilled entries conclude with a note about a certain Lieutenant Rogers who, with thirty men from the Brigade Grenade School, had recaptured eight bays of trench before dark. Then, there is this remark in the diary: 'It is now so late I can't write any more and report ends.'* The writer of this War Diary and others like him could never have imagined how much their efforts would be appreciated by researchers and historians many years later. They were providing the raw material of history books.

Fresh troops were coming to the battle, fortunate to have missed the dangers of the day just ending but destined to be in the thick of it next morning. This soldier happens to be British but his feelings could equally be those of the German soldiers coming up to the battle area that night.

Soon it was dark and we moved on in open formation to take up our position. Things had quietened down for the time being and, after sentry duties had been arranged, we prepared to snatch what rest we could, hoping the enemy were doing the same.

What were my own feelings? Well, I had never been an aggressive person, preferring the quiet ways of life. I hated war and dreaded the thought of being involved in close combat. I don't think I could have bayonetted an enemy to save my life. But I did realise my limitations and had decided from the start that I would do what I was told to do, to the best of my ability, without taking foolhardy risks. That night, I prayed that I would not let my chums down and that the fates who had been so kind to me during my eleven months in France and Belgium, from Ypres to the Somme, would continue to favour me – for no reason I could think of – during the days ahead. (Private F. J. Spragg, 1st Wiltshires)

* Public Record Office WO 95/1608.

13

An Analysis

The first day of the *Kaiserschlacht* was over. In the numbers of men involved and in the total casualties, it had been the biggest day's fighting up to that time on the Western Front and those records would stand for the remainder of that blood-letting war. The scale of this day's fighting would not be exceeded until 10 May 1940, when the Germans attacked France, Belgium and Holland. But the importance of this day to military history is not just in numbers of men involved or casualties suffered, important though these are. 21 March 1918 was the beginning of the end of the First World War. When the German storm troops crossed the shell-battered remnants of the British front line a few minutes before 10 a.m. that day, they set in motion a chain of events that was to end the war. Those events are not the subject of this limited work but the results of that first day's fighting and the manner in which that fighting was conducted are of sufficient importance to merit a close study. Before starting this, I would like to pay my tribute to the great privilege of hindsight enjoyed by anyone writing more than half a century later and any criticisms made of participants in that battle are made only in an attempt to achieve an historical accuracy that is as near absolute as possible.

*

The first, and easiest, task is to present the most obvious results of the day's fighting. By midnight, the German soldiers had taken, by direct assault and capture, ninety-eight and a half square miles of ground previously held by the British Third and Fifth Armies – nineteen square miles from the Third Army and the remainder from the Fifth. In this area of ground there were the ruins of forty-six French villages. It is not suggested that this battle was only about the capture or loss of ground and ruined villages, but this was very much a war of maps with generals and civilians alike watching for the slightest change in the front lines of the armies.

The German successes on 21 March mocked the results of earlier Allied efforts, when the capture of a few trenches, a few acres of ground and a couple of ruined villages had been trumpeted as major victories. The battle that started on this day would later become known, unofficially, as the Second Battle of the Somme, and it is a comparison with the results of the first battle that highlights so vividly the German success on 21 March 1918. On the Somme in 1916, the British and French had captured ninety-eight square miles of ground and forty-six villages in 140 days of hard fighting and at a cost of over half a million casualties. This was almost exactly the same as the ground and villages just taken by the Germans in one day! Furthermore, on the night of 21 March, the British were voluntarily withdrawing from a further forty square miles of ground, containing eleven more villages, in an effort to save certain units from being encircled and over-whelmed. The new lines that would appear on maps, showing reverses which were massive by all preceding standards in that war, were a source of great embarrassment to the British military and political war leaders and would place a great strain on relations between the two groups and also between Britain and her allies, particularly with less en-lightened Frenchmen who were disgusted at the extent to which the British had given ground.*

But this battle was really about men – their casualties and the extent to which those who had not been hurt were still willing to fight. The Western Front had been a battlefield of attrition since 1916, and the German aim in this battle was no less than the destruction of the British Expeditionary Force. In an earlier chapter it was shown that, in the question of manpower, Germany could not hope to win if the war

* A minor example of this can be found in a letter from Captain H. Ward, who was the R.F.C. Liaison Officer at the French Sixth Army Aviation Head-quarters:
'The news concerning our unfortunate Fifth Army produced an instantaneous and bitter anti-British reaction. No one would speak to me in the Mess, a barrage of newspapers being raised the moment I came into the room. I learnt from Major Sewell, our Liaison Officer at the French Aviation G.H.Q., that he had been similarly boycotted.'

dragged on so long that the Americans were able to develop their full strength. The Germans had to break the Allied alliance before this happened and they had chosen the British as the target for the series of blows to be administered by the *Kaiserschlacht* attacks. The yardstick by which the German effort on the first day could be regarded as successful or not was whether the losses they were able to inflict on the British were sufficiently severe to shake Britain's morale and so hasten her exit from the war, and whether the German casualties had been sufficiently low to keep their forces intact for future operations. So, while the Allied watchers of lines on maps were appalled at the loss of ground to the Germans, more realistic observers were studying the important issues of casualty figures and morale.

The problem of how to calculate the exact casualties for the first day of the battle is a challenging one, because detailed figures have never been compiled before for either side. The first casualty return submitted by a unit that had been in battle was always a rough and ready one. A 'casualty' was simply a soldier who was not still present with his unit and fit enough to carry out his duty. There were the obvious casualties – men who were known to be dead and those known to have been evacuated to the rear with wounds. Any other man not present was usually marked as 'missing' – a term that causes much trouble. Such a man might well be dead, his body lost on the battlefield, or he might have been taken prisoner. But he might also have become separated from his unit and later turn up safe and sound. It is the extent to which 'missing' men returned that causes so much trouble for interpreters of casualty figures. Both sides used systems of reporting casualties that did not record properly the numbers of such men who later returned to duty. As for the genuine 'missing', it was many months before it became known who had been killed and who had become prisoners.

It is convenient to deal with the German casualty figures first. The side that remained in occupation of the battlefield at the end of the day always had an advantage. It knew the number of its men that had been wounded; it could count and often identify the bodies of its dead. Unless it had lost many men as prisoners, there was not usually a large number of missing. The War Diaries of the German units involved no longer exist – they were probably destroyed or dispersed in the Second World War – but, fortunately, equally useful documents are available because a large number of German regimental histories were published during the 1920s and 1930s. The German is a formidable archivist and historian, and these works often give precise details of casualties in regiments on 21 March 1918, even to naming every man who died. Such material would have come from the regiment's personnel records that existed then.

Thirty-two German divisions were in the first wave of the attack on 21 March 1918 and, of the ninety-six regiments in these divisions, forty histories, of regiments spread evenly down the battle front, contain detailed casualty figures. These forty regiments suffered the following *average* casualties during the first day of the battle:

Killed	70·6 men
Wounded	262·7 men
Missing	31·3 men
Total	364·6 men

From this it is reasonable to assume that the approximate total infantry casualties of the thirty-two first-wave German divisions were:

Killed	6,778 men
Wounded	25,219 men
Missing	3,004 men
Total	35,001 men

It is possible to clarify the 'missing' figure a little. It is assumed that the German regimental records accounted for the missing who later turned up safely and that the 'missing' still remaining were those men who had been taken prisoner, or who had died and whose bodies could not be identified. The only reliable British statistic for German prisoners taken at this time is a figure of 576 men taken prisoner by the whole of the British Expeditionary Force in the period 19–25

March.* It is unlikely that much more than half of these —
say 300 — were captured on 21 March, and the remainder of
the German missing were probably killed. The figures now
read:

Killed	9,482 men
Wounded	25,219 men
Prisoners	300 men
Total	35,001 men

Unfortunately we are on less sure ground when it comes to
calculating the further casualties in the German artillery and
other arms supporting the infantry regiments, in the two
divisions carrying out feint attacks on the Flesquières
Salient and in the second-wave divisions which would have
suffered some casualties from British artillery fire and aircraft attacks and some of which were committed to the fighting late in the day. Reliable figures for these units are not
available, but an estimate can be made by comparing them
with British units which operated in similar circumstances
during the day. When suitable calculations have been made,
these are the final estimates for the overall casualties of the
Germans on 21 March 1918:

Killed	10,851 men
Wounded	28,778 men
Prisoners	300 men
Total	39,929 men

It must be stressed that these figures are only approximate,
but they are, as far as is known, the first to be produced for
this important day's fighting and they are the best that are
ever likely to become available.

*

The compilation of the British casualties for the day presents
a different set of problems. The normal prime source for such
figures would be the unit War Diaries and the casualty
returns that these units submitted to higher formations.
Although many units have very useful War Diaries, those of

* From *Statistics of the Military Effort*, H.M.S.O., 1922, page 632.

the battalions in the Forward Zone, among which most of the casualties occurred, are in a pathetic condition. Here are a few examples.

It is impossible to give any connected or detailed information or account for the doings of the battalion for the month of March, as none of the officers or men in the front line came out of the 21st March battle. (8th King's Royal Rifle Corps)

Enemy attacked at 9 a.m., which resulted in the loss of 22 officers and 539 men including Lieutenant-Colonel Johnson, battalion H.Q. and staff. Remnants in reserve. No parades. (5th North Staffords)

The Diary now deals with the movement of battalion details, which consist of transport personnel, of Quartermaster Stores, personnel left out of action, O.R.s arriving back from leave, from courses and from hospital, together with a draft of some 100 O.R.s which arrived today. The battalion itself was gone, killed, wounded and prisoner. (15th Royal Irish Rifles)

By the evening of the 21st, the battalion ceased to exist. A few stragglers, under Sgt Beresford of B Company, were attached to the 9th Rifle Brigade. (9th Kings Royal Rifle Corps)

Battalion surrounded. 22 officers and 566 men all missing. (12th Royal Irish Rifles)

21st   No definite information was forthcoming as the battalion was cut off, but a message was received by pigeon at 1.30 p.m., from Lieutenant-Colonel A. V. P. Martin, that he was still holding out in the redoubt with fifty men.

22nd   No news from the battalion.

23rd   No news from the battalion.

24th   10 a.m., a voluntary church service held.

26th   No news from the battalion. (2nd Wiltshires)*

Details such as these were all that could be supplied by the officers who had been left out of the battle and who had the difficult task of starting up a new War Diary. The Army would not know until after the war what had happened to most of the missing men, and even then the information was scattered among the records of dozens of regiments. The

* The above War Diaries are Public Record Office WO 95/1895, 3021, 2503, 1900, 2506 and 2329.

Official Historian was faced with the problem of producing accurate casualty figures many times in his works covering the war years. For the important battle of 1 July 1916, he appointed a member of his staff to examine regimental records and establish what had happened to the men who were 'missing' on that day. This work took six months and 'for reason of economy could not be pursued further'. No investigation was undertaken for the battle fought on 21 March 1918, or at least none was ever published. Because divisional records were in little better state than battalion ones, the Official Historian did not even total the divisional losses, and he presented no estimate at all of the British casualties during the day. The question of how many casualties were suffered by the British units on 21 March 1918 has remained unanswered for sixty years. However, there are means of calculating reasonable figures for the British casualties, although different methods are required for different categories of casualty.

After the war, the Imperial War Graves Commission (now the Commonwealth War Graves Commission) took over from the Army the task of establishing permanent cemeteries for the dead soldiers of the British Empire, and each of the Commission's cemeteries now has a register giving details of the men who are known to be buried there. The men who had died but had no identifiable grave were commemorated by name on special 'Memorials to the Missing' erected on each of the major battlefields. The 'unknown' dead of the Third Army are named on a memorial in a suburb of Arras and those of the Fifth Army on a memorial at Pozières, on the old Roman road between Albert and Bapaume. These memorials also have comprehensive registers. Thus, every dead soldier had his name, rank, unit and date of death in the register of a cemetery or of a memorial. It was interesting to study the registers for the Arras and Pozières Memorials and for the 164 cemeteries which are now located in the area of the 21 March 1918 fighting. Cemeteries well to the east and west of the limits of the battlefield were included in the search in order to take in places where men who had been wounded and evacuated from the battlefield by one side or the other had later died.

This search resulted in a mass of useful information which can be presented to illustrate many different aspects of the fighting on 21 March 1918. The only slight drawback is that the resulting figures do not include wounded men who were evacuated great distances from the battlefield and died before midnight or those who died of wounds on succeeding days, but, except for this, it can be stated with some certainty that the total of British soldiers and airmen who died on 21 March 1918 was 7,512–3,057 in units belonging to the Third Army and 4,455 in the Fifth Army.

The proportion of the dead in the two armies is significant. The Third Army had only been attacked on a frontage equivalent to that held by three divisions. The fighting had been fierce here and the *average* Third Army division attacked had lost 1,019 men killed. By comparison, nine and two thirds divisional frontages had been attacked in the Fifth Army and the *average* casualties of each of its divisions was 461 men killed.

The casualties of individual divisions are also interesting.

Division	Type of division*	Men killed
59th (N. Midland)	T.F. (2nd L)	807
66th (E. Lancs)	T.F. (2nd L)	711
6th	Reg.	602
16th (Irish)	N.A.	572
14th (Light)	N.A.	370
61st (S. Midland)	T.F. (2nd L)	361
51st (Highland)	T.F. (1st L)	309
21st	N.A.	305
24th	N.A.	276
36th (Ulster)	N.A.	267
30th	N.A.	245
18th (Eastern)	N.A.	182

Only divisions which had at least two of their three brigades in the Forward and Battle Zone under German attack are

* Reg. – Regular; T.F. (1st or 2nd L) – Territorial Force (First- or Second-Line); N.A. – New Army. Many of the New Army divisions contained a proportion of Regular battalions.

included in this table. Thirteen other divisions – in the Flesquières Salient, on the flanks of the attack, or coming up from reserve during the day – suffered a total of 1,064 fatal casualties. The very heavy casualties of the 59th (North Midland) Division, which had only two brigades in the line for most of the day, show how heavy the fighting was around the Bullecourt Salient. Some of the heaviest German regimental casualties were also in this area. It is not suggested that the number of dead in a unit is the only yardstick of its fighting qualities and of the bravery of its men, but the presence of the 59th Division and the other two Second-Line Territorial Divisions near the head of the table shows that these sometimes-derided divisions had at least stood and fought and had not run off or surrendered without a fight.

Seven battalions – four Territorial and three Regular – had lost more than 100 of their men killed.

Battalion	Men killed
7th Sherwood Foresters	171
2/6th Sherwood Foresters	131
2nd Durham Light Infantry	122
2/6th South Staffords	112
2/5th Sherwood Foresters	109
2nd Royal Dublin Fusiliers	108
1st West Yorks	107

All these battalions, except the Dublin Fusiliers, were fighting in the Third Army area.*

The British deaths can also be distributed among the different types of fighting units.

Arm	Men killed
Infantry†	6,082
Artillery	644
Machine-gun companies	467
Royal Engineers	139

* The three Sherwood Forester battalions which suffered so heavily were recruited as follows: the 7th Sherwood Foresters in Nottinghamshire and the 2/5th and 2/6th Sherwood Foresters in Derbyshire. All were in the 178th Brigade, 59th Division.

† The infantry casualties include men from light trench-mortar batteries whose names are recorded by the War Graves Commission with the original battalion from which they had been detached.

Arm	Men killed
Royal Army Medical Corps	67
Labour Corps	35
Cavalry	23
Others	55

These figures show that the infantry casualties were 81 per cent of the total and those of the artillery 8·6 per cent. The dead artillerymen were made up of 446 Royal Field Artillery men, 192 from the Royal Garrison Artillery and six from the Royal Horse Artillery. Many of the casualties among the Labour Corps and those under the heading of 'others' were a result of the far-reaching German bombardment of the rear areas. Among such men killed were two military policemen, one man from a cyclist battalion and one from a Mobile X-Ray Company. There is some irony in the experiences of two senior N.C.O.s who had been on the staff of the head-quarters of the 30th Division. One, awaiting a posting to an Officer Cadet Battalion in England, decided to return to his old battalion when it went into the line and he became a prisoner-of-war when Manchester Hill fell. The other, at the supposed safety of divisional headquarters, was killed by a shell while walking to his lunch.

The ranks of all the dead men are known. The 450 dead officers ranged from thirteen lieutenant-colonels* to 265 second lieutenants. The highest proportion of officers killed to men of other ranks was in the artillery and reflects the dangers run by forward observation officers. One chaplain, the Reverend Alan Judd, attached to the 2/5th Sherwood Foresters, was killed, and several more were captured. 1,327 warrant officers and N.C.O.s and 5,736 private soldiers were killed.

It is not enough just to quote statistics. These were all individual human beings, young men killed in the prime of life, their bodies in trenches, in shell holes, in dug-outs, in gun-pits or littered across the open ground of the battlefield. Some had died mercifully quickly, others in protracted agony. Nearly all left behind sorrowing relatives. Most of these men

* Appendix 8 gives details of all senior officer casualties, killed, wounded or taken prisoner.

were from humble families that would never benefit from their deaths. Some had volunteered to face this risk of death, but most were conscripts, men unlucky enough to be born in a certain country the appropriate number of years before that country's leaders called upon them to fight against the young men of other countries.

BEAMENT, Rfn Stanley William. 9th King's Royal Rifle Corps. Age 20. Son of William and Fanny Beament of Croxley Green, Watford, Herts. Twice previously wounded.

CATES, 2nd Lt Geoffrey. 2nd Durham Light Infantry. Aged 24. Son of George and Alice Ann Cates, of Wimbledon. His brother, 2nd Lt George Cates, V.C., also fell, and his brother William Frederick was lost at sea.

CONSIDINE, C.S.M. Michael. 6th Connaught Rangers. Age 44. Son of the late Michael and Mary Considine; husband of Bridget Considine of Limerick. Served 24 years with the Colours.

DUNCAN, Lce Cpl Robert, M.M. 1st Regt South African Inf. Age 24. Son of Robert Duncan of Wynberg, Cape Province.

EVANS, Pte John. Bedfordshire Regt, posted to Hertfordshire Regt. Age 31. Son of Thomas Evans of Maengwyn House, Trawsfynydd, Merioneth.

GORNELL, 2nd Lt Noel Christopher. 157th Field Coy Royal Engineers. Died of wounds. Age 20. Son of Mr and Mrs C. Gornell of Royton, Oldham. Head Prefect in Lancaster Royal Grammar School prior to joining the Royal Engineers.

HOBHOUSE, Capt. Paul Edward. 6th Somerset Light Inf. Mentioned in Despatches. Age 23. Son of the Rt Hon. Henry Hobhouse of Hadspen House, Castle Cary, Somerset. Educated at Eton College and New College, Oxford. Volunteered August 1914.

HUTSON, 2nd Lt William Cecil. 51st Bde Royal Field Artillery. Age 19. Son of Harry and Annie Hutson of Toronto, Canada. Gazetted from Royal Military College, Kingston, Canada.

KING, Serjt Gerald, D.C.M., M.M., 7th/8th Royal Inniskilling Fusiliers. Age 22. Son of Martin King, of Kentucky, U.S.A., and Kathleen King, of Belfast.

LORD, Pte Joe. 2nd Bn York and Lancaster Regt. Age 26. Son of Tom and Elizabeth Lord of Elland, Yorks.

MERGA, Pte Fred Walter. 43rd Field Amb. Royal Army Medical Corps. Age 21. Son of Herbert Harding and Edith Merga of Atherton, Manchester.

PERRIE, Pte James, M.M. 5th Seaforth Highlanders. Age 20. Son of George and Jessie Perrie of Burghead, Morayshire.

POLLARD, A.B. Allen Henry. Hood Bn R.N. Div. Age 32. Son of the late William Pollard; husband of Annie Midgley Pollard of Finsbury Park, London.

RICHARDSON, 2nd Lt David Alexander. 7th Black Watch. Age 27. Only son of Mr and Mrs John Richardson of Edinburgh.

SPINKS, Pte Edward. 25th (Tyneside Irish) Bn Northumberland Fusiliers. Age 29. Son of George and Elizabeth Spinks of South Moor; husband of Annie Spinks, South Moor, Stanley, Co. Durham.

WALTER, Spr Frederick William John. Postal Section Royal Engineers. Age 28. Husband of Ethel Mary Walter of Surbiton, Surrey. A Postman.*

The vast majority of the dead were United Kingdom men, and there were particularly heavy losses among men from Nottinghamshire, Derbyshire and Staffordshire, who had been in the 59th (North Midland) Division, men from Manchester and towns in East Lancashire, who had been in the 66th (East Lancs) Division, the Irish, in their two divisions, and men from the Highlands of Scotland. London, although having two divisions in the front line, had been fortunate. One of its divisions was in the Flesquières Salient, and two brigades of the other were south of the River Oise where the Germans had not attacked. Fifty-five South Africans were killed. The War Graves Commission registers list one solitary Australian sapper from a railway company near Péronne and one Canadian cavalryman from the Fort Garry Horse, both of whom were probably killed by shell-fire, and a Maltese officer serving with the 2nd Royal Munster Fusiliers. No American casualties have been found, although at least three of their medical officers became prisoners while serving with British battalions.

One sad aspect of the study of the registers was the high proportion of the men killed on 21 March 1918 who have no known grave. It was common practice for the victor in a big

* The names of these men, all killed on 21 March 1918, are taken from the registers of the Arras and Pozières Memorials and of the Villers-Faucon Communal Cemetery.

battle to recover his own dead from the battlefield first, identify the bodies where possible, and then bury them. The bodies of the enemy were usually buried without identification or ceremony in shell holes and other forms of multiple graves. For this reason, only 978 of the 7,485 British soldiers killed on 21 March 1918 have individually identified graves; the remainder are commemorated on the Memorials to the Missing. There were six battalions – 2/2nd, 2/4th and 18th Londons, 9th Norfolks, 22nd Northumberland Fusiliers and 7th Royal West Kents – which each had more than fifty men killed, but out of which not a single soldier has his own marked grave.

*

The calculation of the number of British soldiers wounded was an easier task, but the results are less accurate. The only useful figure that could be reached was that of the number of wounded men who were evacuated by the British medical services from the battlefield; the number of men wounded and then taken prisoner by the Germans can only be estimated very roughly.

Reliable figures for wounded British soldiers who were evacuated were found in the records of only one corps, two divisions and ten battalions. Figures by R.A.M.C. units for the *reception* of casualties are almost non-existent. They were too busy dealing with wounded men and moving their locations back to avoid capture; paper work was abandoned. Using what figures are available, averaging them out, making allowances for the difficulty or ease of evacuating men from the Forward and Battle Zones, for the different circumstances of the units in the Flesquières Salient or coming up from reserve – all this resulted in a figure of 10,339 British soldiers wounded and evacuated from the battlefield. It must be stressed that this is no more than an estimate and it might be better to say that 'approximately 10,000' men were thus wounded. The vast majority of these were men wounded in the preliminary bombardment or in the later Battle Zone fighting. Very few wounded men returned from the Forward Zone after the German attack commenced. No estimate is made for the men affected by gas. One report says that 3,000 gas casualties were evacuated in the Flesquières Salient alone, but this figure seems a high one and may be an accumulation of the gas casualties here over the several days of gas shelling that preceded the German attack.

The most intriguing question of all about the British casualties is the one concerning the number of men taken prisoner. The unit War Diary keepers naturally had no means of knowing how many of their men had been captured. The Official Historian is of very little help: he made no effort to estimate a figure for prisoners for the first day. German figures for the day are vague.

The attempt to calculate the number of British prisoners starts with the battalion War Diaries, which usually show the number of officers and men missing. As explained earlier, the 'missing' figures include not only those men killed on the battlefield or taken prisoner, but also the men who had become separated from their units and who later returned unharmed. The Official Historian found that the figure for such men who returned to duty during the March 1918 fighting was, in three divisions, equivalent to *10 per cent* not of the missing but *of the total casualties* of those divisions. He suggested that this proportion should be applied to all units in that battle. Although his three divisions were not heavily involved on the first day and I think this figure is an over-generous one to apply on 21 March, when so many battalions in the Forward Zone were completely surrounded in the fog in the first hour of the battle, I have applied it to all the battalions on that day in order to avoid the danger of over-estimating the number of prisoners.

After deducting, therefore, a figure for the men who were missing and later returned to duty and a further figure for missing men known from the War Graves Commission registers to have been killed, it was found that approximately 19,544 men – 641 officers and 18,903 other ranks – from infantry battalions alone had become prisoners. Four divisions are estimated to have lost more than 2,000 prisoners each during the day: 59th (North Midland) – 3,142 prisoners; 36th (Ulster) – 2,392 prisoners; 14th (Light) – 2,238 prisoners; and the 6th Division – 2,116 prisoners. These figures are for infantry only, and a further number should now be added for units of the supporting arms that were present on the battlefield – machine-gunners, trench-mortar men, engineers, tank men and field gunners. Because these men were not present in such strength in the Forward Zone as the infantry, a comparatively low figure – perhaps no more than 1,500 – should be allowed for these men becoming prisoners. This gives a total of approximately 21,000 British prisoners for the day. An unknown number of these men were wounded or gassed and a proportion of these would later die.

This figure for British prisoners is a high one and it represents the fighting strength of nearly three full divisions. It was certainly the largest total of British soldiers to surrender in one day during the First World War and would not be matched until the Germans captured some 25,000–30,000 British prisoners at Dunkirk in 1940. There will be further comment on the 21 March 1918 prisoners later in this chapter.

*

It is now possible to present a table showing the casualties of both sides in the fighting on 21 March 1918.

	Killed	Wounded	Prisoners	Total
German	10,851	28,778	300	39,929
British	7,512	10,000	21,000	38,512

It must be stressed again that many of these figures are only estimated, but they are the most reliable that are likely to be produced for one of the First World War's most important day's fighting. The total casualty figures – more than 78,000 from both sides – were the highest for a single day's fighting in the whole war, exceeding the 65,470 (57,470 British and approximately 8,000 German) of the first day of the Battle of the Somme on 1 July 1916. But the July 1916 day had been a more lethal one, with some 5,000 more men being killed.

In interpreting these figures, the first thing that can be said is that both sides had suffered remarkably similar *total* casualties; but any similarity ends there. From the human point of view, the British had been more fortunate, with a total of fatal casualties less than three quarters of that of the Germans. Once again, as so often in the First World War, the side that attempted to break the trench-warfare stalemate by attacking its enemy had suffered the greater loss of life. In a strictly military study, however, particularly of a battle in that year of 1918 in which manpower considerations were so important, what counted was the number of men permanently lost to the military service of each side. There can be no doubt that here the Germans had the advantage. Only 11,151 of their men were dead or prisoners, compared to 28,485 of the British, and the Germans could expect a greater number of lightly wounded men to return to service.

*

I must confess that the German breakthrough on 21 March 1918 should never have occurred. There was no cohesion of command, no determination, no will to fight, and no unity of companies or of battalions.

This comment was made by a platoon sergeant who had fought on the Western Front with his division since 1915 and who was wounded and taken prisoner when his battalion was overwhelmed in the Forward Zone that morning. It does not matter which division he was in; it is a comment that might have been made about many of the sectors facing the German attack. It is a convenient introduction to the study of how the British commanders and their units had performed on the battlefield, once Haig had laid down his overall policy and allocated his available divisions. The British plans had been based on the expectation that the Forward Zone defences would hold for at least several hours, that the main redoubts in the Forward Zone would hold for up to two days, and that the first German attack would have been held and broken at the front of the Battle Zone. Why had these hopes not materialised?

A too direct comparison of the performances of General Byng's Third Army and General Gough's Fifth Army would be unprofitable and might be misleading. Byng's defences were well established and well manned, and he had little room to manoeuvre. The conditions under which Gough fought were the opposite, and the early loss of his forward defences and the necessity to give ground were both predictable. But Gough's front that had been attacked must be looked at in two halves. In Gough's north, his men had held as well as had Byng's; in fact, the only sizeable sector of either army where the British Battle Zone had not been breached by the Germans was the 14,000-yard one held by the 30th and 61st (South Midland) Divisions opposite St Quentin. North of that point, Gough's divisions had held the German attack within the Battle Zone on every sector except that of the 16th (Irish) Division. It was only in this Irish sector and on the long frontage south of St Quentin, on that part of the line which the British had taken over from the French late in January, that the British divisions were pushed clean out of their Battle Zone. If the British had never taken over the line south of St Quentin, it would have been the French, with their notoriously weak defence works, who would have faced the German attack here. It is quite likely that they would have fared no better than the weak and extended British divisions did, and then it would have been a French general and not Gough who collected the odium for the disaster that occurred here.

The main factor in any comparison of the two armies was the numbers of men and lengths of front held. Those divisions of the Third Army that were attacked lost, on average, far more men than did the Fifth Army ones on the first day – 3,109 killed and prisoners in an average Third Army division, 1,834 in a Fifth Army division. The number of wounded men evacuated from the Third Army divisions was also probably higher. Gough did not have many reserves and he was forced to adopt a policy that would keep his army as intact as possible; on the above figures he was successful in achieving this by not packing his front line too densely with troops and by judicious withdrawals. Despite this, Gough was in deep trouble at the end of the day. Byng had a continuing flow of reserves arriving on the battlefield to plug gaps; Gough committed all his reserves within the first twenty-four hours.

Byng fought a conventional, defensive battle in the style of the typical Western Front commander – stand and fight where you are, give as little ground as possible. He could do so in the knowledge that he had plenty of reserves with which to replace his losses. Gough showed far more flexibility, although it should be stated that he had the authority of his Commander-in-Chief to do so. Byng's attitude was exemplified in his handling of the Flesquières Salient situation. Haig must have urged him to pull his men out of this exposed position several times; it is a pity that he did not issue a direct order. Troops urgently needed elsewhere were tied up in the salient and unnecessary casualties were suffered there from the German gas shelling before the attack. The British Official History comments:

Regimental officers at the time protested against being left in a salient deluged with gas shell and from the front line of which the field of fire was indifferent, whereas by withdrawal, the enemy, if he attacked, would be forced to advance over ground where he could be dealt with far more easily.*

Even when Byng did allow a withdrawal from here on the first night of the battle, it was of too limited an extent and many casualties were later suffered as a result. Compare this rigidity of Byng with the bold action shown by Gough in pulling more than three divisions back over the Crozat Canal on that first night. Gough's divisions would undoubtedly have suffered more casualties if he had not been so bold, but his reputation might have remained more intact.

Coming to a lower level of command, there is scope for a few comments on the performance of some of the divisions involved, but again the factors affecting the fighting on different sectors were so varied that too many comparisons and judgements should be avoided. The first division to attract attention was the 16th (Irish), which had lost the whole of its Battle Zone in the fighting north of St Quentin. On 22 March, Haig was writing in his diary:

Our 16th (Irish) Division, which was on the right of VII Corps and lost Ronssoy village, is said not to be so full of fight as the others. In fact, certain Irish units did very badly and gave way immediately the enemy showed.†

* British Official History, page 249 footnote.
† *The Private Papers of Douglas Haig*, page 296.

This comment by Haig was only partly justified. This was the division where the corps commander had insisted that the front line be heavily manned, against the wishes of the newly appointed divisional commander, Major-General Hull. The reader will remember that Gough had been consulted over this and had backed up the corps commander – 'The Germans are not going to break my line', Gough had said. The division had been in the line for almost a month and was very tired. Five battalions had been posted in a Forward Zone where two or three would have been enough. These battalions suffered the full weight of the bombardment and then of the main German infantry assault that was intended to encircle the Flesquières Salient from the south. It is true that some of the Irish battalions did break but only after suffering numbers of men killed exceeded by only three other divisions during the day. There were four other divisions, besides the Irish, which lost their entire Battle Zones during the day. Among these four were the two other 'Celtic' divisions, the 36th (Ulster) and the 51st (Highland), and it seems possible that these troops, who all had such fine reputations in offensive operations, did not have the temperament for defence.

The much-derided Second-Line Territorials, however, had come out of the fighting with enhanced reputations. The 59th (North Midland) had lost all of its Battle Zone but only after suffering the highest fatal casualties of the day. The 61st (South Midland) and 66th (East Lancs) had held most of their Battle Zones against heavy attack and their fatal casualties had also been heavy. It might be assumed that these later arrivals on the Western Front were perhaps less skilful in battle than older divisions but that their men were, at least, prepared to stand and fight.

The biggest collapse of a division had occurred in the 14th (Light) Division in the sector south of St Quentin newly taken over from the French. Major-General Sir Victor Couper had only brought his New Army division down from Ypres in January 1918. As late as one week before the battle, there had been a dispute between this division and its neighbours on the left, the Ulster Division. Ulster officers had complained that, while they were deploying in depth, the

14th Division was deployed in line, with too much strength in the front line. Major-General O. S. W. Nugent, the veteran commander of the Ulster Division, complained to his corps commander and, through him, to General Gough. 'The reply was most unsatisfactory and was to the effect that XVIII and III Corps should settle it among themselves.'* A meeting of officers took place on the ground, but only slight adjustments were made. The 14th Division did not fight well on 21 March. Its forward positions fell quickly; many men surrendered, and some hasty flights to the rear were observed. The Ulster Division later blamed the 14th for collapsing and exposing a flank, although the Ulster Division itself did not hold well against the frontal attacks of the Germans. It was all part of a familiar scene, of weak and war-weary divisions with extended frontages, of successful German attacks and the collapse of the defence, and all followed by recriminations with the blame for failure always going to another unit on a flank.

The commander of the 14th Division was sent home on the evening of the second day of the battle. His corps commander charitably recorded in the III Corps War Diary that

Major-General Sir Victor Couper, officer commanding 14th Division, was suffering from want of sleep and rest and, in my opinion, was not in a fit state to handle the situation for the time being. I, therefore, in the afternoon, ordered Major-General W. H. Greenly of the 2nd Cavalry Division to take over.†

Couper's own divisional War Diary recorded that 'Major-General Couper left to assume command of a division in England.'‡ The plain truth is that Major-General Couper was sacked, the first senior officer to lose his command for the handling of his unit in this battle. His replacement did not fare much better. The cavalry officer, Major-General Greenly, had to be returned to England, a man broken in health, on 1 April. The remnants of the poor 14th Division, like most of the Fifth Army, were not relieved and had to fight on to the end of the battle. Major-General Greenly,

* Letter by Major G. S. S. Hodgson, G.S.O.2, 36th Division, to Official Historian, Public Record Office CAB 45/193.
† Public Record Office WO 95/678.
‡ Public Record Office WO 95/1880.

according to Haig's diary, 'went off his head with the strain.'

*

The comments on army and divisional performances may be of interest but they do not really provide the explanation as to why the British defences did not hold as well as their commanders had hoped. Despite the high hopes of the German commanders and the number of men that they had employed in this battle, the basic nature of the German attack on 21 March did not vary all that much from that of previous Allied attacks. It is true that the preliminary bombardment was more intense and placed a greater emphasis on the use of gas and that the infantry attack had relied more on infiltration than confrontation, but these were really refinements of an old concept rather than the unfolding of a new method of breaking the stalemate of trench warfare. Nor was the German superiority in guns and men any greater than the Allies had assembled for their previous attacks. Yet the Germans had achieved a major battlefield success and come nearer to breaking through the rigid trench defences than any other Western Front army. A tribute must be paid to the skill of the Germans, especially of their marvellous infantry, but the explanation of the British failure really lies in three separate but interwoven factors: the nature of the defence system relied upon by the British on this occasion, the weather conditions, and the morale and fighting spirit of the British soldiers.

It don't suit us. The British Army fights in line and won't do any good in these bird cages.

This is what a March 1918 N.C.O., who had been on the Western Front since 1914, told one of his officers when discussing the new principle of redoubts in the Forward Zone defences.* It might be thought that a major reason for the British setback was the new defensive system, with its Forward Zone, thinly held with all-round defence positions rather than in a continuous line, and with the main Battle Zone much farther back. The principles of this defence 'in

* British Official History, page 258.

depth' were not really understood by most of the ordinary soldiers who manned the positions, nor even by many of the officers. It was unfortunate that this new defence concept was first put to the test on this particular day because the idea itself was basically a sound one. It is true that the layout of the defences was very much on a 'trial and error' basis and many mistakes were made; in particular, the large redoubt – the 'bird cage' of the veteran N.C.O. – does not seem to have been successful, tying up as it did a large proportion of the men available in the Forward Zone and being so vulnerable to mortar and light howitzer fire once the smaller surrounding posts had fallen. But the situation was aggravated and the outcome distorted by other factors, and it cannot be said that the new system had a fair trial on 21 March 1918. One obvious factor was the serious shortage of men on many parts of the front, this again being complicated by the too-recent reorganisation in which every brigade had lost one of its four battalions. All this has been covered in earlier chapters, and there is no need to say more here than that the units manning the British defences that morning were not strong enough, had not been properly trained for and did not fully understand their new role, and had not yet recovered from a fundamental change in their structure.

The thick fog that covered the battlefield for the first hours of the battle was another factor, and a very important one, that affected the efficient working of the defence plan. Whether the fog was of more assistance to one side or to the other is one of the open questions of the battle. Certain advantages, all very early in the day, were obvious. The German artillery, firing blindly by the map, could not be corrected by visual observation in the last two hours of the preliminary bombardment. This advantage for the British was immediately cancelled out by the ability of the German storm troops to deploy in No Man's Land, silently and unseen by the British. Once the German attack had commenced, however, the balance of advantage became harder to judge. The British machine-gunners and riflemen were blind until the Germans were almost upon them. The British artillery could not bring down close defensive fire. British commanders could find out nothing about the progress of the battle in the

Forward Zone. For their part, the Germans frequently lost their way on the battlefield; they blundered into defended positions and failed to exploit sufficiently swiftly the gaps between the British positions. The German artillery could not engage those British positions that were still holding out and could only fire a prearranged creeping barrage that usually left the leading German infantry behind.

The question of who benefited most from the fog has been much considered by historians. One of these, W. Shaw Sparrow, devoted a complete chapter to the subject in his book *The Fifth Army in March 1918* and had a correspondence with General Gough on the subject. Both Shaw Sparrow and Gough agreed that the fog had been a slight advantage to the British troops, but both stated that this advantage increased after the first few hours, that is after the British forward defences had been penetrated. I would like to venture the opinion that the advantage was clearly with the Germans and that, had there been no fog, there might not have been any other but a first phase of the battle on many parts of the front attacked, or, at least, that the first phase would have been far more prolonged than it was with the fog present.

The important factor is surely that of how the fog affected the use of weapons. The German infantry were in the open; the British were in the shelter of trenches. The Germans were vulnerable to machine-gun and rifle fire and to observed artillery fire, especially when the British guns were firing shrapnel shells, which burst in the air over the heads of the Germans and blew down on them a plunging shower of lethal shrapnel balls. The main German weapon on 21 March was the hand grenade, which could not be used until the attackers were within throwing distance, and the mortar and light howitzer, which had to be brought up and sited near their targets. It does not require too much imagination to envisage the scene if there had been no fog around the British front-line defences on the morning of 21 March when the Germans attacked at 9.40 a.m. Many a British and French infantry attack in the past had foundered against German machine-gun fire. It has been estimated that the British attack on 1 July 1916, which sustained 57,470 casualties, was stopped by just 200 German machine-guns whose crews had survived a seven-day bombardment. The British divisions on 21 March 1918 had approximately 2,000 machine-guns in the Forward Zone and 4,000 in the Battle Zone on the sectors that were attacked!

The very first line of the British forward defences would probably have fallen quickly, whether there was fog or not, because of the intensity of the German preliminary bombardment; but the main part of the Forward Zone, particularly the all-round defended keeps and redoubts, many of which had not been hit too hard by the German shelling, could have inflicted a veritable slaughter on the German infantry, whose tactics, although skilful and in some ways novel, were not proof against machine-gun bullets. What happened at Epéhy, where the fog lifted early and exposed the Germans deployed in No Man's Land to the fire of well-entrenched British infantry, could have been repeated at most other places where the Germans attacked had there been no fog.

The Germans would probably have battered down the British Forward Zone eventually but with much greater loss of their own men and after a much longer delay than that actually experienced in the fog. The Germans would then have approached the Battle Zone in clear conditions and over ground fully exposed to fire from the Battle Zone defences. This is what actually happened on 21 March in the area of Lieutenant-General Maxse's XVIII Corps, where the fog lifted before the Germans arrived and the 30th and 61st (South Midland) Divisions held off the Germans all afternoon, inflicted heavy losses, and kept their Battle Zone intact until nightfall. Again, the same favourable result could have been achieved by the British on other sectors if the day had been clear. In all this fighting, the British artillery could have played its full part. It is true that the German artillery fire could also have been better controlled and directed in clear conditions, but let it be said again that the German artillery would have been firing on men in the cover of good entrenched positions while the German infantry were advancing over open ground.

It is my opinion that if there had been no fog the German infantry casualties on 21 March 1918 would have greatly exceeded the 40,000 men actually killed and wounded in the fog and that the German advance could have been halted in most places in front of the Battle Zone, as intended by the British defensive planners. The second phase of the battle would then have started under conditions much more favourable to the British. The presence of thick fog on the battlefield on 21 March 1918 completely distorted the outcome of the fighting and led to many false conclusions being drawn about it.

*

Did some of the British units facing the German attack collapse without putting up a reasonable resistance? Did the Fifth Army, as John Keegan, the Sandhurst lecturer, suggested, collapse 'as much morally as physically'? A large proportion of German accounts tell of finding British Forward Zone positions in which the defenders surrendered after only the briefest of fights. Is it true that many of the 20,000 British prisoners surrendered in the first hour or so of the German attack? If one reads only the regimental and battalion histories of British units, the situation presented is of one position after another 'fighting to the end', with the utmost bravery and heavy loss of life. This does not fit in with the German accounts of premature surrenders by the British, and the Germans had nothing to gain by exaggerating the ease of their early successes. Nor does it fit in with the reliable fatal casualty figures extracted from the Commonwealth War Graves Commission records.

Another aspect of this became apparent when I was looking at accounts sent to me by British contributors. Those battalions in the Forward Zone who had the most men taken prisoner provided the fewest personal accounts of the battle and hardly any at all from officers. There was one significant interview with an officer who, on the first day of the battle, had been absent from his battalion on a course. He was the only contributor from that battalion.

Morale wasn't high. Everyone was tired of the war. If we'd had the guts we'd had eighteen months earlier, the Germans would never have knocked a hole in the line as they did that time. I heard later that most of the battalion became prisoners without putting up much of a fight. I know it was foggy but they had wire out and they should have heard the Germans coming through. After the war, I met some of the officers who had been taken prisoner and had the feeling that they were all rather ashamed of what had happened. (Lieutenant R. A. France, 2/5th Manchesters)

It was a situation that probably existed in many other units. Let a few examples be given of Forward Zone battalions which suffered a great loss of prisoners. All have been met in earlier chapters. All were in the Forward Zone.

The 2/8th Worcesters were just north of St Quentin. 'They simply fought it out on the spot and their heroism will live forever in the annals of their regiments.' This was written by an unknown officer in their division, the comment being upon all three battalions in the division's Forward Zone.* But former Private S. Bromell, the only contributor from this battalion, says, 'When my position surrendered, we joined up with practically every man jack of our battalion who had been captured – transport, Red Cross, even the band. We were all marched into St Quentin.' The regimental history published after the war says that one quarter of the battalion were killed. The actual numbers killed were five officers and twenty-one men – only about 4 per cent of those in action. Approximately 600 men surrendered. The same history names nine officers as 'killed' of whom six were certainly prisoners.

The 16th Manchesters had held Manchester Hill and many smaller positions near by. 'The stand made round the Colonel by the garrison of this small Redoubt [Manchester Hill] is an epic in our military history . . . Of the original garrison of eight officers and 160 other ranks, only two officers and fifteen other ranks survived.'† The fatal casualties among the 168 men on Manchester Hill could not have been more than thirty or forty men. Four officers and sixty-nine men died from the whole battalion; the remainder – including at least three quarters of the men on Manchester Hill – surrendered. When the battalion history was published after the war, it named no fewer than fifteen officers 'killed'. Eleven of these had become prisoners.

* Public Record Office WO 95/3061.
† *The Manchester regiment, 16th, 17th, 18th and 19th Battalions, 1914–1918*, no author, published by Sherratt and Hughes, 1923, pages 49 and 53.

'Surrounded on all sides by overwhelming forces, smothered with trench-mortar shells, subjected to constant bombing and *Flammenwerfer* attacks, they had no thought of surrender until further resistance was impossible . . . There were very few of the defenders left alive and unwounded.'* This was a regimental historian's view of Boadicea Redoubt, held by the men of the 2nd Royal Inniskilling Fusiliers. But the German captors of this position say that, far from most of the defenders being killed and wounded, the garrison filed out of the redoubt in good order after a negotiated surrender. At least sixteen officers and 500 men surrendered from Boadicea Redoubt and the remainder of this battalion's defences.

There was rarely such a blunt admission as that of Lieutenant-Colonel G. Flint, the commander of the 2nd Yorks and Lancasters, who recorded in his War Diary how 'no resistance was offered [by a company posted in a reserve trench] and the garrison surrendered without fighting, being plainly visible leaving their trench with their hands up as the enemy approached.'†

It would be commonly accepted that the duty of a soldier in action is to offer resistance to an enemy as long as he has a weapon and ammunition to do so and has not been incapacitated by a serious wound or run out of food. The soldier will risk death in doing this, but that was the sacrifice that he was prepared to make when he volunteered or which he was called upon by his country to make if he had been conscripted. A soldier who fights on to the death, inflicting as much loss as possible on the enemy in doing so, is performing his ultimate duty. A soldier who surrenders while still in possession of a weapon, ammunition and food, and while remaining unwounded, is of no further use to his country in time of war. These rules, so rarely written out or explicitly stated, are the harsh facts of a soldier's life. It must be obvious from examples quoted above and throughout this book that these 'conditions of service' were not fulfilled by thousands of men on 21 March 1918.

* *The Royal Inniskilling Fusiliers in the World War*, by Sir Frank Fox, Constable, 1928, page 137.
† Public Record Office WO 95/1610.

But there is a world of difference between these cold-blooded statements and the actual conditions experienced by the men on the battlefield of that day. Let us visualise the scene. It was not a battalion, nor even a company or a platoon, that occupied a defensive position. Few men saw their commanding officer that day and many never saw any officer at all. The surroundings in which most soldiers fought consisted of only a few yards of trench with a handful of comrades, the highest ranking of whom was probably a corporal. A sergeant or second lieutenant might have appeared for a minute, told them to 'hang on, lads', and disappeared again. There had been a five-hour bombardment that might have slaughtered or maimed men in the most terrible manner only a few feet away and had left every man dazed and concussed – sometimes shuddering, whimpering, temporary nervous wrecks. There was thick fog from out of which came all manner of military noises and human sounds. The soldier was often in a position which may have looked fine on some general's map as a redoubt or smaller link in the Forward Zone defences but which was, for the soldier, no more than a hole in the ground from which he knew there was no safe communication trench to the rear. No one had bothered to explain to him the finer points of 'defence in depth'; all he knew was that once the Germans got in behind him he was caught like a rat in a trap. 'It don't suit us', the old N.C.O. had said. 'The British Army fights in line and won't do any good in these cages.' The men of twenty-seven battalions in the Fifth Army were locked up in these 'bird cages'.

There was still more to it than the actual conditions of that morning in March 1918. Whatever duty may have been expected of the soldiers, the natural instincts of the men and the amount of willpower they could summon up were important factors. Jingoistic historians may write glibly of 'fighting to the end', but men in Western armies do not normally fight on to certain death, although the award of posthumous medals and the official honouring of dead heroes is usually done to encourage men to hold out longer in hopeless situations. The real limit of a Western soldier's resistance is that point at which he feels his individual honour is satisfied. If they cannot be certain of coming out of a battle safely, then most men are prepared to put up a resistance that varies in length of time according to the circumstances, but the average soldier inevitably thinks of surrender when he feels that he has satisfied his own standards of honour. The moment at which different men reach that point – what might be called the 'threshold of resistance' – varies immensely from man to man and from army to army, but not so much from one war to another. Consider the following casualty figures for a British infantry battalion, cut off and under heavy attack.

Killed	59 men
Wounded	180 men
Taken prisoner	526 men

A battalion in the British Forward Zone in March 1918? No, these are the casualty figures of the 1st Gloucesters in April 1951 when cut off by the Chinese on Gloucester Hill in Korea! There were slightly fewer Gloucesters killed here than the seventy-three men of the 16th Manchesters killed on and around Manchester Hill on 21 March 1918.

For the men of an infantry unit, 'fighting to the end' really means fighting on until an honourable period of resistance has been offered and some delay or casualties have been inflicted on the enemy. But then, even in a well-disciplined unit with good morale, the enemy starts to overrun outlying posts and will be seen to be working his way round to the rear; leaders will become casualties; communications will begin to fail. Men will see their friends near by killed or hideously wounded and, all the time, the air will be full of stupefying noise. There will be the explosions of shells and mortar bombs to which the infantryman is powerless to reply. Finally, a few men in one post will surrender. It is infectious. No upbringing or training has prepared the soldier to face certain death when there is an alternative. The temptation to live overcomes the will to die. The defence fails. The actual timing of a surrender is of utmost importance. It is considered 'dirty' for a soldier to carry on firing and killing until the very last minute, then throw down his weapon and expect to be able to surrender. It is a rare event in any army for such late surrenders to be accepted.

This is the way of it in all Western armies, whether in Flanders or Korea, North Africa or Vietnam. I can think of no army, except the Japanese in the Second World War, that does not conform to these general rules of resistance and surrender.

What of the negotiated surrenders, such as the one at Boadicea Redoubt, when commanders decided that the garrison of a position would surrender long before its powers of resistance were exhausted? The commanders of such redoubts knew that there could be no relief for them from the Battle Zone. As the day drew on, they could see that their position was no longer doing anything useful to delay the German advance. The Germans had brought up mortars and howitzers, to which the redoubt defenders had no reply. What choice did Lieutenant-Colonel Lord Farnham have? Fight on, and incur dreadful bloodshed and suffering for little or no military gain? Surrender, and save much life but risk shame? Lord Farnham obtained a piece of paper that satisfied his honour and then he surrendered. Some commanders did as Lord Farnham did; others fought to the end. It is significant that the only two commanders who died in the chain of redoubts near St Quentin were both awarded posthumous Victoria Crosses. As soon as they died, their men surrendered. Two more redoubt commanders, who were wounded before being taken prisoner, were awarded Distinguished Service Orders.* The officers who surrendered while still unwounded risked court-martial and all had to face courts of enquiry on their return to England after the war. But who can say that such officers were not the more civilised, realistic and humane in the circumstances.

Having made all these points, let us get back to the original question. Did the British troops of 21 March 1918, especially men of the Fifth Army, collapse unreasonably? The Regular Army of 1914 and 1915 would never have surrendered as some of the March 1918 men did. Kitchener's New Army men would not have done so in the early years of their

* Lieutenant-Colonel W. Elstob, 16th Manchesters and Second Lieutenant E. de Wind, 15th Royal Irish Rifles, were the V.C.s; Lieutenant-Colonel A. V. P. Martin, 2nd Wiltshires, and Major H. W. Davies, 2/8th Worcesters, were the D.S.O.s.

service on the Western Front. The 'Army of March 1918' was a hybrid army. There were a few Regulars, more New Army volunteers, and many conscripts. It was a tired and war-weary army. The veterans in it had seen many of their friends die in past years – for what? Victory seemed as far away as ever. The dead of 1914–17 seemed to have died in vain. When the Germans came over in the fog that morning, such men usually fought well as long as their flanks were holding, but when the Germans came in behind them and cut them off then that was it.

Yes, there was a premature collapse of resistance in many places that day, but in circumstances that are perfectly understandable. It was often the older soldiers who gave up first. 'Gerry is past us and nothing we can do will stop him now. Why should I be killed looking after these new men? I've done my bit. Surrender. And quick. Leave it too long and Gerry will get mad and then it's a bayonet in the guts or a grenade to share between us.' So the reasoning would have gone. It was the smaller positions that went first. 'Nobody much to see what's happening here.' The larger positions held until the officers commanding them had come to an agonising decision. Some officers cannot have waited long: four battalions in the Forward Zone collapsed and surrendered without a single one of their officers being killed.* The Sandhurst lecturer, John Keegan, in suggesting that the Fifth Army had collapsed morally, was probably generalising and intended to include the smaller number of Third Army divisions involved. There is certainly no evidence that General Byng's divisions were not as prone to surrendering that morning as General Gough's. Both armies contained ordinary divisions of the British Expeditionary Force that had been allocated to one army or the other, although Gough did receive only New Army and Second-Line Territorial divisions. There was no such thing as an 'army spirit' – or rather lack of spirit – before the battle. Not one man in a dozen knew to which army he belonged or the name of its commander. There were simply a lot of soldiers, weary of the war and unwilling to die for the defence of these par-

---

* The four battalions were the 8th King's Royal Rifle Corps, 2/8th Lancashire Fusiliers, 2/2nd Londons and 2nd Royal Inniskilling Fusiliers.

ticular positions. Their 'threshold of resistance' had been worn away. In another battle and under better conditions, they would have fought better. It is significant that other battalions of the same divisions fought well in the more favourable conditions in the Battle Zone later in the day.

*

All these observations about casualties and the battlefield performance of the British forces lead into the question: 'Who really won the battle of 21 March 1918?' There is no doubt that the Germans had achieved a major battlefield success, in both the capture of ground and the infliction of permanent casualties on the British. But was this enough? To answer this vital question, it is necessary to examine again the German intentions for 21 March 1918 and here, for the first time in the book, it is impossible to isolate completely the battle of that one day from the fighting in the days that would follow. It has been stated several times that the overall plan of the Germans in their spring attacks in 1918 was to so weaken the British Expeditionary Force that either the British soldiers would break or their military and political leaders would lose the will to continue playing a major role in the war. It is against this background that the achievements of the Germans on 21 March should be judged.

The Germans had actually set themselves quite clear objectives for the first day of the battle. Oberst Georg Bruchmüller, the German artillery specialist who had planned the bombardment for the opening of the battle, was later nicknamed *'Durchbruchmüller'* (Breakthrough Müller) by his German colleagues; this was a tribute to his work in the 21 March battle and in the later German blows. It was this concept of the 'breakthrough' that had dominated the thinking, planning and hopes of the German leaders on 21 March, just as it had dominated the Allied offensives over the past years. Ludendorff had aimed to break clean through the British defences on the first day of this battle *within the first twenty-four hours*. His great artillery and infantry blow was designed to overrun the entire Forward and Battle Zones of the British sectors attacked, destroying their defenders, capturing their artillery and, for good measure, encircling the

Flesquières Salient. There is plenty of evidence to support this statement. Having achieved this, at a cost in casualties that his armies could afford, Ludendorff would then be free to turn to the north and roll up the remainder of the British Expeditionary Force from the breakthrough he had achieved on the first day.

It must be obvious, from a reading of the 'battle chapters' of this book, that the Germans had fallen well short of their objectives. It is true that the British Forward Zone had been taken at all points, but the British had been prepared to lose these positions anyway. It was the holding or capture of the Battle Zone that was regarded by both sides as vital. It is an easy matter to measure on a map the balance of success in the Battle Zone fighting. This was the position at the end of the day:

Germans right through Battle Zone on 18,000-yard frontage

Germans held only at rear of Battle Zone on 16,000-yard frontage

Germans held within Battle Zone on 19,000-yard frontage

Germans held at front of Battle Zone on 14,000-yard frontage

The Germans had achieved their full hopes on only a little over one quarter of the front that they had attacked. This was all at the southern end of the front, where Gough had decided to save his troops by pulling them back to the Crozat Canal. Nowhere else were the Germans through the Battle Zone, nor had the Flesquières Salient been encircled. In the north, opposite the British Third Army, the Germans were particularly disappointed, and General Otto von Below, commander of the Seventeenth Army, reported that night that the combination of fierce British infantry resistance and heavy artillery fire had prevented him achieving the 'hoped-for breakthrough . . . The main battle of his army was still to come.'*

It was the same with the capture of British guns. The German Official History only claims 138 guns captured on the first day, but this was a grossly underestimated figure

* German Official History, page 114.

which was updated to 400 two days later. The British Official History gives details of 382 guns – 293 field guns and eighty-nine heavies – lost by Fifth Army artillery units, and goes on to suggest that the Third Army may have lost 120 to 140 guns. The total loss of British guns on the first day seems, therefore, to have been 500. This seems a heavy loss, but it represents no more than one fifth of the British artillery on the front attacked, and many of the artillerymen who had lost their guns escaped and were able to draw new ones at once from the large reserves of new guns in ordnance parks. Several British soldiers taken prisoner by the Germans in the Third Army fighting were immediately questioned by German officers with maps, who demanded to know where the British guns were located. There is no doubt that the action of those British commanders who pulled back their guns the night before the battle saved many of the guns from being lost, despite what the British infantry thought about the artillery's 'desertion'; this frustrated the German hopes for a massive capture of guns.

It can be seen, therefore, that the Germans had not achieved more than a fraction of what they hoped for on the first day and, moreover, what German successes had been achieved were at the cost of casualties that could not be replaced. Although the British had suffered a permanent loss of men greater than the Germans', there were more than enough Americans on the way to cover the British casualties many times over. The Germans could not look forward to any such renewal of strength; their losses had permanently diminished a tiring army.

A further aspect was that the German success, where it had come, in the south, led them into a fatal error. It is natural for an army to reinforce and exploit success, and this is what the Germans did here. Crown Prince Wilhelm had, before the battle, secured a greater role for his army group than Ludendorff intended. Now Wilhelm was able to satisfy his ambitions further. In the ensuing days of this battle, the Germans fed more and more men into the south, at the expense of their centre and north. This resulted in spectacular advances, much glory for Wilhelm, and a continual hammering of Gough's poor Fifth Army. But this was a complete betrayal of the original German plan; it took pressure off the British forces to the north and forced the French to face a greater part of the German attack.

This change of emphasis by the Germans to the south leads into the final consideration of 'who won?' Although the politicians and the civilian population in England were appalled at the massive German advances in the south, Haig was not. He was a clever enough general to know where his priorities were, and his policy, both before this battle and in the handling of it, was quite sound. He was right to keep his north and centre strong and, because Lloyd George had kept him short of the necessary troops, to risk his less important southern front. He was right to allow Gough to fall back in order to keep his divisions as intact as possible. It was Haig's generalship as much as the Crown Prince's ambition which led the Germans to divert their main effort to the vacuum in the south. This, in turn, affected the extent to which the morale of the British Expeditionary Force was put to the test. Whether the British morale would have broken if the Germans had stuck to their original plan and let the French off more lightly is an interesting question. It is probable that the British would not have broken. After all the British soldier was the only one who fought from the first day to the last in two world wars without losing and without suffering any major breakdown in morale.

The final comment in this summary of German generalship is that, in retrospect, Ludendorff can be seen to have been wildly overambitious in his plans. However considerable his resources after the collapse of Russia, and however skilful and brave his soldiers, there never really had been a chance that he could capture nearly forty miles of the British defence works on 21 March and that he could break the spirit of the British Expeditionary Force in the ensuing days and weeks. After the First World War, the verdict of German military historians was that the whole series of spring offensives, the whole concept of the decisive *Kaiserschlacht*, had been a mistake, bringing heavy losses to German manhood and merely hastening the humiliation of defeat eight months later. This is valid comment. The truth is that Germany had lost the war before 21 March 1918, the vital factor being that of manpower and the arrival of the Americans. The Germans would have done well to keep their divisions on the defensive and bargain, still from a position of some strength, for peace. But the military men who controlled Germany had to play out their last cards in such a way that thousands of good young men died. The real tragedy of the battles of early 1918 was that it was so unnecessary to fight them at all.

It was not, of course, so clear and obvious at that time as it became later.

14

The Aftermath

The Germans did 'come on' again at dawn on 22 March and the fighting was resumed with much of the intensity of the previous day. The battle that later became known as the Battle of St Quentin or as the March Offensive – although it lasted until 5 April – has been described many times and it is not the main subject of this book. Its progress need only be described briefly. Initially, the Germans persisted with their main effort in the north but General Byng's army, strong and in good defences, held well. General Gough's Fifth Army never recovered from its heavy losses on the first day, its starvation of reserves, and the failure of the French to station a central reserve near by. Its weak and exhausted units were rarely relieved and had to fight on, day after day. They were soon pushed out of all prepared defence works and had to retreat over open ground. New lines of resistance were designated and manned, but, always, the Germans found a weak place or a gap and the British soldiers had to retreat again to avoid being surrounded. Yet there was never a complete German breakthrough. Whatever reverses were suffered, there was always a thin line of men to be found who were prepared to offer a fight. Divisions shrank in size to that of weak brigades and brigades to the size of a poor battalion; many battalions ceased to exist altogether. Make-shift fighting units, made up of men from schools and administrative organisations, were put into the line as temporary expedients and fought for days. The best known of these was 'Carey's Force', formed on 26 March, mainly of men from engineer units including two companies of American and one of Canadian engineers. Four days later it had dwindled in size and was merged with the remnants of the 16th (Irish) Division and some cavalry to become 'Whitemore's Cosmopolitan Force', in which form it fought on to the end of the battle. The French divisions arrived in strength and there were nineteen of them in action when the

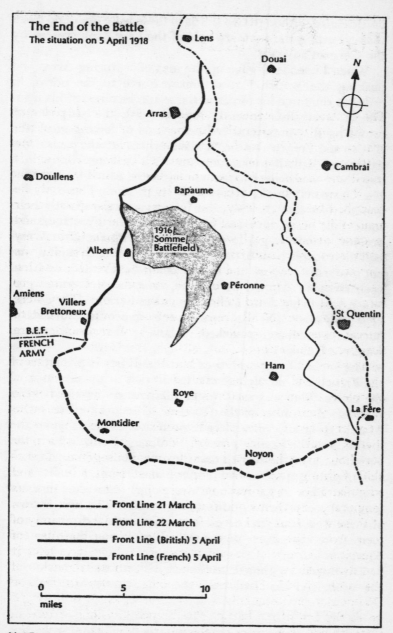

The End of the Battle
The situation on 5 April 1918

Lens
Douai
N
Arras
Cambrai
Doullens
Bapaume
1916
Somme
Battlefield
Albert
Amiens
Péronne
Villers
Bretoneux
St Quentin
B.E.F.
FRENCH
ARMY
Ham
Roye
La Fère
Montidier
Noyon

- - - - - - - - Front Line 21 March
———————— Front Line 22 March
━━━━━━━━ Front Line (British) 5 April
▬ ▬ ▬ ▬ Front Line (French) 5 April

0   5   10
miles

Map 7

battle ended, although two thirds of these were doing no more than guarding the southern side of the long flank created by the German advance.

When Ludendorff gave up the idea of capturing Arras and pushing the British Expeditionary Force to the north, in order to reinforce his forces in the south, he directed his main weight westwards towards Amiens with the purposes of capturing that important rail centre and of forcing apart the British and French armies. While German attacks pushed the exhausted British back, sometimes six or more miles in a day, there was consternation among some Allied leaders that the Germans would succeed in their aim. There was a genuine fear that the Germans might reach the sea and even some talk of an invasion of England. The French almost decided, at one stage, to break contact with the British and pull their forces back to protect Paris. The French capital was not really in danger, but it was being bombarded, and had been since 23 March, by a huge, long-range German gun which was firing from a clearing in the Forest of St Gobain near La Fère.* The gun was seventy-five miles from Paris but the inhabitants panicked, believing that the Germans were much closer.

The rapid German advance and the different priorities of the French and the British created a crisis in the direction of the battle. This was resolved at a famous conference held in the council chamber of the Hôtel de Ville at Doullens on 26 March. Haig offered to place himself and his forces under the direction of the French general, Ferdinand Foch. In turn, the French assured the British that they would keep in touch with the British Expeditionary Force and stand fast in front of Amiens. This was a great turning point, and although there was still much hard fighting to come the worst was passed. For the first time, there was a genuine central direction and purpose to the efforts of the Allied armies on the Western Front.

The retreat continued, and the British troops fell back over the wasteland that had been the old Somme battlefield of

---

* This gun is sometimes erroneously called Big Bertha. Big Bertha was, however, the 420-millimetre howitzer built to bombard the forts around Liége in 1914. The 210-millimetre gun that shelled Paris had no special name.

1916. The survivors of that earlier battle who were still with the 1918 divisions were almost heartbroken at having to give up the ground that had been taken from the Germans at the cost of the lives of so many of their comrades two years earlier. Most of the gains of 1916 were now lost in just one day. Even Albert, the town that had been so secure behind the 'old front line' of 1916, was lost. Just after the British troops evacuated Albert, a heavy artillery battery was ordered to fire on the famous basilica until the tower collapsed. The British did this to deny the Germans the use of the tower for artillery observation but it also brought nearer the fulfilment of the legend, believed by many British soldiers, that the war would not end until the statue of the Golden Virgin on the tower fell.

The battle ended on 5 April, the last actions taking place at Villers Bretonneux with Australian and French troops holding the last, dying German efforts. It was at Villers Bretonneux that General Gough had stopped the dismantling of the old defences covering Amiens before the battle. Now the Germans were only ten miles from the city. They had come forty miles to reach this point and had captured, in all, over 1,000 square miles of ground, but they were still fifty miles from the sea and the same distance from Paris. The British units in the battle had suffered approximately 160,000 casualties – 22,000 killed, 75,000 prisoners, 63,000 wounded evacuated to medical units. It is unfortunate that the best available French and German figures only give totals to the end of April, by which time another, but smaller, battle had been fought elsewhere. It is possible that the French casualties in the fighting up to 5 April had been 80,000 and those of the Germans 250,000, although these are only rough proportions and the German total probably did not include large numbers of lightly wounded men. From these figures, it seems that British and French casualties in the battle totalled 240,000 and those of the Germans 250,000, plus the German lightly wounded.*

The Germans had inflicted a huge reverse on the Allies, particularly on the British, but they had achieved neither their

* These details are based on casualty figures quoted in the British Official History 1918, volume II, pages 489–90.

first objective – the capture of Arras and the rolling-up of the British Expeditionary Force to the north – nor their second – the capture of Amiens and the splitting of the British and the French armies. They had captured no town of real importance, and most of the ground they had captured consisted of the wastelands of the 1916 battlefields and the ground they had themselves devastated in 1917 before withdrawing to the Hindenburg Line. The Allies were left exhausted but not beaten. Their morale was still intact and their leadership was united for the first time in the war.

*

There are two further comments that can be made on the progress and outcome of the battle that started on 21 March 1918. The theory that attacking armies on the Western Front always suffered greater losses than defending ones has been vigorously debated since 1918, usually in connection with arguments about Sir Douglas Haig's handling of the British Expeditionary Force from early 1916 until the end of the war. Haig's critics say that he bled the British Army almost to death with his obsession for attack and his belief that the German Army was always on the verge of collapse; they believe that the British always lost more men than the enemy in these offensives. Supporters of Haig say that this was not so, that the defenders usually suffered the same number of casualties as the attackers and that the war could only be won by means of attacks and the eventual defeat of the Germans on the battlefield. This argument has always been a difficult one to resolve because the method of reporting casualties varied so much between the two armies. The March Offensive is particularly relevant in this argument because it was now the Germans who were attacking, the first time they had done so in any strength since their offensive at Verdun in early 1916. In the battle which ended on 5 April 1918, there is a clear advantage in casualties in favour of the Allies. The British and French losses were approximately 240,000 men, those of the Germans 250,000, plus the lightly wounded who may well have totalled another 50–60,000.

When I think of all those brave German infantry, walking calmly and with poise, into our murderous machine-gun fire, now, and as then, we had nothing but admiration for them. Unqualified courage! Poor devils! It was the weight of numbers; as fast as we knocked them down, another wave would appear. It was a shattering experience. When I was hit at Corbie, some ten days later, give or take a day or two, we were still knocking them down. (Trooper C. H. Somerset, 9th Machine Gun Squadron)

The situation which Mr Somerset describes could so easily have been British or French troops attacking in the years 1915 to 1917 and being mown down by German machine-gunners. Nothing had changed. Whatever else may be said about March 1918 fighting, it was a very good example of a First World War offensive being more costly than the defensive.

A number of the great battles of the Western Front were intended to be 'decisive' in that the commander of the attacking forces intended to strike a knock-out blow. The objective of all these attacks was ultimately the destruction of the enemy army; capture of ground was of secondary importance. Victory in such a battle was the dream of every Western Front commander. Loos, Verdun, the first Somme, Passchendaele – these were all 'strategic' battles that were intended to be decisive; Arras and Cambrai were more 'tactical' battles with more limited objectives. One school of thought insists that the concept of the 'decisive battle' under conditions prevailing on the Western Front was an illusion, that the defence would always overcome the attack, that neither side could attack and win, in fact that an absolute stalemate existed. Now the Germans had tried and, despite apparent success, had gained none of their objectives, but had lost more casualties than the defenders.

To counter this argument it can be said that the Allies, particularly the British, did achieve decisive victories in their offensives later in 1918, after the German spring offensives had run their course. But these Allied successes were not achieved under the same conditions as had previously been present. They were not the achievements solely of superior military skill shown by Allied commanders. It is true that there were improved tactics, but, after so many attempts had been made since 1915, it would have been surprising if nothing new had been learnt, especially in the use of the tank, the new weapon which the Germans could not produce because their industry was under too much pressure. But the vital factor all the time was that of manpower. The Americans came, and in the summer and autumn of 1918 the Allied generals were fighting with an ever-growing army against an ever-weakening one. The Germans were there for the plucking after their losses in the spring. There could only be one result, and the eventual Allied victory was more to the credit of the remorseless processes of attrition than to hard-earned improvements in the skill shown by Allied generals. The cost of victory, when it did come, had been so great that the victors insisted on imposing the most vindictive of terms on the Germans, and this led to a second conflict. The great tragedy of the First World War is that none of the many opportunities presented for negotiated peace was ever grasped. A combination of national pride, on both sides, and of militaristic ambitions, on both sides, demanded that the battlefield solution and not the political one was played out to the end. Again, it is realised that this was not at all clear at the time and such views are a luxury enjoyed with the advantage of hindsight. It is against this greater background, however, that the March Offensive and the other 1918 campaigns should be viewed.

*

Let us look back on what had become of the soldiers who had fought on 21 March 1918. There were not many of these men from either side still left in front-line units when the war ended in November. The German divisions had been thrown into one attack after the other during the spring and then, so weary, had been forced to face the growing power and the relentless attacks of their enemies. They had fought hard but they could not hold the forces against them indefinitely. They were assailed, too, by other threats. The continuing blockade by the Royal Navy was imposing intolerable stresses on German civilian morale and on war production. When the Germans had advanced into captured British positions in March and April, they had captured immense quantities of food and stores of a quality that they had not seen for years. The German propaganda myth that Britain was also near starvation had been blown sky high. It badly shook the morale of the German soldiers, and the later stages of the German offensives were badly affected by the desire of their men to drink and loot stores, rather than to fight. The years of battle had also removed too many of their superb officers and N.C.O.s. The losses of the spring offensives were only partially replaced by new men, and an increasing number of these were affected by the civilian dissatisfaction with the war. When the Allies attacked in the late summer and autumn, the Germans did not resist as well as in earlier years and, for the first time, there were many surrenders. The Allied advances were always costly, mainly because of the rearguard action of German machine-gunners, but, basically, the Germany army was a beaten one, ground down by the superior weight of their enemies.

Reference was made earlier in this book to the British 'Army of March 1918'. This was gone, as surely as the original army of Regulars and their successors, the New Armies, had gone. When the German attacks started, Lloyd George had immediately released the large force of men that he had been holding in England and it was largely these men – often half-trained and inexperienced boy conscripts – who formed the main strength of the army that finally overcame the Germans eight months later, although the Empire units remained strong to the end and provided the most reliable divisions in the final stages of the fighting.

Even those reinforcements that were sent were not sufficient to replace all the losses, and some of the divisions and battalions which fought on 21 March had to be disbanded. A typical example was the 7th Sherwood Foresters, the Nottingham Territorial battalion that had fought at Bullecourt on 21 March and suffered the heaviest casualties of that day. The battalion's predecessors, the 1/7th Battalion, had twice before been reduced to only a few dozen men – at the Hohenzollern Redoubt in the Battle of Loos, 1915, and at Gommecourt in the 1916 Battle of the Somme. After the battle at Bullecourt, no more than a dozen men again remained of the fighting part of the battalion. These survivors were paraded in a village street and inspected by King George V on 30 March. Even so, the battalion was rebuilt in April when 700 new men arrived; most of these were recovered wounded and young conscripts from Lancashire and Yorkshire regiments. By the middle of April, this hotchpotch unit had to go into the line again, on the Ypres front near Kemmel Hill, but immediately lost one third of its strength when the Germans mounted a new attack here. This time there were no more reinforcements available and the battalion was disbanded, its remaining members being dispersed to other units. Battalion headquarters was retained in the hope that new men could again be found, but they never were and a proud battalion finally died. There were many battalions which faded away like the 7th Sherwood Foresters.*

Another unit that nearly disappeared was the South African Infantry Brigade. On the fourth day of the March Offensive, the South Africans were ordered to hold their positions on a hill near Marrières Wood 'at all costs'. The troops on either side gave way and the Germans surrounded the brigade. The ensuing battle lasted eight hours, and at the end of it the entire brigade was either dead or taken prisoner. The history of a German regiment which crossed the battlefield on the following day described how its men found the trenches full of dead from bayonet and hand-grenade wounds, 'a proof that there had been bitter hand-to-hand fighting'.† Those South Africans who had not been present at the brigade's last battle formed a composite battalion which served to the end of the war.

*

Many thousands of the men who fought in March had become

---

* The battalion was re-formed in Nottingham after the war but in December 1936, like many Territorial units, it became a searchlight regiment of the Royal Engineers and later of the Royal Artillery. It served in England until September 1944, when it crossed to France. In the final stage of the war it was often called upon to produce 'artificial moonlight' for British night attacks.

† From the history of an unidentified regiment in the German 1st Division, quoted in the British Official History, page 417, footnote. Over 5,000 South Africans, more than the original strength of the brigade, were killed during the war. It may have been this experience that induced the South African Government to decide that its forces would not be permitted to fight outside the continent of Africa in the Second World War.

prisoners. The badly wounded among these had a very hard time. The German medical units were at full stretch and were hard put to it even to tend all their own wounded. Several British soldiers who had been wounded tell how they were left out on the battlefield for several days but, with youth and strong constitutions, they survived. Others, more seriously hurt, must have died slowly out in the open before help reached them, and more died in the German hospitals. The Germans were short of all medicines and food, and had only crêpe-paper bandages.

For most of the unwounded prisoners, there was a long, hard march away from the battle area under the escort of guards who were never as considerate as the front-line Germans they had met on the battlefield. The prisoners were usually channelled through three towns – Guise, Le Cateau and Cambrai; it is surprising how many British soldiers refer to the last of these as 'Cambria'. Some prisoners were shown great kindness by French civilians, but other prisoners were shocked to see the population of some villages, chiefly women, laughing and joking with the Germans and on obviously good terms with them. One party of captured British officers met the Kaiser.

There was a large party of us on the march, very bedraggled. We were suddenly ordered to stand at the side of the road and several cars came along, in one of which were two men, one in magnificent uniform with decorations. The other was possibly Hindenberg. They were both sat in the back of an open car which pulled up. The Kaiser had kindly features; he was benevolent, nothing like all the caricatures we had seen in the newspapers. He said, 'There is no need for you to be ashamed of being prisoners.' He congratulated us on the tremendous fight we had put up but said, 'My victorious troops are advancing everywhere and you will soon be home with your families once more.'

I looked at two near-by guards; they were stood so rigidly to attention that they were shivering like a jelly. (Lieutenant A. A. Simpson, 197th Trench Mortar Battery)

After up to a week's hard marching, on the scantiest of rations and sleeping in fields by night, the prisoners were loaded on to trains and reached their permanent prison camps in Germany. The 'other ranks' spent most of the remaining months of the war working hard for the Germans and being saved from starvation only by the food parcels supplied by the Red Cross. After the war ended on 11 November, conditions in Germany were so confused that some of these prisoners were not able to return to their homes until after Christmas. Some of the prisoners had been retained by the Germans in France to provide labour immediately behind the fighting area. These men undoubtedly had a harder time and they suffered great privations. There were no Red Cross parcels for them and 'we only kept going on what we could pinch; we became experts.'

*

One soldier from the March 1918 fighting had become a different type of casualty. General Sir Hubert Gough, commander of the Fifth Army, had been relieved of his command on 28 March and was sent home less than a week later. When the Germans pushed the British out of their defences and went on to advance across the old Somme battlefield by daily stages of several miles, those at home who watched maps and saw the ground captured at such cost in 1916 being lost so easily demanded to know what had gone wrong. A scapegoat was required. There were several possibilities – Lloyd George, who was responsible for the British Expeditionary Force's shortage of men, General Sir Henry Wilson, Chief of the Imperial General Staff, Sir Douglas Haig, the Commander-in-Chief in France, General Gough, the commander whose army was mainly involved in the retreat.

It is not surprising that the choice fell on the most junior of these. Haig sent a senior officer to inform Gough that he was to be 'rested' and replaced by General Sir Henry Rawlinson, then a military representative at the Supreme War Council at Versailles. Gough's staff were to be replaced by the staff of the Fourth Army, which had earlier been Rawlinson's command but was then a spare army headquarters organisation without troops. Gough and his staff departed the following day and Haig gave them the task of reconnoitering a new line of defences between Amiens and the sea in case the Germans took the city. A few days later, however, Haig was forced to tell Gough that London had demanded his return to England and that there would be no further work for him in France.

What had happened behind the scenes was that Lloyd George had chosen Gough as the scapegoat. Sir Henry Wilson could hardly be blamed; he had only recently been appointed Chief of the Imperial General Staff. As for Haig, public opinion would have been badly affected if he had been ordered home at this time; he had so often been favourably mentioned in the Press. It would actually have been an injustice if Haig had been sacrificed for the setbacks; he had not been responsible for the weakness in men of his command and the dispositions he had made for dealing with the German attack were reasonable ones.

Sir Henry Wilson had probably been prepared to support the sacrifice of Gough. It is said that he wanted the strong-minded Rawlinson away from Versailles. When it was asked why Gough had to go, Wilson stated, according to his deputy who noted the exact words in his diary, 'Hubert Gough has got to go because he had lost the confidence of his troops'.* Who were these 'troops' who had lost confidence in Gough and how could senior officers in London know what they thought? It was, of course, an excuse, and the only 'troops' who had lost confidence were probably those corps and divisional commanders whom Gough had sent home during the Passchendaele fighting the previous autumn. It is true that there was some talk among wounded men from the Fifth Army now in hospital in England, but such talk was surely based on only the most limited personal experiences. Most of the 'troops' still in France were not yet aware that they belonged to an army commanded by a general called Gough, and they had little thought of whether they had confidence or not in that officer.

So Gough went home. There was a debate in Parliament in which Lloyd George was pressed about the conduct of the war and the setbacks in France. He used all his skill in oratory and presented some dubious statistics to refute the charge that he had kept the British Expeditionary Force short of men. He praised General Byng and the Third Army for

* British Official History 1918, volume II, page 28, footnote.

holding their lines intact and suggested that Byng's units had only had to withdraw to conform to the retreat of the Fifth Army. He implied that the whole blame lay with Gough and the Fifth Army. Gough had few influential friends and those friends he had could not, at that time, expose the false statistics used by Lloyd George, although they did so later. The enemies Gough had made over the Curragh incident in 1914 and again when he gained his 'Butcher' reputation at Passchendaele were happy to see him take the blame. A study of the earlier chapters in this book would surely show that Gough had fought well with the meagre forces allocated to him by Haig, had conformed at all times with the policy laid down by Haig, and had made the best of the almost impossible circumstances in which he and his army found themselves.

One interesting question is whether Haig had behaved correctly in the affair. It is known that he had no hand in the decision to remove Gough and that he offered to resign his command if the Government wanted him out of the way too. Lloyd George may have been tempted to accept that offer, but he realised that he could not shift Haig in the middle of the German attacks. But should Haig have gone on to insist on resigning as a protest against what he saw as the unfair treatment of a subordinate? After the war, Haig is reputed to have told Lieutenant-Colonel E. H. L. Beddington, who had been acting as Gough's temporary Chief of Staff at the time of the March Offensive, that

after considerable thought, I decided that public opinion at home, whether right or wrong, demanded a scapegoat, and that the only possible ones were Hubert or me. I was conceited enough to think that the army could not spare me.*

On the face of it, this is a disgraceful statement, but it must be remembered that it was an episode that developed over several weeks and that it must have been difficult for Haig to pinpoint the exact moment when Gough should have been supported, especially as Haig was fully occupied with the German attacks at the time and as both Gough and Haig had been promised an enquiry. Lloyd George ensured that this

* *Goughie*, page 324.

was never held. Haig might have chosen his words better, but he was not one to cover up a nasty moment in soft words and he was probably right to stay at his post. A fascinating subject for speculation is who would have become Commander-in-Chief if Haig had gone as well as Gough and what effect would this change have had on the remaining months of the war.

The incident was not closed, however, and there were several unusual repercussions. Ordinary soldiers rarely care about which army commander they have served under, but most of the thousands of men who fought in the Fifth Army in March 1918 – it was redesignated the Fourth Army on 2 April – assumed a strong and lasting pride in the army and in its disgraced commander. They knew that they had done nothing shameful and they were very bitter at the treatment of Gough and the slur on their own fighting qualities. To be known as having once been a member of 'Gough's Fifth Army' was later the proudest boast of many of Gough's men who survived the war.

Gough behaved with much dignity, but he had to wait many years for his name to be cleared. It was not until the 1930s that there was much investigation into the affair but the wrongs of it were then recognised. In 1936, Lloyd George wrote to Gough, admitting that Gough had done well in the March 1918 fighting and Gough was created a Knight Cross of the Bath. He survived all his contemporaries, organised part of the London Home Guard in 1940, and did not die until 1963, at the age of ninety-two.

Some years ago I made a sort of pilgrimage to Gough's grave at St Michael's Church at Camberley in Surrey. Alas, there was the grave of Sir Hubert and Lady Gough, totally ignored and covered with weeds. Poor man, from such a brave family and such a brave soldier he was. To think how this man suffered after 1918 in life and, now in death, he was deserted once again. It was all very sad. (Captain E. P. Hall, 2nd Leinsters)

Thus writes one of Gough's loyal soldiers. There were others, who served with both the Third and Fifth Armies in March 1918, who can contribute their thoughts of later years to the conclusion of this book.

From my 'worm's eye view', I would strongly disagree with any impression given that the British Army was completely routed and demoralised. We were forced back in stages, but resisting all the way. The proof is surely that the Germans never really broke through and were eventually held. We may have been un-imaginative, but we never looked upon this retreat as more than one of those temporary setbacks such as we had seen on the Somme and at Cambrai. (Lieutenant F. Mansfield, 8th Siege Battery)

I'm not educated, having left school at thirteen, and am now nearly seventy-eight. I should like to give some of my own thoughts as an ordinary infantryman of that war. Youngsters like me, after a few months of action, soon became tough and hard and very quick minded, not professional, but good fighters. We put up a great show to stop the German counter-attack at Cambrai on the morning of 1 December 1917 and would have done our best on 21 March if the morning had been clear. However, as we got battle hardened, things were either '*cushy*', if all went well, or, if not, we said '*san fairy an*'. That is as near as I can get with the spelling but we meant, 'What the hell does it matter'. And, when we were in a German prison camp, the verdict we passed on the 21 March fighting was that it was 'all a proper balls-up'. (Private J. Cummings, 2/4th Oxford and Bucks Light Infantry)

The morale and courage of the troops I fought with during those distressing days was wonderful and that was why we survived. (Lieutenant K. Pearce Smith, 2/4th Royal Berkshires)

I have read many books about World War One, written mostly from the point of view of the officer class, most of whom, in my opinion, above the rank of lieutenant-colonel should have been suffocated at birth. For God's sake and common humanity do not write about honour and glory. There was none. War, especially ours, was a stinking, ugly, horrible business. Please treat it as such.

I am no angel and do not suppose I ever shall be one. I joined the British Army in 1914, aged eighteen, a sensitive and patriotic boy. I left some six years later, a bitter old man, but, by the grace of God, whole in body and mind. (Private W. W. Francis, 7th King's Shropshire Light Infantry)

Soldiers' Tales

Several particularly well written accounts were received of individual men's experiences of the fighting on 21 March 1918, or of the period immediately beforehand, but it was not possible to include them in the main chapters of this book, usually because the length of such accounts would have thrown the contents of the relevant chapter out of balance. Extracts from eight of the best of these accounts are presented here.

The Hungry German Soldiers by Vizefeldwebel Wilhelm Prosch, 463rd Regiment, 238th Division.

The only cause for grumbling was the rations, which were still poor; they were out of all proportion to the physical exertions from us. The old hands knew how to look after themselves. On our daily march to the exercise ground we passed a large army bakery. The smell of fresh loaves stacked high behind the gratings of the windows made our mouths water. One night, some of our men sneaked to the building, cut the grating of one window and filled their sandbags. The whole company had a proper fill.

Passing the bakery next day, we had a big surprise. The stacked loaves were now two metres away from the windows, the grating repaired. We marched past, very disappointed, and our faces showed how we felt; there was only one who laughed, a boy from Hamburg – St Pauli – who knew all the tricks from his early days. This boy said quite casually, 'That won't stop us. Tonight we will fetch a double ration', and he asked for volunteers. We all stepped forward. He picked three. They had a long pole, a bayonet fixed to it. The window and grating were removed in no time, the sandbags filled to capacity.

Next evening the boy announced that bread and nothing to go with it isn't good enough. We stared at him and asked what he meant. He looked at us pityingly and said that the missing things, like sausages, ham, bacon and other items, could be 'organised' tonight. It was the same gang. The target was the storeroom behind the kitchen of the officers' mess of a posh cavalry regiment newly arrived from the Baltic front, where they had requisitioned those good things we hadn't seen for years. Why should they fill their bellies while we had to do with so little? A knock at the kitchen door was answered by a sleepy cook. He couldn't have believed his eyes, seeing the four with blackened faces, hand grenades in the belts, sandbags in hand. He was pushed aside and told to open the store. What could the poor fellow do but comply? There were rows of sausages and ham; only those were taken, other delicacies did not interest us. The cook had to go with the raiders and was locked up in a dug-out outside the village. In our quarters we had a feast undreamed of, nothing to be left over, otherwise the devil would get us next day.

On parade next morning, we had to wait a long time for the company commander. He said it had been reported to him that the officers' mess had been raided; an investigation had been initiated. He hoped that none of his men were involved. On our return from exercise, military police were present, searching our quarters and interviewing everybody. Nothing doing. They left, our officer grinning behind their backs. We had to fall in once more. He walked along the line looking all of us in the eyes. We expected a rocket. Standing in front of us he kept still for a while, keeping us on tenterhooks. Then he said, 'You are a daring lot, ready for everything. I trust you are prepared to fetch the devil from hell if need be. I expect you to show the same spirit when the time comes to go over the top.'

A Day at the Races by Lieutenant E. M. Payne, 1/23rd Londons, 47th (London) Division.

Yes, a race meeting! What better tonic than that, for a division of Londoners with their Sandown, Kempton and Hurst Parks and, of course, Epsom Downs. Many of us had never ridden or even handled a horse until we joined the army, when we learned to ride the hard way, bareback with just a snaffle and tosses galore until we got the knack. Horses played a bigger part in the first war and each unit had its quota of riding and transport horses and mules.

An aerodrome of suitable size was found and marked out with ropes and posts to provide the right sort of course, from about 6-furlong sprints up to a mile. A tote was set up and there were plenty of chaps – bookies' clerks, tic-tac men and other horsey experts – to arrange the betting and the starting gate. A large farm wagon was placed to form a grandstand for the top brass, and by midday all was ready. Soon horses and men from all over the Divisional area began to converge on the 'race course' until a crowd worthy of Sandown was there.

At Zero Hour General Gorringe (known to the men as the old 'blood orange') and his staff rode up and took their place on the 'grandstand', and all eyes were soon turned towards the starting area, in expectation of the first 'off'.

But shouts from another quarter drew attention to a group of some six persons, heading for the general on the stand. They resembled strangely a bunch of clowns entering a circus ring. One was clad in the full uniform of a London policeman with tall helmet and twirling a truncheon. Another, with very red nose, was dressed like a down-and-out tramp. A pearly king, a barrow boy and so on. Making their way across, they asked the general whether he knew he was breaking the law by running a betting show without a licence and so on. It was all good fun and the general took it all with a good laugh. The sight of a policeman and that Cockney group struck just the right note, and in good humour the races began.

Race after race took place with almost professional smoothness. There was a race for heavy draught horses, and it was delightful to see a dozen or so of these dear old things coming along in a fast canter, which never seemed to reach a gallop. Then the funniest thing of the afternoon. A race for mules, those reputedly obstinate creatures. Along they came, in a bunch, going at a good gallop. Suddenly, instead of making for the winning post, they seemed to spot the hangar in which they had apparently been fed and quartered and they just jumped out of the course and all made for that hangar in spite of the efforts of their jockeys . . . and there they stayed. Race void!

All good things come to an end. Racing over, working parties started to clear up the tent, the 'grandstand', the ropes and posts, and all that. Slowly, riding and on foot, the 47th Division made its way back to billets and duties.

A week or so later, we were fighting a rearguard action across the site of the racing, and the history books record that we were as obstinate in retreat as those mules.

A Night Raid by Second Lieutenant A. A. Lamb, 2/7th Manchesters, 66th (East Lancs) Division.

I was ordered to command the raiding party, and Second Lieutenant Shaw was to assist me. Brigade decided to carry out the venture in a big way and, from aerial photographs, reproduced the trench system at the point of proposed action behind our lines for rehearsal. The plan was to set Zero Hour on the setting of the moon; preparation was to be by a box barrage, the wire to be blown by the R.E.s with a Bangalore Torpedo.

There was a preliminary conference with Staff, Gunners and R.E.s to settle the logistics and timetable. The signal for the barrage was to be the explosion of the Bangalore Torpedo observed by a Staff Officer, who would immediately signal to the Artillery by Very Light. After one of the conferences, when the Gunners were offering their wares, 'I can do the five-point-nines fairly accurately for the box' or the trench mortars saying 'We can blast that wire' and the Field Artillery offering their contribution for the frontal blasting of the enemy line 'to keep their heads down', Frank Shaw said they were 'like a lot of enthusiastic commercial travellers'. Shaw didn't take part; he was recalled to England at the last minute because his father died.

On the night of the 18th, my raiding party set out in motor transport for the line, to be in position for the action. That it was my 21st birthday had seeped through to the troops, who regaled me with the music hall song 'I am twenty-one today'. According to the timetable, I had my men outside our wire and in position and the Sappers were forward preparing the torpedo. I joined the Sappers and discussed with Beaumont (their officer) the situation, because the moon was one hour behind our timetable. It seemed that the planning staff had not amended between the G.M.T. moon chart and British Summer Time adjustment. There was to be desultory heavy and light artillery fire to hide our preparations. Unfortunately, one of the heavy shells, being mistaken for the torpedo, triggered off the artillery 'go'. The barrage came down; flares went up. Enemy retaliation was immediate and all hell let loose with the Sapper party exposed only half-way through their job.

Beaumont sent his party back, or what was left of them, and I sent my party back into our trench. I joined Beaumont, who intended to complete the blowing. He said, 'I came out here to blow the wire and I will damn well blow it.' I can still hear Beaumont twanging the enemy wire regardless of the alarm it might provide to the enemy and his curse on dropping a monocle while we were crawling a few yards from the enemy line. I found this amusing and it somehow gave one confidence in the insouciance of this man while stumbling in the dark in No Man's Land. He must have known the raid could not continue, with the warning given to the enemy. He lost some of his men. However, he blew it with a very short fuse – almost direct contact. He was awarded the M.C. posthumously, on my report and recommendation, for he was killed in the action of the 21st.

Of course the whole thing was an utter failure, but I never knew who was responsible for the awful gaff in timing. My reward was ten days' leave, but this was cancelled by the Germans' unsympathetic action of the 21st March.

Getting up the Ammunition for a Counter-Preparation Barrage by Captain F. N. Broome, Adjutant of the 173rd Brigade R.F.A., 36th (Ulster) Division.

Early in the morning of March the 20th, orders were received to prepare for one last great counter-preparation bombardment, after which all batteries were to move behind the Battle Line, and I had to set about providing the necessary ammunition. It was an enormous job. The only method of supplying battery positions by day-light was by a tramline, and very few trucks were available. However, I set out soon after breakfast to do my best. The ammunition dump was behind Grand Seraucourt. On arriving there I found plenty of ammunition but no labour to do the loading. I rushed off to Grand Seraucourt to the Trench Mortar billets, where I found Gimson who very kindly lent me all his available officers, servants, cooks, etc. These people, at least, realised the emergency and helped me most willingly and, in less than no time, the first truck was sent off up the line behind a couple of mules. While the next trucks were being loaded I went back to H.Q. and telephoned to the various batteries to provide guides and off-loading parties.

I soon realised two things: first, that if I were to rely on mule traction I should never finish the job, and, secondly, that the tramline was so congested with traffic that, unless I went forward myself, my trucks would never reach their destination.

Somewhere in Grand Seraucourt was a Tramway Officer who had a number of motor tractors. I set out to find him. He was out. I interviewed his sergeant-major, who was sorry but couldn't lend me any tractors without the authority of his officer. I pleaded with him but it was no good. Faced with the failure of my whole ammunition supply and the consequent failure of the artillery bombardment, I made one last effort. I said to him 'Sergeant-major, it is quite possible that by this time tomorrow the Bosche will have taken over your entire garage. This is a great emergency. The situation calls for men who will do things on their own initiative. The man who waits for an order from his superior now will be too late.' Without another word, he led the way to his shed and from that moment and for the rest of the day I controlled the whole of the divisional tramline.

At the dump I found a whole string of trucks ready loaded. I linked them up to my tractor, seated myself beside the driver, and the whole train moved off up the line. I had not gone far when I realised the need for the presence of an officer with the ammunition train. The tramline was only a single track with very few sidings and it was hopelessly congested with traffic moving the other way – trollies loaded perilously high with all the impedimenta of officers' messes – stretchers, beds, cases of whisky, huge looted iron stoves and the like. These were all being pushed by hand. To every party I met I gave the choice of two alternatives and one minute within which to decide. Either they had to pull their truck off the line and let me pass, or they could join on to my train, come up the line again with me and return with my empties. There was much grumbling and much talking of definite orders from their officers, but I was firm. In some cases I turned out my own men to pull their trucks off the line if they seemed inclined to hesitate. Some chose one alternative and some the other and, by the time we reached the forward areas, we had as many trucks in front of the engine as behind.

My scheme worked splendidly. At various points of the line my train was met by off-loading parties from the various batteries. I soon overtook the four mules which had been sent off hours before. I sent them off home and joined their trucks to my train.

The last battery was D/173. When I reached there it was about 2.30 p.m., and the bulk of my work was done. I left my empty train to find its own way back and returned to H.Q. cross-country. As I walked over the crest of the ridge, I paused for a moment and took one last look at the massive bulk of St Quentin Cathedral and wondered, incuriously, where I should be that time tomorrow.

I had had nothing to eat since breakfast and the rush and excitement of working at high pressure had brought on the headache which tormented me the day before almost every battle in which I took part. It had been an intensely busy day, and I have always looked back upon what I did on the 20th March 1918 as about the best day's work I ever did in France. Had I set out to arrange for the ammunition supply by the ordinary regular official methods, hardly a round of ammunition would have ever reached any battery position and there would have been no counter-preparation bombardment that night, so far as my brigade was concerned.

Only one hitch occurred in all my arrangements. Among the batteries I had to supply was D/232, belonging to another brigade and not tactically attached to us. I rang up the Major and asked him to send a guide down to the railway line at the point nearest to his position to meet the trucks containing his ammunition, which I sent off with a separate tractor. I did not personally accompany the train. It was the one detail of my day's work which I did not personally superintend, and it was the only thing that went wrong. In the evening the Major rang me up and asked me why the hell his ammunition hadn't arrived. He was a certain Major 'the Honourable something' Anson, a nice enough fellow but rather conscious of his aristocratic connection. By that time my temper was getting a little short and I didn't like the way he spoke to me, so I told him that if his ammunition hadn't arrived it was because he was a damned fool and I refused to speak with him further. Later on his Colonel rang up and twenty minutes of wordy warfare ensued in the course of which I told him that what his battery commander required was a wet nurse and that I refused to act in that capacity. It was one of those rare occasions when differences of rank are forgotten and two persons of very different standing speak to one another as man to man. I cannot remember all I said to him but I know that I said things to him that I wouldn't have said to the most junior subaltern in the brigade. In due course we recovered ourselves and parted on excellent terms. His name was Colonel Eley, a Territorial and an excellent soldier of the get-on-with-it type and quite unhampered by the more devastating of the old army traditions. But he was rather highly strung and he reached his breaking point a few days later.

The Battalion Commander by Major V. V. Pope, D.S.O., M.C., temporary commander of the 1st North Staffords, 24th Division.

The 18th, 19th, and 20th March passed tranquilly, for until just before dusk on the last day not a round was fired by the Germans; then, for no apparent reason, four rounds fell suddenly on an unoccupied hillside and all was peace again. I was very uneasy but, remembering how I had alarmed the company commanders once before, I did not tell them of my certainty that we would be attacked but merely warned them of the great probability. When, on the evening of the 20th, I returned from the front line, I found a message from Brigade to say that prisoners who had been captured that day further down the line reported that the attack would start on the 21st. Captain Stamer, the Adjutant, pooh-poohed this, adding that even if they were truthful it was extremely improbable that we should be attacked. So I made one more bet, this time of 100 francs, that we should be attacked before we were relieved on the 23rd March.

The Brigade, however, agreed with me, and reinforcements were sent up that night to Essling Redoubt and to Maissemy, and bursts of harassing fire were arranged throughout the night upon the German front line. These preparations kept me busy, but at 4 a.m. I lay down fully dressed on my bunk. I did not sleep and at 4.25 I heard our guns open one of their periodic bursts of fire. Five minutes later their petulant yapping was utterly drowned by the simultaneous muzzle-explosions of some 6,000 German guns. The offensive had begun.

I ran the twenty yards from my bunk to the signal office, but as I pulled back the blanket which screened the doorway, the signaller on duty looked up and said, 'All lines dissed, Sir.' There was not a buried cable in the whole area. I went up to the trench. The night was still dark and there was a heavy mist. I could see nothing, but I breathed deeply of gas before I realised that gas shells were falling about us. Our information, which had so far proved correct, was that the German bombardment would last some five hours, so, beyond doubling our sentries, I kept the men under cover. Then I went to my dug-out and destroyed all secret papers. I did not know what to do with my diary, which contained a complete record of all our doings; I could not bring myself to destroy it, so reluctantly I hid it behind the skirting. Our canteen money I put in my haversack. Then I returned to the mess-room and waited.

I felt very ill as a result of the gas I had inhaled, but I took the opportunity to ask Stamer to pay up on our debt. He, however, followed St Thomas and said that he would pay only when he saw for himself that the Germans had attacked.

Dawn came at last and we went up to a concrete O.P. outside headquarters, but the mist was impenetrable and the bombardment continued. Presently a very gallant motor cyclist arrived on foot from Brigade bearing an order telling me to man battle positions. His cycle had been hit by a shell but he persisted in delivering his message. A little later a subaltern of the Argylls arrived to tell me that his battalion had moved up into position on my right. This relieved my mind a little, for there was a very nasty re-entrant there which it was the role of the 61st Division to hold. He could give me no information except that the shelling was intense everywhere and that his colonel, a man I knew and liked, had been killed before the battalion had left its reserve billets.

I felt intensely depressed for I could do nothing but wait. The mist showed no signs of clearing and the bombardment was still intense. At 9 o'clock, four and a half hours after the bombardment had begun, I moved the men out into the trench. We had two Vickers guns, two Lewis guns and some twenty-five to thirty riflemen. We were now being shelled with high explosive only.

At half past ten the German barrage passed over us, very intense but strangely enough not very effective. Immediately behind it came a young officer of one of the front-line companies with a few men. He told me that the Germans had broken through the front line but that they were some distance behind their barrage. I put him into the line and reviewed the situation.

The visibility was now about twenty yards but, provided my flanks were secure, I thought we could give a good account of ourselves. On the left flank there was a gap between headquarters and 'C' Company, but I had posted a machine-gun to cover that and the ground between was open. On the right there was that danger-ous re-entrant, but the Argylls would see to that. I walked round the line and told the men what to expect. All shelling of our trench had now ceased and the men were generally cool and confident. When I reached our right, however, I found that nobody had seen anything of the Argylls. I thought they must be near, but I determined that they must be nearer if our flank was not to be turned. I could hear rifle and machine-gun fire from the direction of Essling Redoubt and I hoped that the Germans might have been held up by it. It was essential, however, that the Germans should not be free to attack us via the covered re-entrant and, remembering Sadleir-Jackson's injunction, 'Go and see for yourself', I told Stamer that I was going to find the Argylls, taking Byas, the Intelligence Officer, with me. Stamer did not view this suggestion with any great favour and asked me whether he was to hold on to the last if they were attacked. 'I shall be back long before that can happen,' I replied, 'but, if things do go wrong, I don't want you uselessly to throw away the men's lives. Hold on while you have a fighting chance and then fall back fighting.'

I climbed on to the top and went along the trench, but it was empty. There was another system a little further behind and I realised that, in the dark, the Argylls must have gone there by mistake, so I hurried towards it. As I went I heard firing from the direction of battalion headquarters. Telling Byas to find the Argylls at all costs and bring them up into line I turned back to rejoin Stamer. I had not gone far before I saw three figures moving towards me in the mist. I did not know whether they were British or Germans so, dropping on one knee, I took out my field glasses and then recognised the silhouette of the German helmet. Like a fool, I picked up my rifle and fired at the leading man. The man dropped, but as he fell the second German fired at me and hit me in the right elbow, which was still bent in the act of firing. The bone was shattered and, dropping my rifle, I ran back into the mist whilst more bullets cracked round me. Then, by chance, I came across the very people I had been so earnestly seeking. The trench was full of men standing idly about. I found their officer, a subaltern, told him what was happening and ordered him to move up to assist my headquarters; then, for I was bleeding freely and feeling faint, I looked about for a strong man and, finding one, told him, 'You must help me back to an Aid Post.'

I was determined not to be taken prisoner and that was the only clear thought in my mind. Private McCall (I found out his name later) took me by my left arm and we set off together through the mist. My right arm was dangling loose and hitting against my revolver holster, so I stopped and strapped it in to my side with my Sam Browne belt. 'Come on, Sir,' said the Highlander, 'ye're doing fine.' We passed through the 18-pdr lines, now abandoned; we passed through the lines of a 4·5-how battery and they fired their last shot as we went. There was something very like panic abroad, but I was the last man to deny it. I struggled back a mile or more, bleeding like a pig, and then at last I found a company of the Pioneer Battalion, the 12th Sherwood Foresters, in position. They had a stretcher, and I collapsed into it. There too I found our Quartermaster and to him I gave the canteen money and made him promise to send me my Highlander's name. I was about done, when I saw standing beside me a company commander, unwounded, whose place was in the line. 'What in God's name are you doing here?' I said, and then I finally collapsed.

At the Dressing Station I was lucky enough to be dealt with by a doctor I knew well. He dressed my wound, gave me brandy and assured me that, though I might have a stiff arm, I ought not to lose it. A friendly padre offered his service and I bade him write to my mother and some friends telling them not to worry. Then I was whisked away in an ambulance to the Casualty Clearing Station. They looked at me there and said I had been so well dressed that they would put me on the train that night, but there was no room. So they took me into the operating tent and put tubes into the wound. When I came out the wards were full, and my stretcher was left in a corridor. It was very draughty and I grew very cold. At last I stopped an orderly and begged for brandy. He fetched a doctor who looked at me and, clearly thinking 'The poor devil is going to die anyway,' gave it to me. That brandy saved my life, for it put warmth into me and I slept.

(Major Pope became very ill and his arm had to be amputated

because of gas gangrene. Every year, after 1918, he drank a glass
of port on 21 March in memory of his comrades who had fallen in
the battle. Major Pope remained in the army and, between the
wars, concentrated on the development of armoured warfare. He
became Armoured Adviser to Lord Gort during the Battle of
France, 1940, and in 1941 he was a lieutenant-general and was
Director of Armoured Fighting Vehicles at the War Office when
General Auchinleck asked for him to take command of XXX
(Armoured) Corps in the North African fighting. Just after taking
up this command, however, Pope was tragically killed when the
Hudson aircraft in which he was a passenger crashed on taking
off from a desert airstrip on 5 October 1941. The manuscript above
has been kindly provided by his family.)

The Trench Mortar Officer by Lieutenant A. A. Simpson, 197th
Trench Mortar Battery, 66th (East Lancs) Division.

(Because it had been his turn to be out of the trenches, Lieutenant
Simpson was at the headquarters of his battery when the bombard-
ment started. The 'Coombes' to whom he refers several times was
Captain Coombes, the battery commander.)

I was sleeping in a very flimsy canvas hut near the cottage,
which was our headquarters, with another officer called Guthrie,
who had come up, 'slumming', from some unit in the rear –
possibly a Corps Signal Unit – to visit Coombes. We woke up
when these huge shells started coming just over our heads. Guthrie
got his kit together, told me this wasn't his war, and disappeared.
I decided to get to the cottage and rushed across to it. I can
remember that, when I opened the door, I then deliberately walked
in nonchalantly as though I had just strolled over from my hut.

We soon realised that he was sending gas shells across. We had
got used to gas long ago but I noticed what appeared to be tendrils
forming in the fog; I suppose it must have been a mixture of fog,
gas and lyddite, but I was very worried that this might be a new
German secret weapon. Our pet cat didn't like all this and she
brought in her kittens as though she wanted us to look after them
for her. Later on, I saw her stretched out dead – gas, I suppose –
but I don't know what happened to the kittens.

There was a bang on the door, so I took out my revolver thinking
it might be a German. There was an R.A.M.C. captain – I could
tell he was a new arrival by his new uniform and kit. He was a bit
startled to find a revolver under his nose. He was looking for a
Dressing Station. We couldn't help him; I told him there was.

nothing farther up our road, 'only a war', and off he went. Eventually, we officers decided it would be safer down in the men's dug-out and I took down a gramophone and some records. Coombes was highly amused at the idea of playing records in a bombardment.

Eventually, the bombardment lifted and Coombes decided that we should form ourselves into a defensive position, but our present area was not much good; there would have been no field of fire. We got some aerial photographs of our locality out and found what appeared to be a good trench to our left rear. Coombes started destroying our papers and we wondered what we should do about the spare mortar we had; we had strict orders never to abandon a mortar. We had a special red-painted bomb for this situation. We were supposed to put it in, retire and, five seconds later, it would blow up. We did this but it didn't work. I was always a show-off in front of people so I nipped out, dragged the mortar with its live shell still in it and threw it down a well. The shell still didn't go off.

We took up position in this trench but found that it was only dug out a little. We had about forty of our men and there were odd stragglers coming back from the front line. I stood in the road stopping these; I had often heard about this sort of thing but never dreamed that it would happen to me. As each man came along, I casually told him we were planning to make a show here and suggested he join us, making sure to wave my revolver about a bit as I talked to him. They all came with us. Then two officers came down the road; they were from my old unit, the Lancashire Fusiliers. They said all their men had gone and they couldn't do any more. I told them that they would only get court-martialled if they went farther back and, rather grudgingly, they agreed. I think Coombes was pleased to get them; by then, we had seventy or eighty men altogether.

A German machine-gun opened up from our right flank, firing at extreme range. Our trench was too shallow and bullets were falling in it, causing casualties. One of my gunners was hit in the thigh, and while I was bandaging him up, I looked over my shoulder and these two Lancashire Fusilier officers were legging it down the road. (The next time I saw them was when I rejoined the Lancashire Fusiliers after I came back from Germany; they both had the Military Cross then.) We continued to get casualties, so we decided to move back to an old village that we could see about 200 yards back.

While the main body was taking up position near a church with thick walls, Lieutenant Anderson and myself went into the village to scout round. All we could find was one Lewis-gunner, dead in the road – I removed his revolver and ammunition – and, amazingly, a brand-new Vauxhall car. We tried to start this with a view to going back for more ammunition, but we couldn't start it. I was hopping mad so I put six rounds from my revolver through the radiator and engine so that the Germans wouldn't be able to use it. Anderson was laughing his head off at me, shooting a car.

All at once, my left leg was gripped; the pain was so severe that, at first, I thought I had stepped into a mantrap. I looked down and found a chap was clutching my leg. He said, 'Will you shoot me. I'm not falling into the hands of those bastards.' He was injured in the back and paralysed in his legs. That took the grin off my face quickly. I didn't know what to do. He refused to leave go and I hadn't got the heart to clout him over the head, so I agreed to shoot him. 'Andy' looked awful at this; he thought I was going to do it. I showed him that my revolver was empty and promised to shoot him if he would let go and let me get at my ammunition. He did let go and I immediately grabbed Andy and we ran up the road like hell to join the others.

There was still no sign of any other unit of our side but we hoped for a counter-attack; all old soldiers expected this. We were worried that we might be fired on by British artillery and decided to send someone back. I would have liked to have gone but Anderson was chosen instead. He disappeared down a hedgerow to the rear. The next thing that happened was that we spotted a wounded man between us and the Germans. I went out with another man and we managed to fetch him in under covering fire. The wounded man turned out to be an artillery officer, Lieutenant Hammond.*

The Germans kept up a fire on us for most of the afternoon but it was never serious. I volunteered to reconnoitre to our left to find out who was there. My batman and one other man insisted on coming with me. We reached a small barn and got into the roof and prised up a tile to look out. Surprise! Surprise! There were Germans marching along the road in fours only 250–300 yards farther away to the left. I took the batman's rifle, set the sights and started taking pot shots. I carried on firing for some time; I wished I had a machine-gun. We kept concealed under the tiles and the batman kept reloading my rifle. I was careful not to keep shooting in the same place. I was certainly scoring hits and causing

* This was probably Lieutenant Richard Martin Hammond, X/66th Heavy Trench Mortar Battery, who died of wounds on 20 May 1918 while a prisoner-of-war.

some confusion but the Germans kept marching. It was just like shooting at a fair. Suddenly, an infantry officer with binoculars appeared from God knows where. He was soon anxious to be off again, but I insisted on borrowing the binoculars. I could see that a little party had detached itself from the German column. They were setting up a light mortar and bombs soon started falling around the barn. The infantry officer was very cross; he got a small wound in his ear. He insisted on having his binoculars back and then disappeared.

I rejoined Coombes and the main party then. Anderson had returned and reported that he had found the brigadier and the brigade major on horseback. Andy had reported the situation and asked that we not be shelled and for a counter-attack. The brigadier had told him that there would be no counter-attacks; he had no troops. Andy repeated the brigadier's exact words. 'I've lost my bloody brigade. I'm waiting here, and the first Germans to appear over the ridge, I'm galloping to hell out of it.' He had offered Anderson a spare horse for him to ride off to the rear also, but Andy had insisted on returning to us. The brigadier said, 'I admire you but you're a bloody fool.' The whole of our party was full of admiration for Anderson's return.

We were very tired by now and very hungry. It was still fairly quiet but we were badly hoping for fresh troops to take over from us. Anderson and myself then reconnoitred out to the right and found a Dressing Station. The R.A.M.C. officer in charge was the one that we had met early that morning during the bombardment. He was worried about the many wounded in his care. We reassured him that fresh troops were bound to come up but the words were hardly out when a machine-gun opened up down the road outside the Dressing Station. We were prepared to make a fight of it but were amazed when the doctor pushed a rifle in our backs and insisted that there was going to be no fighting at the Dressing Station. 'Go and do your fighting somewhere else.' While we were still arguing, what appeared to be a whole company of Germans poured into the yard and surrounded us. I was too mad for words. After two and a half years and feeling so clever, to be caught in such a stupid manner. I later met the doctor in a prison camp and he told me that he regretted surrendering in view of the way the Germans had failed to treat our wounded and the general poor conditions of our prisoners. I also met my batman after the war, and he told me that Coombes had seen this large body of Germans taking us prisoner and had withdrawn his party safely.

The Field Gunner by Gunner W. W. Lugg, C Battery, 83rd Brigade R.F.A., 18th (Eastern) Division.

At about one o'clock, the survivors of our four forward guns, which had been overrun by the Germans, arrived at our position. Among them was Captain Heybittle, who immediately took command. The few survivors who had escaped took up positions flanking our two guns; each was equipped with a rifle and we had plenty of ·303 'ammo'.

I was the gunlayer on No. 1 gun, and my pal Charlie Drake was on No. 2. Charlie was blessed with keen eyesight and suddenly said to our captain, 'There are Germans over there on our right, sir.' The captain climbed on to the top of No. 1 gun-pit and scrutinised the area through his binoculars. 'It's all right,' he said, 'they are probably French.' We had a shrewd suspicion that our captain knew that Charlie was right, for he immediately gave orders to pull the guns out of the pits into the open.

We commenced firing at about 3,000 yards. After a short while we came under rifle and machine-gun fire as well as artillery bombardment. A red-painted German aeroplane passed several times a few feet above us and we could see an observer with goggles on looking over the side at us. An Irish gunner on my gun said to me, 'Wally, we are going to have a rough time later' – as though we weren't already! Poor old Paddy was hit shortly after and wounded again on the way down the line.

That left Gunner Syd Taylor and myself on my gun, with Charlie Drake, Gunner Heap and Corporal McKay on the other. It was very exciting at this stage, with no obvious fixed targets, as associated with trench warfare. We had plenty of 'ammo' and kept firing at various ranges. Our captain said jokingly, 'You'd better stop firing, you are getting too enthusiastic!' It was during this lull that the Jerry plane came over again, and Mr Goggles waved to us and we shook our fists in return. When we discussed this incident later we concluded that Fritz was in effect indicating that it was 'curtains' for us.

I kept looking through the telescope sight, which had a magnification of 5¼ and a field of view of 5½ degrees and, all of a sudden, I saw the enemy 300 yards away. We opened fire with our rifles and could see them duck. In the foreground was a derelict house into which we could see the Germans running. I remember saying to the captain, 'Shall I put some shells into it, sir?' He replied 'No, no, you'd better not.' Why not, I never knew; perhaps he thought some of our wounded were in there. At about this time we were amazed to see a Tommy go quite near to the house and pick up a wounded man, carrying him past us on our left. Someone said he was a Somerset Light Infantryman. He was right out in the open with no cover. He sure had a charmed life – made us proud to be British!

For us the real battle started now. We had always been regaled by our 1914 instructors with the glories of firing over open sights, never dreaming it would come to pass. Captain Heybittle, in full view of the Germans, stood on the top of No. 1 Gun-pit, scanning the area in front of us, and decided that we were going to hang on. We then reopened fire with our fuses cut to 0·5 seconds, which was a dangerous operation for the gunners by reason of premature detonation. I once had one burst in the bore at Arras.

Our rate of fire created difficulties after a few hours. My gun was so hot that the expansion of the breech block made it difficult to open it by hand, and it became necessary to prise it open by inserting a pickaxe to increase the leverage. After a while, the breech lever broke, putting the gun out of action. By this time the light was fading. Meanwhile, our boys kept up a steady rate of rifle fire; the situation was so novel that one seemed proof against fear. No. 2 gun developed its troubles, the extractor broke (the extractor ejects the cartridge case from the bore after firing a shell) and, thereafter, every round fired had the shellcase ejected by means of a ramrod which was pushed down the muzzle. After a short while our three boys on No. 2 gun were pretty tired, and Syd Taylor and I transferred our activities to assist them. It was a dangerous job going to the front of the gun to push out the shell case but Gunner Heap, a Lancashire lad, revelled in it. At the finish, it required two of us to force out the cartridge case.

Eventually No. 2 gun became inoperative, but what marvellous service both guns had given us for almost seventeen hours. By this time darkness had fallen, and our superb Captain Heybittle decided to make a fighting withdrawal. We removed the No. 7 dial sights, and burned No. 2 breech block. We also took off the wheel dust caps and removed the retaining keys, deriving much pleasure in imagining Fritz moving the guns and the wheels falling off!

We left the gun position in twos and met about 300 yards to the rear, just behind recently erected barbed wire. When we were fully assembled and about to move off, a group of Germans were seen quite near to our left. We recognised them as such by an obvious command. Gunner Charlie Stone and two others approached them, rifles at the ready. I remember Charlie (a most kindly man) calling in a friendly voice 'Come on, Fritz', whereupon shots were fired. Our return fire scattered the Germans, two being taken prisoners together with a machine-gun. We had great difficulty in restraining our Gunner Stan Hilling from beating the prisoners with his rifle butt. His brother was in the line in front of us.

One of the Germans who ran away was killed and, from his body, religious pamphlets and a revolver were taken. I remember feeling a curious affinity with the dead German – an officer – by reason of our common Christian adherence. I've thought of the sorrow with which his death was received by his relatives. The revolver was claimed by Charlie Drake. Charlie later sold it for 70 francs.

With the two prisoners we marched off to the rear, keeping very quiet and in close touch, as a thick fog was settling. After a short while we challenged two men who, on scrutiny, turned out to be Royal Scots Greys and they teamed up with us. They had become detached from their unit and had lost their bearings. They were the only British troops we had seen since the gallant exploit of the Somerset infantryman. Eventually we arrived at our wagon lines and found, to our amazement, that it had been evacuated, obviously in a hurry. Our Captain Heybittle, whose leadership on that day had been beyond praise, thought that, despite the risks, we should have a meal, using the rations left behind by our drivers.

(One of Mr Lugg's comrades in this day's exploits, Gunner Charlie Stone M.M., was recommended by Captain Heybittle for a decoration and was subsequently awarded the Victoria Cross.)

Captured by Private W. Greenhalgh, 2/6th Manchesters, 66th (East Lancs) Division.

(Early in the day, Private Greenhalgh had been detached from his battalion to act as a runner at the headquarters of the 199th Infantry Brigade. After several adventures, he found himself looking after a badly wounded artillery corporal at an abandoned gun-site in the Battle Zone. The advancing German infantry had paused a few yards away. They were probably Prussian soldiers of the 4th Guard Division.)

So I had to await events, sitting on the bunk beside the wounded corporal, and peeping cautiously now and then at the German machine-gunners in the shell hole. They did not seem very anxious or alert. They probably felt the intense weariness that follows the nerve-strain of hours in battle. I was hungry and tired. Somehow it felt like late afternoon, but it never occurred to me to look at my watch. My thought processes must have been confused with the excitements of the day. My recollection is that there was no shell or small-arms fire in the neighbourhood. The mist was uncanny. I remember thinking that it reminded me of King Arthur's 'last great battle in the mist', before he was wafted away, according to Tennyson, to the island valley of Avilion.

Then, one or two shouts outside reminded me that my affairs were approaching a crisis. There was the sound of heavy feet pounding along the top of the bank above me. Then the sound of heavy feet entering my valley from the enemy end, feet that paused from time to time, and came on again. I wondered, 'What will they do to me? Will they toss one of their "tater-masher" grenades into this bivvy? Would they be as savage as I had seen our men, sometimes, with prisoners?' Anything could happen. They might shoot. I swiftly thought it best to declare my presence. I knew no German, so I shouted 'Hello, there' a couple of times and, within a matter of seconds, a huge German, loaded with his battle equipment, appeared at the door. I remained sitting on the bunk, and I indicated to the German the wounded man. Without a word, he strode into the bivvy, seized a rifle, which I had not noticed standing in the corner, and threw it behind him and outside with his left hand, keeping me covered with the rifle in his right hand. Then he stepped outside and called to someone.

I stepped to the door, and even as I did so, half a dozen other Germans arrived, all of whom seemed to me to be in their middle twenties, except one who looked about my own age. Each one seemed to have two or three days' growth of beard on his face, due, no doubt, to their having been crowded in their assembly positions for a couple of days before the attack. They were obviously in very high spirits, as well they might be after their success. The man in charge (I took him to be a sergeant) was a smiling young man with slightly sticking out teeth. He asked me 'Sprechen Sie deutsch?' I just knew what that meant and I answered him in French, at which I was fairly expert. At that, he seized my hand with a great laugh and shouted 'Mon ami, pourquoi la guerre?' With that, we were all friends. The Germans crowded round me, and each one clicked his heels, bowed and shook my hand.

It was evident that those Germans had reached their objective for the day. They were such splendid men, and their behaviour was so generous and exemplary as soldiers, that later I was loth to believe many of the things attributed to Hitler's men in the 1939–45 War. The first care of the sergeant was my wounded corporal. He examined and bandaged him, and had him taken away on a stretcher, though it was all too late. He showed me that the corporal must have been hit from behind by two machine-gun bullets as he was bending forward. One bullet had shattered his right arm, and the other had hit him low in the back, traversed his body, and passed out through the left lung. I found out later that he died that day.

In that bank where the bivvy was, there was another bivvy and also the entrance to a deep, shell-proof dug-out, which was a battery H.Q. Somewhere my captors had found a British 'iron ration' dump. They were gloating over the small tins of sugar, packets of tea, and the famous 'dog-biscuits'. The sergeant said to me, 'We will take the English "five-o'clock",' and, when they had 'brewed-up' on a thing like a 'tommy-cooker', he said 'You must drink first; it is your tea', and they gave me a piece of their German brown bread spread with some of our jam they had found. The German sergeant asked me, 'What did you think of our gas?' I said it had been a bit of a nuisance. He laughed at that and said, 'As a matter of fact, it was quite harmless. It was only used to deceive and harass you. We were told to disregard it completely.'

My captors continued to treat me as an honoured guest. The front locally was dead quiet and they were settling down for the night. Several strange things happened soon after darkness fell.

The first was that the German sergeant asked me to walk to the wood, through which I had first approached the scene of my capture, to see whether there was a well there. He said they needed water. I told him that there certainly was no well there. He said 'Go, all the same. One of my men will go with you.' So I went and the youngest of his men accompanied me, quite unarmed, I noticed. We found our way through the apron wire, and looked around in the misty darkness for a few minutes, but of course there was no well and I suddenly became convinced that I was being invited to escape! I considered the point. That little wood was Corpeza Copse. It was wired both front and back, and at both sides, I knew, and there was a trench line behind it which had been manned by our men in the morning. I felt sure that trench line was now manned by nervous British infantrymen, perhaps my own D Company, and I remembered the wire I would have to crawl through on the other side if I got through the wood. I thought the odds would be ten to one against my survival if I tried to get away at that point, so I said nothing and the young German and I walked back.

I was allowed to take my ease in the bivvy where the wounded corporal had been. The young German soldier came in and out from time to time and we tried to communicate, but there was the language difficulty. It was perhaps an hour and a half after darkness fell, and I was alone, when the door opened and two British artillerymen staggered in. One was a sergeant and he was supporting the other, a private, who could only hop on one leg; he had been wounded in the other leg, and was obviously exhausted. The sergeant said, when he saw me, 'Thank God the Jerries haven't got here yet.' I said, 'But they have. They got here some hours ago.' But he thought I was distraught or something like that, and tried to reassure me. He said, 'Never mind, chum. You'll be all right now. We'll look after you.' He was still unbelieving and trying to reassure me, when a few moments later my young German walked in. Then he believed me. 'That explains it,' he said. 'We've been hopping about in the mist since it went dark, trying to find this place. We did meet a chap out there on top, and tried to talk to him, but we couldn't understand a bloody word he said. We thought he must be a Jock. He must have been a Jerry.' The two were escorted away and I saw no more of them.

Later the German sergeant stayed talking with me in the dug-out. He said I had nothing at all to fear as a prisoner in Germany; in any case, he said, the war would be over in three months. That, I thought, was the most significant thing I had heard that day. Here was an experienced N.C.O. of first-class combat troops, after one day of surprising success, fully persuaded that this was the final battle! How, I wondered, had the Germans managed to imbue those men of the 21st March with that tremendous vision after the disappointments of three and a half years.

While we were talking, the bell of a telephone fixed to the dug-out wall started buzzing. The instrument was quite close to our faces. I suppose it was someone of the Divisional Artillery staff, hoping against hope to get some news of the 331st Battery. The sergeant saw my look of regret, I suppose. He smiled, drew his bayonet, and hacked the instrument off the wall. I thought, 'There goes my last link with the British Army.'

I squatted down for the night in that compartment on a box. I had found some candles, otherwise there would have been a complete absence of light. There was dead quiet outside. Once or twice I moved to glance up the steps, and each time I saw the form of a German sentry against the sky line at the top.

German Ranks

No attempt has been made to translate the ranks of the German soldiers mentioned in the text of this book. This was done partly to preserve the distinctive character of the German soldiers and partly because direct translations into British equivalents are sometimes misleading. Below are the best translations possible.

Musketier	
Grenadier	
Fusilier	
Jäger (light infantry)	Private
Soldat	
Infanterist (Bavarian)	
Schütze (machine-gunner)	
Pionier	Sapper, engineer, pioneer
Funker	
Signalist	Signaller
Telefonist	
Luftschiffer	Balloonist
Gefreiter	Lance corporal, corporal
Unteroffizier	Sergeant
Vizefeldwebel	Staff sergeant
Feldwebel (infantry)	
Wachtmeister (artillery, cavalry)	Sergeant-major
Offizier Stellvertreter	Deputy officer (non-commissioned)
Fähnrich	Officer cadet
Leutnant	Second lieutenant
Oberleutnant	Lieutenant
Hauptmann	Captain
Major	Major
Oberst	Colonel
Generalleutnant	Lieutenant-general

Appendix 2

Order of Battle of German Infantry Divisions, 21 March 1918

(The three German armies involved are set out below in a north to south order. The corps in each army are also presented from north to south, and the British divisions that each corps was attacking are also given. Within each corps, the first-line divisions are shown first, followed by the second- and third-line divisions. All the first-line divisions and some of the second-line divisions were involved in the attack on 21 March. The recruiting areas or depot towns for divisions and regiments are also shown where possible.)

SEVENTEENTH ARMY (General Otto von Below)

XVIII CORPS (Generalleutnant Albrecht) – attacking the British 34th and 59th (North Midland) Divisions.

1st Line: 111th Division – 73rd (Hanover), 76th (Hamburg) and 164th (Hamelin) Regiments

221st Division – 41st and 45th (East Prussia) Regiments, 60th Reserve Regiment (Weissenburg, Lorraine)

234th Division – 451st, 452nd and 453rd (Brandenburg and Prussian Saxony) Regiments

2nd Line: 2nd Guard Reserve Division. 15th (Minden), 77th Reserve (Celle) and 91st (Oldenburg) Reserve Regiments

6th Bavarian Division – 6th, 10th and 13th Bavarian Regiments

3rd Line: 239th Division – 466th (Hesse), 467th (Thuringia) and 468th (Hesse and Nassau) Regiments

VI RESERVE CORPS (Generalleutnant von dem Borne) – attacking the left and centre of the British 6th Division.

1st Line: 17th Division – 75th (Bremen) Regiment, 89th (Mecklenburg) Grenadier Regiment, 90th (Rostock and Wismar) Fusilier Regiment

195th Division – 6th, 8th and 14th *Jäger* Regiments

2nd Line: 1st Guard Reserve Division – 1st and 2nd Guard Reserve Regiments, 64th (Prenzlau) Reserve Regiment

5th Bavarian Division – 7th (Bayreuth), 19th (Erlangen) and 21st (Fürth) Bavarian Regiments

3rd Line: 24th Division – 133rd, 139th and 179th Regiments (all Saxony)

XIV RESERVE CORPS (Generalleutnant von Lindequist) – attacking the right of British 6th Division and left of 51st (Highland) Division.

1st Line: 3rd Guard Division – Guard Fusilier Regiment (Berlin), Lehr Regiment (Potsdam), 9th Grenadier Regiment (Pomerania)

20th Division – 77th (Hanover), 79th (Hildesheim) and 92nd (Brunswick) Regiments

2nd Line: 39th Division – 126th (Württemberg), 132nd and 172nd Regiments

XI CORPS (Generalleutnant Kühne) – attacking the centre and right of 51st (Highland) Division and northern flank of the Flesquières Salient.

1st Line: 24th Reserve Division – 104th (Chemnitz), 107th (Leipzig) and 133rd (Zwickau) Reserve Regiments

53rd Reserve Division – 241st, 242nd and 243rd Reserve Regiments (all Saxony)

119th Division – 46th and 58th Regiments, 46th Reserve Regiment (all Saxony)

2nd Line: 4th Division – 14th, 49th and 140th Regiments (all Pomerania)

SECOND ARMY (General Georg von der Marwitz)

XXXIX RESERVE CORPS (General der Infanterie von Staabs) – holding attacks on 63rd (Naval) and 47th (London) Divisions in Flesquières Salient.

16th Reserve Division – 29th (Trier), 30th (Saarlouis) and 68th (Coblenz) Reserve Regiments

21st Reserve Division – 80th (Wiesbaden), 87th and 88th (both Mainz) Reserve Regiments

XIII CORPS (General der Infanterie Freiherr von Watter) – attacking the 9th (Scottish) and 21st Divisions.

1st Line: 27th Division – 120th, 123rd and 124th Regiments (all Württemberg)

107th Division – 448th Regiment, 52nd and 232nd Reserve Regiments (all Prussian Saxony and Hanover)

183rd Division – 184th (Prussian Saxony) and 418th (Hesse) Regiments, 440th (Hanover and Oldenburg) Reserve Regiment

2nd Line: 54th Reserve Division – 246th, 247th and 248th Reserve Regiments (all Württemberg or Saxony)

3rd Line: 3rd Marine Division – 1st, 2nd and 3rd Marine Regiments

XXIII RESERVE CORPS (General der Infanterie von Kathen) – attacking the 16th (Irish) and left of 66th (East Lancs) Divisions.

1st Line: 18th Division – 31st (Altona) and 85th (Rendsburg) Regiments, 86th Fusilier Regiment (Flensburg)

50th Reserve Division – 229th, 230th and 231st Reserve Regiments (all Hanover and Brunswick)

79th Reserve Division – 261st, 262nd and 263rd Reserve Regiments (all Prussia)

2nd Line: 9th Reserve Division – 6th (Posen), 19th (Lauban) and 395th Reserve Regiments

13th Division – 13th (Munster), 15th (Minden) and 55th (Detmold) Regiments

3rd Line: 199th Division – 114th (Baden) and 357th (Pomerania) Regiments and 237th Reserve Regiment (Rhineland)

XIV CORPS (Generalleutnant von Gontard) – attacking the centre and right of the 66th (East Lancs) Division and the left of the 24th Division.

1st Line: 4th Guard Division – 5th Foot Guard and 5th Guard Grenadier Regiments (both with depots at Spandau), 93rd Reserve Regiment (Dessau)

25th Division – 115th *Leibgarde* Grenadier Regiment (Darmstadt), 116th Regiment (Giessen) and 117th Leib Regiment (Mainz)

2nd Line: 1st Division – 1st and 3rd Grenadier Regiments, 43rd Regiment (all Königsberg)

3rd Line: 228th Division – 35th Fusilier Regiment, 48th Regiment and 207th Reserve Regiment (all Brandenburg)

LI CORPS (Generalleutnant von Hofacker) – attacking the centre of the 24th Division.

1st Line: 208th Division – 25th (Rhineland) and 185th (Baden) Regiments, 65th Reserve Regiment (Rhineland)

2nd Line: 19th Division – 74th (Hanover), 78th (Osnabrück) and 91st (Oldenburg) Regiments

3rd Line: Guard Ersatz Division – 6th and 7th Guard Regiments, 299th Regiment (all Prussia)

EIGHTEENTH ARMY (General Oskar von Hutier)

III CORPS (Generalleutnant von Lüttwitz) – attacking the right of the 24th Division and the left and centre of the 61st (South Midland) Division.

1st Line: 28th Division – 40th Regiment, 109th Leib-Grenadier Regiment and 110th Grenadier Regiment (all Baden)

88th Division – 352nd, 353rd (both Silesia) and 426th (Hansa towns) Regiments

113th Division – 36th Fusilier and 66th Regiments, 32nd Reserve Regiment (all Saxony)

2nd Line: 5th Division – 8th Leib-Grenadier, 12th Grenadier and 52nd Regiments (all Brandenburg)

6th Division – 24th (Neuruppin), 64th (Prenzlau) and 396th Regiments

206th Division – 359th (Brandenburg) and 394th (Schleswig-Holstein) Regiments, 4th Reserve Ersatz Regiment (Hanover)

3rd Line: 23rd Division – 100th Leib-Grenadier Regiment, 101st Grenadier Regiment and 108th *Schützen* Regiment (all Saxony)

IX CORPS (Generalleutnant Ritter und Edler von Oetinger) – attacking the right of the 61st (South Midland) Division and the 30th Division.

1st Line: 45th Reserve Division – 210th, 211th and 212th Reserve Regiments (all Pomerania)

50th Division – 39th Fusilier, 53rd and 158th Regiments (all Westphalia)

2nd Line: 5th Guard Division – 2nd Guard and 3rd Guard Grenadier Regiments, 20th Regiment (Wittenberg)

231st Division – 442nd, 443rd and 444th Regiments (all Prussia)

3rd Line: 1st Guard Division – 1st, 2nd and 4th Foot Guard Regiments (all Prussia)

XVIII CORPS (Generalleutnant von Werern) – attacking the 36th (Ulster) Division and the left of the 14th (Light) Division.

1st Line: 1st Bavarian Division – 1st and 2nd Bavarian Regiments (both Munich), 24th Bavarian Regiment (Lower Franconia)

36th Division – 5th Grenadier (East Prussia), 128th (Danzig) and 175th (Prussia) Regiments

238th Division – 463rd (Hansa towns), 464th (Schleswig) and 465th (Hanover) Regiments

2nd Line: 9th Division – 7th Grenadier, 19th and 154th Regiments (all Lower Silesia)

10th Division – 6th Grenadier, 47th and 398th Regiments (all Posen)

3rd Line: 7th Reserve Division – 36th, 66th and 72nd Reserve Regiments (all Prussian Saxony)

10th Reserve Division – 37th Fusilier and 37th Reserve Regiments (both Krotoschin), 155th Regiment (Ostrowo)

IV RESERVE CORPS (Generalleutnant von Conta) – attacking the centre and right of the 14th (Light) Division and the left of the 18th (Eastern) Division.

1st Line: 34th Division – 30th (Saarlouis), 67th (Madgeburg) and 145th King's (Lorraine) Regiments

37th Division – 147th (Lyck), 150th (Allenstein) and 151st (Sensburg) Regiments

103rd Division – 32nd (Mainingen) and 71st (Erfurt) Regiments, 116th (Hesse) Reserve Regiment

2nd Line: 33rd Division – 98th, 130th and 135th Regiments (all Lorraine)

GRUPPE GAYL (General Freiherr von Gayl) – attacking the centre and right of the 18th (Eastern) Division and the 173rd Brigade, 58th (London) Division.

1st Line: 13th Landwehr Division – 15th, 60th and 82nd Landwehr Regiments (all Westphalia)

47th Reserve Division – 218th, 219th and 220th Reserve Regiments (all Pomerania)

2nd Line: 223rd Division – 144th and 173rd Regiments (both Lorraine), 29th Ersatz Regiment (Baden)

3rd Line: 211th Division – 27th (Halberstadt) and 390th (Prussian Saxony) Regiments, 75th Reserve Regiment (Bremen)

Order of Battle of British Infantry and Cavalry Divisions, 21 March 1918

(Corps are set out in a north to south order. The locations of army, corps and divisional headquarters are given. Divisions were in the front line unless it is stated that they were in reserve. The original recruiting areas or sponsors of Territorial and New Army battalions are given where possible.)

THIRD ARMY (General Hon. Sir Julian H. G. Byng) H.Q. Albert

XVII CORPS 4th and 15th (Scottish) Divisions in line, Guards Division in reserve, not in action on 21 March 1918.

VI CORPS (Lieutenant-General Sir J. A. L. Haldane) H.Q. Bretencourt

3RD DIVISION (Major-General C. J. Deverell) H.Q. Boisleux-au-Mont

8th Brigade
1st Royal Scots Fusiliers
2nd Royal Scots
7th King's Shropshire Light Infantry

76th Brigade
1st Gordon Highlanders
2nd Suffolks
8th King's Own

9th Brigade
1st Northumberland Fusiliers
4th Royal Fusiliers
13th King's (Liverpool)

Pioneers
20th King's Royal Rifle Corps (British Empire League Pioneers)

34TH DIVISION (Major-General C. J. Nicholson) H.Q. Gomiecourt

101st Brigade
11th Suffolks (Cambridge)
15th Royal Scots (1st City of Edinburgh)
16th Royal Scots (2nd City of Edinburgh)

102nd Brigade
22nd Northumberland Fusiliers (3rd Tyneside Scottish)
23rd Northumberland Fusiliers (4th Tyneside Scottish)
25th Northumberland Fusiliers (2nd Tyneside Irish)

103rd Brigade
1st East Lancashires
9th Northumberland Fusiliers
10th Lincolns (Grimsby Chums)

Pioneers
18th Northumberland Fusiliers

59TH (2ND NORTH MIDLAND) DIVISION (Major-General C. F. Romer) H.Q. Behagnies

176th Brigade
5th North Staffords
2/6th North Staffords
2/6th South Staffords

177th Brigade
4th Lincolns
2/5th Lincolns
2/4th Leicesters

178th Brigade
2/5th Sherwood Foresters
2/6th Sherwood Foresters
7th Sherwood Foresters

Pioneers
6/7th Royal Scots Fusiliers

40TH DIVISION (Major-General J. Ponsonby) H.Q. Basseux. The division was in G.H.Q. Reserve but was released to VI Corps at noon and came into action

119th Brigade
13th East Surreys
(Wandsworth)
18th Welch (2nd Glamorgans)
21st Middlesex (Islington)

120th Brigade
10/11th Highland Light
Infantry
14th Highland Light Infantry
14th Argyll and Sutherland
Highlanders

121st Brigade
12th Suffolks
13th Green Howards
20th Middlesex (Shoreditch)

Pioneers
12th Green Howards

IV CORPS (Lieutenant-General Sir G. M. Harper) H.Q. Grevillers

6TH DIVISION (Major-General T. O. Marden) H.Q. The monument at trench-map reference H.15.c.

16th Brigade
1st Buffs
1st King's Shropshire Light
Infantry
2nd York and Lancasters

18th Brigade
1st West Yorks
2nd Durham Light Infantry
11th Essex

71st Brigade
1st Leicesters
2nd Sherwood Foresters
9th Norfolks

Pioneers
11th Leicesters (City of
Leicester)

51st (highland) division (Major-General G. T. C. Carter-Campbell) H.Q. Fremicourt

152nd Brigade
5th Seaforth Highlanders
(Sutherland and Caithness)
6th Seaforth Highlanders
(Morayshire)
6th Gordon Highlanders
(Banff and Donside)

153rd Brigade
6th Black Watch (Perthshire)
7th Black Watch (Fifeshire)
7th Gordon Highlanders
(Deeside)

154th Brigade
4th Gordon Highlanders
4th Seaforth Highlanders
(Ross-shire)
7th Argyll and Sutherland
Highlanders

Pioneers
8th Royal Scots

19th (western) division (Major-General G. D. Jeffreys) H.Q. Haplincourt. The division was in V Corps reserve but was transferred to IV Corps and came into action during the day.

56th Brigade
1/4th King's Shropshire
Light Infantry
8th North Staffords
9th Cheshires

57th Brigade
8th Gloucesters
10th Royal Warwicks
10th Worcesters

58th Brigade
6th Wiltshires
9th Royal Welch Fusiliers
9th Welch

Pioneers
5th South Wales Borderers

25th division (Major-General Sir E. G. T. Bainbridge) H.Q. Achiet-le-Petit. The division was in reserve and came into action during the day.

7th Brigade
1st Wiltshires
4th South Staffords
10th Cheshires

74th Brigade
3rd Worcesters
9th Loyal North Lancashires
11th Lancashire Fusiliers

75th Brigade
2nd South Lancashires
8th Border
11th Cheshires

Pioneers
6th South Wales Borderers

v corps (Lieutenant-General Sir E. A. Fanshawe) H.Q. Villers-au-Flos

17TH (NORTHERN) DIVISION (Major-General P. R. Robertson) H.Q. Bertincourt

50th Brigade
6th Dorsets
7th East Yorks
10th West Yorks

51st Brigade
7th Border
7th Lincolns
10th Sherwood Foresters

51st Brigade
9th Duke of Wellington's
10th Lancashire Fusiliers
12th Manchesters

Pioneers
7th York and Lancasters

47TH (2ND LONDON) DIVISION (Major-General Sir G. F. Gorringe) H.Q. Ytres Château

140th Brigade
1/15th Londons (Civil Service)
1/17th Londons (Poplar and Stepney)
1/21st Londons (Surrey Rifles)

142nd Brigade
1/22nd Londons (The Queens)
1/23rd Londons
1/24th Londons (The Queens)

141st Brigade
1/18th Londons (London Irish)
1/19th Londons (St Pancras)
1/20th Londons (Blackheath and Woolwich)

Pioneers
10th Duke of Cornwall's
Light Infantry

63RD (ROYAL NAVAL) DIVISION (Major-General C. E. Lawrie) H.Q. Neuville Bourjonval

188th Brigade
1st Royal Marine Light Infantry
2nd Royal Marine Light Infantry
Hood Battalion

190th Brigade
1st Artists Rifles
4th Bedfords
7th Royal Fusiliers

189th Brigade
Anson Battalion
Hawke Battalion
Drake Battalion

Pioneers
14th Worcesters

2ND DIVISION (Major-General C. E. Pereira) H.Q. Etricourt.
The division was in reserve and did not see serious action during the day although it suffered casualties from shellfire.

5th Brigade
2nd Highland Light Infantry
2nd Oxford and Bucks Light Infantry
24th Royal Fusiliers

6th Brigade
1st King's (Liverpool)
2nd South Staffords
17th Royal Fusiliers

99th Brigade
1st King's Royal Rifle Corps
1st Royal Berkshires
23rd Royal Fusiliers

Pioneers
4th Royal Welch Fusiliers

FIFTH ARMY (General Sir Hubert Gough) H.Q. Nesle

VII CORPS (Lieutenant-General Sir W. N. Congreve V.C.) H.Q. Templeux-la-Fosse

9TH (SCOTTISH) DIVISION (Brigadier-General H. H. Tudor, in temporary command) H.Q. Nurlu

26th Brigade
5th Cameron Highlanders
7th Seaforth Highlanders
8th Black Watch

27th Brigade
6th King's Own Scottish
Borderers
11th Royal Scots
12th Royal Scots

South African Infantry Brigade
1st South Africans
2nd South Africans
4th South Africans

Pioneers
9th Seaforth Highlanders

16TH (IRISH) DIVISION (Major-General Sir C. P. A. Hull) H.Q. Tincourt

47th Brigade
1st Royal Munster Fusiliers
2nd Leinsters
6th Connaught Rangers

48th Brigade
1st Royal Dublin Fusiliers
2nd Royal Dublin Fusiliers
2nd Royal Munster Fusiliers

49th Brigade
2nd Royal Irish
7th Royal Irish
7/8th Royal Inniskilling Fusiliers

Pioneers
11th Hampshires

21ST DIVISION (Major-General D. G. M. Campbell) H.Q. Longavesnes

62nd Brigade
1st Lincolns
2nd Lincolns
12/13th Northumberland
Fusiliers

64th Brigade
1st East Yorks
9th King's Own Yorkshire
Light Infantry
15th Durham Light Infantry

110th Brigade
6th Leicesters
7th Leicesters
8th Leicesters

Pioneers
14th Northumberland
Fusiliers

39TH DIVISION (Brigadier-General M. L. Hornby, in temporary command) H.Q. Haut Allaines. The division was in reserve and came into action during the day.

116th Brigade
1/1st Hertfords
11th Royal Sussex (3rd South Downs)
13th Royal Sussex

117th Brigade
16th Sherwood Foresters
16th Rifle Brigade
17th King's Royal Rifle Corps

118th Brigade
1/1st Cambridge
4/5th Black Watch
9th Cheshires

Pioneers
13th Gloucesters

XIX CORPS (Lieutenant-General Sir H. E. Watts) H.Q. Catelet

24TH DIVISION (Major-General C. A. Daly) H.Q. Bouvincourt

17th Brigade
1st Royal Fusiliers
3rd Rifle Brigade
8th Queens

72nd Brigade
1st North Staffords
8th Royal West Kents
9th East Surreys

73rd Brigade
7th Northamptons
9th Royal Sussex
13th Middlesex

Pioneers
12th Sherwood Foresters

66TH (2ND EAST LANCS) DIVISION (Major-General N. Malcolm) H.Q. Nobescourt Farm

197th Brigade
6th Lancashire Fusiliers
2/7th Lancashire Fusiliers
2/8th Lancashire Fusiliers

198th Brigade
4th East Lancashires
2/5th East Lancashires
9th Manchesters

199th Brigade
2/5th Manchesters
2/6th Manchesters
2/7th Manchesters

Pioneers
5th Border (West Cumberland)

The 50th (Northumbrian) Division was allocated from G.H.Q. Reserve to XIX Corps at 3.20 p.m. but did not arrive until 22 March.

XVIII CORPS (Lieutenant-General Sir I. Maxse) H.Q. Ham

30TH DIVISION (Major-General W. de L. Williams) H.Q. Dury

21st Brigade
2nd Green Howards

89th Brigade
17th King's (1st Liverpool Pals)

21st *Brigade*
2nd Wiltshires
17th Manchesters (2nd Pals)

90th *Brigade*
2nd Bedfords
2nd Royal Scots Fusiliers
16th Manchesters (1st Pals)

89th *Brigade*
18th King's (2nd Liverpool Pals)
19th King's (3rd Liverpool Pals)

Pioneers
11th South Lancashires

36TH (ULSTER) DIVISION (Major-General O. S. W. Nugent)
H.Q. Ollezy

107th *Brigade*
1st Royal Irish Rifles
2nd Royal Irish Rifles
15th Royal Irish Rifles
(North Belfast)

108th *Brigade*
1st Royal Irish Fusiliers
9th Royal Irish Fusiliers
(Armagh, Monaghan and
Cavan)
12th Royal Irish Rifles
(Central Antrim)

109th *Brigade*
1st Royal Inniskilling Fusiliers
2nd Royal Inniskilling Fusiliers
9th Royal Inniskilling Fusiliers
(Tyrone)

Pioneers
16th Royal Irish Rifles (2nd
Co. Downs)

61ST (2ND SOUTH MIDLAND) DIVISION (Major-General C. J.
Mackenzie) H.Q. Aurior

182nd *Brigade*
2/6th Royal Warwicks
(Birmingham)
2/7th Royal Warwicks
(Coventry)
2/8th Worcesters

184th *Brigade*
2/4th Oxford and Bucks
Light Infantry
2/4th Royal Berkshires
2/5th Gloucesters

183rd *Brigade*
1/5th Gordon Highlanders
(Buchan and Formartin)
1/8th Argyll and Sutherland
Highlanders (Argyllshire)
1/9th Royal Scots

Pioneers
1/5th Duke of Cornwall's
Light Infantry

20TH (LIGHT) DIVISION (Major-General W. Douglas Smith)
H.Q. Ercheu. The division was in G.H.Q. Reserve but was
released to XVIII Corps at 1.0 p.m. and came into action.

58th *Brigade*
2nd Scottish Rifles
11th Rifle Brigade

60th *Brigade*
6th King's Shropshire Light
Infantry

58th Brigade
11th King's Royal Rifle Corps

60th Brigade
12th Rifle Brigade
12th King's Royal Rifle Corps

61st Brigade
7th Duke of Cornwall's Light
Infantry
7th Somerset Light Infantry
12th King's (Liverpool)

Pioneers
11th Durham Light Infantry

III CORPS (Lieutenant-General Sir R. H. K. Butler) H.Q. Ugny-le-Gay

14TH (LIGHT) DIVISION (Major-General Sir V. A. Couper)
H.Q. Clastres

41st Brigade
7th Rifle Brigade
8th Rifle Brigade
8th King's Royal Rifle Corps

42nd Brigade
5th Oxford and Bucks Light
Infantry
9th Rifle Brigade
9th King's Royal Rifle Corps

43rd Brigade
6th Somerset Light Infantry
7th King's Royal Rifle Corps
9th Scottish Rifles

Pioneers
11th King's (Liverpool)

18TH (EASTERN) DIVISION (Major-General R. P. Lee) H.Q.
Rouez

53rd Brigade
7th Royal West Kents
8th Royal Berkshires
10th Essex

54th Brigade
6th Northamptons
7th Bedfords
11th Royal Fusiliers

55th Brigade
7th Buffs
7th Queens
8th East Surreys

Pioneers
8th Royal Sussex

58TH (2/1ST LONDON) DIVISION (Major-General A. B. E.
Cator) H.Q. Quierzy. The 174th and 175th Brigades were south
of the River Oise and not heavily involved on 21 March.

173rd Brigade
2/2nd Londons
3rd Londons
2/4th Londons

174th Brigade
6th Londons
7th Londons
8th Londons (Post Office Rifles)

175th Brigade
9th Londons (Queen Victoria's Rifles)
2/10th Londons (Hackney)
12th Londons (Rangers)

Pioneers
1/4th Suffolks

CAVALRY CORPS (Lieutenant-General Sir C. T. McM. Kavanagh)
The Cavalry Corps did not operate as a united force, and its divisions were split up to give dismounted support to various infantry corps in the Fifth Army.

1ST CAVALRY DIVISION (Major-General R. L. Mullens)

1st Cavalry Brigade
2nd Dragoon Guards
5th Dragoon Guards
11th Hussars

2nd Cavalry Brigade
4th Dragoon Guards
9th Lancers
18th Hussars

9th Cavalry Brigade
8th Hussars
15th Hussars
19th Hussars

2ND CAVALRY DIVISION (Major-General W. H. Greenly)

3rd Cavalry Brigade
4th Hussars
5th Lancers
16th Lancers

4th Cavalry Brigade
6th Dragoon Guards
3rd Hussars
1/1st Oxfordshire Hussars

5th Cavalry Brigade
2nd Dragoons
12th Lancers
20th Hussars

3RD CAVALRY DIVISION (Brigadier-General A. E. W. Harman)

6th Cavalry Brigade
3rd Dragoon Guards
1st Dragoons
10th Hussars

7th Cavalry Brigade
7th Dragoon Guards
6th Dragoons
17th Lancers

Canadian Cavalry Brigade
Royal Canadian Dragoons
Fort Garry's Horse
Lord Strathcona's Horse

The 1st and 2nd Life Guards, the Royal Horse Guards and several unidentified Yeomanry regiments were attached to the Fifth Army as 'army troops' but were not in action on 21 March.

Artillery Guns and Howitzers Available to the British Third and Fifth Armies, 21 March 1918

	Third Army	Fifth Army
18-pounder guns	495	864
4·5-inch howitzers	164	288
60-pounder guns	96	108
6-inch guns	20	28
6-inch howitzers	217	260
8-inch howitzers	52	60
9·2-inch guns	5	4
9·2-inch howitzers	53	61
12-inch howitzers	15	10
15-inch guns	3	1
Total	1,120	1,684

NOTE 1. The Official History (pages 126 and 130) gives only combined totals for the 18-pounder field guns and 4·5-inch howitzers in field artillery brigades. The separate figures given above are on the basis that these two types of gun were everywhere distributed in the normal proportion of eighteen field guns to six howitzers per artillery brigade.

NOTE 2. Approximately 20 per cent of the Third Army and 6 per cent of the Fifth Army artillery could take no part in the battle because their positions were beyond the northern and southern limits of the German attack.

Royal Flying Corps Air Order of Battle on the Front of the German Attack, 21 March 1918

An R.F.C. 'brigade' was part of the ground army of the same number, so III Brigade was part of the Third Army. 'Corps wings' provided one reconnaissance/observation squadron to work closely with each of the infantry corps in the army. The 'army wings' contained scout and bomber squadrons for more general work within the army.

III BRIGADE (Brigadier-General J. F. A. Higgins) H.Q. Albert

TWELFTH (CORPS) WING (Lieutenant-Colonel W. G. S. Mitchell)

Squadron	Main Type of Aircraft	Airfield	Corps to which attached
12	R.E.8	Boiry St Martin	VI
13	R.E.8	Etrun	XVII
15	R.E.8	Lechelle	V
59	R.E.8	Courcelles-le-Comte	IV

Total aircraft — 78

THIRTEENTH (ARMY) WING (Lieutenant-Colonel P. H. L. Playfair)

3	Sopwith Camel	Warloy
11	Bristol Fighter	Bellevue
41	S.E.5a	Lealvillers
46	Sopwith Camel	Le Hameau
49	D.H.4	Bellevue
56	S.E.5a	Baisieux
64	S.E.5a	Le Hameau

| 70 | Sopwith Camel | Marieux |
| 102 | F.E.2b | Le Hameau |

Total aircraft — 183

THIRD BALLOON WING (Lieutenant-Colonel F. H. Cleaver)
Nos. 10, 12, 18 and 19 Balloon Companies

V BRIGADE (Brigadier-General L. E. O. Charlton) H.Q. Mesnil St Nicaise

FIFTEENTH (CORPS) WING (Lieutenant-Colonel I. A. E. Edwards)

8	Armstrong-Whitworth	Templeux-la-Fosse	VII
35	Armstrong-Whitworth	Estrées-en-Chaussée	XIX
52	R.E.8	Bonneuil	XVIII
53	R.E.8	Villeselve	IX
82	Armstrong-Whitworth	Bonneuil	III

Total aircraft — 102

TWENTY-SECOND (ARMY) WING (Lieutenant-Colonel F. V. Holt)

5 (Naval)	D.H.4	Mons-en-Chaussée
23	Spad	Matigny
24	S.E.5a	Matigny
48	Bristol Fighter	Flez
54	Sopwith Camel	Flez
84	S.E.5a	Flez
101	F.E.2b	Catigny

Total aircraft — 141

FIFTH BALLOON WING (Lieutenant-Colonel Hon. A. S. Byng)
Nos. 13, 14, 15, 16 and 20 Balloon Companies

In addition to their own wings, both the Third and the Fifth Army received help during the day from wings outside their armies. The Third Army was helped by the squadrons of the Tenth Wing (Second Army) and the Fifth Army by the Ninth (Day) Wing, which was a group of squadrons under the control of G.H.Q. The orders of battle of these two wings are given below.

TENTH (ARMY) WING (Lieutenant-Colonel C. T. Maclean)

2*	S.E.5a	Savy
3(Naval)	Sopwith Camel	Mont St Eloi
4*	Sopwith Camel	Bruay
18	D.H.4	Treizennes
22	Bristol Fighter	Serny
40	S.E.5a	Bruay
43	Sopwith Camel	La Gorgue

Total aircraft – 141

* Australian

NINTH (DAY) WING (Lieutenant-Colonel W. R. Freeman)

25	D.H.4	Villers-Bretonneux
27	D.H.4	Villers-Bretonneux
62	Bristol Fighter	Cachy
73	Sopwith Camel	Champien
79	Sopwith Dolphin	Champien
80	Sopwith Camel	Champien

Total aircraft – 114

___

Timetable for the German Preliminary Bombardment of the British Fifth Army Positions, 21 March 1918*

4.40 a.m. First period, 120 minutes. General surprise fire on the enemy batteries, trench mortars, command posts, telephone exchanges, billets and bivouacs, beginning with a crash, and fired by all batteries and trench mortars (mixed gas and high-explosive shell). After twenty minutes the trench mortars stop. At 5.30 a.m. ten minutes surprise fire on the infantry positions, beginning suddenly from all batteries except super-heavy (against the First and Intermediate Positions, high-explosive only, against the Second Position, mixed gas, lethal and lachrymatory). During this ten minutes no counter-battery work.

6.40 a.m. Second, Third and Fourth Periods, each of ten minutes, during each of which a proportion of the batteries of the infantry groups check the range on named trench lines, whilst the rest fire on other defences.†

7.10 a.m. Fifth Period, seventy minutes. Whilst counter-batteries and long-range batteries continue to fire on their normal targets, the others bombard the infantry defences for effect, the areas being defined by a map. After thirty minutes' fire, some howitzers in each group sweep the ground between the trenches of the First Position for fifteen minutes; the other howitzers shell certain centres of resistance for ten minutes, and then sweep backwards; the field guns sweep the ground between the Second and Intermediate Positions for ten minutes with lachrymatory and high-explosive shell.

8.20 a.m. Sixth Period, 75 minutes. Shooting as in the Fifth Period, with slight variation of targets for the long-range batteries: the same special bombardments after thirty minutes' fire, also with slight variation of targets.

9.35 a.m. Seventh Period. The five minutes before Zero. All

* Translation of German orders, British Official History, pages 159–60.
† It was not possible to carry out this visual ranging because of the fog.

howitzers fire as near to the front line of the First Position as is possible without endangering their own infantry; beyond them the light and medium trench mortars fire, and beyond them again the field guns, but only with high explosive; beyond them again the super-heavy guns, flanking batteries and heavy trench mortars fire on the second line of the First Position; long-range guns (other than flanking batteries) and some of the guns not to be used in the creeping barrage fire on the Second Position; the others continue counter-battery work. At the end of this period, the infantry will assault without 'hurrahs'.

The creeping barrage (fired in principal by the field artillery, 5·9-inch howitzers and light trench mortars) proceeds by deep bounds, the first bound being 300 metres, other bounds 200 metres for field artillery, and 400 for the heavy artillery; after the first bound the field artillery to halt the barrage for three minutes, the heavy for two; after the other bounds for four and eight minutes, respectively. Signals for advancing the barrage on emergency, 200 metres at a time, to be by use of green rockets and the small flame projectors; no signals for halting it.

Victoria Cross Awards for 21 March 1918

Second Lieutenant E. F. Beal, 13th Green Howards, 40th Division. For actions on the evening of 21 March and on the 22nd, when he was killed. No known grave; commemorated on the Arras Memorial to the Missing.

Second Lieutenant J. C. Buchan, 1/8th Argyll and Sutherland Highlanders, 61st (South Midland) Division. For actions on 21 and 22 March; he was presumed killed on 22 March and is buried in Roisel Communal Cemetery Extension.

Second Lieutenant E. de Wind, 15th Royal Irish Rifles, 36th (Ulster) Division. Killed on 21 March. No known grave; commemorated on the Pozières Memorial to the Missing.

Lieutenant-Colonel W. Elstob, D.S.O., M.C., 16th Manchesters, 30th Division. Killed on 21 March. No known grave; commemorated on the Pozières Memorial to the Missing.

Captain R. F. J. Hayward, M.C., 1st Wiltshires, 25th Division. For actions on 21-23 March. Survived.

Captain M. A. James, M.C., 8th Gloucesters, 19th (Western) Division. For actions on 21-23 March. Wounded and taken prisoner.

Lieutenant A. E. Ker, 61st Machine Gun Battalion, 61st (South Midland) Division. For actions on 21 March. Survived.

Lance Corporal J. W. Sayer, 8th Queens, 24th Division. For actions on 21 March. Wounded and taken prisoner but died on 18 April 1918; buried in Le Cateau Military Cemetery.

Gunner C. E. Stone, M.M., 83rd Brigade Royal Field Artillery, 18th (Eastern) Division. For actions on 21 March. Survived. (See further references to this soldier in Gunner Lugg's account in Soldiers' Tales', pages 374-5.)

Second Lieutenant C. L. Knox, 150th Field Company Royal Engineers, 36th (Ulster) Division, was awarded his Victoria Cross for an action in the early hours of 22 March. A further twenty Victoria Crosses were awarded before the end of March 1918.

Senior Officer Casualties, 21 March 1918

The list below gives the known officers of battalion commander or equivalent position to become casualties during the day. Temporary battalion commanders are included.

6TH DIVISION

Lieutenant-Colonel H. M. Smith, 1st King's Shropshire Light Infantry	Taken prisoner
Lieutenant-Colonel C. A. M. Boyall, 1st West Yorks	Wounded and prisoner
Lieutenant-Colonel B. H. L. Prior, 9th Norfolks	Wounded

9TH (SCOTTISH) DIVISION

Lieutenant-Colonel C. W. W. MacLean, Acting C.R.A.	Wounded

14TH (LIGHT) DIVISION

Major J. H. Jerwood, 6th Somerset Light Infantry	Killed
Lieutenant-Colonel A. J. H. Sloggett, 7th Rifle Brigade	Taken prisoner
Lieutenant-Colonel R. H. Brown, 8th King's Royal Rifle Corps	Taken prisoner
Lieutenant-Colonel H. Bury, 9th King's Royal Rifle Corps	Taken prisoner

16TH (IRISH) DIVISION

Lieutenant-Colonel H. R. H. Ireland, 2nd Royal Munster Fusiliers	Died of wounds
Lieutenant-Colonel J. D. Scott, 2nd Royal Irish	Killed
Major F. Call, 7th Royal Irish	Taken prisoner
Lieutenant-Colonel A. Walkey, 7/8th Royal Inniskilling Fusiliers	Wounded

18TH (EASTERN) DIVISION

Lieutenant-Colonel J. D. Crosthwaite, 7th Royal West Kents	Wounded and prisoner

20TH (LIGHT) DIVISION

Lieutenant-Colonel A. N. Vince, 12th King's (Liverpool)	Killed

21ST DIVISION

Major G. White, 12/13th Northumberland Fusiliers	Taken prisoner
Lieutenant-Colonel H. W. Festing, 15th Durham Light Infantry	Killed

24TH DIVISION

Major V. V. Pope, 1st North Staffords	Wounded
Lieutenant-Colonel L. J. Le Fleming, 9th East Surreys	Killed

30TH DIVISION

Lieutenant-Colonel A. V. P. Martin, 2nd Wiltshires	Wounded and prisoner
Lieutenant-Colonel W. Elstob, 16th Manchesters	Killed

34TH DIVISION

Lieutenant-Colonel S. Acklom, 22nd Northumberland Fusiliers	Killed
Lieutenant-Colonel G. Charlton, 23rd Northumberland Fusiliers	Taken prisoner
Lieutenant-Colonel Lloyd, 25th Northumberland Fusiliers	Taken prisoner

36TH (ULSTER) DIVISION

Lieutenant-Colonel Lord Farnham, 2nd Royal Inniskilling Fusiliers	Taken prisoner
Major A. H. Hall, 12th Royal Irish Rifles	Taken prisoner
Lieutenant-Colonel C. G. Cole-Hamilton, 15th Royal Irish Rifles	Taken prisoner

47TH (LONDON) DIVISION

Lieutenant-Colonel G. E. Milner, 24th Londons	Wounded

51ST (HIGHLAND) DIVISION

Lieutenant-Colonel J. Robertson, 2/1st Highland Field Ambulance	Killed

58TH (LONDON) DIVISION

Lieutenant-Colonel A. R. Richardson, 2/2nd Londons	Taken prisoner

59TH (NORTH MIDLAND) DIVISION

Lieutenant-Colonel H. Johnson, 5th North Staffords	Wounded and prisoner
Lieutenant-Colonel T. B. H. Thorne, 2/6th North Staffords	Killed
Lieutenant-Colonel J. Stuart-Wortley, 2/6th South Staffords	Killed
Lieutenant-Colonel H. R. Gadd, 2/5th Sherwood Foresters	Taken prisoner
Lieutenant-Colonel H. S. Hodgkin, 2/6th Sherwood Foresters	Taken prisoner
Lieutenant-Colonel W. S. N. Toller, 7th Sherwood Foresters	Taken prisoner

61ST (SOUTH MIDLAND) DIVISION

Lieutenant-Colonel J. H. S. Dimmer, 2/4th Royal Berkshires	Killed
Lieutenant-Colonel H. E. de R. Wetherall, 2/4th Oxford and Bucks Light Infantry	Taken prisoner but escaped
Lieutenant-Colonel M. F. McTaggart, 1/5th Gordon Highlanders	Taken prisoner
Lieutenant-Colonel J. R. Macalpine-Downie, 1/8th Argyll and Sutherland Highlanders	Died of wounds
Major H. W. Davies, 2/8th Worcesters	Wounded and prisoner

66TH (EAST LANCS) DIVISION

Lieutenant-Colonel A. L. Wrenfold, 4th East Lancashires	Wounded and prisoner
Lieutenant-Colonel W. A. Baillie-Hamilton, 2/7th Manchesters	Taken prisoner
Lieutenant-Colonel A. E. Stokes-Roberts, 2/8th Lancashire Fusiliers	Taken prisoner

IV CORPS

Lieutenant-Colonel G. B. Hinton, 26th
Army Field Brigade R.F.A.   Killed

SUMMARY

Killed	12
Died of wounds	2
Wounded	5
Taken prisoner (6 wounded)	24
Prisoner but escaped	1
Total	44

'The Three-Week Subaltern' or Pilot

Many legends have sprung up since the First World War. Among the most prevalent are those which say that the life expectation of a subaltern in a front-line infantry battalion or of a pilot in a front-line fighter squadron was only three weeks. While it is true that both groups of men suffered severe losses, the 'three-week life expectation' is an exaggeration. The reader may be interested in actual figures from one average infantry battalion and from an R.F.C./R.A.F. squadron.

The history of an infantry brigade in the 17th (Northern) Division contains an appendix giving the names of every officer who served in three of the brigade's four original battalions.* The first battalion listed is the 10th West Yorks, an early New Army battalion which served with its division on the Western Front continuously from its arrival in France in August 1915 until the Armistice. The battalion took part in the Battle of the Somme in 1916, the Battles of Arras and Passchendaele (Third Ypres) in 1917, and the March Retreat and the Final Advance in 1918. There is no reason to believe that this was not a typical Western Front battalion during more than three years of fighting.

The officers' details in the brigade history give the date of joining the battalion, the date of the final departure from the battalion and the reason for that departure. There is one unfortunate omission: temporary absences because of light wounds or for other reasons are not noted. To allow for this, all subalterns remaining with the battalion for more than two years have had twelve months deducted from their service to allow for such temporary absences, and those remaining between one and two years have had six months deducted. It is believed that these deductions err on the generous side.

It was found that 174 officers joined the battalion as lieutenants or second lieutenants. After the allowances for temporary absence had been made, it was found that the average subaltern spent not three weeks but 6·17 months of front-line service with the battalion before becoming a casualty or leaving for some other reason.

* *History of the 50th Infantry Brigade 1914–1919*, published privately in 1919, no author named.

Furthermore, only one in five of these subalterns was actually killed, and almost half left the battalion unhurt. The following table shows the circumstances in which their service with the battalion ended.

Killed	37 (21·3%)
Wounded	48 (27·6%)
Prisoners	6 (3·4%)
Other reasons	83 (47·7%)

The 'wounded' total does not include those slightly wounded subalterns who returned to the battalion. The 'other reasons' include transfer to other units – usually trench-mortar, machine-gun, tank or flying units – those officers returned to England for various reasons, and those still with the unit at the Armistice. The shortest stay was by Second Lieutenant H. Banks, who arrived at the battalion on 23 August 1918 and was killed four days later near Flers, on the old Somme battlefield, during the final advance of the British Expeditionary Force.

Although these figures debunk the 'three-week subaltern' legend, it should not be forgotten that the figure of 174 subalterns serving with the 10th West Yorks during its period of thirty-eight months service on the Western Front shows that the battalion had to replace its original complement of junior officers six times.

＊

Details for length of service of pilots joining a front-line fighter squadron are also available. This is No. 56 Squadron, which served on the Western Front from April 1917 until the end of the war, except for a very short period when it was withdrawn to England at the height of the German Gotha bomber attacks on London. The squadron flew S.E.5a single-seat fighters and, again, there is no reason to believe that it was other than an average fighter squadron during that part of the war which saw the greater part of the war's air fighting; this squadron did, however, miss the worst of the spring 1917 air battles, when the R.F.C.'s aircraft were so inferior to those of the Germans and when excessive British casualties were suffered. (The active-service details of this squadron's pilots – all commissioned officers at this stage of the war – have been kindly provided by Alex Revell of Hatfield, England, from his, as yet unpublished, history of the squadron.)

A total of 109 pilots were included in the survey; a further small number, who were transferred to other squadrons almost as soon as they arrived or who were returned home, presumably as unsuitable for front-line flying duties, have been omitted. There were no temporary absences among the 109 pilots, and their average stay with the squadron worked out at ten weeks and five days. The reasons for departure were as follows.

Killed	45 (41·3%)
Wounded	17 (15·6%)
Prisoners	31 (28·4%)
To home establishment	16 (14·7%)

The shortest stay was by an American, Lieutenant J. N. Offut, who was killed two days after his arrival.

It can be seen from these figures that, although the 'three-week pilot' is a myth, life for a fighter pilot was considerably more hazardous than for the junior infantry officer.

It would be interesting to see figures for equivalent German units. It is probable that neither their infantry-officer nor their fighter-pilot casualty rate would have been so high as that of the British. German infantry officers were not exposed to danger as frequently as their British counterparts because German senior N.C.O.s carried out many of the duties that British subalterns performed. The German fighter pilots fought mostly within their own lines and the prevailing westerly wind prevented many a British pilot in a damaged aircraft from returning to safety.

Acknowledgements to the British and German Armies

Before all others I would like to thank the following men, British and German, who were all present at the battle fought on 21 March 1918. This book could not have been written without their generous and willing help.

THE BRITISH ARMY*

2ND DIVISION *2nd Oxford and Bucks L.I.:* Pte R. Hill. *24th R. Fus.:* Pte J. F. J. Nicholson. *1st K.R.R.C.:* 2/Lt D. G. Buxton. *1st R. Berkshires:* 2/Lt H. J. Odell, L/Cpl J. Wallace. *23rd R. Fus.:* Sgt J. H. Phillips. *2nd Bn M.G.C.:* Lt A. J. Powell.

3RD DIVISION *7th King's Shropshire L.I.:* Pte W. W. Francis. *4th R. Fus.:* L/Cpl A. T. A. Browne. *1st Gordons:* Pte W. J. Stephen. *2nd Suffolks:* Pte F. H. Drane. *76th T.M.B.:* Sgt E. C. Bird. *3rd Bn M.G.C.:* Pte W. Gandy, Pte A. Rheinheimer. *40th Bde R.F.A.:* Lt E. K. Page. *3rd Signal Coy:* Spr W. Sellars.

6TH DIVISION *1st King's Shropshire L.I.:* Pte T. Link, Pte W. J. Pullinger. *1st Buffs:* Lt E. Foster Hall, Pte F. Moore, Pte F. Powell. *1st W. Yorks:* Pte E. Atkinson, Pte H. A. Mason. *11th Essex:* Cpl C. W. Dale, Lt F. S. Pinney, 2/Lt J. C. H. Willett. *1st Leicesters:* Pte C. Frost, L/Cpl G. H. Leedham, Pte H. Walklate. *2nd Sherwood Foresters:* Capt. N. H. Beedham, Pte R. H. Bryan. *9th Norfolks:* Pte J. Jolly, Cpl J. E. Osler. *2nd Bde R.F.A.:* Cpl A. Rush.

9TH (SCOTTISH) DIVISION *5th Camerons:* Pte G. Barrie, L/Cpl T. Chamberlain, Cpl J. J. Sellars. *6th King's Own Scottish Borderers:*

* The contributors are listed by unit, in alphabetical order of surname; ranks shown are those held on 21 March 1918. Abbreviations for ranks are used as follows: Private – Pte, Rifleman – Rfmn, Gunner – Gnr, Driver – Dvr, Trooper – Tpr, Sapper – Spr, Lance Corporal – L/Cpl, Corporal – Cpl, Bombardier – Bdr, Sergeant – Sgt, Company (or Battery) Sergeant Major – C. (or B.) S.M., Second Lieutenant – 2/Lt, Lieutenant – Lt, Captain – Capt., Major – Maj., Lieutenant-Colonel – Lt Col. Abbreviations for units are used as follows: Royal – R., Light Infantry – L.I., Fusiliers – Fus., Battalion – Bn, Company – Coy, Battery – Bty, Brigade – Bde, King's Royal Rifle Corps – K.R.R.C., Trench Mortar Battery – T.M.B., Divisional Ammunition Column – D.A.C., Machine Gun Corps – M.G.C., Royal Field Artillery – R.F.A., Royal Garrison Artillery – R.G.A., Royal Horse Artillery – R.H.A.

Pte G. Cathcart. *11th R. Scots:* Pte C. A. G. McMaren. *1st S. Africans:* Pte H. L. Adler, Pte F. G. Aupiais, Pte W. Gray, L/Cpl A. H. Lawrence, Pte C. W. Levey, Capt. A. W. Liefeldt, Pte D. P. Marais. *2nd S. Africans:* Pte L. B. Maund, Capt. G. V. Merriman, Pte A. Pechey. *4th S. Africans:* Pte R. F. Attwell, Pte G. N. Dunn, L/Cpl R. J. Grimsdell, 2/Lt G. Leighton, Lt R. J. Read, Sgt F. J. L. Van Hasselt, Pte C. E. Whillier. *S. African T.M.B.:* L/Cpl A. F. Lilford. *9th Bn M.G.C.:* Pte G. H. McMillan. *51st Bde R.F.A.:* L/Bdr R. F. Durley. *63rd Field Coy:* Spr N. Paterson. *90th Field Coy:* Cpl G. D. Spencer. *27th Field Ambulance:* Pte A. H. Flindt. *9th Signal Coy:* Spr B. G. Watts.

14TH (LIGHT) DIVISION *8th K.R.R.C.:* Rfmn C. Brown, L/Cpl H. W. Cook, Rfmn A. J. Murcott. *8th Rifle Bde:* Rfmn R. Airley, 2/Lt W. G. F. Dewar. *5th Oxford and Bucks L.I.:* Cpl R. Long. *9th Rifle Bde:* L/Cpl F. E. Dorey, Rfmn W. Stevens. *9th K.R.R.C.:* Rfmn H. J. Bird (died 1976). *6th Somerset L.I.:* Pte A. Frampton, Lt W. D. Scott. *7th K.R.R.C.:* Rfmn J. W. J. Austin. *9th Scottish Rifles:* L/Cpl C. R. G. Wells. *14th Bn M.G.C.:* L/Cpl E. Depledge, Cpl E. Palmer. — *Bde R.F.A.:* Gnr H. P. Southall. *47th Bde R.F.A.:* Cpl J. Tyler, Dvr A. Wakerley. *246th Bde R.F.A.:* Bdr T. Wood. *14th Heavy T.M.B.:* Capt. J. Thomson-Evans. *42nd Field Ambulance:* Pte W. E. Illingworth. *62nd Field Coy:* Spr G. Storer. *41st Bde Signal Section:* Rfmn W. Collins.

16TH (IRISH) DIVISION *1st R. Munster Fus.:* Pte J. Connolly. *2nd Leinsters:* Capt. E. P. Hall. *6th Connaught Rangers:* Cpl T. McCarthy, Sgt D. J. O'Donovan. *7th R. Irish:* Sgt N. D. Hood, Pte J. T. McGuire. *7/8th R. Inniskilling Fus.:* Pte C. Coward. *11th Hampshires:* Pte E. G. Marlow, Sgt A. V. Young. *Divisional H.Q.:* Maj. K. S. Mason. *16th Bn M.G.C.:* 2/Lt G. F. Greaves, Pte J. Parkinson, Pte W. Wilson. *77th Bde R.F.A.:* Bdr G. A. Sheffield. *177th Bde R.F.A.:* Dvr E. Carrington. *16th Heavy T.M.B.:* Cpl C. Steward. *16th D.A.C.:* Cpl A. E. Barger. *156th Field Coy:* Spr F. S. Hicking. *157th Field Coy:* L/Cpl A. Jackson — *Field Ambulance:* Pte A. W. Pettit. *16th Signal Coy:* Spr G. Stewart.

17TH (NORTHERN) DIVISION *6th Dorsets:* Pte A. Pryor. *7th E. Yorks:* Pte A. A. McDonald. *10th W. Yorks:* Capt. P. Howe. *7th Border:* Pte J. Hully, Pte H. C. Little. *7th Lincolns:* Pte R. T. Gibson. *10th Sherwood Foresters:* Pte R. W. Davey, Cpl J. A. Sturges. *9th Duke of Wellington's:* Pte A. V. Simpson. *10th Lancashire Fus.:* Pte A. S. Hulme, Pte W. A. Orton, Pte G. Ready. *17th Bn M.G.C.:* Maj. J. Gowring, Pte A. Hensher. *79th Bde R.F.A.:*

Lt W. A. Carne, Dvr G. M. Colville. *78th Field Coy:* Spr J. Meldrum.

18TH (EASTERN) DIVISION *7th R. W. Kents:* Pte C. S. Smith. *8th R. Berkshires:* L/Cpl W. J. Atkins, 2/Lt W. C. A. Hanney, Lt J. W. Randall. *10th Essex:* Pte J. A. G. Bourne. *7th Bedfords:* Sgt J. J. Cousins. *11th R. Fus.:* Pte C. Clark, Pte C. East, 2/Lt G. M. Gibbs. *7th Buffs:* Cpl T. Bailey, 2/Lt F. C. Winter. *7th Queens:* Pte S. G. Cane, L/Cpl G. A. Fleet. *8th E. Surreys:* Lt Col A. P. B. Irwin, 2/Lt J. Moore, Pte B. P. Simpson. *8th R. Sussex:* L/Cpl C. A. R. Cook, Pte E. F. Walter. *18th Bn M.G.C.:* Cpl W. Fraser, Pte D. A. S. Leitch. *82nd Bde R.F.A.:* Gnr T. H. Woodgate. *83rd Brigade R.F.A.:* Gnr W. W. Lugg. *54th Field Ambulance:* Pte F. J. Law.

19TH (WESTERN) DIVISION *8th Gloucesters:* Sgt E. Chadband, Capt. M. A. James, V.C. (died 1975), Pte H. B. Mugridge, Pte R. E. Summers. *1/4th King's Shropshire L.I.:* Pte J. R. Richards. *8th N. Staffords:* Capt. D. O. Jones. *9th Cheshires:* Pte H. H. Bull. *6th Wiltshires:* Pte B. J. Dasson, Capt. N. L. Flower (died 1976). *88th Bde R.F.A.:* Gnr G. W. Sadler.

20TH (LIGHT) DIVISION *6th King's Shropshire L.I.:* L/Cpl A. R. Hartley, L/Cpl W. E. Staples. *11th K.R.R.C.:* Rfmn R. W. Otley. *20th Bn M.G.C.:* L/Cpl E. I. Roberts (died 1976).

21ST DIVISION *1st Lincolns:* Lt H. M. Boxer. *2nd Lincolns:* Pte F. Chilton, Pte H. Nangle. *12/13th Northumberland Fus.:* Cpl J. Gibson, Pte L. Straugheir, Pte J. P. Turner. *9th King's Own Yorkshire L.I.:* Cpl J. Anderson. *15th Durham L.I.:* Pte J. H. Maiden. *6th Leicesters:* L/Cpl O. Parkin, Pte F. E. Pothecary, Pte R. H. Taylor. *7th Leicesters:* L/Cpl A. D. Carpenter, Pte W. R. Carter, L/Cpl S. T. North, Pte N. Walton, Pte J. Wignall. *8th Leicesters:* 2/Lt J. C. Farmer. *Divisional H.Q.:* Capt. A. C. Sparks. *21st Bn M.G.C.:* Maj. H. W. Clarke (died 1976). *95th Bde R.F.A.:* Dvr B. Leafe.

24TH DIVISION *1st R. Fus.:* Pte H. H. Wells. *3rd Rifle Bde:* Rfmn W. J. Nunn, Rfmn C. Woods. *8th Queens:* Pte A. E. Bury, Pte E. F. Harrison, C.S.M. W. Hitchcock, Pte C. C. Jenner. *1st N. Staffords:* Pte D. H. Johnson. *9th E. Surreys:* Pte H. E. Arnold, Pte J. Crimmins. *7th Northamptons:* Pte D. Thomsett. *9th R. Sussex:* Lt-Col M. V. B. Hill. *13th Middlesex:* Cpl H. Hulks. *Divisional H.Q.:* Pte R. E. Wilde. *24th Bn M.G.C.:* Capt. C. G. C. Gilbert, Pte A. Hawkins, Pte T. Hood, Pte F. Plimmer, Pte W. R.

Stowers, Pte A. G. Toms. *106th Bde R.F.A.*: Lt W. F. Lawrence. *107th Bde R.F.A.*: Dvr S. Barton, Lt A. G. Everett. *24th Heavy T.M.B.*: 2/Lt S. Horscroft. *104th Field Coy*: Spr F. J. Austin. *24th Signal Coy*: Cpl A. G. Raby.

25TH DIVISION *1st Wiltshires*: Pte F. J. Spragg. *10th Cheshires*: Cpl F. Elson, Lt G. H. Gadsden. *3rd Worcesters*: Pte S. Sheppard. *11th Lancashire Fus.*: Capt. G. A. Potts. *2nd S. Lancashires*: Pte C. R. Harry. *8th Border*: Pte J. Bailey. *25th Bn M.G.C.*: Lt W. C. Curry. *105th Field Coy*: Spr H. Brown. *76th Field Ambulance*: Colour-Sgt P. Webb.

30TH DIVISION *2nd Wiltshires*: Pte F. B. Cook, Pte C. H. Manning, Pte S. S. Taylor. *2nd Green Howards*: Capt. J. S. A. Bunting. *17th King's*: Pte A. Tyrer, Pte W. J. Yendall. *18th King's*: L/Cpl W. Lloyd. *19th King's*: Pte B. Connor, Cpl E. G. Williams. *2nd R. Scots Fus.*: Pte G. H. Bennett, Capt. E. Hakewill Smith. *2nd Bedfords*: 2/Lt W. F. Billingham. *16th Manchesters*: Cpl R. Crossley, R.Q.M.S. P. E. Jenkins, Pte W. E. Smith, Pte A. E. Turner, L/Cpl A. Twiggs. *30th Bn M.G.C.*: 2/Lt E. Field, Pte S. N. Preece. *148th Bde R.F.A.*: Lt F. R. J. Peel. *149th Bde R.F.A.*: Spr A. Barton. *30th Heavy T.M.B.*: Bdr D. Holmes. *200th Field Coy*: Spr A. Turner. *201st Field Coy*: Spr T. Cass. *30th Signal Coy*: Spr H. E. Hopthrow, Cpl L. Jackson, Spr F. Waldron.

34TH DIVISION *11th Suffolks*: Pte H. J. Matthews. *16th R. Scots*: Pte A. W. Smith. *22nd Northumberland Fus.*: L/Cpl J. H. Brown, 2/Lt H. V. Crees. *23rd Northumberland Fus.*: 2/Lt F. A. Bailey, Pte T. Easton, Lt A. R. Liddell. *25th Northumberland Fus.*: Pte H. Bell (died 1973).* *9th Northumberland Fus.*: Cpl H. J. Smith. *10th Lincolns*: Pte H. Baumber. *102nd Bde H.Q.*: Capt. H. H. Davies. *34th Bn M.G.C.*: Pte G. H. Banfield, Cpl W. Hutton. *152nd Bde R.F.A.*: Dvr D. C. Brown. *160th Bde R.F.A.*: Artificer W. W. Mason.

36TH (ULSTER) DIVISION *15th R. Irish Rifles*: Sgt A. W. Colville. *1st R. Inniskilling Fus.*: Pte J. B. Hodgins. *9th R. Inniskilling Fus.*: Pte E. V. Cleverly, Capt. T. D. Morrison. *16th R. Irish Rifles*: Pte J. Potts. *36th Bn M.G.C.*: Pte S. H. Smith. *153rd Bde R.F.A.*: Gnr G. Langdon, B.Q.M.S. S. J. Sherman. *173rd Bde R.F.A.*: Capt. F. N. Broome. *36th D.A.C.*: Cpl J. Tully.

---

* Mr Bell's contribution was in the form of a manuscript written before he died; this was kindly provided by his son, Rev. J. G. Bell of Worsley, Manchester.

39TH DIVISION *1/1st Hertfords:* 2/Lt H. Knee, Pte W. H. Weller, Pte H. E. Winter. *11th R. Sussex:* Pte A. E. Beeney, L/Cpl T. R. Tompkins. *13th R. Sussex:* Pte C. J. May. *16th Rifle Bde:* Rfmn H. Griffiths. *16th Sherwood Foresters:* Pte J. R. Leese. *1/1st Cambridgeshire:* Pte O. W. Banks, Pte T. Newton. *4/5th Black Watch:* Pte J. Miller. *13th Gloucesters:* L/Cpl E. C. Vickery. *212th Field Coy:* 2/Lt H. Lawrie. *133rd Field Ambulance:* Pte J. H. Forman. *39th Signal Coy:* Spr T. F. Sinclair.

40TH DIVISION *13th E. Surreys:* 2/Lt H. M. S. Bailey. *12th Suffolks:* Pte J. Gray. *20th Middlesex:* 2/Lt R. J. Lucas.

47TH (LONDON) DIVISION *15th Londons:* Pte C. Hughes, Pte T. C. H. Jacobs, Pte F. J. Mummery, 2/Lt L. W. Pickard, Pte A. L. Robins, Pte B. Tombleson. *18th Londons:* Rfmn E. Chapman, Rfmn F. Hancock, Rfmn H. S. Woolacott. *19th Londons:* L/Cpl S. W. Lanfear, Capt. J. J. Sheppard. *20th Londons:* Pte G. T. Chew. *22nd Londons:* L/Cpl A. G. Elam. *23rd Londons:* Capt. G. A. Brett, Pte A. R. Brewin, Capt. E. M. Payne, Cpl T. J. Phillips. *24th Londons:* Pte P. J. Monk. *140th T.M.B.:* Lt M. B. Owen-Jones. *47th Bn M.G.C.:* Pte F. E. Heninghem. *236th Bde R.F.A.:* Capt. L. B. Tansley. *142nd Bde Signal Section:* Pte H. Bridgen.

51ST (HIGHLAND) DIVISION *5th Seaforths:* Pte T. Johnston, Pte D. McKay. *6th Black Watch:* Sgt D. J. Martin. *7th Black Watch:* Pte E. R. Savage. *7th Gordons:* Pte J. L. Smith, Sgt H. J. Strachan. *4th Gordons:* Pte G. A. Anderson, L/Cpl A. Milligan. *4th Seaforths:* Pte S. M. Calder, Pte W. M. Millar. *7th Argyll and Sutherlands:* L/Cpl J. B. Forgan, Sgt R. Kirkland, Pte A. MacDonald, Pte J. B. Stewart. *Divisional H.Q.:* Pte A. E. Camp. *51st Bn M.G.C.:* Pte J. McCormick. *255th Bde R.F.A.:* Gnr R. Thomas. *256th Bde R.F.A.:* 2/Lt W. H. Crowder. *400th Field Coy:* Maj. J. Kiggell, 2/Lt J. B. Longmuir, Capt. R. W. McCrone, Cpl F. Y. Thomson. *2/1st Highland Field Ambulance:* Pte J. Harper.

58TH (LONDON) DIVISION *2/2nd Londons:* Pte L. H. Jeapes, L/Cpl F. Miller, Cpl J. Price. *3rd Londons:* Drummer A. Sparrow. *7th Londons:* Capt. P. B. Berliner, 2/Lt R. C. R. Richards. *8th Londons:* L/Cpl A. Hardy, Rfmn G. H. Muggleton. *9th Londons:* Sgt B. G. Ashman, Rfmn P. W. Hunt, Rfmn E. Packman, Capt. A. N. Philbrick. *2/10th Londons:* Pte C. W. R. Firman. *12th Londons:* Cpl L. Tebbutt. *291st Bde R.F.A.:* Gnr H. D. Hatswell. *58th D.A.C.:* Dvr M. L. Hunt. *58th Signal Coy:* Cpl V. J. Loram.

59TH (NORTH MIDLAND) DIVISION *2/6th S. Staffords:* L/Cpl

J. Fetch, Pte R. T. Smith, Pte G. S. Taylor. *2/6th N. Staffords:*
Pte J. E. Barnes, Pte F. Beardsell, Pte J. C. Owen, Pte J. F.
Spencer, Cpl G. Wright. *4th Lincolns:* Pte C. Hankins, Pte B.
Pepper, Pte C. Pocklington. *2/4th Leicesters:* Pte A. Allen, 2/Lt C.
Greaves, L/Cpl C. E. Palmer, Pte A. C. Stodd, Sgt E. J. J. Vincent.
2/5th Lincolns: Cpl B. Whyers (died 1977), L/Cpl J. Wortley.
2/5th Sherwood Foresters: L/Cpl A. Bowler, Pte F. Cunnington,
Pte W. J. Haycroft, Pte L. H. Henchliffe, Pte A. J. Lane, L/Cpl A.
Wallace. *2/6th Sherwood Foresters:* Pte W. Cockayne. *7th Sherwood
Foresters:* Pte J. T. Goodwin, Pte F. H. Holmes, L/Cpl B.
Lambert, Pte J. Lear, Bugler H. Waldram. *6/7th R. Scots Fus.:*
Pte F. S. Hutchinson. *Divisional H.Q.:* S.Q.M.S. L. H. Goadby.
177th T.M.B.: Pte M. A. Joice. *178th T.M.B.:* Pte A. B. Ainslie,
Pte W. H. Arnold. *295th Bde R.F.A.:* Sgt J. Sellars. *296th Bde
R.F.A.:* Gnr F. W. Woodward. *59th D.A.C.:* Dvr L. E. William-
son. *2/2nd North Midland Field Ambulance:* Pte R. Lloyd.

61st (south midland) division *2/7th R. Warwicks:* L/Sgt
S. Aris, Pte H. G. Cox, Pte A. C. Fearn, Pte J. H. Keasey, Pte
R. D. Matthews. *2/8th Worcesters:* Pte S. Bromell. *1/8th Argyll
and Sutherlands:* Lt W. S. Mitchell. *1/9th R. Scots:* Pte W.
Stothard. *2/4th Oxford and Bucks L.I.:* Pte J. Bridges, Pte J.
Cummings, Pte L. A. Howard, 2/Lt H. Jones, Lt-Col H. E. de R.
Wetherall. *2/4th R. Berkshires:* L/Cpl H. Moore, Lt K. Pearce
Smith, Pte M. Ramplee. *2/5th Gloucesters:* Cpl W. A. Davis, Pte
S. W. Foote, Sgt F. B. Stanton, Pte W. C. Suter, Cpl M. G.
Wakefield. *61st Bn M.G.C.:* Pte W. H. Ware. *306th Bde R.F.A.:*
Capt. J. R. A. Evans. *307th Bde R.F.A.:* 2/Lt G. K. Stanley. *478th
Field Coy:* Sgt W. Donoghue, L/Cpl W. E. P. Hague. *2/1st South
Midland Field Ambulance:* Dvr A. W. Isaac. *61st Signal Coy:*
Pioneer C. Gaffney.

63rd (naval) division *1st R. Marine L.I.:* Pte G. McArdle,
Pte E. Wilson. *2nd R. Marine L.I.:* Pte A. Meadowcroft. *Drake
Bn:* Able Seaman F. H. Stretton. *Hawke Bn:* Able Seaman A. C.
Williams. *1st Artists Rifles:* Pte D. G. Kenney, Pte F. R. Wagstaffe.
63rd Bn M.G.C.: Sgt F. Cooper.

66th (east lancs) division *2/8th Lancashire Fus.:* Pte C.
Lewis, Sgt H. Murnaghan, Pte W. A. Reed. *4th E. Lancashires:*
L/Cpl T. Quinn, Pte A. T. Shaw. *2/5th E. Lancashires:* Pte S. N.
Camm. *9th Manchesters:* Pte A. J. Biss, Pte T. Braddock. *2/5th
Manchesters:* Lt R. A. France. *2/6th Manchesters:* Sgt J. Fitz-
patrick, Pte W. Greenhalgh, Pte C. H. Martin. *2/7th Manchesters:*

L/Cpl W. Brittan, Pte R. C. A. Frost, Pte H. James, 2/Lt A. A. Lamb, Pte R. G. Minns. *5th Borders:* Pte J. Bell, Pte W. H. Hartley, Pte A. V. Mason. *199th Bde H.Q.:* Capt. R. L. Bond. *197th T.M.B.:* Lt A. A. Simpson. *330th Bde R.F.A.:* Bdr H. Oddie. *331st Bde R.F.A.:* Bdr H. J. Hewetson. *432nd Field Coy:* L/Cpl J. Kyffin. *2/1st E. Lancs Field Ambulance:* Dvr H. Booth.

CAVALRY *2nd Dragoon Guards:* Lt W. R. Beddington (died 1975). *2nd Dragoons:* Tpr A. W. Bradbury (died 1972).* *10th Hussars:* Pte F. Turner. *15th Hussars:* Lt J. Cormack-Thompson. *16th Lancers:* Tpr G. Oxlade. *19th Hussars:* Cpl L. J. Shaw. *Northumberland Hussars:* Tpr O. Hall. *9th Machine Gun Squadron:* Tpr C. H. Somerset. *'O' Battery R.H.A.:* Lt I. R. H. Probert.

ARTILLERY (non divisional) *Field Bdes – 14th:* Dvr S. R. Wright. *23rd:* Gnr A. R. Fulwood, Lt A. W. Rowlerson, Bdr J. Wright. *65th:* Bdr N. Howdill. *83rd:* Cpl P. Dollin. *108th:* 2/Lt G. K. Thornton. *150th:* Bdr J. H. H. Burrows. *169th:* Bdr J. P. Barker. *189th:* Dvr B. A. McConnell, Lt F. E. Payne. *293rd:* Spr F. W. Hart. *298th:* Gnr H. A. Harris, Gnr H. Johnson. *— Bde:* Bdr W. Stemp. *77th Bty:* Gnr R. P. Knappitt.
V Bde R.H.A.: Sgt C. W. Archer.
Siege Btys R.G.A. – 8th: Lt F. Mansfield. *42nd:* Bdr J. O. Peacock. *51st:* 2/Lt L. W. White. *81st:* 2/Lt F. A. Rimer. *95th:* Maj. R. B. Pargiter. *126th:* Lt F. C. Greene-Price. *150th:* 2/Lt L. T. Whitaker. *169th:* Bdr P. H. Biddle. *205th:* Lt B. H. Baylis. *214th:* Bdr W. T. Davison. *245th:* Gnr H. B. Mills (died 1966).† *295th:* Gnr J. Turner. *303rd:* Bdr T. L. Latimer. *327th:* Lt C. H. Mapp. *409th:* Lt H. J. C. Millett.
Heavy Btys R.G.A. – 113th: Lt L. Rushforth Ward. *124th:* Gnr H. V. Kearsey. *138th:* Lt F. G. Browning. *144th:* Dvr C. Kettlewell, Bdr L. J. Ounsworth. *1st (Kent):* B.S.M. S. F. Jacob. *1st (Hants):* Gnr J. A. James.
56th Heavy Bde H.Q.: Pte W. M. Greenwood.

ROYAL FLYING CORPS *5 (Naval) Squadron:* Flight Commander C. P. O. Bartlett, Flight Lt J. Gamon. *41 Squadron:* Lt H. J. D. Arkell. *59 Squadron:* Capt. C. E. Williamson Jones. *82 Squadron:*

* Mr Bradbury's contribution was in the form of a manuscript written before he died; this was kindly provided by his son, Mr A. Bradbury of Marnhull, Dorset.
† Mr Mills's contribution was in the form of a manuscript written before he died; this was kindly provided by his son, Mr A. B. Mills of Ponteland, Newcastle-upon-Tyne.

Lt R. M. Montgomery. Liaison officer with French Sixth Army Aviation H.Q.: Capt. H. Ward.

TANK CORPS *5th Bn:* Gnr W. L. M. Francis. *8th Bn:* L/Cpl E. A. Bond, Cpl F. S. Franklin (died 1975), Capt. G. A. Grounds. *10th Bn:* L/Cpl H. W. Brown, L/Cpl G. S. Western.

OTHER UNITS *Royal Engineers – 5th Field Squadron:* Cpl H. P. Seaton. *577th Coy:* Spr H. J. Paine. *III Corps Signals:* Lt J. W. N. Orton. *XIX Corps Signals:* Cpl C. H. James, Lt N. McConnies. *Meteorological Section:* Spr J. H. R. Body. *Field Survey Coys:* Spr A. E. Johnson, Spr W. Lord. *'G' Special Coy:* Pioneer F. W. J. Hayward. *22nd Light Train Crew Coy:* Spr T. R. Berriman. *Army and Corps H.Q.s – Third Army:* Cpl R. L. Roughsedge. *Fifth Army:* Staff Sgt S. Cooke. *VII Corps:* Pte J. L. Deighton. *XVIII Corps:* Capt. N. Stronge, Capt. W. N. C. Van Grutten. *Entrenching Bns – 16th:* Pte S. A. Starkey. *17th:* Pte P. J. Kennedy, L/Cpl B. E. Laurence. *23rd:* Capt. L. S. Duncan, Rfmn J. McAteer. *Corps Cyclist Bns – IV:* Sgt H. Vaughan, L/Cpl H. A. Woodgate. *XIX:* Pte C. N. Levett. *33rd Reserve Machine Gun Coy:* Sgt D. J. Freeman.

THE GERMAN ARMY*

1ST GUARD DIVISION *1st Guard Regt:* Unt. Sedlacek.

1ST GUARD RESERVE DIVISION *64th Res. Regt:* Musk. W. Kownatzki.

1ST BAVARIAN DIVISION *1st Bav. Regt:* Lt R. Spengler. *2nd Bav. Regt:* Infanterist F. Scharl. *24th Bav. Regt:* Infanterist P. Karpfser.

2ND GUARD RESERVE DIVISION *77th Res. Regt:* Telefonist A. Turk. *91st Res. Regt:* Musk. A. Boehm.

3RD GUARD DIVISION *Lehr Regt:* Fus. W. Adams. *2nd Guard Fussartillerie Regt:* Unt. O. Jaffé. *5th Guard Field Regt:* Lt W. Lindner. *28th Pion. Bn:* Gef. P. Kretschmer.

3RD MARINE DIVISION *3rd Marine Regt:* Marine O. Kranz.

4TH GUARD DIVISION *5th Guard Gren. Regt:* Fus. M. Kappus

---

* Abbreviations for ranks are used as follows: Musketier – Musk., Fuselier – Fus., Grenadier – Gren., Pionier – Pion., Gefreiter – Gef., Unteroffizier – Unt., Leutnant – Lt. Units: Regiment – Regt, Reserve – Res., Bataillon or Abteilung – Bn, Bavarian – Bav.

(died 1977), Fus. W. Schmielau. *93rd Res. Regt:* Musk. W. Ehrenberg.

5TH DIVISION *12th Gren. Regt:* Gren. W. Both.

5TH BAVARIAN DIVISION *7th Bav. Regt:* Unt. M. Strobel. *19th Bav. Regt:* Lt M. J. Strauss. *21st Bav. Regt:* Infanterist K. Badewitz.

6TH DIVISION *396th Regt:* Unt. F. Schaffrath.

6TH BAVARIAN DIVISION *13th Medical Coy:* Soldat A. Lauterbach. *Divisional Intelligence:* Lt H. Baum.

9TH DIVISION *154th Regt:* Gef. K. Huland.

10TH DIVISION *6th Gren. Regt:* Lt R. Brettschneider. *398th Regt:* Musk. O. Maraun.

12TH DIVISION *62nd Regt:* Unt. H. Fiedler.

13TH LANDWEHR DIVISION *60th Landwehr Regt:* Musk. J. Noll.

16TH RESERVE DIVISION *30th Res. Regt:* Musk. R. Behringer, Lt F. Schemm.

17TH DIVISION *89th Gren. Regt:* Vizefeldwebel M. Gerchow, Gren. K. Rothenburg.

18TH DIVISION *31st Regt:* Musk. O. Lund. *85th Regt:* Musk. O. Erichsen. *45th Field Regt:* Wachmeister B. Lauritzen. *9th Pion. Bn:* Unt. H. Kage.

19TH DIVISION *91st Regt:* Musk. R. Hillringhaus.

20TH DIVISION *77th Regt:* Unt. F. Flohr, Musk. K. Petersen. *79th Regt:* Musk. O. Fick, Lt H. Wedekind. *92nd Regt:* Gef. O. Wiegand. *20th Telephone Bn:* Signalist W. Rose.

21ST RESERVE DIVISION *80th Res. Regt:* Musk. P. Knibbe, Musk. P. Schlegel, Vizefeldwebel K. Uttecht.

24TH RESERVE DIVISION *107th Res. Regt:* Gef. H. Müller.

25TH DIVISION *115th Leibgarde Gren. Regt:* Unt. F. Bohl (died 1976).

27TH DIVISION *123rd Regt:* Gef. M. Brenner, Gren. H. Schüle. *124th Regt:* Lt O. Moser.

28TH DIVISION *109th Leib Gren. Regt:* Gef. W. Reinhard. *110th Gren. Regt:* Feldwebel H. Gasser. *28th Mortar Coy:* Pion. N. Schubert.

34TH DIVISION *67th Regt:* Offizier Stellvertreter H. Drees. *145th Konigs Regt:* Fähnrich A. Bruntsch, Musk. H. Telöken.

39TH DIVISION *126th Regt:* Unt. W. Eberbach.

45TH RESERVE DIVISION *210th Res. Regt:* Musk. O. Klingbeil, Gef. R. Loss. *211th Res. Regt:* Gef. C. Clemp. *20th Fussart. Regt:* Unt. E. Kubatzki. *Divisional Intelligence:* Soldat H. Mühlhausen.

47TH RESERVE DIVISION *219th Res. Regt:* Unt. O. Rottmann. *9th Jager Bn:* Gef. H. Bartel, Jäger H. Rautenberg.

50TH DIVISION *39th Fus. Regt:* Gef. W. Jobst. *158th Regt:* Gef. F. Leifert. *95th Fussart. Bn:* Gef. H. Schwartz.

50TH RESERVE DIVISION *230th Res. Regt:* Musk. F. Ballhausen, Musk. W. Boscheinen, Lt O. Heilmann, Musk. W. Raschow, Musk. O. Seibt.

54TH RESERVE DIVISION *13th Pion. Bn:* Lt K. Kräutle.

79TH RESERVE DIVISION *3rd Jägersturmbataillon:* Jäger H. Schroeter. *63rd Res. Field Regt:* Lt A. Seiffert.

111TH DIVISION *73rd Regt:* Gef. W. Junk. *76th Regt:* Musk. H. Borchert.

119TH DIVISION *46th Regt:* Feldwebel M. Schulz. *46th Res. Regt:* Lt F. Wellhausen.

183RD DIVISION *184th Regt:* Feldwebel W. Schulze. *418th Regt:* Gef. W. Jachmann. *440th Regt:* Gef. E. Meul.

195TH DIVISION *16th Res. Jäger Bn:* Gef. M. Pitsch.

206TH DIVISION *359th Regt:* Unt. R. Weber. *394th Regt:* Unt. H. Maass, Musk. A. Vogelsang.

208TH DIVISION *25th Regt:* Unt. G. Bastin, Musk. G. Schulz. *185th Regt:* Gef. A. Renschler. *65th Res. Regt:* Gef. K. Pütz.

211TH DIVISION *27th Pion. Bn:* Pion W. Niebuhr.

221ST DIVISION *41st Regt:* Gef. J. Herber.

231ST DIVISION *443rd Regt:* Gren. O. Wesche. *90th Fussart. Bn:* Unt. W. Best. *353rd Pion. Coy:* Pion. G. Zobel.

234TH DIVISION *452nd Regt:* Musk. P. Kollmann.

236TH DIVISION *459th Regt:* Gef. A. Gleim, Gef. A. Ostermann. *Divisional Signals:* Funker T. Schepers.

238TH DIVISION *463rd Regt:* Lt R. Hoffmann, Telefonist R. Müller, Vizefeldwebel W. Prosch, Musk. P. Sass. *464th Regt:* Schütze H. Beeck, Lt K. Fischer, Musk. H. Hinrichsen, Musk. W. Offen, Unt. H. Petersen, Musk. A. Schoen, Gef. A. Timm. *465th Regt:* Schütze K. Brunotte, Lt H. Möller.

NON-DIVISIONAL UNITS *12th Sturmbn:* Gren. P. Meyer. *Fussart. Regts – 4th Bav.:* Feldwebel O. Luban. *10th:* Unt. H. Jericho. *13th:* Unt. K. Heimgartner. *M.G. Scharfschützen Bns – 14th:* Schütze B. Kolks. *19th:* Unt. A. Eilers. *36th:* Gef. A. Bender. *302nd Minenwerfer Coy:* Pion. J.-B. Hilmer. *Balloon Platoons – 117th:* Luftschiffer L. Reineking. *148th:* Luftschiffer E. Lange, Luftschiffer K. Löffelholz. *210th Flieger Bn:* Feldwebel F. Reinecken. *71st Lichtmessetruppe:* Unt. F. Ihlenfeldt. *214th Meteorological Section:* Soldat K. Richard.

Personal Acknowledgements

I should like to express my grateful appreciation to many people in England and Germany for their generous and friendly help with the preparation of this book.

Pride of place must go to Neville Mackinder of Finchley who bravely volunteered to carry out the Public Record Office search of the War Diaries of the British Army units involved in the fighting on 21 March 1918 and who also carried through many items of supplementary research. This work was performed with a calm and methodical efficiency which must have enhanced the quality of the written work. I am most grateful for this marvellous help, and also for Julia Mackinder's hospitality on many occasions. My thanks also to an old friend and colleague, Patrick Mahoney, of Chadwell Heath, who performed the search of Royal Flying Corps War Diaries with his customary efficiency, and to Norman Franks, of Morden, who gave much valuable advice on flying matters. Another old friend, Norbert Krüger, of Essen, provided valuable material on German casualty figures by his prolonged search of German regimental histories.

The translation of German letters and documents is always a problem. A major breakthrough for me was the offer by Otto Jaffé, a German gentleman now living in Oakham, Rutland, to translate the more useful passages from more than 120 letters sent by German participants in the battle. Herr Jaffé's selection from this material was particularly reliable because he had served as an artilleryman in the German 3rd Guard Division on 21 March 1918. I am also grateful for equally valuable, if less voluminous, translation work carried out by Annemarie Lamb, of Boston, and by Helen Laurence and her daughter Elizabeth of Finchley. I should like to thank Alan Taylor, of Boston, for his valuable help also.

The research for this book involved a vast correspondence which, at one time, required the help of four part-time typists – Bridget Bemrose, Frances Grebby, Karen Kilshaw and Cherrie Robinson. My thanks are due to these efficient ladies. I am particularly grateful to Janet Mountain, who typed two drafts of a long manuscript with her customary expertise. My daughter Jane gave valuable help with the sorting and filing of the correspondence from the participants in the battle and with the compilation of the index, and my wife, Mary, checked the final typescript with great diligence.

Of the more official organisations, I should like to express my thanks for the ever-willing and valuable help of the staff of the Commonwealth War Graves Commission and the Imperial War Museum – particularly to Mr David Nash. I also received valuable help from the historians and secretaries of many British Army regiments and from A. Roughton of the 16th Manchesters Old Boys' Association. I should like also to thank the Librarian of the Macnaughten Library, Eton College, for help given to Neville Mackinder, and the staff of the Boston Branch of the Lincolnshire County Library Service for their usual efficient help to myself.

Acknowledgements for permission to include quotations from *The Official History of the War, France and Belgium 1918* and from Crown copyright records in the Public Record Office are made to the Controller of H.M. Stationery Office; from *Storm of Steel*, by Ernst Jünger, to Chatto and Windus; and from *Not the Whole Truth*, by Captain F. N. Broome, to the author. The three reproductions of *Punch* cartoons are from *Mr Punch at War* and are reproduced by kind permission of *Punch*. The diagram of the defences of Manchester Hill on page 264 is based on a similar diagram in *The Sixteenth, Seventeenth, Eighteenth and Nineteenth Battalions of the Manchester Regiment*, and I am grateful to Messrs Sherratt and Hughes of Manchester for permission to use this.

THE PRESS

Many newspapers and magazines published my appeals for participants in the battle of 21 March 1918, and I am pleased to record my gratitude for this valuable help.

UNITED KINGDOM: *Daily Telegraph, Aberdeen Evening Express, Accrington Observer and Times, Belfast Telegraph, Bradford Telegraph and Argus, Brighton and Hove Gazette, Bristol Evening Post, Bucks Advertiser, Burton Daily Mail, Bury Free Press, Bury Times, Cambridge Evening News, Coventry Evening Telegraph, Croydon Advertiser, Cumberland Evening News and Star, Derby Evening Telegraph, Derbyshire Advertiser, Derry Journal, Dover Express and East Kent News, Dudley Herald, Durham Advertiser, Eastbourne Herald, Eastern Daily Press, Folkestone and Hythe Gazette, Glasgow Daily Record, Glasgow Herald, Gloucester Journal, Gloucestershire Echo, Grimsby Evening Telegraph, Hampshire Chronicle, Hemel Hempstead Gazette, Hereford Evening News, Herts Advertiser, Hexham Courant, Ilford Recorder, Inverness Courier, Ipswich Evening Star, Kent and Sussex Courier, Kent Messenger, Lancashire Evening Post, Lancaster Guardian, Leek Post and Times,*

Leicester Mercury, Lincolnshire Echo, Lincolnshire Standard, Liverpool Daily Post, Loughborough Monitor, London Evening News, Luton News, Maidenhead Advertiser, Manchester Evening News, Newcastle Evening Chronicle, Nottingham Evening Post, Notts Free Press, Oxford Mail, Oban and West Highland Times, Perthshire Advertiser, Salford City Reporter, Salisbury and Winchester Journal, Sheffield Morning Telegraph, Shrewsbury Chronicle, Shropshire Star, Southend Standard, Southern Evening Echo, Southport Journal Visiter, Stafford Newsletter, Staffordshire Weekly Sentinel, Stoke Evening Sentinel, Stirling Observer, Sunderland Echo, Surrey Comet, Surrey Daily Advertiser, Walsall Observer, Western Gazette, Western Morning News, West Herts and Watford Observer, West Lancashire Evening Gazette, Westmorland Gazette, Whitehaven News, Wigan Evening Post and Chronicle, Wiltshire Times, Wolverhampton Express and Star, Worcester Evening News, Worthing Gazette, Yorkshire Evening Press, Yorkshire Post.
The Green Howards Gazette, Royal British Legion Journal, Royal United Services Institution Journal.

REPUBLIC OF IRELAND: *Cork Examiner, Dublin Evening Press, Limerick Advertiser, Wexford People.*

SOUTH AFRICA: *Bloemfontein Friend, Cape Times, Cape Town Argus, East London Daily Dispatch, Johannesburg Star, Natal Witness, Pretoria News, Rand Daily Mail.*

GERMANY: *Badische Neueste Nachrichten, Berliner Morgenpost, Braunschweiger Zeitung, Cellesche Zeitung, Darmstädter Tagblatt, Der Abend* (Berlin), *Düsseldorfer Nachrichten, Flensburger Tageblatt, Frankfurter Rundschau, Hamburger Abendblatt, Hannoversche Allgemeine Zeitung, Hildesheimer Allgemeine Zeitung, Kölner Stadt-Anzeiger, Lippische Landes-Zeitung, Lübecker Nachrichten, Münchener Merkur, Neue Hannoversche Presse, Neue Rhein Zeitung, Neue Ruhr Zeitung, Neue Westfälische, Nordbayerischer Kurier, Nordsee Zeitung, Rheinische Post, Rhein-Neckar Zeitung, Saarbrücker Zeitung, Schwäbische Zeitung, Stuttgarter Nachrichten, Stuttgarter Zeitung, Unsere Altmark, West Deutsche Zeitung, Westfälische Rundschau, Westfälische Volksblatt.*
Der Leibgardist, Die Fackel, Kyffhäuser.

Bibliography

OFFICIAL HISTORIES

Edmonds, Brigadier-General Sir James E., *Military Operations France and Belgium 1918*, Macmillan, 1935.

Janes, H. A., *The War in the Air*, Vol. IV, Oxford University Press, 1934.

Der Weltkrieg 1914–18, Vol. 14, published by Oberkommando der Wehrmacht in 1944 and by Bundesarchiv in 1956.

OTHER PUBLICATIONS

Behrend, Arthur, *As From Kemmel Hill*, Eyre, 1963.

Coombs, Rose, *Before Endeavours Fade*, Battle of Britain Prints International, 1976.

Dunham, Frank, *The Long Carry*, edited by R. H. Haigh and P. W. Turner, Pergamon, 1970.

Farrar-Hockley, Anthony, *Goughie*, Hart-Davis, MacGibbon, 1975.

Fielding, Rowland, *War Letters to a Wife*, Medici Society, 1929.

Godspeed, D. J., *Ludendorff*, Hart-Davis, 1966.

Gough, General Sir Hubert, *The Fifth Army*, Hodder and Stoughton, 1931.

Jünger, Ernst, *Storm of Steel*, Chatto and Windus, 1929.

Keegan, John, *The Face of Battle*, Cape, 1976.

Maze, Paul, *A Frenchman in Khaki*, Heinemann, 1934.

Sparrow, W. Shaw, *The Fifth Army in March 1918*, John Lane, 1922.

Terraine, John, *Impacts of War 1914 and 1918*, Hutchinson, 1970.

The Private Papers of Douglas Haig 1914–1919, edited by Robert Blake, Eyre and Spottiswoode, 1952.

Index

READ MORE IN PENGUIN

In every corner of the world, on every subject under the sun, Penguin represents quality and variety – the very best in publishing today.

For complete information about books available from Penguin – including Puffins, Penguin Classics and Arkana – and how to order them, write to us at the appropriate address below. Please note that for copyright reasons the selection of books varies from country to country.

In the United Kingdom: Please write to *Dept. EP, Penguin Books Ltd, Bath Road, Harmondsworth, West Drayton, Middlesex UB7 ODA*

In the United States: Please write to *Consumer Sales, Penguin Putnam Inc., P.O. Box 12289 Dept. B, Newark, New Jersey 07101-5289.* VISA and MasterCard holders call 1-800-788-6262 to order Penguin titles

In Canada: Please write to *Penguin Books Canada Ltd, 10 Alcorn Avenue, Suite 300, Toronto, Ontario M4V 3B2*

In Australia: Please write to *Penguin Books Australia Ltd, P.O. Box 257, Ringwood, Victoria 3134*

In New Zealand: Please write to *Penguin Books (NZ) Ltd, Private Bag 102902, North Shore Mail Centre, Auckland 10*

In India: Please write to *Penguin Books India Pvt Ltd, 11 Community Centre, Panchsheel Park, New Delhi 110017*

In the Netherlands: Please write to *Penguin Books Netherlands bv, Postbus 3507, NL-1001 AH Amsterdam*

In Germany: Please write to *Penguin Books Deutschland GmbH, Metzlerstrasse 26, 60594 Frankfurt am Main*

In Spain: Please write to *Penguin Books S. A., Bravo Murillo 19, 1° B, 28015 Madrid*

In Italy: Please write to *Penguin Italia s.r.l., Via Benedetto Croce 2, 20094 Corsico, Milano*

In France: Please write to *Penguin France, Le Carré Wilson, 62 rue Benjamin Baillaud, 31500 Toulouse*

In Japan: Please write to *Penguin Books Japan Ltd, Kaneko Building, 2-3-25 Koraku, Bunkyo-Ku, Tokyo 112*

In South Africa: Please write to *Penguin Books South Africa (Pty) Ltd, Private Bag X14, Parkview, 2122 Johannesburg*

READ MORE IN PENGUIN

PENGUIN CLASSIC BIOGRAPHY

 Highly readable and enjoyable biographies and autobiographies from leading biographers and autobiographers. The series provides a vital background to the increasing interest in history, historical subjects and people who mattered. The periods and subjects covered include the Roman Empire, Tudor England, the English Civil Wars, the Victorian Era, and characters as diverse Joan of Arc, Jane Austen, Robert Burns and George Melly. Essential reading for everyone interested in the great figures of the past.

Published or forthcoming:

E. F. Benson	As We Were
Ernle Bradford	Cleopatra
David Cecil	A Portrait of Jane Austen
Roger Fulford	Royal Dukes
Christopher Hibbert	Charles I
	The Making of Charles Dickens
Christopher Hill	God's Englishman: Oliver Cromwell
Marion Johnson	The Borgias
James Lees-Milne	Earls of Creation
Edward Lucie-Smith	Joan of Arc
Philip Magnus	Gladstone
John Masters	Casanova
Elizabeth Mavor	The Ladies of Llangollen
Ian McIntyre	Robert Burns
George Melly	Owning Up: The Trilogy
Raymond Postgate	That Devil Wilkes
Peter Quennell	Byron: The Years of Fame
Lytton Strachey	Queen Victoria
	Elizabeth and Essex
Gaius Suetonius	Lives of the Twelve Caesars
	translated by Robert Graves
Alan Villiers	Captain Cook

READ MORE IN PENGUIN

PENGUIN CLASSIC HISTORY

 Well written narrative history from leading historians such as Paul Kennedy, Alan Moorehead, J. B. Priestley, A. L. Rowse and G. M. Trevelyan. From the Ancient World to the decline of British naval mastery, from twelfth-century France to the Victorian Underworld, the series captures the great turning points in history and chronicles the lives of ordinary people at different times. Penguin Classic History will be enjoyed and valued by everyone who loves the past.

Published or forthcoming:

Leslie Alcock	**Arthur's Britain**
John Belchem/Richard Price	**A Dictionary of 19th-Century History**
Jeremy Black/Roy Porter	**A Dictionary of 18th-Century History**
Ernle Bradford	**The Mediterranean**
Anthony Burton	**Remains of a Revolution**
Robert Darnton	**The Great Cat Massacre**
Jean Froissart	**Froissart's Chronicles**
Johan Huizinga	**The Waning of the Middle Ages**
Aldous Huxley	**The Devils of Loudun**
Paul M. Kennedy	**The Rise and Fall of British Naval Mastery**
Margaret Wade Labarge	**Women in Medieval Life**
Alan Moorehead	**Fatal Impact**
Samuel Pepys	**Illustrated Pepys**
J. H. Plumb	**The First Four Georges**
J. B. Priestley	**The Edwardians**
Philippa Pullar	**Consuming Passions**
A. L. Rowse	**The Elizabethan Renaissance**
John Ruskin	**The Stones of Venice**
G. M. Trevelyan	**English Social History**
Philip Warner	**The Medieval Castle**
T. H. White	**The Age of Scandal**
Lawrence Wright	**Clean and Decent**
Hans Zinsser	**Rats, Lice and History**

READ MORE IN PENGUIN

PENGUIN CLASSIC MILITARY HISTORY

 This series acknowledges the profound and enduring interest in military history, and the causes and consequences of human conflict. Penguin Classic Military History covers warfare from the earliest times to the age of electronics and encompasses subjects as diverse as classic examples of grand strategy and the precision tactics of Britain's crack SAS Regiment. The series will be enjoyed and valued by students of military history and all who hope to learn from the often disturbing lessons of the past.

Published or forthcoming:

Correlli Barnett	**Engage the Enemy More Closely**
	The Great War
David G. Chandler	**The Art of Warfare on Land**
	Marlborough as Military Commander
William Craig	**Enemy at the Gates**
Carlo D'Este	**Decision in Normandy**
Michael Glover	**The Peninsular War**
	Wellington as Military Commander
Winston Graham	**The Spanish Armadas**
Heinz Guderian	**Panzer Leader**
Christopher Hibbert	**Redcoats and Rebels**
Heinz Höhne	**The Order of the Death's Head**
Anthony Kemp	**The SAS at War**
Ronald Lewin	**Ultra Goes to War**
Martin Middlebrook	**The Falklands War**
	The First Day on the Somme
	The Kaiser's Battle
Desmond Seward	**Henry V**
John Toland	**Infamy**
Philip Warner	**Sieges of the Middle Ages**
Leon Wolff	**In Flanders Fields**
Cecil Woodham-Smith	**The Reason Why**